IMAGES: A READER

IMAGES: A READER

EDITED BY

SUNIL MANGHANI, ARTHUR PIPER *and* JON SIMONS

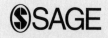

Los Angeles | London | New Delhi
Singapore | Washington DC

Editorial introductions and arrangement © Sunil Manghani,
Arthur Piper and Jon Simons 2006

First published 2006
Reprinted 2009, 2010 (twice), 2011

SAGE Publications Ltd
1 Oliver's Yard
55 City Road
London EC1Y 1SP

SAGE Publications Inc.
2455 Teller Road
Thousand Oaks, California 91320

SAGE Publications India Pvt Ltd
B 1/I 1, Mohan Cooperative Industrial Area
Mathura Road
New Delhi 110 044

SAGE Publications Asia-Pacific Pte Ltd
33 Pekin Street #02-01
Far East Square
Singapore 048763

British Library Cataloguing in Publication data

A catalogue record for this book is available
from the British Library

ISBN 978-1-4129-0044-7
ISBN 978-1-4129-0045-4 (pbk)

Library of Congress Control Number: 2005910541

Typeset by C&M Digitals (P) Ltd., Chennai, India
Printed and bound in Great Britain by the MPG Books Group
Printed on paper from sustainable resources

CONTENTS

ACKNOWLEDGEMENTS

Having been a student the first time the module 'Thought, Image, Critique' ran, Sunil Manghani would like to acknowledge his debt to Jon Simons. It was out of the experience of his very interactive, interdisciplinary forum that not only has this book emerged, but also my own doctoral research. I would also like to thank my own students who, over the last couple of years, have taken my module 'Words and Images'. This has afforded many new and untold insights, keeping the topics of the *Reader* very much alive and lively. I am grateful for the collaboration of my co-editors — it has been a long process of devising, editing, writing and 'of course' emailing; but nonetheless a process which has been extremely formative and always led by a certain shared intellectual curiosity. I'd also like to express my thanks to Gurdeep Mattu and Katherine Haw at Sage for all their help and patience in finalising the book. Finally, a personal thanks (always) to Kyoko Fukukawa whose critical eye/mind never fails.

Arthur Piper would like to thank Peter Bennett for help with sourcing material on Byzantine icons and Richard Woodfield for suggesting the relevant passages from Thomas Hobbes. He would also like to thank his co-editors for a collaboration which has been both stimulating and extremely rewarding. But most thanks are reserved for his wife Sarah whose support made his involvement with this project a possibility.

Jon Simons would like to thank his co-editors for proposing the idea of the *Reader* and for taking on the bulk of the technical work required in order to produce it. The inspiration for the *Reader* came from a graduate seminar called 'Thought, Image, Critique' that I taught as part of the Critical Theory Masters programme at the University of Nottingham. I am grateful to all the students who have participated in the seminar since 2000 for helping me appreciate the richness and excitement of 'image studies'. Thanks also to Lisa Walsh for advice about the 'Psychoanalysis' selections. I would also like to thank my partner, Claire Swallow, whose paintings *are* rich and inspiring images.

All the editors are extremely grateful to Julia Hall at Sage for her encouragement and patience.

PUBLISHERS' PERMISSIONS

4:1
Extract from *Studies in Iconology: Humanistic Themes in the Art of the Renaissance* by Erwin Panofsky (1972, Westview Press Inc.). Reprinted by permission of Westview Press, a member of Perseus Books, L.L.C.

4:2
GOMBRICH, E.H.; ART AND ILLUSION Copyright © 1960 Princeton University Press, 1988 renewed PUP, 2000 paperback edition. Reprinted by permission of Princeton University Press.

4:3
'Interpretation without Representation, or the Viewing of Las Meninas' by Svetlana Alpers from Representations, Svetlana Alpers (UCP). Reprinted by permission of the University of Chicago Press.

4:4
Extract from 'Eye and Mind' by Susan Buck-Morss, originally in *October 77, Summer 1996*. Reprinted by permission of the author.

5:2
C. S. Pierce 'The Sign: Icon, Index and Symbol'. Reprinted by permission of the publisher from THE COLLECTED PAPERS OF CHARLES SANDERS PEIRCE: VOLUME II, edited by Charles Hartshorne and Paul Weiss, pp. 135, 143–44, 169–173, Cambridge, Mass: The Belknap Press of Harvard University Press. Copyright © 1932, 1960 by the President and Fellows of Harvard College.

5:3
Extract from *The Responsibility of Forms, Roland Barthes* (Farrar, Straus and Giroux/Hill and Wang), New York, pp. 41–44, 47–48, 51, 54–59. Reprinted by permission of Blackwell Publishing.

5:4
'From Sub- to Suprasemiotic: The Sign as Event' from Mieke Bal, Remembering Rembrant. Reprinted by kind permission of the author.

5:5
'The Semiotic Landscape' by Gunter Kress and Theo van Leeuwen from *Reading Images* (Routledge, 1996). Reprinted by permission of Taylor and Francis Books Ltd.

6:1
"Thing and Work", *Basic Writings*, Martin Heidegger (1993, Routledge). Reprinted by permission of Taylor and Francis Books Ltd.
Excerpt from "The Origin of the Work of Art" from BASIC WRITINGS, REVISED AND EXPANDED EDITION by Martin Heidegger and EDITED by DAVID FARRELL KRELL English Translation © 1977, 1993 by HarperCollins Publishers Inc. General Introduction and Introductions to Each Selection Copyright © 1977, 1993 by David Farrell Krell. Reprinted by permission of HarperCollins Publishers.

6:2
Extract from *L'oeil et l'esprit* by Maurice Merleau-Ponty (1985, Editions Gallimard, Paris). Reprinted by permission from Editions Gallimard.

6:3
Extract from *The Psychology of the Imagination,* Jean-Paul Sartre (New York Philosophical Library). Reprinted by permission of Taylor and Francis Group.

6:4
Extract from Mikel Dufrenne, *Phenomenologie de l'experience esthetique* (1967, Presses Universitaire de France). Reprinted by permission of PUF.

6:5
Extract from Idhe, Don, *Expanding Hermeneutics: Visualism in Science* (Evanston: Northwestern University Press, 1998 pp. 159–163 (excerpts)). Reprinted by permission of Northwestern University Press.

7:1
The Four Fundamental Concepts of Psycho-Analysis by Jacques Lacan, translated by Alan Sheridan. Copyright © 1973 by Editions du Seuil. English translation © 1977 by Alan Sheridan. Used by permission of W. W. Norton & Company, Inc.
Extract from *The Four Fundamental Concepts of Pyscho-Analysis* by Jacques Lacan, translated by Alan Sheridan, published by Chatto & Windus. Reprinted by permission of The Random House Group Ltd.

7:2
pp. 45–47 from *Psychoanalysis and Cinema,* Christian Metz trans. Celia Britton et al. (1982, Palgrave Macmillan). Reprinted by permission from Macmillan.

7:3
pp. 19–26 from *Visual and Other Pleasures,* Laura Mulvey (Macmillan). Reprinted by permission from Macmillan.

7:4
Extract from Joan Copec, *Imagine There's No Woman: Ethics and Sublimation* (2004, MIT Press). Reprinted by permission of The MIT Press.

7:5
Extract from *The Hidden Order of Art,* Anton Ehrenzweig (2000, Orion). Reprinted by permission of The Orion Publishing Group.

8:2
"Icon and Image" pp. 207–214, extract from Paul Ricoeur, *The Rule of Metaphor* (2003, Routledge). Reprinted by permission of Taylor and Francis Books Ltd.
"Icon and Image" pp. 207–214, extract from Paul Ricoeur, *The Rule of Metaphor.* Reprinted by permission of University of Toronto Press [USA and Canadian rights].

8:3
Extract from 'This is Not a Pipe' by Michel Foucault (1983, University of California press). Reprinted by permission of The University of California Press.

10:1
pp. 16–19 and p. 21 from *Pedagogical Sketchbook* by Paul Klee. Reprinted by permission from Faber & Faber.

10:2
Extract from "The Filmic Fourth Dimension" in *Film Form: Essays in Film Theory* by Sergei Eisenstein, English translation by Jay Leyda. Copyright © 1949 by Harcourt Inc. and renewed 1977 by Jay Leyda. Reprinted by permission of the publisher.

10:3
Extract from William Mitchell, 'The Reconfigured Eye: Visual Truth in the Post-photographic Era' (1994, The MIT Press). Reprinted by permission of the publishers.

10:4
Extract from SECRET KNOWLEDGE (pp. 12–17, 66–67 only) by David Hockney, (2001, Thames and Hudson Ltd.) Copyright © 2001 David Hockney. Reproduced by permission of the author c/o Rogers, Coleridge & White Ltd., 20 Powis Mews, London, W11 1JN.

10:5
Extract from material first published in 'Iconoclash: Beyond the Image Wars in Science, Religion and Art' eds. Bruno Latour and Peter Weibel, (ZKM, Centre of Art and Media, Karlsruhe, The MIT Press, Cambridge, MA, 2002). Reprinted by kind permission of the publishers.

11:1
Extract from *Understanding Media: The Extensions of Man* by Marshall McLuhan (2001, Routledge). Reprinted by permission of T & F Informa plc. Extract from *Understanding Media: The Extensions of Man* by Marshall McLuhan (1994, MIT Press). Reprinted by permission from the MIT Press.

11:2
pp. 1–2, 8–13 from *The Image of the City*, Kevin Lynch (1960, MIT Press). Reprinted by permission of the MIT Press.

11:3
Extract from ON PHOTOGRAPHY by Susan Sontag (1978, Allen Lane). Reprinted by permission of The Penguin Group UK.
"The Image-World" from ON PHOTOGRAPHY by Susan Sontag. Copyright © 1977 by Susan Sontag. Reprinted by permission of Farrar, Straus and Giroux, LLC.

11:4
Extract from 'The Philosopher as Andy Warhol' in *Philosophizing Art* (1999, University of California Press), pp 65 and 80–82. Reprinted by kind permission of the author and Georges Borchardt Inc.

11:5
Extract from 'Symbol, Idol and Mūrti' by Gregory Price Grieve from *RCTCI – Culture, Theory and Critique*. Reprinted by permission of T & F Group journals.

11:7
Extract from *Feminism and Visual Culture Reader*, ed Amelia Jones (2003, Routledge). Reprinted by kind permission of Meiling Cheng. This piece is dedicated to his son, Ashtin Natshi Wang.

12:3
Extract from *White: Essays on Race and Culture* by Richard Dyer (1997, Routledge). Reprinted by permission of the Taylor and Francis Group.

12:5
Extract from *Inner Vision* by Semir Zeki (1999, Oxford University Press). Used by permission of the publishers.

13:1
Extract *From Iconology: Image, Text, Ideology* by W.J.T. Mitchell (Chicago: University of Chicago Press, 1986). Reprinted by permission of University of Chicago Press.

13:2
Reprinted from James Elkins, *The Domain of Images*. Copyright © 1999 by Cornell University. Used by permission of the publisher, Cornell University Press.

13:3
Extract from Barbara Stafford, *Good Looking*: *Essays on the Virtue of Images*. Reprinted by permission of the MIT Press.

13:4
p. 171 'Mediological Tables' from *Media Manifestos* by Régis Debray (1993, Verso). Reprinted by permission of Verso.

13:5
Bruno Latour, from 'What is Iconoclash Or is There a World Beyond the Image Wars?' in *Iconoclash: Beyond the Image Wars in Science, Religion and Art*, ed. Bruno Latour and Peter Weibel, Cambridge, MA and London: The MIT Press: and, ZKM, Centre for Art and Media, Karlsruhe, Germany, 2002, pp. 14–15 and 25–32.
Copyright © Bruno Latour. Reproduced with permission of Bruno Latour.

Figure 3.1
Conservative Party Election Poster, 1983. Reprinted by permission of the Conservative Party.

Figure 4.2
Barr, Alfred Hamilton Jr (1902–1981): Cover of the exhibition catalogue "Cubism and Abstract Art", MoMA 1936. New York, Museum of Modern Art (MoMA). The Museum of Modern Art Library, New York © 2005. Digital image, The Museum of Modern Art, New York/Scala, Florence.

Figures 5.1 and 5.2
Film stills from 'Ivan The Terrible' and 'Obyknovennyi Fashizm (Ordinary Fascism)' used by permission of the BFI.

Figure 5.3
Vermeer, Johannes, *Woman Holding a Balance,* Widener Collection. Image © 2006 Board of Trustees, National Gallery of Art, Washington.

Figure 6.1
Van Gogh, Vincent, *A Pair of Shoes*. © Van Gogh Museum, Amsterdam.

Figure 7.1
Hans Holbein the Younger, Jean de Dinteville and Georges de Selve ('The Ambassadors') © National Gallery London.

Figure 7.2
Cindy Sherman, Untitled Film Still #2 (1977). Courtesy of Metro Pictures.

Figure 7.3
Cindy Sherman, Untitled Film Still #35 (1979). Courtesy of Metro Pictures.

Figure 8.2
Magritte René, *Les Deux Mystères* (1966) © ADAGP, Paris and DACS, London, 2006.

Figure 10.11
Paul Klee, Fabtafel (auf maiorem Grau)/ Colour Table (in grey major), 1930, 83 from Zentrum Paul Klee © DACS, London.
Paul Klee, Specielle Ordnung/ Pedagogical Sketchbook, PN30, M60/101 Recto from Zentrum Paul Klee © DACS, London.

Figure 10.12
Giotto (1266–1336): Scenes from the Life of Saint Francis: Death of the Knight of Celano – detail. Assisi, San Franceso © 1990. Photo Scala, Florence.

Figure 10.14
Masolino (1383–1447): Healing of the Lame Man and Raising of Tabitha. Florence, Santa Maria del Carmine © 1991. Photo Scala, Florence/Fondo Edifici di Culto – Ministero dell'Interno.

Figure 10.15
Robert Campin, 'A Man' © National Gallery London.

Figure 12.1
Ersnt, Max, *A Little Girl Dreams of Taking the Veil* (1930) © ADAGP, Paris and DACS, London, 2006.

Figure 12.3
Duchamp, Marcel, Rotorelief No.1. 'Carolles' (1935) © Succession Marcel Duchamp/ADAGP, Paris and DACS, London 2006.
Duchamp, Marcel, Rotorelief No.3 'Chinese Lantern' (1935) © Succession Marcel Duchamp/ADAGP, Paris and DACS.

GENERAL INTRODUCTION

IMAGES, IMAGE CULTURE AND IMAGE STUDIES

The approach to the study of images proposed by this book is interdisciplinary, concerned with the notion of the 'image' in all its theoretical, critical and practical contexts, uses and history. The *Reader* is, in part, a response to W.J.T. Mitchell's regret (1986: 155), that 'there is, at present, no real "field" in the humanities ... no "iconology" that studies the problem of perceptual, conceptual, verbal and graphic images in a unified way'. In our response to this call, the *Reader* suggests a holistic field of inquiry rather than a single disciplinary practice. The approach of the *Reader* is interdisciplinary in that it creates an interdisciplinary space for the study of images, not limited to the humanities. The *Reader* accommodates and examines the different types of objects of study that various disciplines and perspectives make of images, rather than designating images as a new object of study. In so far as images are objects of study and enquiry in disciplines from art history to neuroscience, from political science to cultural studies, it cannot be assumed that the interdisciplinary terrain is already mapped out, ready for scholarly investigation. The creation of a single 'interdiscipline' would, therefore, be inappropriate. The *Reader* instead encourages users to pursue imaginative combinations of theories, images, disciplines and debates in the interdisciplinary field. In presenting the historical and philosophical trajectories along which the study of images has developed, the *Reader* also provides a guide to some of the differences and similarities between the various disciplinary approaches to images.

This book is also a response to the fact that images appear to be a prominent feature of contemporary life. Today images seem to inhabit every part of our lives, and everything seems to be or have an image. Our eyes are bombarded by visual images, most obviously those produced and disseminated by commercial entertainment and information media, from advertising billboards, newspaper photography, the internet, television, films and computer games. The urban environment is replete with the visual displays of architectural design, interior décor, landscape, shop and business fronts, and traffic signals. Print culture has gradually expanded its ability to include many visual images along with text at relatively low cost, in technical instruction manuals, educational publications, tourist brochures, magazines and shopping catalogues, to name but a few. In the sciences, the possibility of seeing what is to be known has progressed from attendance at experiments and autopsies to the viewing and production of electronic

images. Visual scientific images of previously invisible or unseen realms –
from a nebula across the galaxy to a strand of DNA – are no longer limited
to what our eyes can see through optical instruments such as the telescope
and microscope, but are generated by electronic instruments and computer
programs that translate data into images, such as those made by MRI
scanners and radio telescopes. The general technical capacity to produce
visual images has vastly increased, from manual crafting to chemical and
then digital photography, from draftsmanship to computer-aided design.
The past can be visually reconstructed and the future imagined not only in
our minds but also before our eyes. At the point at which electronic,
computer-generated images become simulations or virtual realities, it is no
longer a question of seeing images but rather of inhabiting them.

But the ubiquity of visual imagery is only half the story of contemporary
image culture. In capitalist consumerism, there has been increasing emphasis
on advertising not the product, but the image or identity of the brand.
Consumers buy trainers and cars for their logos, for the lifestyle or
experience associated with brand image, such that the image has become the
commodity (Jameson, 3.4; Klein, 2000). The corporations that produce such
commodity images, such as Nike and Microsoft, also have their own images
that constitute a large part of their financial value. Politics, particularly
electoral competition, is said to have become a matter of images and their
professional marketing. In this context image is understood as 'the reputation,
trustworthiness and credibility of the candidates or parties' (Scammel, 1995:
20). Writing in the United States in 1961, Daniel Boorstin (1992: 185–6)
observed the confluence between political and commercial images,
characterising an image as a 'pseudo-ideal', as 'a studiously crafted personality
profile of an individual, institution, corporation, product or service'. This
notion of images reaches into our very sense of our selves, not only in terms
of how we and others perceive our personality, but also in terms of body and
gender images that inform our physical shape and the different ways we
display ourselves visually, such as through cosmetics and fashion (Bordo, 3.6).
We seem to be images living in a world of images.

A key motivation for this anthology is to provide an aid for making sense of
contemporary image culture in the West. The *Reader* critically examines
images and debates about them in various historical, theoretical and cultural
contexts. We understand image culture to include not only the institutionalised culture of galleries, museums and performance spaces, not only
the popular culture of the mediasphere, not only the commercialised
culture of consumerism; but also the culture of politics, of the economy, of
science and technology, of ideas, thought and knowledge, of bodies, social
classes, gender and race, of subjectivity and identity. Image culture is as
broad as the culture of everyday life and as pertinent to each specialised
sphere of activity as any other.

Yet, despite the sheer prevalence of images, despite the many academic
engagements with them, despite the frequent acknowledgements that we

live in an image culture, there is a persistent, even consistent, lack of coherence and understanding about what images are. Images thus constitute a problematic field for contemporary intellectual endeavour. If image culture is one of the spurs for collating this book, another is an acute need to understand the various meanings of the term 'image' as it is used in different contexts. When we say the word 'image' we do not always seem to know what we mean, or, rather, we may mean too much or too little. Wittgenstein argues that attempts to define the essence of a vague term such as 'image' are futile. A word does not show us the essence of a thing, but for the most part 'the meaning of a word is its use in language' (Wittgenstein, 1958: §43). We often know what words such as 'image' mean when they crop up in everyday use without being able to explain that meaning in precise terms. There is no single definition or 'essential nature' of images, different meanings having only some semantic overlap in common. Wittgenstein further suggests that we make sense of a term such as image by perceiving a complex network of relations, which he calls 'family resemblances', between different meanings. Rather than striving for absolute clarity in a philosophical concept that can guide our research in advance, we should take our cues from the everyday language in which 'image culture' is used.

Mitchell (13.1) directly invokes a Wittgensteinian approach to the multiple meanings of the word 'image' by figuring images as a family that includes graphic, optical, perceptual, mental and verbal forms. His 'family tree of images' is a graphic illustration of the many different 'institutionalized discourses', types and sites of images and of how difficult it is to develop an adequate taxonomy of images that will serve every purpose. Mitchell points out that only some images, such as the ones mentioned in the first paragraph above, are visual. Dreams, fantasies, memories, literary images, metaphors, ideas and sense impressions have also been understood as images. The corporate, political, personal, bodily and commodity images mentioned above that are so integral to image culture are also not predominantly visual images, though they generally have visual manifestations.

This collection of readings, then, does not attempt to define the image as such, but instead presents a representative but not exhaustive range of the historical contexts, institutionalised discourses, theoretical approaches and debates that are pertinent to the study of images. Only by figuring out the family resemblances between the use of the term images in all of these settings, only by understanding the meaning of images across theories and debates, will an appreciation of the significance of images for contemporary culture emerge. Not least among the relations to be mapped are those between the allegedly strict, literal or 'proper' meanings of images in visual senses and extended, figurative meanings. Mitchell (13.1) advises us not to overlook the latter as 'bastard children' in the family of images. The relations between the proliferation of visual imagery and the transformation (or experience) of objects, events and ideas as images is crucial to any characterisation of contemporary image culture.

Yet, the analysis of images through history, theory and culture requires, therefore, not only the analysis of different types of visual and non-visual images, in terms of their conditions of production, dissemination and interpretation. It also requires an appreciation of the roles of and attitudes to images in their various academic, cultural and economic contexts. A brain scan can be enjoyed aesthetically, but in a hospital setting its functional use as evidence for pathology is paramount, requiring specialised interpretative skills. Each of the various domains of images deserves study in its own right as well as an aspect of the network of relations that constitute image culture. Moreover, the interdisciplinary study of image culture must also be historical and comparative. What is the justification for considering it more imagistic than previous cultures? How have the roles of images changed over time, such as in relation to other modes of signification (Debray, 13.4)? One of the central themes of this bsook is how images have been discussed and contested from some of the first writings on the subject to the present day. The study of image culture entails a history of the past as well as of the present.

Another motivation for compiling this volume is to array the discursive apparatus required for the study of images. In this respect, we have been influenced most immediately by those writers we have gathered together under the heading 'Image Studies' (Section 13), especially W.J.T. Mitchell, James Elkins and Barbara Maria Stafford. The *Reader* aims both to define the interdisciplinary field of 'image studies' and create the discursive conditions for making image studies a reality. In presenting a selection of key readings across the domains of philosophy, art, literature, science, critical theory and cultural studies, the *Reader* tells the story of the image through intellectual history from the Bible to the present. By including both well-established writings and more recent and innovative research, the *Reader* outlines the specific developments of the forms of discourses about images emerging today.

Each of the pioneers in this incipient, interdisciplinary field has provided the impetus to reconsider how, why, and in relation to what we might examine and understand images. They consider what demarcates the field of images, the historical, social and cultural complexes that images reveal and what role images can play in the broader interests of thought and critique. There is an overriding concern among these and other writers in the field to do justice to images, rather than treat them reductively through the twin orientations of iconophobia and iconophilia – the hatred or love of images, respectively. This entails an effort to understand images in their own terms and to allow for the many different types of images. As a result, the interdisciplinary study of images is not restricted to a single theorisation. The *Reader* – through its variety of entries – therefore explores different contexts and methodologies.

The need for an interdisciplinary study of images is dictated by the limitations of the current disciplines and multidisciplinary arrangements, particularly by the division between the sciences and the humanities. By and large, images have been studied academically through the disciplines of art and art history, traditionally divided between either aesthetic or social and cultural history enquiry. Even today those best suited to understand images in the broader sense have been those trained in practical criticism – the study of art, for example, sitting somewhere between theory and practice. The capacity of art history and criticism to deal with images of all sorts has also been enhanced by catering for a far greater complexity of artistic production and performance, including those using new technologies. It is thus not surprising that two of the pioneers of image studies named above are art historians. Elkins (1999), for example, has called into question the whole 'domain of images' by applying critical and analytical tools to 'non-art' images. Stafford (1996) urges art history to re-invent itself as 'imaging studies'. Art history as it stands currently, she suggests, is too narrow a base from which to study all the relatives within a 'family of images'. It is soon apparent, for example, that Stafford's interests in cognitive science and computer screens, through which she aims to demonstrate the 'intelligence of sight', cannot be contained, or sustained, by her home discipline.

Given that there is already a relatively established interdisciplinary area of visual studies, and given that even the scholars mentioned above do not unequivocally call for the institutionalisation of image studies or a clear differentiation from visual culture (Elkins, 2003: 7), why is there a need for yet another new academic field? Mitchell's (1986) plea for the revival of iconology as the study of all members of the family of images opens the door to a truly multi-disciplinary approach to the subject that transcends the strictures of art history. It is clear from his inclusion of perceptual, mental and verbal images in the family of images that the interdisciplinary study of images is not to be understood as concerned solely with the narrower concepts such as 'vision' and 'visuality'. Image studies thereby marks itself out from the recent growth in visual cultural studies, which works largely from within a cultural studies perspective (Evans and Hall, 1999; Mirzoeff, 1998). In our framework, visual cultural studies can be subsumed into a wider frame of analysis and critical perspective, though not all of its practices should be welcomed uncritically. For example, Elkins (2003: 83) suggests that 'visual images might not always be the optimal place to look for signs of gender, identity, politics, and the other questions that are of interest to scholars'. The interdisciplinary study of images turns to a broader set of perspectives from which to explore the purported 'pictorial turn' identified by Mitchell (1994: 11). The perceived predominance of the visual is, in this light, examined as both an object of enquiry – a visual culture open to interpretation – and equally as a perspective of enquiry.

At the risk of establishing an overly antagonistic relationship with visual studies, we offer some further justification for the distinct development of image studies. The usage of visual culture to refer to all types of images and all aspects of image culture is a feature of the 'picturalising of the domain of images' that has 'continued inexorably till the full spectrum of invisible and inner-bodily images were modelled on, or reconceived in pictorial terms'

(Van Den Berg, 2004: 10). The colonisation of the image categories by visual or pictorial ones is not an innocent process but one that expresses an ideology of ocularcentrism that privileges vision above other senses, ennobling vision with the authority of knowledge of and power over that which is seen. Similarly to Romanyshyn (8.4), Van Den Berg argues that Western culture is deeply implicated with ocularcentric ideology, through practices and institutions such as the invention of perspective in realistic visual representation, detached, objectifying scientific observation, Panoptical social surveillance, and in short all aspects of the 'gaze'. Even if this argument is exaggerated or even unfounded, some explanation is required for the tendency of visual meanings of the word image to colonise the others, as if a mental image is an object looked at in the mind, or as if an idea must conjure up a picture. Image studies resists the 'picturalising' of images (or even the visualising of the invisible) because it is inappropriate to consider all forms of images as if they are visual.

An example that illustrates the significance of the distinction between visual images or pictures and non-visual images is Susan Sontag's (2004) essay on the photographs of the torture of Abu Ghraib prisoners. The photographs are undoubtedly pictures of enormous political importance. The predominant trope of Sontag's essay is nicely summed up by the first-page subheading: 'Susan Sontag on the real meaning of the Abu Ghraib pictures'. Sontag treats the pictures to a political hermeneutic, arguing that 'complex crimes of leadership, policies and authority [are] revealed by the pictures'. By looking at the pictures, Sontag can read the pathologies of US political power and socio-cultural existence.

Sontag's essay, though, is as much about what the photographs do, or she would like them to do, as what they reveal or mean. First, she notes that photographs have accrued 'an insuperable power to determine what people recall of events'. Despite the Pentagon's planning, then, these pictures of torture would stick in people's minds as much as, say, the contrived toppling of Saddam Hussein's statue. Second, they 'tarnish and besmirch the reputation – that is the image – of America'. Bush was 'sorry that people seeing these pictures didn't understand the true nature of the American heart', while Rumsfeld worried about the reputation of the US armed forces 'who are courageously and responsibly and professionally protecting our freedoms across the globe'. Sontag reports that the Bush administration principally deplored the damage done to America's image by the pictures. There is an important distinction between the visual images, the photographs that have political meanings and effects, and the political image, or reputation that is affected. While there are certainly visual aspects to whatever image of America Bush and Rumsfeld were concerned about (the flag, an apple pie, George Washington's face, the Statue of Liberty), these pictures are not enough to capture the concepts of freedom and democracy that they so often invoke. An aspect of living in visual culture is that there are so many visual associations even for such abstract ideas, but they do not provide the complete picture.

Having said that, there is considerable overlap between image studies and the more thoughtful forms of visual studies. Image studies in an extensive and inclusive sense might be achieved by following what Elkins (2003: 7) suggests needs to be risked for a future visual studies, which he describes as a kind of 'unconstricted, unanthropological interest in vision', an interest that, importantly, can go beyond any 'niche in the humanities'. Elkins advocates that the current remit of visual studies 'be *even more* general, welcoming scientists from various disciplines, moving beyond premodern Western visuality and into non-Western art, archaeology, and the visual elements of linguistics' (p. 41). This conception of visual studies accords for the most part with our vision for image studies. Yet, whilst Elkins refers to an extremely broad 'image domain', his account is still very much attached to what he describes as 'a love for the visual world' (p. viii). We add to that a 'love' of other kinds of images in the broad, complex family. We do not propose a discipline of image studies as a 'master science'. The current excitement (and continued concern) about images will perhaps temper and be better sustained as an underlying interest or condition, rather than a discipline. And the 'condition' of image studies will gain greater depth through interdisciplinary understanding and dialogue.

HOW TO USE THE *READER*

The *Reader* is divided into three parts, with a total of 13 separate sections. Each section is preceded by a short introduction, which explains the significance of the section for image studies, as well as the major theoretical concepts, main themes and contentious issues in the section. Paragraphs on each selection show how they relate to the understanding of images and some of the more general themes traced by individual writers. We also refer within these introductions to connections with selections from other sections, so that the threads of debates focused in one section can be followed beyond it. We also draw attention to some texts that we were unable to include for reasons of space, so that the short bibliographies that appear at the end of the introduction to each section can be used for further research. Also, included below, are four alternative tables of contents. While the *Reader* neither advocates any particular theorisation of images nor makes any general overriding point about the meaning of images, it is possible to discern some recurring themes and tropes that resonate today. We have attempted to reflect these views in the structure(s) of this book. The selections that we have made fall into three major parts.

Part One, **Historical and Philosophical Precedents**, sets the background for contemporary debates about images. Images have always played a central role in helping to define social orders, from the cave paintings of Lascaux, Chauvet and Altamira, to the pedagogical frescos in mediaeval churches and the iconography of military regimes. Before assuming that contemporary culture is more predominantly an image culture than other and previous cultures, more historical reflection is required on what images meant in and to past societies. Some of the readings in this part introduce major theoretical approaches to images covered in the second part, notably Marx (2.3, 2.4) for ideology critique (Section 3) and Freud (2.8) for psychoanalysis (Section 7).

More significantly, though, these selections indicate the extent to which attitudes expressed thousands and hundred of years ago still frame current debates about images. As the introduction to Section 1 explains, the antagonism to images, or iconophobia, expressed in the rejection of idolatry is still prevalent today. Mitchell (1994: 15) claims that there is a paradox peculiar to the contemporary 'pictorial turn':

> On the one hand, it seems so overwhelmingly obvious that the era of video and cybernetic technology, the age of electronic reproduction, has developed new forms of visual stimulation and illusionism with unprecedented powers. On the other hand, the fear of the image, the anxiety that the 'power of images' may finally destroy even their creators and manipulators, is as old as image-making itself.

In other words, we are both fascinated by the seemingly pervasive power of these new images, yet, at the same time, bring age-old fears to the debate about their meaning. Manifestations of iconoclasm can thus be found not only in the first section, but also in contemporary cultural analysis (Debord, 3.2; Baudrillard, 3.3) and science (Galison, 10.5). In a similar way, earlier conceptions about the forms of thought, ideas and mental images in the mind, as well as the relation between mind and body (Aristotle, 1.7; Descartes 1.12, 1.13; Locke, 1.14; Kant, 2.1) have had an enormous influence on later and contemporary psychological and cognitive theories (Merleau-Ponty, 6.2; Sartre, 6.3; Dufrenne 6.4; Damasio, 9.2; Zeki, 12.5).

Part Two, on **Theories of Images**, provides key texts of the major approaches through which images have been conceptualised in the twentieth century and beyond. Ideology critique is not so much a theoretical perspective itself as an offshoot of Marxism that can be understood, as it is by Mitchell (1986), as an iconoclastic form of iconology, one which is particularly suited to criticism of the images of mass, consumer, popular culture. Art history is also a discipline, rather than a single theoretical approach, but its own sense of crisis about its current pertinence has provided much of the impetus for establishing image studies. Moreover, its practices of aesthetic judgement, close attention to detail, elaboration of historical and contextual issues and its variety of interpretative techniques are invaluable to any conception of image studies. Semiotics, as the study, or even science, of signs has made the strongest claims to holding the key for understanding both visual and linguistic signs, but its ambitious scope and scientific aspirations have been challenged. Phenomenology is philosophically rooted, focusing on the conscious and unconscious perception and experience of images, while also providing insights for scientific, cognitive approaches to images. Psychoanalysis' scientific claims are hotly contested, but that has not diminished its reputation for acute analysis of the unconscious processes at work in making and interpreting images, particularly of subjectivity.

Part Three, **Image Culture**, introduces some of the more recent debates about images and today's visual environment. The debate about the relative value of words and images, language and pictures easily escalates into fierce disputes about the rational, cognitive and aesthetic value of each mode of signification. Similarly, debates about the linguistic or imagistic character of human thought, particularly cognitive and critical thinking, are often heated and loaded. This brings us to some of the issues prevalent in contemporary image culture. One feature of such culture is the sheer power, scope and diversity of image production, institutions and techniques. We cover some of this diversity in readings from scientists, philosophers of science and technology and various image-makers in Section 10. In Section 11 the readings address different aspects of visual culture as well as approaches for understanding the significance of different visual practices and experiences. A key feature of visual cultural studies has been analysis of visuality as the cultural, historical and socio-political shaping of vision. As well as identifying the social impact of different forms of visuality, these analyses lead into debates about the cultural relativism and cultural construction of vision. The *Reader* closes with selections from the three pioneers of image studies, mentioned above, as well as others whose work establishes frameworks for image studies.

We recognise that tables of contents and introductions, no matter how short, can carry too much authority in setting out an approach. We have, therefore, also provided alternative tables of contents to pave the way for other possible readings and constellations of texts, as alternative ways to approach the selections in this *Reader* and as alternative frameworks for considering images. In listing the readings under different headings, we have erred on the side of inclusiveness, in the spirit of allowing connections to emerge from the reading rather than being imposed from above by the structure of the volume.

For alternative tables of contents, see pages 10–17.

Table 1 Theoretical approaches to the analysis of images

Theoretical approaches to the analysis of images	Relevant readings
Marxist ideology critique	Marx and Engels (2.3), Marx (2.4), Adorno (3.1), Debord (3.2), Jameson (3.4), Benjamin (9.6), Berger (9.7)
Non-Marxist ideology critique	Gilroy (3.5), Bordo (3.6), Kress & van Leeuwen (5.5), Lacan (7.1), Metz (7.2), Mulvey (7.3), Romanyshyn (8.4), Sontag (11.3), Lury (11.6), Cheng (11.7), Dyer (12.3), Mitchell (13.1)
Psychoanalysis	Freud (2.8), Adorno (3.1), Lacan (7.1), Metz (7.2), Mulvey (7.3), Copjec (7.4), Ehrenzweig (7.5), Romanyshyn (8.4), Krauss (12.2)
Semiotics	Baudrillard (3.3), Gilroy (3.5), Saussure (5.1), Peirce (5.2), Barthes (5.3), Bal (5.4), Kress & van Leeuwen (5.5), Lacan (7.1), Metz (7.2), DeLuca (8.5), Berger (9.7)
Aesthetic value analysis	Plato (1.5), Lessing (2.2), Panofsky (4.1), Gombrich (4.2), Alpers (4.3), Barthes (5.3), Bal (5.4), Heidegger (6.1), Merleau-Ponty (6.2), Ehrenzweig (7.5), Fenollosa (8.1), Hockney (10.4), Danto (11.4), Elkins (13.2), Stafford (13.3)
Feminism/Gender studies	Bordo (3.6), Mulvey (7.3), Copjec (7.4), Lury (11.6), Cheng (11.7)
Postcolonialism and race	Gilroy (3.5), Lury (11.6), Dyer (12.3)

Table 1 lists selections according to **theoretical or methodological approaches** to images that are not treated in separate sections in Part Two, while also indicating which selections could also be included in those sections but are located elsewhere. Interested readers can thus choose to read as a set the selections pertinent to aesthetic value analysis (the judgement of images according to aesthetic criteria), feminism and gender studies, postcolonial theory and critical race studies.

Table 2 Disciplines dealing with images

Disciplines dealing with images	Relevant readings
Art and art history	Plato (1.5), Lessing (2.2), Panofsky (4.1), Gombrich (4.2), Alpers (4.3), Buck-Morss (4.4), Bal (5.4), Heidegger (6.1), Merleau-Ponty (6.2), Lacan (7.1), Copjec (7.4), Ehrenzweig (7.5), Foucault (8.3), Klee (10.1), (William) Mitchell (10.3), Hockney (10.4), Danto (11.4), Krauss (12.2), Elkins (13.2), Stafford (13.3)
Architecture	Lynch (11.2)
Film studies	Barthes (5.3), Metz (7.2), Mulvey (7.3), Copjec (7.4), Deleuze (9.5), Eisenstein (10.2), Dyer (12.3)
Cultural, communication and media studies	Adorno (3.1), Debord (3.2), Baudrillard (3.3), Jameson (3.4), Gilroy (3.5), Bordo (3.6), Saussure (5.1), Peirce (5.2), Barthes (5.3), Kress and van Leeuwen (5.5), Lacan (7.1), Metz (7.2), Mulvey (7.3), Copjec (7.4), Romanyshyn (8.4), DeLuca (8.5), Deleuze (9.5), Benjamin (9.6), Berger (9.7), Eisenstein (10.2), (William) Mitchell (10.3), McLuhan (11.1), Sontag (11.3), Danto (11.4), Grieve (11.5), Lury (11.6), Dyer (12.3), Jay (12.4), Debray (13.4), Latour (13.5)
Visual culture studies	Debord (3.2), Bordo (3.6), Alpers (4.3), Buck-Morss (4.4), Barthes (5.3), Bal (5.4), Kress and van Leeuwen (5.5), Ihde (6.5), Lacan (7.1), Metz (7.2), Mulvey (7.3), Copjec (7.4), Foucault (8.3), Romanyshyn (8.4), DeLuca (8.5), Deleuze (9.5), Berger (9.7), Hockney (10.4), Galison (10.5), Lynch (11.2), Sontag (11.3), Danto (11.4), Grieve (11.5), Lury (11.6), Cheng (11.7), Crary (12.1), Krauss (12.2), Dyer (12.3), Jay (12.4), Mitchell (13.1), Elkins (13.2), Stafford (13.3), Debray (13.4), Latour (13.5)
Neuroscience	Damasio (9.2), Zeki (12.5)
Science studies	Ihde (6.5), Galison (10.5), Latour (13.5)
Historical studies	Alpers (4.3), Benjamin (9.6), Crary (12.1)
Literary studies	Aristotle (1.6), Lessing (2.2), Saussure (5.1), Bal (5.4), Fenollosa (8.1), Ricoeur (8.2), Proust (9.3), Le Doeuff (9.4)
Anthropology and sociology	Marx and Engels (2.3), Marx (2.4), Debord (3.2), Baudrillard (3.3), Gilroy (3.5), Kress and van Leeuwen (5.5), Sontag (11.3), Grieve (11.5), Lury (11.6), Dyer (12.3), Jay (12.4), Debray (13.4)

(Continued)

Table 2   (Continued)

Disciplines dealing with images	Relevant readings
Philosophy	Plato (1.4, 1.5), Aristotle (1.6, 1.7), Hobbes (1.11), Descartes (1.12, 1.13), Locke (1.14), Kant (2.1), Marx and Engels (2.3), Marx (2.4), Nietzsche (2.5), Bergson (2.7), Heidegger (6.1), Merleau-Ponty (6.2), Sartre (6.3), Dufrenne (6.4), Ihde (6.5), Wittgenstein (9.1), Le Doeuff (9.4), Deleuze (9.5), Benjamin (9.6), Danto (11.4)
History of psychology	Hobbes (1.11), Descartes (1.12, 1.13), Locke (1.14), Kant (2.1), Bergson (2.7), Freud (2.8), Merleau-Ponty (6.2), Sartre (6.3)
Education	Buck-Morss (4.4), Kress and van Leeuwen (5.5)

Table 2 lists selections according to the **academic disciplines** to which they belong or within which they are likely to be read. The categories in this table should be self-explanatory, but as several selections appear under more than one heading, the interdisciplinary nature of image studies is highlighted.

Table 3   Types of images

Types of images	Relevant readings
Drawing and illustration	Kress and van Leeuwen (5.5), Ehrenzweig (7.5), Benjamin (9.6), Klee (10.1), Hockney (10.4), Krauss (12.2), Elkins (13.2)
Paintings	Plato (1.5), Lessing (2.2), Panofsky (4.1), Gombrich (4.2), Alpers (4.3), Bal (5.4), Heidegger (6.1), Merleau-Ponty (6.2), Lacan (7.1), Foucault (8.3), Hockney (10.4), Danto (11.4), Elkins (13.2)
Photographs (chemical)	Barthes (5.3), Copjec (7.4), Berger (9.7), Hockney (10.4), Sontag (11.3), Crary (12.1), Dyer (12.3)
TV	Adorno (3.1), Romanyshyn (8.4), DeLuca (8.5), Dyer (12.3)
Film	Barthes (5.3), Mulvey (7.3), Copjec (7.4), Deleuze (9.5), Eisenstein (10.2), Dyer (12.3), Jay (12.4)
Magazine, newspaper and still ads	Gilroy (3.5), Bordo (3.6), Danto (11.4), Lury (11.6)
Computer screen images (internet)	(William) Mitchell (10.3), Hockney (10.4), Stafford (13.3), Debray (13.4)
Scientific images (incl. human sciences)	Kress and van Leeuwen (5.5), Ihde (6.5), Damasio (9.2), Hockney (10.4), Galison (10.5), Zeki (12.5), Elkins (13.2), Stafford (13.3), Latour (13.5)

(Continued)

Table 3 (Continued)

Types of images	Relevant readings
3-D artefacts (sculptures and buildings)	McLuhan (11.1), Lynch (11.2), Grieve (11.5)
Optics	Plato (1.4), Descartes (1.13), Marx and Engels (2.3), Lacan (7.1), Hockney (10.4), Crary (12.1), Zeki (12.5), Mitchell (13.1)
Verbal images	Aristotle (1.7), Lessing (2.2), Nietzsche (2.5, 2.6), Saussure (5.1), Peirce (5.2), Bal (5.4), Sartre (6.3), Fenollosa (8.1), Ricoeur (8.2), Foucault (8.3), Wittgenstein (9.1), Proust (9.3), Le Doeuff (9.4), Mitchell (13.1), Stafford (13.3)
Mental images	Plato (1.4), Aristotle (1.7), Hobbes (1.11), Descartes (1.12, 1.13), Locke (1.14), Kant (2.1), Marx and Engels (2.3), Nietzsche (2.5), Bergson (2.7), Freud (2.8), Baudrillard (3.3), Bordo (3.6), Panofsky (4.1), Gombrich (4.2), Saussure (5.1), Peirce (5.2), Sartre (6.3), Dufrenne (6.4), Lacan (7.1), Metz (7.2), Ehrenzweig (7.5), Wittgenstein (9.1), Damasio (9.2), Proust (9.3), Le Doeuff (9.4), Deleuze (9.5), Benjamin (9.6), Berger (9.7), Mitchell (13.1)
Perceptual images	Plato (1.4, 1.5), Aristotle (1.7), Hobbes (1.11), Descartes (1.12, 1.13), Locke (1.14), Kant (2.1), Marx and Engels (2.3), Bergson (2.7), Adorno (3.1), Debord (3.2), Baudrillard (3.3), Jameson (3.4), Gilroy (3.5), Bordo (3.6), Panofsky (4.1), Saussure (5.1), Peirce (5.2), Barthes (5.3), Bal (5.4), Kress and van Leeuwen (5.5), Heidegger (6.1), Merleau-Ponty (6.2), Sartre (6.3), Dufrenne (6.4), Ihde (6.5), Lacan (7.1), Metz (7.2), Mulvey (7.3), Copjec (7.4), Ehrenzweig (7.5), Romanyshyn (8.4), DeLuca (8.5), Wittgenstein (9.1), Damasio (9.2), Deleuze (9.5), Berger (9.7), Eisenstein (10.2), Hockney (10.4), McLuhan (11.1), Lynch (11.2), Sontag (11.3), Danto (11.4), Grieve (11.5), Lury (11.6), Cheng (11.7), Krauss (12.2), Dyer (12.3), Mitchell (13.1), Stafford (13.3)
Icons, idols, symbols and logos	Genesis (1.1), Exodus (1.2), Midrash Rabbah (1.3), Iconodules and Iconoclasts in Byzantium (1.8, 1.9, 1.10), Hobbes (1.11), Marx (2.4), Freud (2.8), Jameson (3.4), Panofsky (4.1), Saussure (5.1), Peirce (5.2), Ihde (6.5), Fenollosa (8.1), Foucault (8.3), McLuhan (11.1), Lynch (11.2), Danto (11.4), Grieve (11.5), Lury (11.6), Mitchell (13.1), Latour (13.5)

Table 3 lists selections according to the **type of image** discussed. However, as mentioned above, no particular typology of images is satisfactory for all issues and approaches. In addition to the types of image included in Mitchell's (13.1) family tree, we have categorised selections according to everyday types of media and art images.

Table 4   Issues and debates in image studies

Issues and debates in image studies	Relevant readings
Contemporary culture as image culture (hyper-reality, media and science images)	Adorno (3.1), Debord (3.2), Baudrillard (3.3), Jameson (3.4), Bordo (3.6), Buck-Morss (4.4), Bal (5.4), Kress and van Leeuwen (5.5), Ihde (6.5), Copjec (7.4), Foucault (8.3), Romanyshyn (8.4), DeLuca (8.5), Damasio (9.2), Berger (9.7), Galison (10.5), McLuhan (11.1), Sontag (11.3), Danto (11.4), Lury (11.6), Cheng (11.7), Crary (12.1), Krauss (12.2), Dyer (12.3), Jay (12.4), Mitchell (13.1), Elkins (13.2), Stafford (13.3), Debray (13.4), Latour (13.5)
Tension between word and image (logosphere/videosphere)	Plato (1.4), Lessing (2.2), Nietzsche (2.6), Saussure (5.1), Bal (5.4), Kress and van Leeuwen (5.5), Fenollosa (8.1), Ricoeur (8.2), Foucault (8.3), Romanyshyn (8.4), DeLuca (8.5), Wittgenstein (9.1), Le Doeuff (9.4), Benjamin (9.6), Galison (10.5), Grieve (11.5), Jay (12.4), Mitchell (13.1), Stafford (13.3), Debray (13.4), Latour (13.5)
Visual semiotics and rhetoric (verbal interpretation of the visual)	Gilroy (3.5), Bordo (3.6), Panofsky (4.1), Gombrich (4.2), Alpers (4.3), Buck Morss (4.4), Saussure (5.1), Peirce (5.2), Barthes (5.3), Bal (5.4), Kress and van Leeuwen (5.5), Heidegger (6.1), Merleau-Ponty (6.2), Ihde (6.5), Lacan (7.1), Metz (7.2), Mulvey (7.3), Copjec (7.4), Ehrenzweig (7.5), Fenollosa (8.1), Foucault (8.3), DeLuca (8.5), Deleuze (9.5), Berger (9.7), Galison (10.5), Grieve (11.5), Lury (11.6), Dyer (12.3), Elkins (13.2), Stafford (13.3)
Power of images (iconophobia, ideology critique, political images)	Genesis (1.1), Exodus (1.2), Midrash Rabbah (1.3), Plato (1.4, 1.5), Iconodules and Iconoclasts in Byzantium (1.8, 1.9, 1.10), Hobbes (1.11), Descartes (1.12), Marx and Engels (2.3), Marx (2.4), Adorno (3.1), Debord (3.2), Baudrillard (3.3), Jameson (3.4), Gilroy (3.5), Bordo (3.6), Barthes (5.3), Kress and van Leeuwen (5.5.), Heidegger (6.1), Lacan (7.1), Metz (7.2), Mulvey (7.3), Copjec (7.4), Romanyshyn (8.4), DeLuca (8.5), Le Doeuff (9.4), Deleuze (9.5), Benjamin (9.6), Berger (9.7), McLuhan (11.1), Sontag (11.3), Danto (11.4), Grieve (11.5), Lury (11.6), Cheng (11.7), Krauss (12.2), Dyer (12.3), Jay (12.4), Mitchell (13.1), Stafford (13.3), Debray (13.4), Latour (13.5)

(Continued)

Table 4   (Continued)

Issues and debates in image studies	Relevant readings
Relation of images to language and thought	Plato (1.5), Aristotle (1.7), Hobbes (1.11), Descartes (1.13), Locke (1.14), Kant (2.1), Nietzsche (2.5, 2.6), Bergson (2.7), Freud (2.8), Panofsky (4.1), Saussure (5.1), Peirce (5.2), Barthes (5.3), Kress and van Leeuwen (5.5), Heidegger (6.1), Merleau-Ponty (6.2), Sartre (6.3), Dufrenne (6.4), Ihde (6.5), Lacan (7.1), Metz (7.2), Mulvey (7.3), Copjec (7.4), Ehrenzweig (7.5), Fenollosa (8.1), Ricoeur (8.2), Foucault (8.3), Romanyshyn (8.4), DeLuca (8.5), Wittgenstein (9.1), Damasio (9.2), Proust (9.3), Le Doeuff (9.4), Deleuze (9.5), Benjamin (9.6), Berger (9.7), Klee (10.1), Galison (10.5), McLuhan (11.1), Grieve (11.5), Cheng (11.7), Krauss (12.2), Mitchell (13.1), Stafford (13.3), Debray (13.4), Latour (13.5)
Relation of visual to other perceptual modes, aurality/music	Plato (1.5), Iconodules and Iconoclasts in Byzantium (1.8, 1.9, 1.10), Lessing (2.2), Bergson (2.7), Barthes (5.3), Romanyshyn (8.4), DeLuca (8.5), Damasio (9.2), Proust (9.3), Eisenstein (10.2), McLuhan (11.1), Debray (13.4)
Scopic regimes, techniques of visibility	Debord (3.2), Gilroy (3.5), Alpers (4.3), Barthes (5.3), Bal (5.4), Metz (7.2), Mulvey (7.3), Copjec (7.4), Ehrenzweig (7.5), Romanyshyn (8.4), Deleuze (9.5), Eisenstein (10.2), (William) Mitchell (10.3), Hockney (10.4), Galison (10.5), McLuhan (11.1), Lynch (11.2), Grieve (11.5), Lury (11.6) Crary (12.1), Krauss (12.2), Dyer (12.3), Debray (13.4)
What is an image? (object, way of seeing, physical perception)	Genesis (1.1), Plato (1.4), Aristotle (1.7), Iconodules and Iconoclasts in Byzantium (1.8, 1.9, 1.10), Hobbes (1.11), Descartes (1.13), Locke (1.14), Kant (2.1), Marx (2.4), Nietzsche (2.6), Bergson (2.7), Freud (2.8), Baudrillard (3.3), Jameson (3.4), Panofsky (4.1), Gombrich (4.2), Peirce (5.2), Barthes (5.3), Heidegger (6.1), Merleau-Ponty (6.2), Sartre (6.3), Dufrenne (6.4), Ihde (6.5), Lacan (7.1), Copjec (7.4), Ehrenzweig (7.5), Foucault (8.3), Wittgenstein (9.1), Damasio (9.2), Proust (9.3), Le Doeuff (9.4), Deleuze (9.5), Benjamin (9.6), Klee (10.1), Lynch (11.2), Krauss (12.2), Mitchell (13.1), Elkins (13.2), Stafford (13.3), Debray (13.4), Latour (13.5)

(Continued)

Table 4   (Continued)

Issues and debates in image studies	Relevant readings
Theories as images	Exodus (1.2), Midrash Rabbah (1.3), Plato (1.4), Iconodules and Iconoclasts in Byzantium (1.8, 1.9, 1.10), Hobbes (1.11), Descartes (1.13), Locke (1.14), Kant (2.1), Marx and Engels (2.3), Marx (2.4), Nietzsche (2.5), Adorno (3.1), Debord (3.2), Jameson (3.4), Gilroy (3.5), Bordo (3.6), Gombrich (4.2), Barthes (5.3), Bal (5.4), Ihde (6.5), Lacan (7.1), Metz (7.2), Mulvey (7.3), Ricoeur (8.2), Romanyshyn (8.4), Wittgenstein (9.1), Le Doeuff (9.4), Deleuze (9.5), Benjamin (9.6), Berger (9.7), Klee (10.1), Eisenstein (10.2), Galison (10.5), McLuhan (11.1), Lynch (11.2), Sontag (11.3), Danto (11.4), Grieve (11.5), Lury (11.6), Cheng (11.7), Krauss (12.2), Dyer (12.3), Mitchell (13.1), Stafford (13.3), Debray (13.4)

Table 4 lists selections according to **issues and debates in image studies**. Some of the headings here include fuller listings of selections relevant to issues and debates identified in Part Three of the reader, notably Section 8 on relations between words and images, and Section 9 on relations between images and thought. The category on contemporary image culture includes readings that both characterise contemporary culture as an image culture and explore different aspects of it. The 'visual semiotics or rhetoric' heading covers selections that address the fraught question, discussed in the introduction to Section 5, of whether particular modes of analysis can work for both linguistic and imagistic (or visual) signs and representations. The category about the power of images expands the discussion on iconophobia (in the introduction to Section 1) and ideology critique (Section 3) to cover the range of readings that address the power that images are said to have over our minds and in establishing or legitimising social power relations. One of the main doubts about the pertinence of characterising contemporary culture as visual culture is that so many of its features are multimedia, normally including sound. The relation between visuality and aurality, as well as other senses and modes of perception of images, is therefore covered by another heading. Visuality, the mode of seeing and looking, is not uniform but, as discussed in the introduction to Section 12, is organised by varying 'scopic regimes' or techniques of rendering visible, readings about which are also listed under that heading. The vexed question of how to define or conceive images also deserves its own category, which includes readings pointing to some clear differences between, for example, images as static or moving objects that are produced and viewed, images as human, physical perceptions that come from or with the act of viewing, and images that are not viewed physically at all. Finally, the Greek etymological roots of the word 'theory' refer to seeing, such that theories are ways of

perceiving the world and images. The readings under this heading relate to that sense of theorising.

We are, of course, aware of the irony of producing a *Reader* about images, especially as some of the readings question the validity of analysing visual images verbally. That we have done so is a reflection of the limitations of our situation as scholars working in the humanities, where instruction and research are still largely conducted textually, even in fields such as visual culture. Were we compiling a science textbook, the budget might well have allowed for an accompanying disk packed with visual images, though the cost of copyright for the media images that are so prevalent in image culture would be prohibitive. Our background in the humanities also explains the limited range of disciplines in Table 2. Elkins (2003) notes that the sciences tend to be far more visual as disciplines than the humanities, so there is a wealth of academic visual material, as well as a whole series of issues about the imagistic character of scientific theorising, that we have barely tapped in to. Like Elkins, our inter- or transdisciplinary ambitions for image studies include the study of image making and interpreting across the natural and social sciences as well as the humanities. We are also aware that the *Reader* deals predominantly with Western image culture and Western approaches to analysing images, especially regarding the historical and philosophical background in Part One. No single volume could do justice to the range and depth of writings on images. We could not hope to map the entire territory of images, but we do hope that the *Reader* will open a few new pathways for novices and professionals alike. Overall, this volume sets out a range of materials that readers can draw on and use in fashioning their own approach to image studies.

EDITING CONVENTIONS

Many of the texts chosen have been edited. Where we have cut words, we have used '…' to indicate an omission of a few words within a sentence; '[…]' either embedded in a paragraph, or appearing at the beginning or end, to indicate the elision of a sentence or two of that paragraph; '[…]' on a new line to indicate that anything from a paragraph to more is missing; and a centred '*' to indicate a significant break in the text, the removal of a subheading or chapter.

We have also removed many of the footnotes to the texts chosen, which has allowed us to include more selections. We have occasionally added our own footnotes, which are identified as such. References such as '(Kant, 2.1)' are to selections in this volume, giving their ordering according to the section in which they are located.

REFERENCES

Boorstin, D.J. (1992) *The Image: A Guide to Pseudo-Events in America*, 25th anniversary edition. New York: Vintage Books.

Elkins, J. (1999) *The Domain of Images*. Ithaca, NY: Cornell University Press.

Elkins, J. (2003) *Visual Studies: A Skeptical Introduction*. London: Routledge.

Evans, J. and Hall, S. (eds) (1999) *Visual Culture: The Reader*. London: Sage.

Klein, N. (2000) *No Logo*. London: Flamingo.

Mirzoeff, N. (ed.) (1998) *The Visual Culture Reader*. London: Routledge.

Mitchell, W.J.T. (1986) *Iconology: Image, Text, Ideology*. Chicago: University of Chicago Press.

Mitchell, W.J.T. (1994) *Picture Theory: Essays on Verbal and Visual Representation*. Chicago: University of Chicago Press.

Scammell, M. (1995) *Designer Politics: How Elections are Won*. New York: St Martin's Press.

Sontag, S. (2004) 'What have we done?', *The Guardian*, G2 section, 24 May, pp. 2–5.

Stafford, B. (1996) *Good Looking: Essays on the Virtue of Images*. Cambridge, MA: MIT Press.

Van Den Berg, D. (2004) 'What is an image and what is image power?', *Image and Narrative*, 8 (May) Published on-line at www.imageandnarrative. be/issue08/dirkvandenbergh.htm

Wittgenstein, L. (1958) *Philosophical Investigations*, 3rd edn, tr. G.E.M. Anscombe. New York: Macmillan.

PART ONE:

HISTORICAL & PHILOSOPHICAL
PRECEDENTS

I: FROM GENESIS TO LOCKE

INTRODUCTION

Current debates about the meaning, interpretation and status of images are based on a rich and complex history dating from the beginning of writing in the West. Many of these early arguments have formed the basis for a great deal of writing on images down to the present time. Knowledge of this tradition is, therefore, crucial for understanding what kind of issues are at stake in talking about images.

Two predominant attitudes held about images by modern-day thinkers arise first in both biblical writing and early Greek philosophy: iconophobia and iconophilia – the fear (or hatred) of images and the love of images, respectively. Iconophobia is associated with a deep mistrust of images, or particular kinds of images, and can be seen at work in writers as diverse as Plato (1.4 and 1.5), Karl Marx (2.4), Sigmund Freud (2.8), Jean Baudrillard (3.3) and among many modern scientists. Iconophobes have often sought to challenge established beliefs by breaking or decrying images and are also known as iconoclasts.

This impulse can be found at work in the first pages of the Bible and in the Torah. Abraham, for example, literally smashed the idols in his father's shop because he was concerned that people would worship false gods rather than the one, true God (1.3). Similarly, in one of the most influential passages on images in the history of philosophy, Plato (1.4) has Socrates describe how ordinary people are like slaves chained in a dark cave awaiting enlightenment. In dispelling the illusion, rational thought – the right way of seeing – provides access to true knowledge and emancipation.

Both W.J.T. Mitchell (1986) and Bruno Latour (13.5) have written recently about how iconoclastic arguments share certain assumptions. First, iconoclasts purport to possess a truth denied to ordinary people because they cannot see beyond the appearances of everyday, sensory reality. They mistake images for truths and, in doing so, threaten the fabric of the social order. Second, iconoclasts have access to the truth hidden behind these superficial images either through divine insight, or because of the acquisition of a special method of inquiry. Third, only by the iconoclastic action of smashing our everyday beliefs in the images that surround us can the rest of society become privy to the real truth, while at the same time being freed from the dangerous and illusory world of the senses. Finally, in both biblical and philosophical texts the false images of this world, or way of life, are replaced by the true ones of the next.

As Mitchell has noted, iconoclasm entails both an epistemological and an ethical claim (1986: 197). So it is perhaps no accident that Plato's analogy of the cave appears as a centre piece of his political text *The Republic* (1955), which aimed to show how an ideal state would be run. Painting the existing political status quo as a false reality has been a tactic employed by many later thinkers, including Marx and Engels (2.3), Friedrich Nietzsche (2.5 and 2.6), Guy Debord (3.2) and Theodor Adorno (3.1) – most of whom grounded their ethical claims in epistemological terms.

The influence of such thinkers on later commentators owes a great deal to the strength of the critical images that they deploy in their own work. Plato's prisoners in the cave, or René Descartes' (1.12) evil demon of images, are such powerful pictures that they have become complex reference points for a whole way of thinking. For example, when Susan Bordo (3.6) talks about learning to live with the images in Plato's cave she is acknowledging her debt to his ideas, at the same time as making them relevant for today.

Given the central role afforded to icons, statuary and, later, paintings in those early Western societies dominated by religious life, the stakes over the ownership, meaning and interpretation of images were high. More often than not, debates on images were underpinned by real social upheaval. The controversy over icons in eighth-century Byzantium (1:8–1:10) was not a debate about art, but a crisis over the place and role of the holy in society, as Peter Brown (1982) has argued. Successive Arab invasions in the late seventh century created the need for social cohesion. The liberal iconodules, who had seen pictorial icons as having holy status, suddenly looked like idolaters. Fearing further divine retribution, the iconoclasts destroyed the icons and replaced them with the simple, unifying political symbol of the cross. Similar trajectories could be traced during the English Civil War – see Thomas Hobbes' writing on idolatry (1.11) – and the Cultural Revolution in China.

Iconophobia has extended to art itself. Plato (1.5) suggested that the reality depicted in paintings ends up being an image of a shadow; a corrupting influence on society. Many writers have followed Plato's mistrust of art as a vehicle for truth and marginalise the importance of art theory in their work. In contrast, Aristotle's (1.6) discussion of mimesis – or the human capacity for making meaningful representations of their social world – acted as a counter to Plato's iconophobia and informed eighteenth-century debates on the nature of representation that still remain relevant to art history.

Despite the concerns raised by Plato and others about the unreliability of sensory experience, images have frequently been used by theorists as a way of describing how we can have true knowledge of the world. Aristotle's (1.7) famous remark about 'the soul's never thinking without an image' placed images at the centre of epistemological theory, a trend that can be traced from the sixteenth century to the present day. For example, Immanuel Kant (2.1), Henri Bergson (2.7), Ludwig Wittgenstein (9.1) and Antonio Damasio (9.2) have each argued that mental images are repositories of knowledge.

It may appear today that the cognitive sciences have answered many of the traditional questions posed by philosophers such as Hobbes (1.11), Descartes (1.12 and 1.13) and John Locke (1.14). New brain-imaging technologies have promised to open up thought itself to direct observation. But, as Howard Gardner (1987) has noted, the new sciences of the brain are attempting to answer some of the very questions posed by these earlier thinkers. For example, the philosopher Daniel Dennett (1991) and the neuroscientist Antonio Damasio (1994) have published major works that explicitly acknowledge their conceptual debt to Descartes. They ask, for example, is it right to talk about images in the mind as though they represented the external world? If we only know the world through such representations can we have access to any unmediated truth? And what could it mean for images to represent? In doing so, they either implicitly rely on seventeenth-century assumptions about the nature of mental images as representations of the external world, or attempt to prove that such arguments are wrong.

But it would be a mistake to think that epistemological theory is not influenced by social forces, even when it is divorced from the kind of ethical injunction required by iconoclasm. The questions about images raised by Hobbes, Descartes and Locke emerged out of a social world coming to terms with its new-found empiricism, as Steven Shapin (1988) has argued. Locke's (1.14) image of the solitary philosopher observing his own experiences and drawing universal conclusions solely on the basis of the images reflected in his mind is mirrored by the figure of the scientific experimenter demonstrating how objective knowledge could be possible and legitimate in a world where God still provided ultimate authority. Epistemological theory helps make the social enterprise of science seem as natural as looking at a piece of wax.

Without knowledge of the reach and richness of this tradition, our understanding of images is greatly impoverished.

REFERENCES

Brown, P. (1982) 'A Dark Age crisis: aspects of the iconclastic controversy', in P. Brown (ed.), *Society and the Holy in Late Antiquity*. London: Faber & Faber. pp. 251–301.

Damasio, A.R. (1994) *Descartes' Error: Emotion, Reason and the Human Brain*. New York: G.P. Putnam's Sons.

Dennett, D.C. (1991) *Consciousness Explained*. Boston, MA: Little, Brown & Co.

Gardner, H. (1987) *The Mind's New Science: A History of the Cognitive Revolution*. New York: Basic Books.

Mitchell, W.J.T. (1986) *Iconology: Image, Text, Ideology*. Chicago: University of Chicago Press.

Plato (1955) *The Republic*, tr. Desmond Lee. London: Penguin Books.

Shapin, S. (1988) 'House of experiment in seventeenth-century England', *Isis*, 79: 373–404.

MAN CREATED IN GOD'S IMAGE

26: And God said, Let us make man in our image, after our likeness: and let them have dominion over the fish of the sea, and over the fowl of the air, and over the cattle, and over all the earth, and over every creeping thing that creepeth upon the earth.

27: So God created man in his *own* image, in the image of God created he him; male and female created he them.

1:2 GRAVEN IMAGES

4: Thou shalt not make unto thee any graven image, or any likeness *of any thing* that *is* in heaven above, or that *is* in the earth beneath, or that *is* in the water under the earth:

5: Thou shalt not bow down thyself to them, nor serve them: for I the LORD thy God *am* a jealous God, visiting the iniquity of the fathers upon the children unto the third and fourth *generation* of them that hate me;

6: And shewing mercy unto thousands of them that love me, and keep my commandments.

1:3 ABRAHAM AND THE IDOL SHOP OF HIS FATHER TERAH

Rabbi Hiya the son of Rabbi Ada said that Terah [Abraham's father] was an idol worshipper. One day Terah had to leave the store [in which he sold idols]. He left Abraham to manage the store in his absence. A man came and wanted to buy an idol. Abraham asked him: 'How old are you?' And he responded: 'Fifty or sixty years old.' Abraham then said: 'Pitiful is the man who is sixty and worships idols that are only a day old.' So the man left in embarrassment. Once, came a woman with an offering of fine flour. She said to him [Abraham]:

'Genesis, Chapter 1' and 'Exodus, Chapter 20', in *The Bible: Authorized King James Version with Apocrypha*, Oxford and New York: Oxford University Press, 1997, pp. 1. and 89–90.

From 'Midrash Rabbah, Noah, Portion 38, Section 13', tr. Shai Lavi, in *Iconoclash: Beyond the Image Wars in Science, Religion, and Art*, ed. Bruno Latour, and Peter, Weibel, Cambridge, MA: MIT Press 2002, p. 38.

'Here, take it and bring it before [the idols].' Abraham stood up, took a stick, broke all the idols, and put the stick back in the hands of the biggest idol among them. When his father returned he asked: 'Who did this to them?' Abraham answered: 'I will not deny you the truth. A woman came with an offering of fine flour and asked me to bring it before them. So I brought it before them, and each said, 'I shall eat first.' Then the biggest one stood among them, he took a stick in his hand and broke them all.' So Terah said to him: 'Why do you mock me? Do these [idols] know anything [to speak and move]?' And Abraham replied: 'Won't your ears hear what your mouth speaks?'

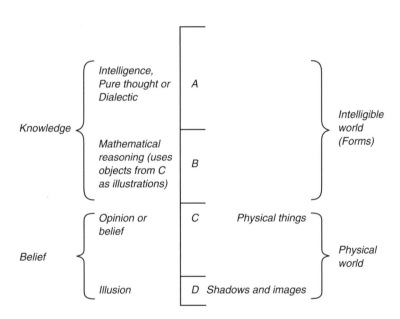

FIGURE 1.1
Plato's *The Divided Line*

1:4 THE SIMILE OF THE CAVE
PLATO

'I want you to go on to picture the enlightenment or ignorance of our human conditions somewhat as follows. Imagine an underground chamber, like a cave with an entrance open to the daylight and running a long way underground. In this chamber are men who have been prisoners there since they were children, their legs and necks being so fastened that they can only look straight ahead of them and cannot turn their heads. Behind them and above them a fire is burning, and between the fire and the prisoners runs a road, in front of which a curtain-wall has been built, like the screen at puppet shows between the operators and their audience, above which they show their puppets.'

'I see.'

'Imagine further that there are men carrying all sorts of gear along behind the curtain-wall, including figures of men and animals made of wood and stone and other materials, and that some of these men, as is natural, are talking and some not.'

'An odd picture and an odd sort of prisoner.'

'They are drawn from life,' I replied. 'For, tell me, do you think our prisoners could see anything of themselves or their fellows except the shadows thrown by the fire on the wall of the cave opposite them?'

'How could they see anything else if they were prevented from moving their heads all their lives?'

'And would they see anything more of the objects carried along the road?'

'Of course not.'

'Then if they were able to talk to each other, would they not assume that the shadows they saw were real things?'

'Inevitably.'

'And if the wall of their prison opposite them reflected sound, don't you think that they would suppose, whenever one of the passers-by on the road spoke, that the voice belonged to the shadow passing before them?'

'They would be bound to think so.'

'And so they would believe that the shadows of the objects we mentioned were in all respects real.'

'Yes, inevitably.'

'Then think what would naturally happen to them if they were released from their bonds and cured of their delusions. Suppose one of them were let loose, and suddenly compelled to stand up and turn his head and look and walk towards the fire; all these actions would be painful and he would be too dazzled to see properly the objects of which he used to see the shadows. So if he was told that what he used to see was mere illusion and that he was now nearer reality and seeing more correctly, because he was turned towards objects that were more real, and if on top of that he were compelled to say what each of the passing objects was when it was pointed out to him, don't you think he would be at a loss, and think that what he used to see was more real than the objects now being pointed out to him?'

'Much more real.'

'And if he were made to look directly at the light of the fire, it would hurt his eyes and he would turn back and take refuge in the things which he could see, which he would think really far clearer than the things being shown him.'

'Yes.'

'And if,' I went on, 'he were forcibly dragged up the steep and rocky ascent and not let go till he had been dragged out into the sunlight, the process would be a painful one, to which he would much object, and when he emerged into the light his eyes would be so overwhelmed by the brightness of it that he wouldn't be able to see a single one of the things he was now told were real.'

'Certainly not at first,' he agreed.

'Because he would need to grow accustomed to the light before he could see things in the world outside the cave. First he would find it easiest to look at shadows, next at the reflections of men and other objects in water, and later on at the objects themselves. After that he would find it easier to observe the heavenly bodies and the sky at night than by day, and to look at the light of the moon and stars, rather than at the sun and its light.'

'Of course.'

'The thing he would be able to do last would be to look directly at the sun, and observe its nature without using reflections in water or any other medium, but just as it is.'

'That must come last.'

'Later on he would come to the conclusion that it is the sun that produces the changing seasons and years and controls everything in the visible world, and is in a sense responsible for everything that he and his fellow-prisoners used to see.'

'That is the conclusion which he would obviously reach.'

'And when he thought of his first home and what passed for wisdom there, and of his fellow-prisoners, don't you think he would congratulate himself on his good fortune and be sorry for them?'

'Very much so.'

'There was probably a certain amount of honour and glory to be won among the prisoners, and prizes for keen-sightedness for anyone who could remember the order of sequence among the passing shadows and so be best able to predict their future appearances. Will our released prisoner hanker after these prizes or envy this power or honour? Won't he be more likely to feel, as Homer says, that he would far rather be "a serf in the house of some landless man",[1] or indeed anything else in the world, than live and think as they do?'

'Yes,' he replied, 'he would prefer anything to a life like theirs.'

'Then what do you think would happen,' I asked, 'if he went back to sit in his old seat in the cave? Wouldn't his eyes be blinded by the darkness, because he had come in suddenly out of the daylight?'

'Certainly.'

'And if he had to discriminate between the shadows, in competition with the other prisoners, while he was still blinded and before his eyes got used to the darkness – a process that might take some time – wouldn't he be likely to make a fool of himself? And they would say that his visit to the upper world had ruined his sight, and that the ascent was not worth even attempting. And if anyone tried to release them and lead them up, they would kill him if they could lay hands on him.'

'They certainly would.'

'Now, my dear Glaucon,' I went on, 'this simile must be connected, throughout, with what preceded it.[2] The visible realm corresponds to the prison, and the light of the fire in the prison to the power of the sun. And you won't go wrong if you connect the ascent into the upper world and the sight of the objects there with the upward progress of the mind into the intelligible realm – that's my guess, which is what you are anxious to hear. The truth of the matter is, after all, known only to God. But in my opinion, for what it is worth, the final thing to be perceived in the intelligible realm, and perceived only with difficulty, is the absolute form of Good; once seen, it is inferred to be responsible for everything right and good, producing in the visible realm light and the source of light, and being, in the intelligible realm itself, controlling source of reality and intelligence. And anyone who is going to act rationally either in public or private must perceive it.'

'I agree,' he said, 'so far as I am able to understand you.'

'Then you will perhaps also agree with me that it won't be surprising if those who get so far are unwilling to return to mundane affairs, and if their minds long to remain among higher things. That's what we should expect if our simile is to be trusted.'

'Yes, that's to be expected.'

'Nor will you think it strange that anyone who descends from contemplation of the divine to the imperfections of human life should blunder and make a fool of himself, if, while still blinded and unaccustomed to the surrounding darkness, he's forcibly put on trial in the law-courts or elsewhere about the images of justice or their shadows, and made to dispute about the conceptions of justice held by men who have never seen absolute justice.'

'There's nothing strange in that.'

'But anyone with any sense,' I said, 'will remember that the eyes may be unsighted in two ways, by a transition either from light to darkness or from darkness to light, and that the same distinction applies to the mind. So when he sees a mind confused and unable to see clearly he will not laugh without thinking, but will ask himself whether it has come from a clearer world and is confused by the unaccustomed darkness, or whether it is dazzled by the stronger light of the clearer world to which it has escaped from its previous ignorance. The first state is a reason for congratulation, the second for sympathy, though if one wants to laugh at it one can do so with less absurdity than at the mind that has descended from the daylight of the upper world.'

NOTES

1. *Odyssey*, XI, 489.

2. That is, the simile of the Sun and the analogy of the Line. The detailed relations between the three figures have been much disputed. The translation assumes the following main correspondences:

Tied prisoner in the cave	Illusion
Freed prisoner in the cave	Belief
Looking at shadows in the world outside the cave	Reason
Looking at real things in the world outside the cave	Intelligence
Looking at the sun	Vision of the Form of Good. [...]

ART AND ILLUSION
PLATO

1:5

'Can you give me a general definition of representation? I'm not sure that I know, myself, exactly what it is.'

'Then it's not very likely I shall!'

'Oh, I don't know,' I said. 'Short sight is sometimes quicker than long sight.'

'True enough,' he replied. 'But with you here, if I did see anything, I shouldn't much want to say so. You must use your own eyes.'

'Then shall we start where we always do? You know that we always assume that there is a single essential Form corresponding to each class of particular things to which we apply the same name?'

'Yes, I know.'

'Then let us take an instance. For example, there are many particular beds and tables.'

'Yes.'

'But there are only two Forms, one of Bed and one of Table.'

'Yes.'

'Then we normally say that the maker of either of these kinds of furniture has his eye on the appropriate Form; and similarly with other things. For no one could possibly make the Form itself, could he?'

Plato, 'Part Ten [Book Ten]', in *The Republic*, tr. H.D.P. Lee. London: Penguin Classics, 1955, pp. 371–4. Copyright © H.D.P. Lee, 1953, 1974 and 1987. Reproduced by permission of Penguin Books Ltd.

'No.'

'I wonder what you would call a man who could make all the objects produced by individual craftsmen?'

'He would be a remarkably clever man.'

'Just a minute, and you'll be more surprised still. For this same craftsman can not only make all artificial objects, but also create all plants and animals, himself included, and, in addition, earth and sky and gods, the heavenly bodies and the underworld.'

'An astonishing bit of craftsmanship!' he exclaimed.

'You don't believe me?' I asked. 'Tell me, do you think that a craftsman of this sort couldn't exist, or (in one sense, if not in another) create all these things ? Do you know that there's a sense in which you could create them yourself?'

'What sense?'

'It's not difficult, and can be done in various ways quite quickly. The quickest way is to take a mirror and turn it round in all directions; before long you will create sun and stars and earth, yourself and all other animals and plants, and all the other objects we mentioned just now.'

'Yes, but they would only be reflections,' he said, 'not real things.'

'Quite right,' I replied, 'and very much to the point. For a painter is a craftsman of just this kind, I think. Do you agree?'

'Yes.'

'You may perhaps object that the things he creates are not real; and yet there *is* a sense in which the painter creates a bed, isn't there?'

'Yes,' he agreed, 'he produces an appearance of one.'

'And what about the carpenter? Didn't you agree that what he produces is not the essential Form of Bed, the ultimate reality, but a particular bed?'

'I did.'

'If so, then what he makes is not the ultimate reality, but something that resembles that reality. And anyone who says that the products of the carpenter or any other craftsman are ultimate realities can hardly be telling the truth, can he?'

'No one familiar with the sort of arguments we're using could suppose so.'

'So we shan't be surprised if the bed the carpenter makes lacks the precision of reality?'

'No.'

'Then shall we try to define representation now, in the light of this illustration?'

'Yes, please.'

'We have seen that there are three sorts of bed. The first exists in the ultimate nature of things, and if it was made by anyone it must, I suppose, have been made by God. The second is made by the carpenter, the third by the painter.'

'Yes, that is so.'

'So painter, carpenter, and God are each responsible for one kind of bed.'

'Yes.'

'God created only one essential Form of Bed in the ultimate nature of things, either because he wanted to or because some necessity prevented him from making more than one; at any rate he didn't produce more than one, and more than one could not possibly be produced.'

'Why?'

'Because, suppose he created two only, you would find that they both shared a common character or form, and this common character would be the ultimate reality.'

'That's true.'

'And I suppose that God knew it, and as he wanted to be the real creator of a real Bed, and not just a carpenter making a particular bed, decided to make the ultimate reality unique.'

'I suppose so.'

'Then do you think we might call him author of the nature of things or some such name?'

'We could do so with justice; for all his creations are ultimate realities.'

'And what about the carpenter? Doesn't he manufacture the bed?'

'Yes.'

'And what about the artist? Does he make or manufacture?'

'No.'

'Then what does he do?'

'I think that we may fairly say that he represents what the other two make.'

'Good,' said I. 'Then the artist's representation stands at third remove from reality?'

[…]

'The artist's representation is … a long way removed from truth, and he is able to reproduce everything because he never penetrates beneath the superficial appearance of anything.' […]

THE ORIGINS OF IMITATION 1:6
ARISTOTLE

[…] The instinct for imitation is inherent in man from his earliest days; he differs from other animals in that he is the most imitative of creatures, and

Aristotle, 'The origins and development of poetry', from *On the Art of Poetry*, in *Classical Literary Criticism*, tr. T.S. Dorsch. London: Penguin Books, 1965, p. 35. Copyright © T.S. Dorsch 1965.

he learns his earliest lessons by imitation. Also inborn in all of us is the instinct to enjoy works of imitation. What happens in actual experience is evidence of this; for we enjoy looking at the most accurate representations of things which in themselves we find painful to see, such as the forms of the lowest animals and of corpses. The reason for this is that learning is a very great pleasure, not for philosophers only, but for other people as well, however limited their capacity for it may be. They enjoy seeing likenesses because in doing so they acquire information (they reason out what each represents, and discover, for instance, that 'this is a picture of so and so'); for if by any chance the thing depicted has not been seen before, it will not be the fact that it is an imitation of something that gives the pleasure, but the execution or the colouring or some other such cause.

The instinct for imitation, then, is natural to us, as is also a feeling for music and for rhythm – and metres are obviously detached sections of rhythms. Starting from these natural aptitudes, and by a series of for the most part gradual improvements on their first efforts, men eventually created poetry from their improvisations.

1:7 THINKING WITH IMAGES
ARISTOTLE

Perceiving … is analogous to mere saying and thinking, but when it is of the pleasant or painful the soul engages in pursuit or avoidance and these are analogous to assertion and denial.

In fact, to experience pleasure and pain is to be active with the perceptive mean in relation to good or bad as such. Avoidance, what is more, and desire are, in their actualized state, the same thing, nor are their faculties different either from each other or from the perceptive faculty, but their way of being the same thing is different. For in the thinking soul, images play the part of percepts, and the assertion or negation of good or bad is invariably accompanied by avoidance or pursuit, which is the reason for the soul's never thinking without an image.[1]

NOTE
1. It is interesting that the word translated here as 'image' is not *phantasma* but *aisthema*, a rare word only used once elsewhere in the *De Anima*. As Hamlyn suggests, its use there seems to remind us of the close dependence that Aristotle sees in the intellectual soul on the sensitive soul immediately below it in the hierarchy. [...]

Aristotle, Chapter III.7, *De Anima: On the Soul*, tr. Hugh Lawson-Tancred. London: Penguin Classics, 1986, pp. 208 and 248. Copyright © Hugh Lawson-Tancred 1986.

JOHN OF DAMASCUS 1:8

When we set up an image of Christ in any place, we appeal to the senses, and indeed we sanctify the sense of sight, which is the highest among the perceptive senses, just as by sacred speech we sanctify the sense of hearing. An image is, after all, a reminder; it is to the illiterate what a book is to the literate, and what the word is to the hearing, the image is to sight. All this is the approach through the senses: but it is with the mind that we lay hold on the image. We remember that God ordered that a vessel be made from wood that would not rot, guilded inside and out, and that the tables of the law should be placed in it and the staff and the golden vessel containing the manna – all this for a reminder of what had taken place, and a foreshadowing of what was to come. What was this but a visual image, more compelling than any sermon? And this sacred thing was not placed in some obscure corner of the tabernacle; it was displayed in full view of the people, so that whenever they looked at it they would give honour and worship to the God who had through its contents made known his design to them. They were of course not worshipping the things themselves; they were being led through them to recall the wonderful works of God, and to adore him whose words they had witnessed.

HOROS AT NICAEA, 787 AD 1:9

We define with all accuracy and care that the venerable and holy icons be set up like the form of the venerable and life-giving Cross, inasmuch as matter consisting of colours and pebbles and other matter is appropriate in the holy Church of God, on sacred vessels and vestments, walls and panels, in houses and on the roads, as well as the images of our Lord and God and Saviour Jesus Christ, of our undefiled Lady of the Holy Mother of God, of the angels worthy of honour, and of all the holy and pious men. For the more frequently they are seen by means of pictorial representation the more those who behold them are aroused to remember and desire the prototypes and to give them greeting and worship of honour – but not the true worship of our faith which befits only the divine nature – but to offer them both incense and candles, in the same way as to the form and the venerable and life-giving Cross and the holy Gospel books and to the other sacred objects, as was the custom even of the ancients.

From *Iconoclasm*, eds Anthony Bryer and Judith Herrin. Birmingham; University of Birmingham Press, 1975, pp. 183–4. Reproduced with permission of the editors.

1:10 HOROS AT NIERA, 754 AD

The divine nature is completely uncircumscribable and cannot be depicted or represented by artists in any medium whatsoever. The word Christ means both God and Man, and an icon of Christ would therefore have to be an image of God in the flesh of the Son of God. But this is impossible. The artist would fall either into the heresy which claims that the divine and human natures of Christ are separate or into that which holds that there is only one nature of Christ.

1:11 IMAGE AND IDOLATRY[1]
THOMAS HOBBES

An IMAGE (in the most strict signification of the word) is the Resemblance of some thing visible: In which sense the Phantasticall Formes, Apparitions, or Seemings of visible Bodies to the Sight, are onely *Images*; such as are the Shew of a man, or other thing in the Water, by Reflexion, or Refraction; or of the Sun, or Stars by Direct Vision in the Air; which are nothing reall in the things seen, nor in the place where they seem to bee; nor are their magnitudes and figures the same with that of the object; but changeable, by the variation of the organs of Sight, or by glasses; and are present often-times in our Imagination, and in our Dreams, when the object is absent; or changed into other colours, and shapes, as things that depend onely upon the Fancy. And these are the Images which are originally and most properly called *Ideas*, and IDOLS, and derived from the language of the Graecians, with whom the word signifieth to *See*. They are Εἴδω also called PHANTASMES, which is in the same language, *Apparitions*. And from these Images it is that one of the faculties of mans Nature, is called the *Imagination*. And from hence it is manifest, that there neither is, nor can bee any Image made of a thing Invisible.

It is also evident, that there can be no Image of a thing Infinite: for all the Images, and Phantasmes that are made by the Impression of things visible, are figured: but Figure is a quantity every way determined: And therefore there can bee no Image of God; nor of the Soule of Man; nor of Spirits; but onely of Bodies Visible, that is, Bodies that have light in themselves, or are by such enlightened.

And whereas a man can fancy Shapes he never saw; making up a Figure out of the parts of divers creatures; as the Poets make their Centaures, Chimaeras, and other Monsters never seen: So can he also give Matter to those Shapes, and make them in Wood, Clay or Metall. And these are also called Images, not for the resemblance of any corporeall thing, but for the

Thomas Hobbes, 'Of the kingdome of darknesse', in *Leviathan*, Part IV, Chapter 45. London: Penguin Classics, 1985, pp. 668–75.

resemblance of some Phantasticall Inhabitants of the Brain of the Maker. But in these Idols, as they are originally in the Brain, and as they are painted, carved, moulded, or moulten in matter, there is a similitude of the one to the other, for which the Materiall Body made by Art, may be said to be the Image of the Phantasticall Idoll made by Nature.

But in a larger use of the word Image, is contained also, any Representation of one thing by another. So an earthly Soveraign may be called the Image of God: And an inferiour Magistrate the Image of an earthly Soveraign. And many times in the Idolatry of the Gentiles there was little regard to the similitude of their Materiall Idol to the Idol in their fancy, and yet it was called the Image of it. For a Stone unhewn has been set up for Neptune, and divers other shapes far different from the shapes they conceived of their Gods. And at this day we see many Images of the Virgin Mary, and other Saints, unlike one another, and without correspondence to any one mans Fancy; and yet serve well enough for the purpose they were errected for; which was no more but by the Names onely, to represent the Persons mentioned in the History; to which every man applyeth a Mentall Image of his owne making, or none at all. And thus an Image in the largest sense, is either the Resemblance, or the Representation of some thing Visible; or both together, as it happeneth for the most part.

[…]

To worship an Image, is volunarily to doe those externall acts, which are signes of honoring either the matter of the Image, which is Wood, Stone, Metall, or some other visible creature; or the Phantasme of the brain, for the resemblance, or representation whereof, the matter was formed and figured; or both together, as one animate Body, composed of the Matter and the Phantasme, as of a Body and Soule.

[…]

[…] But to worship God, as inanimating, or inhabiting, such Image, or place; that is to say, an infinite substance in a finite place, is Idolatry: for such finite Gods, are but Idols of the brain, nothing reall; and are commonly called in the Scripture by the names of *Vanity*, and *Lyes*, and *Nothing*. Also to worship God, not as inanimating, or present in the place, or Image; but to the end to be put in mind of him, or of some works of his, in case the Place, or Image be dedicated, or set up by private authority, and not by the authority of them that are our Soveraign Pastors, is Idolatry. For the Commandement is, *Thou shalt not make to they selfe any graven image.* […]

[…]

Besides the Idolatrous Worship of Images, there is also a Scandalous Worship of them; which is also a sin; but not Idolatry. For *Idolatry* is to worship by signes of an internall, and reall honour: but *Scandalous Worship*, is but Seeming Worship; and may sometimes bee joined with an inward, and hearty detestation, both of the Image, and of the Phantasticall Daemon, or Idol, to which it is dedicated; and proceed only from the fear of death, or other grievous punishment; and is neverthelesse a sin in them that so worship, in case they be men whose actions are looked at by others, as lights to guide them by; because following their ways, they cannot but stumble, and fall in the way of Religion: Whereas the example of those we regard not, works not on us at all, but leaves us to our own diligence and caution; and consequently are no causes of our falling.

[…]

The summe of that which I have said hitherto, concerning the Worship of Images, is this, that he that worshippeth in an Image, or any Creature, either the Matter thereof, or any Fancy of his own, which he thinketh to dwell in it; or both together; or beleeveth that such things hear his Prayers, or see his Devotions, without Ears, or Eyes, committeth Idolatry: and he that counterfeiteth such Worship for fear of punishment, if he bee a man whose example hath power amongst his Brethren, committeth a sin: But he that worshippeth the Creator of the world before such an Image, or in such a place as he hath not made, or chosen of himselfe, but taken from the commandement of Gods Word, as the Jewes did in worshipping God before the Cherubins, and before the Brazen Serpent for a time, and in, or towards the Temple of Jerusalem, which was also but for a time, committeth not Idolatry.

NOTE

1. Marginalia and original page numbering that appears within the text have been removed.

1:12 EVIL DEMON
RENÉ DESCARTES

I shall suppose, therefore, that there is, not a true God, who is the sovereign source of truth, but some evil demon, no less cunning and deceiving than powerful, who has used all his artifice to deceive me. I will suppose that the heavens, the air, the earth, colours, shapes, sounds and all external things that we see, are only illusions and deceptions which he uses to take me in. I will consider myself as having no hands, eyes, flesh, blood or senses, but as believing wrongly that I have all these things. I shall cling obstinately to this notion; and if, by this means, it is not in my power to arrive at the knowledge of any truth, at the very least it is in my power to suspend my judgement. This is why I shall take great care not to accept into my belief anything false, and shall so well prepare my mind against all the tricks of this

René Descartes, 'First meditation', in *Discourse on Method and the Meditations*, tr. F.E. Sutcliffe. London: Penguin Classics, 1968, p. 100. Copyright © F.E. Sutcliffe, 1968.

great deceiver that, however powerful and cunning he may be, he will never be able to impose on me.

OPTICS 1:13
RENÉ DESCARTES

[...] [I]t is necessary to beware of assuming that in order to sense, the mind needs to perceive certain images transmitted by the objects to the brain, as our philosophers commonly suppose; or, at least, the nature of these images must be conceived quite otherwise than as they do. For, inasmuch as [the philosophers] do not consider anything about these images except that they must resemble the objects they represent, it is impossible for them to show us how they can be formed by these objects, received by the external sense organs, and transmitted by the nerves to the brain. And they have had no other reason for positing them except that, observing that a picture can easily stimulate our minds to conceive the object painted there, it seemed to them that in the same way, the mind should be stimulated by little pictures which form in our head to conceive of those objects that touch our senses; instead, we should consider that there are many other things besides pictures which can stimulate our thought, such as, for example, signs and words, which do not in any way resemble the things which they signify. And if, in order to depart as little as possible from currently accepted beliefs, we prefer to avow that the objects which we perceive truly transmit their images to the inside of our brain, we must at least observe that there are no images that must resemble in every respect the objects they represent – for otherwise there would be no distinction between the object and its image – but that it is sufficient for them to resemble the objects in but a few ways, and even that their perfection frequently depends on their not resembling them as much as they might. For example, you can see that engravings, being made of nothing but a little ink placed here and there on the paper, represent to us forests, towns, men, and even battles and storms, even though, among an infinity of diverse qualities which they make us conceive in these objects, only in shape is there actually any resemblance. And even this resemblance is a very imperfect one, seeing that, on a completely flat surface, they represent to us bodies which are of different heights and distances, and even that following the rules of perspective, circles are often better represented by ovals rather than by other circles; and squares by diamonds rather than by other squares; and so for all other shapes. So that often, in order to be more perfect as images and to represent an object better, they must not resemble it. Now we must think in the same way about the

René Descartes, 'Optics', Discourses 4–6, in *Discourse on Method, Optics, Geometry, and Meteorology*, tr. Paul J. Olscamp. Revised edition. Indianapolis: Hackett Publishing Company, 2001, pp. 89–91, 97 and 100–1.

images that are formed in our brain, and we must note that it is only a question of knowing how they can enable the mind to perceive all the diverse qualities of the objects to which they refer; not of [knowing] how the images themselves resemble their objects; just as when the blind man … touches some object with his cane, it is certain that these objects do not transmit anything to him except that, by making his cane move in different ways according to their different inherent qualities, they likewise and in the same way move the nerves of his hand, and then the places in his brain where these nerves originate. Thus his mind is caused to perceive as many different qualities in these bodies, as there are varieties in the movements that they cause in his brain.

*

Thus you can clearly see that in order to perceive, the mind need not contemplate any images resembling the things that it senses. But this makes it no less true that the objects we look at do imprint very perfect images on the back of our eyes. Some people have very ingeniously explained this already, by comparison with the images that appear in a chamber, when having it completely closed except for a single hole, and having put in front of this hole a glass in the form of a lens, we stretch behind, at a specific distance, a white cloth on which the light that comes from the objects outside forms these images. For they say that this chamber represents the eye; this hole, the pupil; this lens, the crystalline humor, or rather, all those parts of the eye which cause some refraction; and this cloth, the interior membrane, which is composed of the extremities of the optic nerve.

*

Now, having thus seen this picture in the eye of a dead animal, and having considered its causes, you cannot doubt that an entirely similar one is formed in the eye of a live man, on the interior membrane … and even that it is formed much better there, because its humors, being full of spirits, are more transparent and have more exactly the shape which is requisite to this effect. And also, perhaps in the eye of an ox the shape of the pupil, which is not round, prevents this picture from being so perfect there.

Neither can we doubt that the images which we cause to appear on a white cloth in a dark chamber are formed there in the same way and for the same reasons as on the back of the eye; and indeed, because they are ordinarily much larger there, and form there in many more ways, we can more easily note different details there, of which I here desire to inform you so that you can test for them, if you have not already done so. […]

[…]

[…] not only do the images of objects form thus on the back of the eye, but they also pass beyond to the brain […]

*

Now although this picture, in being so transmitted into our head, always retains some resemblance to the objects from which it proceeds, nevertheless, as I have already shown, we must not hold that it is by means of this resemblance that the picture causes us to perceive the objects, as if there were yet other eyes in our brain with which we could apprehend it; but rather, that it is the movements of which the picture is composed which, acting immediately on our mind inasmuch as it is united to our body, are so established by nature as to make it have such perceptions [...]

OF IDEAS
JOHN LOCKE

1:14

1. Every man being conscious to himself that he thinks, and that which his mind is applied about whilst thinking being the *ideas* that are there, it is past doubt that men have in their minds several *ideas* such as those expressed by the words *whiteness, hardness, sweetness, thinking, motion, man, elephant, army, drunkenness* and others: it is in the first place then to be inquired, how he comes by them? I know it is a received doctrine that men have native *ideas* and original characters stamped upon their minds in their very first being. This opinion I have at large examined already; and, I suppose, what I have said in the foregoing book will be much more easily admitted when I have shown whence the understanding may get all the *ideas* it has, and by what ways and degrees they may come into the mind; for which I shall appeal to everyone's own observation and experience.

2. Let us then suppose the mind to be, as we say, white paper void of all characters, without any *ideas*. How comes it to be furnished? Whence comes it by that vast store which the busy and boundless fancy of man has painted on it with an almost endless variety? Whence has it all the materials of reason and knowledge? To this I answer, in one word, from *experience*; in that all our knowledge is founded, and from that it ultimately derives itself. Our observation, employed either about *external sensible objects, or about the internal operations of our minds perceived and reflected on by ourselves, is that which supplies our understandings with all the materials of thinking*. These two are the fountains of knowledge, from whence all the *ideas* we have, or can naturally have, do spring.

3. First, *our senses*, conversant about particular sensible objects, do *convey into the mind* several distinct *perceptions* of things, according to those various ways wherein those objects do affect them. And thus we come by those *ideas* we have of *yellow, white, heat, cold, soft, hard, bitter, sweet,* and all those which we call sensible qualities; which when I say the senses convey into the mind, I mean, they from external objects convey into the mind what produces there those *perceptions*. This great source of most of the *ideas* we have, depending wholly upon our senses, and derived by them to the understanding, I call SENSATION.

John Locke, 'Of ideas in general and their original', in *An Essay Concerning Human Understanding*, Book II, Chapter 1. London and Vermont: Everyman, 1993, pp. 45–7.

4. Secondly, the other fountain from which experience furnisheth the understanding with *ideas* is the *perception of the operations of our own minds* within us, as it is employed about the *ideas* it has got; which operations, when the soul comes to reflect on and consider, do furnish the understanding with another set of *ideas*, which could not be had from things without. And such are *perception, thinking, doubting, believing, reasoning, knowing, willing,* and all the different actings of our own minds; which we, being conscious of and observing in ourselves, do from these receive into our understandings as distinct *ideas* as we do from bodies affecting our senses. This source of *ideas* every man has wholly in himself; and though it be not sense, as having nothing to do with external objects, yet it is very like it, and might properly enough be called internal sense. But as I call the other *sensation,* so I call this REFLECTION, the *ideas* it affords being such only as the mind gets by reflecting on its own operations within itself. By REFLECTION then, in the following part of this discourse, I would be understood to mean that notice which the mind takes of its own operations, and the manner of them, by reason whereof there come to be *ideas* of these operations in the understanding. These two, I say, viz. external material things as the objects of SENSATION, and the operations of our own minds within as the objects of REFLECTION, are to me the only originals from whence all our *ideas* take their beginnings. The term *operations* here I use in a large sense, as comprehending not barely the actions of the mind about its *ideas,* but some sort of passions arising sometimes from them, such as is the satisfaction or uneasiness arising from any thought.

[…]

6. He that attentively considers the state of a *child,* at his first coming into the world, will have little reason to think him stored with plenty of *ideas,* that are to be the matter of his future knowledge. It is by degrees he comes to be furnished with them. And though the *ideas* of obvious and familiar qualities imprint themselves before the memory begins to keep a register of time order, yet it is often so late before some unusual qualities come in the way, that there are few men that cannot recollect the beginning of their acquaintance with them. And if it were worthwhile, no doubt a child might be so ordered as to have but a very few, even of the ordinary *ideas,* till he were grown up to a man. But all that are born into the world being surrounded with bodies that perpetually and diversely affect them, variety of *ideas,* whether care be taken about it or no, are imprinted on the minds of children. *Light* and *colours* are busy at hand everywhere when the eye is but open; *sounds* and some *tangible qualities* fail not to solicit their proper senses and force an entrance to the mind; but yet, I think it will be granted easily that, if a child were kept in a place where he never saw any other but black and white till he were a man, he would have no more *ideas* of scarlet or green than he that from his childhood never tasted an oyster or a pineapple has of those particular relishes.

2: FROM KANT TO FREUD

INTRODUCTION

In the late eighteenth century and throughout the nineteenth century, European attitudes to images began to radically alter. Images had been linked throughout the Middle Ages and up until the seventeenth century primarily with the sacred. But following the critical revolution initiated by such thinkers as Immanuel Kant (2.1), the products of social activity began to be seen as autonomous objects in need of special forms of interpretation.

In the *Critique of Pure Reason* (1781), Kant made the rational subject the basis of intelligibility for human experience of the world, by showing that the organising framework of the mind regulated how the world could be understood. We need reasoning prior to experience to turn sense impression into knowledge. Experience of the world comes through the basic intuitions of perception, namely time and space, and categories of understanding, such as the notion of causality.

Kant identified and differentiated between particular cognitive capacities. Imagination was shown to organise the 'schema' that the mind applied to empirical sense data in order to produce a unified image of the world in our minds, by linking experience and understanding. Kant's view directly contrasts with Locke's (1.14) empirical concept of the reflected images of the world playing on the 'white paper' of a passive mind. For Kant, the mind's 'imaging' capacity is a precondition for our perception of images of the world.

Kant's ambitious philosophical system includes a sense that different cognitive faculties and forms of reasoning are appropriate to different intellectual realms or forms, such as scientific understanding and aesthetic judgement. An emphasis on cultural forms has deeply influenced analysis and criticism in literary studies and art history. For example, in Gotthold Lessing's (2.2) attempt to delimit the separate domains of art and literature, Lessing justified his argument by saying that the former was concerned primarily with space and the latter with time. Those drawing on Lessing's work argue for the evaluation of different artworks based on the purity of form. For example, the North American art critic Clement Greenberg (1940) denigrated the impurity of Surrealism because of its narrative and temporal qualities. Critics still argue about the relative merits of cultural forms, but, as W.J.T. Mitchell (1986: 10) has argued, such debates tend to serve hidden powers and interests.

Kant believed that when pure reason over-reaches itself by using concepts unempirically, it engages in metaphysical speculation that generates illusions. It was possible to misunderstand the world and the objects within it. Improper reasoning could lead the mind or consciousness to be captivated by illusions, just like the prisoners in Plato's (1.4) cave. Paul Ricoeur (1970: 32) has suggested that the three major iconoclasts of the nineteenth and early twentieth centuries – Karl Marx, Friedrich Nietzsche and Sigmund Freud – belonged to a 'school of suspicion' that aimed to demystify the world through a critique of consciousness.

For Marx, Nietzsche and Freud the ability to see the truth requires an act of interpretation. As Ricoeur (1970: 3–34) says:

> Beginning with them, understanding is hermeneutics: henceforward, to seek meaning is no longer to spell out the consciousness of meaning, but to *decipher its expressions* … What all three attempted, in different ways, was to make their 'conscious' methods of deciphering coincide with the 'unconscious' *work* of ciphering which they attribute to the will to power, to social being, to the unconscious psychism.

If nothing could be taken at face value, then everything in need of interpretation should be considered an image, or an illusion. For Marx and Engels (2.3), that meant that social reality was projected into the minds of citizens like an image in a camera obscura, as social relations produce their own topsy-turvy, ideological version of reality. Critique turns that image the right way up by deciphering its effects on social consciousness, thereby dispelling the power of the false image on the mind of its observers. Marx's (2.4) analysis of the commodity as a religious fetish is one such interpretation of the effects of capitalist production on its consumers – they worship commodities in the same way that those in Abraham's father's shop worshipped their idols (1.3). Marx's analysis was subsequently developed into a genre of ideology critique (see Section 3).

Kant held that the categories in the mind are necessary, universal and accord with the structure of the world. Nietzsche (2.5 and 2.6) reconceives these cognitive concepts as metaphors, as aesthetic forms that are contingent and serve human purposes. For Nietzsche, cognition is a fundamentally metaphorical activity, the concepts through which we interpret reality having no foundation in it. Human artistry translates sense impressions into images and thence into concepts, which appear 'true' to us only because we forget our role in making them. Nietzsche urges us to acknowledge and take responsibility for the human role in 'imaging' or constructing reality, rather than accepting sedimented interpretations of the world as the truth. His emphasis on the metaphorical nature of meaning, if not truth, is taken up by philosophers such as Ricoeur (8.2) and Le Doeuff (9.4).

Freud's (2.8) invention of psychoanalysis as a 'talking cure' for those suffering from mental disorders can be seen as a science for the deciphering and understanding of the repressed, unconscious processes of the psyche, manifest not only in irrational behaviour and beliefs but also in dream images, in which the latent message is hidden behind the manifest content. The rationality of language serves as the ordering principle for bringing to light the sense latent in irrational images. The theory behind Freud's psychoanalysis was to have a major impact on contemporary image culture. His nephew, Edward Bernays, used Freud's understanding of unconscious motivations when establishing the principles of the public relations industry. In the academic world, Freud's methods have been applied to analyse critically a range of cultural symbols, from literature through to art images and films (see Section 7: Psychoanalysis).

Despite the profound influence the 'school of suspicion' exerted on the thinking of many twentieth-century writers, where there is often a merging of these interpretative techniques within a single piece of writing, some philosophers continued to build upon Kant's work in other ways. For example, Henri Bergson (2.7) placed the body at the centre of understanding in a way that is reminiscent of Kant's transcendental subject as the world's unifying principle. For Bergson, the world becomes an *'aggregate of images'* and perception of the world occurs when *'these same images* [are] *referred to the eventual action of one particular image, my body'*. While Bergson implies a non-rational aspect to cognition through the use of the body image, it arises out of a critique of Kant and is meant to help provide a positive, affective aspect to thought which resonates in different fields that have dealt with psychology, such as phenomenology (Maurice Merleau-Ponty (6.2) and Jean-Paul Sartre (6.3)), the philosophy of Gilles Deleuze (9.5) and the neuroscience of Antonio Damasio (9.2).

REFERENCES

Greenberg, C. (1940) 'Toward a newer Laocoon', *Partisan Review,* 7 (July–August): 296–310.

Kant, I. (1929 [1781]) *The Critique of Pure Reason*, tr. N. Kemp Smith. New York: St Martin's Press.

Mitchell, W.J.T. (1986) *Iconology: Image, Text, Ideology*. Chicago: University of Chicago Press.

Ricoeur, P. (1970) *Freud and Philosophy: An Essay on Interpretation*. New Haven, CT: Yale University Press.

REPRESENTATION AND
IMAGINATION[1]
IMMANUEL KANT

2:1

It is a merely empirical law, that representations which have often followed or accompanied one another finally become associated, and so are set in a relation whereby, even in the absence of the object, one of these representations can, in accordance with a fixed rule, bring about a transition of the mind to the other. But this law of reproduction presupposes that appearances are themselves actually subject to such a rule, and that in the manifold of these representations a coexistence or sequence takes place in conformity with certain rules. Otherwise our empirical imagination would never find opportunity for exercise appropriate to its powers, and so would remain concealed within the mind as a dead and to us unknown faculty. [...]

There must then be something which, as the *a priori* ground of a necessary synthetic unity of appearances, makes their reproduction possible. What that something is we soon discover, when we reflect that appearances are not things in themselves, but are the mere play of our representations, and in the end reduce to determinations of inner sense. For if we can show that even our purest *a priori* intuitions yield no knowledge, save in so far as they contain a combination of the manifold such as renders a thoroughgoing synthesis of reproduction possible, then this synthesis of imagination is likewise grounded, antecedently to all experience, upon *a priori* principles; and we must assume a pure transcendental synthesis of imagination as conditioning the very possibility of all experience. For experience as such necessarily presupposes the reproducibility of appearances. When I seek to draw a line in thought, or to think of the time from one noon to another, or even to represent to myself some particular number, obviously the various manifold representations that are involved must be apprehended by me in thought one after the other. But if I were always to drop out of thought the preceding representations (the first parts of the line, the antecedent parts of the time period, or the units in the order represented), and did not reproduce them while advancing to those that follow, a complete representation would never be obtained: none of the above-mentioned thoughts, not even the purest and most elementary representations of space and time, could arise.

The synthesis of apprehension is thus inseparably bound up with the synthesis of reproduction. And as the former constitutes the transcendental ground of the possibility of all modes of knowledge whatsoever – of those

Immanuel Kant, from 'Transcendental deduction', and 'Schematism', in *The Critique of Pure Reason*, tr. Norman Kemp Smith. London: Macmillan Press, 1929, pp. 132–3, 142–3 and 181–3. © Macmillan Press. Reproduced with permission by Macmillan Press.

that are pure *a priori* no less than of those that are empirical – the reproductive synthesis of the imagination is to be counted among the transcendental acts of the mind. We shall therefore entitle this faculty the transcendental faculty of imagination.

*

[...] The transcendental unity of apperception ... relates to the pure synthesis of imagination, as an *a priori* condition of the possibility of all combination of the manifold in one knowledge. But only the *productive* synthesis of the imagination can take place *a priori*; the reproductive rests upon empirical conditions. Thus the principle of the necessary unity of pure (productive) synthesis of imagination, prior to apperception, is the ground of the possibility of all knowledge, especially of experience.

We entitle the synthesis of the manifold in imagination transcendental, if without distinction of intuitions it is directed exclusively to the *a priori* combination of the manifold; and the unity of this synthesis is called transcendental, if it is represented as *a priori* necessary in relation to the original unity of apperception. Since this unity of apperception underlies the possibility of all knowledge, the transcendental unity of the synthesis of imagination is the pure form of all possible knowledge; and by means of it all objects of possible experience must be represented *a priori*.

The unity of apperception in relation to the synthesis of imagination is the *understanding*; and this same unity, with reference to the *transcendental synthesis* of the imagination, the *pure understanding*. In the understanding there are then pure *a priori* modes of knowledge which contain the nec-essary unity of the pure synthesis of imagination in respect of all possible appearances. These are the *categories*, that is, the pure concepts of understanding. The empirical faculty of knowledge in man must therefore contain an understanding which relates to all objects of the senses, although only by means of intuition and of its synthesis through imagination. All appearances, as data for a possible experience, are subject to this understanding. This relation of appearances to possible experience is indeed necessary, for otherwise they would yield no knowledge and would not in any way concern us. We have, therefore, to recognise that pure under-standing, by means of the categories, is a formal and synthetic principle of all experiences, and that appearances have *a necessary relation to the understanding*.

*

[...] For we have seen that concepts are altogether impossible, and can have no meaning, if no object is given for them, or at least for the elements of which they are composed. They cannot, therefore, be viewed as appli-cable to things in themselves, independent of all question as to whether and how these may be given to us. We have also proved that the only manner in which objects can be given to us is by modification of our sensibility; and finally, that pure *a priori* concepts, in addition to the function of understanding expressed in the category, must contain *a priori* certain formal conditions of sensibility, namely, those of inner sense. These conditions of sensibility constitute the universal condition under which alone the category can be applied to any object. This formal and pure condition of sensibility to which the employment of the concept of understanding is restricted, we shall entitle the *schema* of the concept. The procedure of understanding in these schemata we shall entitle the *schematism* of pure understanding.

The schema is in itself always a product of imagination. Since, however, the synthesis of imagination aims at no special intuition, but only at unity in the determination of sensibility, the schema has to be distinguished from the image. [...]

Indeed it is schemata, not images of objects, which underlie our pure sensible concepts. No image could ever be adequate to the concept of a triangle in general. It would never attain that universality of the concept which renders it valid of all triangles, whether right-angled, obtuse-angled, or acute-angled; it would always be limited to a part only of this sphere. The schema of the triangle can exist nowhere but in thought. It is a rule of synthesis of the imagination, in respect to pure figures in space. Still less is an object of experience or its image ever adequate to the empirical concept; for this latter always stands in immediate relation to the schema of imagination, as a rule for the determination of our intuition, in accordance with some specific universal concept. The concept 'dog' signifies a rule according to which my imagination can delineate the figure of a four-footed animal in a general manner, without limitation to any single determinate figure such as experience, or any possible image that I can represent *in concreto*, actually presents. This schematism of our understanding, in its application to appearances and their mere form, is an art concealed in the depths of the human soul, whose real modes of activity nature is hardly likely ever to allow us to discover, and to have open to our gaze. This much only we can assert: the *image* is a product of the empirical faculty of reproductive imagination; the *schema* of sensible concepts, such as of figures in space, is a product and, as it were, a monogram, of pure *a priori* imagination, through which, and in accordance with which, images themselves first become possible. These images can be connected with the concept only by means of the schema to which they belong. In themselves they are never completely congruent with the concept. On the other hand, the schema of a *pure* concept of understanding can never be brought into any image whatsoever. It is simply the pure synthesis, determined by a rule of that unity, in accordance with concepts, to which the category gives expression. It is a transcendental product of imagination, a product which concerns the determination of inner sense in general according to conditions of its form (time), in respect of all representations, so far as these representations are to be connected *a priori* in one concept in conformity with the unity of apperception.

NOTE
1. All footnotes have been removed from this passage.

2:2 SPACE AND TIME
GOTTHOLD LESSING

I reason thus: if it is true that in its imitations painting uses completely different means or signs than does poetry, namely figures and colors in space rather than articulated sounds in time, and if these signs must indisputably bear a suitable relation to the thing signified, then signs existing in space can express only objects whose wholes or parts coexist, while signs that follow one another can express only objects whose wholes or parts are consecutive.

Objects or parts of objects which exist in space are called bodies. Accordingly, bodies with their visible properties are the true subjects of painting.

Objects or parts of objects which follow one another are called actions. Accordingly, actions are the true subjects of poetry.

However, bodies do not exist in space only, but also in time. They persist in time, and in each moment of their duration they may assume a different appearance or stand in a different combination. Each of these momentary appearances and combinations is the result of a preceding one and can be the cause of a subsequent one, which means that it can be, as it were, the center of an action. Consequently, painting too can imitate actions, but only by suggestion through bodies.

On the other hand, actions cannot exist independently, but must be joined to certain beings or things. Insofar as these beings or things are bodies, or are treated as such, poetry also depicts bodies, but only by suggestion through actions.

Painting can use only a single moment of an action in its coexisting compositions and must therefore choose the one which is most suggestive and from which the preceding and succeeding actions are most easily comprehensible.

Similarly, poetry in its progressive imitations can use only one single property of a body. It must therefore choose that one which awakens the most vivid image of the body, looked at from the point of view under which poetry can best use it. From this comes the rule concerning the harmony of descriptive adjectives and economy in description of physical objects.

I should put little faith in this dry chain of reasoning did I not find it completely confirmed by the procedure of Homer, or rather if it had not been just this procedure that led me to my conclusions. Only on these principles can the grand style of the Greek be defined and explained, and only thus can the proper position be assigned to the opposite style of so

Gotthold Ephriam Lessing, *Laocoon: An Essay on the Limits of Painting and Poetry,* tr. Edward Allen McCormick. Baltimore, MD: Johns Hopkins University Press, 1984, pp. 78–9. © 1984 Johns Hopkins University Press. Reprinted with permission of The Johns Hopkins University Press.

many modern poets, who attempt to rival the painter at a point where they must necessarily be surpassed by him.

CAMERA OBSCURA 2:3
KARL MARX AND FRIEDRICH ENGELS

The production of ideas, of conceptions, of consciousness, is at first directly interwoven with the material activity and the material intercourse of men, the language of real life. Conceiving, thinking, the mental intercourse of men, appear at this stage as the direct efflux of their material behaviour. The same applies to mental production as expressed in the language of politics, laws, morality, religion, metaphysics, etc. of a people. Men are the producers of their conceptions, ideas, etc. – real, active men, as they are conditioned by a definite development of their productive forces and of the intercourse corresponding to these, up to its furthest forms. Consciousness can never be anything else than conscious existence, and the existence of men is their actual life-process. If in all ideology men and their circumstances appear upside-down as in a *camera obscura,* this phenomenon arises just as much from their historical life-process as the inversion of objects on the retina does from their physical life-process.

In direct contrast to German philosophy which descends from heaven to earth, here we ascend from earth to heaven. That is to say, we do not set out from what men say, imagine, conceive, nor from men as narrated, thought of, imagined, conceived, in order to arrive at men in the flesh. We set out from real, active men, and on the basis of their real life-process we demonstrate the development of the ideological reflexes and echoes of this life-process. The phantoms formed in the human brain are also, necessarily, sublimates of their material life-process, which is empirically verifiable and bound to material premises. Morality, religion, metaphysics, all the rest of ideology and their corresponding forms of consciousness, thus no longer retain the semblance of independence. They have no history, no development; but men, developing their material production and their material intercourse, alter, along with this their real existence, their thinking and the products of their thinking. Life is not determined by consciousness, but consciousness by life. In the first method of approach the starting-point is consciousness taken as the living individual; in the second method, which conforms to real life, it is the real living individuals themselves, and consciousness is considered solely as *their* consciousness.

Karl Marx and Friedrick Engels, from 'Feuerbach', in *The German Ideology.* 2nd edn, ed. C.J. Arthur. London: Lawrence & Wishart, 1974, p. 47. Translation © 1970 Lawrence & Wishart.

2:4

THE FETISHISM OF COMMODITIES AND THE SECRET THEREOF[1]
KARL MARX

A commodity appears, at first sight, a very trivial thing, and easily understood. Its analysis shows that it is, in reality, a very queer thing, abounding in metaphysical subtleties and theological niceties. So far as it is a value in use, there is nothing mysterious about it, whether we consider it from the point of view that by its properties it is capable of satisfying human wants, or from the point that those properties are the product of human labour. It is as clear as noon-day, that man, by his industry, changes the forms of the materials furnished by Nature, in such a way as to make them useful to him. The form of wood, for instance, is altered, by making a table out of it. Yet, for all that, the table continues to be that common, every-day thing, wood. But, so soon as it steps forth as a commodity, it is changed into something transcendent. It not only stands with its feet on the ground, but, in relation to all other commodities, it stands on its head, and evolves out of its wooden brain grotesque ideas, far more wonderful than 'table-turning' ever was.

The mystical character of commodities does not originate, therefore, in their use-value. Just as little does it proceed from the nature of the determining factors of value. For, in the first place, however varied the useful kinds of labour, or productive activities, may be, it is a physiological fact, that they are functions of the human organism, and that each such function, whatever may be its nature or form, is essentially the expenditure of human brain, nerves, muscles, &c. Secondly, with regard to that which forms the ground-work for the quantitative determination of value, namely, the duration of that expenditure, or the quantity of labour, it is quite clear that there is a palpable difference between its quantity and quality. In all states of society, the labour-time that it costs to produce the means of subsistence, must necessarily be an object of interest to mankind, though not of equal interest in different stages of development. And lastly, from the moment that men in any way work for one another, their labour assumes a social form.

Whence, then, arises the enigmatical character of the product of labour, so soon as it assumes the form of commodities? Clearly from this form itself. The equality of all sorts of human labour is expressed objectively by their products all being equally values; the measure of the expenditure of labour-power by the duration of that expenditure, takes the form of the quantity of value of the products of labour; and finally, the mutual relations of the producers, within which the social character of their labour affirms itself, take the form of a social relation between the products.

Karl Marx, from 'The fetishism of commodities and the secret thereof', in *Capital*, Vol. 1, §. 4, tr. S. Moore and E. Aveling. London: Charles H. Kerr & Co., 1919, pp. 81–4 and 85–6. Copyright 1906.

A commodity is therefore a mysterious thing, simply because in it the social character of men's labour appears to them as an objective character stamped upon the product of that labour; because the relation of the producers to the sum total of their own labour is presented to them as a social relation, existing not between themselves, but between the products of their labour. This is the reason why the products of labour become commodities, social things whose qualities are at the same time perceptible and imperceptible by the senses. In the same way the light from an object is perceived by us not as the subjective excitation of our optic nerve, but as the objective form of something outside the eye itself. But, in the act of seeing, there is at all events, an actual passage of light from one thing to another, from the external object to the eye. There is a physical relation between physical things. But it is different with commodities. There, the existence of the things *quâ* commodities, and the value-relation between the products of labour which stamps them as commodities, have absolutely no connection with their physical properties and with the material relations arising therefrom. There it is a definite social relation between men, that assumes, in their eyes, the fantastic form of a relation between things. In order, therefore, to find an analogy, we must have recourse to the mist-enveloped regions of the religious world. In that world the productions of the human brain appear as independent beings endowed with life, and entering into relation both with one another and the human race. So it is in the world of commodities with the products of men's hands. This I call the Fetishism which attaches itself to the products of labour, so soon as they are produced as commodities, and which is therefore inseparable from the production of commodities.

This Fetishism of commodities has its origin, as the foregoing analysis has already shown, in the peculiar social character of the labour that produces them.

As a general rule, articles of utility become commodities, only because they are products of the labour of private individuals or groups of individuals who carry on their work independently of each other. The sum total of the labour of all these private individuals forms the aggregate labour of society. Since the producers do not come into social contact with each other until they exchange their products, the specific social character of each producer's labour does not show itself except in the act of exchange. In other words, the labour of the individual asserts itself as a part of the labour of society, only by means of the relations which the act of exchange establishes directly between the products, and indirectly, through them, between the producers. To the latter, therefore, the relations connecting the labour of one individual with that of the rest appear, not as direct social relations between individuals at work, but as what they really are, material relations between persons and social relations between things. [...]

Hence, when we bring the products of our labour into relation with each other as values, it is not because we see in these articles the material receptacles of homogeneous human labour. Quite the contrary; whenever, by an exchange, we equate as values our different products, by that very act, we also equate, as human labour, the different kinds of labour expended upon them. We are not aware of this, nevertheless we do it. Value, therefore, does not stalk about with a label describing what it is. It is value, rather, that converts every product into a social hieroglyphic. Later on, we try to decipher the hieroglyphic, to get behind the secret of our own social products; for to stamp an object of utility as a value, is just as much a social product as language. The recent scientific discovery, that the products of labour, so far as they are values, are but material expressions of the human labour spent in their production, marks, indeed, an epoch in the history of the development of the human race, but, by no means, dissipates the mist through which the social character of labour appears to us to be an objective character of the products themselves. The fact, that in the particular form of production with which we are dealing, viz., the production of commodities, the specific social character of private labour carried on independently, consists in the equality of every kind of that labour, by virtue of its being human labour, which character, therefore, assumes in the product the form of value – this fact appears to the producers, notwithstanding the discovery above referred to, to be just as real and final, as the fact, that, after the discovery by science of the component gases of air, the atmosphere itself remained unaltered.

NOTE
1. All footnotes have been removed from this passage.

2:5 HOW THE REAL WORLD AT LAST BECAME A MYTH
FRIEDRICH NIETZSCHE

HISTORY OF AN ERROR
1. The real world, attainable to the wise, the pious, the virtuous man – he dwells in it, *he is it*.

(Oldest form of the idea, relatively sensible, simple, convincing. Transcription of the proposition 'I, Plato, *am* the truth.')[1]

2. The real world, unattainable for the moment, but promised to the wise, the pious, the virtuous man ('to the sinner who repents').

(Progress of the idea: it grows more refined, more enticing, more incomprehensible – *it becomes a woman*, it becomes Christian …)

Friedrich Nietzsche, 'How the "real world" at last became a myth', in *Twilight of the Idols: Or, How to Philosophize with a Hammer; The Anti-Christ*, tr. R.J. Hollingdale. London: Penguin Classics, 1968, pp. 40–1. Copyright © R.J. Hollingdale, 1968. Reproduced by permission of Penguin Books Ltd.

3. The real world, unattainable, undemonstrable, cannot be promised, but even when merely thought of a consolation, a duty, an imperative.

(Fundamentally the same old sun, but shining through mist and scepticism; the idea grown sublime, pale, northerly, Königsbergian.)[2]

4. The real world – unattainable? Unattained, at any rate. And if unattained also *unknown*. Consequently also no consolation, no redemption, no duty: how could we have a duty towards something unknown?

(The grey of dawn. First yawnings of reason. Cockcrow of positivism.)[3]

5. The 'real world' – an idea no longer of any use, not even a duty any longer – an idea grown useless, superfluous, *consequently* a refuted idea: let us abolish it!

(Broad daylight; breakfast; return of cheerfulness and *bon sens*; Plato blushes for shame; all free spirits run riot.)

6. We have abolished the real world: what world is left? the apparent world perhaps? ... But no! *with the real world we have also abolished the apparent world!*

(Mid-day; moment of the shortest shadow; end of the longest error; zenith of mankind; INCIPIT ZARATHUSTRA.)[4]

NOTES

1. The truth = *Wahrheit*, corresponding to *wahre Welt* = real world.
2. That is, Kantian, from the northerly German city in which Kant was born and in which he lived and died.
3. Here meaning empiricism, philosophy founded on observation and experiment.
4. Here begins Zarathustra. [...]

ON TRUTH AND LIES IN A NON-MORAL SENSE
FRIEDRICH NIETZSCHE

2:6

What then is truth? A movable host of metaphors, metonymies, and anthropomorphisms: in short, a sum of human relations which have been poetically and rhetorically intensified, transferred, and embellished, and which, after long usage, seem to people to be fixed, canonical, and binding. Truths are illusions which we have forgotten are illusions; they are metaphors which have become worn out and have been drained of sensuous force, coins which have lost their embossing and are now considered as metal and no longer as coins.

Friedrich Nietzsche, from *Philosophy and Truth: Selections from Nietzsche's Notebooks of the Early 1870s*, ed. and tr. Daniel Breazeale. Atlantic Highlands, NJ: Humanities Press, 1979, p. 84.

2:7 IMAGES, BODIES AND CONSCIOUSNESS
HENRI BERGSON

We will assume for the moment that we know nothing of theories of matter and theories of spirit, nothing of the discussions as to the reality or ideality of the external world. Here I am in the presence of images, in the vaguest sense of the word, images perceived when my senses are opened to them, unperceived when they are closed. All these images act and react upon one another in all their elementary parts according to constant laws which I call laws of nature, and, as a perfect knowledge of these laws would probably allow us to calculate and to foresee what will happen in each of these images, the future of the images must be contained in their present and will add to them nothing new.

Yet there is *one* of them which is distinct from all the others, in that I do not know it only from without by perceptions, but from within by affections: it is my body. I examine the conditions in which these affections are produced: I find that they always interpose themselves between the excitations that I receive from without and the movements which I am about to execute, as though they had some undefined influence on the final issue. I pass in review my different affections: it seems to me that each of them contains, after its kind, an invitation to act, with at the same time leave to wait and even to do nothing. I look closer: I find movements begun, but not executed, the indication of a more or less useful decision, but not that constraint which precludes choice. I call up, I compare my recollections: I remember that everywhere, in the organic world, I have thought I saw this same sensibility appear at the very moment when nature, having conferred upon the living being the power of mobility in space, gives warning to the species, by means of sensation, of the general dangers which threaten it, leaving to the individual the precautions necessary for escaping from them. Lastly, I interrogate my consciousness as to the part which it plays in affection: consciousness replies that it is present indeed, in the form of feeling or of sensation, at all the steps in which I believe that I take the initiative, and that it fades and disappears as soon as my activity, by becoming automatic, shows that consciousness is no longer needed. Therefore, either all these appearances are deceptive, or the act in which the affective state issues is not one of those which might be rigorously deduced from antecedent phenomena, as a movement from a movement; and, hence, it really adds something new to the universe and to its history. Let us hold to the appearances; I will formulate purely and simply what I feel and what I see: *All seems to take place as if, in this aggregate of images which I call the universe, nothing really new could happen except through the medium of certain particular images, the type of which is furnished me by my body.*

Henri Bergson, 'Of the selection of images for conscious presentation. What our body means and does', in *Matter and Memory*, tr. Nancy Margaret Paul and W. Scott Palmer. New York: Zone Books, 1991, pp. 17–22. Reproduced by permission of Zone Books.

I pass now to the study, in bodies similar to my own, of the structure of that particular image which I call my body. I perceive afferent nerves which transmit a disturbance to the nerve centers; then efferent nerves which start from the center, conduct the disturbance to the periphery, and set in motion parts of the body or the body as a whole. I question the physiologist and the psychologist as to the purpose of both kinds. They answer that, as the centrifugal movements of the nervous system can call forth a movement of the body or of parts of the body, so the centripetal movements, or at least some of them, give birth to the representation[1] of the external world. What are we to think of this?

The afferent nerves are images, the brain is an image, the disturbance traveling through the sensory nerves and propagated in the brain is an image too. If the image which I term cerebral disturbance really begot external images, it would contain them in one way or another, and the representation of the whole material universe would be implied in that of this molecular movement. Now to state this proposition is enough to show its absurdity. The brain is part of the material world; the material world is not part of the brain. Eliminate the image which bears the name material world, and you destroy at the same time the brain and the cerebral disturbance which are parts of it. Suppose, on the contrary, that these two images, the brain and the cerebral disturbance, vanish: *ex hypothesi* you efface only these, that is to say very little, an insignificant detail from an immense picture. The picture in its totality, that is to say the whole universe, remains. To make of the brain the condition on which the whole image depends is, in truth, a contradiction in terms, since the brain is by hypothesis a part of this image. Neither nerves nor nerve centers can, then, condition the image of the universe.

Let us consider this last point. Here are external images, then my body, and, lastly, the changes brought about by my body in the surrounding images. I see plainly how external images influence the image that I call my body: they transmit movement to it. And I also see how this body influences external images: it gives back movement to them. My body is, then, in the aggregate of the material world, an image which acts like other images, receiving and giving back movement, with, perhaps, this difference only, that my body appears to choose, within certain limits, the manner in which it shall restore what it receives. But how could my body in general, and my nervous system in particular, beget the whole or a part of my representation of the universe? You may say that my body is matter, or that it is an image: the word is of no importance. If it is matter, it is a part of the material world; and the material world, consequently, exists around it and without it. If it is an image, that image can give but what has been put into it, and since it is, by hypothesis, the image of my body only, it would be absurd to expect to get from it that of the whole universe. *My body, an object destined to move other objects, is, then, a center of action; it cannot give birth to a representation.*

But if my body is an object capable of exercising a genuine and therefore a *new* action upon the surrounding objects, it must occupy a privileged position in regard to them. As a rule, any image influences other images in a manner which is determined, and even calculable, through what are called the laws of nature. As it has not to choose, so neither has it any need to explore the region round about it, nor to try its hand at several merely *eventual* actions. The *necessary* action will take place automatically, when its hour strikes. But I have supposed that the office of the image which I call my body was to exercise on other images a real influence, and, consequently, to decide which step to take among several which are all materially possible. And since these steps are probably suggested to it by the greater or lesser advantage which it can derive from the surrounding images, these images must display in some way, upon the aspect which they present to my body, the profit which my body can gain from them. In fact, I note that the size, shape, even the color, of external objects is modified as my body approaches or recedes from them; that the strength of an odor, the intensity of a sound, increases or diminishes with distance; finally, that this very distance represents, above all, the measure in which surrounding bodies are insured, in some way, against the immediate action of my body. To the degree that my horizon widens, the images which surround me seem to be painted upon a more uniform background and become to me more indifferent. The more I narrow this horizon, the more the objects which it circumscribes space themselves out distinctly according to the greater or lesser ease with which my body can touch and move them. They send back, then, to my body, as would a mirror, its eventual influence; they take rank in an order corresponding to the growing or decreasing powers of my body. *The objects which surround my body reflect its possible action upon them.*

[...] *I call* matter *the aggregate of images, and* perception of matter *these same images referred to the eventual action of one particular image, my body.*

NOTE
1. The word representation is used throughout ... in the French sense, as meaning a mental picture, which mental picture is very often perception. (Translators' note.)

2 : 8
THE DREAM-WORK
Sigmund Freud

Until now every other effort to solve the problems presented by dreams has latched directly on to the dream's manifest content as it is present in the memory, and has attempted to use this as the basis of an interpretation; or, if it dispensed with an interpretation, it sought to substantiate its judgement

Sigmund Freud, from 'Dream work', in *The Interpretation of Dreams*, tr. Joyce Crick. Oxford: Oxford University Press, 1999, pp. 211–12, 232–5 and 254–6. Translation copyright © Joyce Crick, 1999. Reproduced by permission of Oxford University Press.

of the dream by reference to its content. We are alone in confronting a different state of affairs; as we see it, there is a new kind of psychical material intervening between the content of the dream and the results of our reflections: the *latent* dream-content reached by our procedure, or the dream-thoughts. It is from this latent content, not the manifest, that we worked out the solution to the dream. This is why a new task faces us which did not exist before, the task of investigating the relationship of the manifest dream-content to the latent dream-thoughts, and of tracing the processes by which the former turned into the latter.

The dream-thoughts and the dream-content lie before us like two versions of the same content in two different languages, or rather, the dream-content looks to us like a translation of the dream-thoughts into another mode of expression, and we are supposed to get to know its signs and laws of grammatical construction by comparing the original and the translation. Once we have learnt what these are, the dream-thoughts will be easy for us to understand without any further ado. The content of the dream is given as it were in the form of hieroglyphs whose signs are to be translated one by one into the language of the dream-thoughts. We would obviously be misled if we were to read these signs according to their pictorial value and not according to their referentiality as signs. Suppose I have a picture-puzzle, a rebus, before me: a house with a boat on its roof, then a single letter of the alphabet, then a running figure with his head conjured away, and the like. Now I could fall into the trap of objecting that this combination and its constituent parts are nonsense. A boat does not belong on the roof of a house and a person without a head cannot run; besides, the person is bigger than the house, and if the whole is supposed to represent a landscape, then single letters of the alphabet do not fit in there, as they certainly do not occur in Nature. Obviously the correct solution to the rebus can only be reached if I raise no such objections to the whole or to the details, but take the trouble to replace each picture by a syllable or a word which, through some association, can be represented by the picture. The words connected in this way are no longer nonsense, but can yield the most beautiful and meaningful poetic saying. The dream is a picture-puzzle of this kind, and our predecessors in the field of dream-interpretation made the mistake of judging the rebus as if it were a pictorial composition. As such, it seemed to them to have no meaning or value.

*

The first thing the investigator comes to understand in comparing the dream-content with the dream-thoughts is that *work of condensation* has been carried out here on a grand scale. The dream is scant, paltry, laconic in comparison to the range and abundance of the dream-thoughts. Written down, the dream will fill half a page; the analysis containing the dream-thoughts will require six, eight, twelve times as much space. The ratio varies for different dreams; as far as I can check, it never changes its intent. As a rule, in taking the dream-thoughts brought to light to be all the dream-material there is, one is underestimating the degree of compression that takes place, whereas further work of interpretation is able to reveal fresh thoughts hidden behind the dream. We have already had to note that actually one is never certain of having interpreted a dream in its entirety; even when the solution seems satisfying and complete, it is always possible for a further meaning to announce its presence through the same dream. *The quota of condensation* is thus, strictly speaking, indeterminable. One conclusion to be drawn from this disproportion between dream-content and dream-thoughts might be that a wholesale condensation of the psychical material takes place during the dream's formation. [...]

*

While we were collecting examples of dream-condensation, another relationship, probably no less significant, must already have caught our attention. We could not fail to observe that the elements pushing to the fore in the dream-content as essential components certainly did not play the same part in the dream-thoughts. As a corollary, this statement can also be reversed. What is clearly essential in the content of the dream-thoughts does not need to be represented in the dream itself at all. The dream, one might say, is *centred differently*; its content is ordered around a centre made up of elements other than the dream-thoughts. [...] In my patient's Sappho dream, [for example], *climbing up and down, being up above and down below* are made to be its centre; but in fact the dream deals with sexual relations with persons of the *lower* orders, so that only one of the elements in the dream-thoughts seems to have entered the dream-content, but then to an undue extent. [...] Dreams of this kind give the impression of *displacement* with good reason. In complete contrast to these examples, the dream of Irma's injection shows that in the formation of a dream individual elements are also able to retain the place they occupy in the dream-thoughts. When we first recognize this new relation, which is entirely variable in meaning, between dream-thoughts and dream-content, it is likely to fill us with astonishment. If in the course of some normal psychical process we find one idea being singled out from many others and becoming particularly vivid in our consciousness, we usually regard this success as proof that it has been accorded the especially high psychical value (a certain degree of interest) which is its due. But now we discover that this value accorded to particular elements in the dream-thoughts is not retained or not taken into account in forming a dream. After all, there is no doubt as to which are the most valuable elements in the dream-thoughts; our judgement needs no help to tell us. But in dream-formation these essential elements, charged though they are with intense interest, are dealt with as if they were of little value, and instead their place is taken in the dream by other elements which certainly had little value in the dream-thoughts. At first this gives the impression that the psychical intensity[1] of the particular ideas was not taken into consideration at all in their selection for the dream, but only the varying nature and degree of their determination. What enters the dream, one might think, is not what is important in the dream-thoughts, but what appears frequently and variously in them. However, this assumption will not take our understanding of dream-formation much further, as from the outset it leaves no room for thinking that these two factors in selecting elements for the dream – multiple determination and inherent value – must necessarily work along the same lines to produce the same meaning. It supposes that the ideas which are the most important in the dream-thoughts are likely to be the ones that recur in them most often, for the particular dream-thoughts radiate from them as it were from a centre. And yet the dream can reject these elements, even though they are emphasized so intensely and reinforced so variously, and it can take up into its content other elements which are characterized by the second quality, inherent value, alone.

[...]

The thought suggests itself that a psychical power is operative in the dream-work which on the one hand strips the psychically valuable elements of their intensity, and on the other creates new values *by way of over-determination* out of elements of low value; it is the new values that then reach the dream-content. If this is what happens, then *a transference and displacement of the psychical intensity* of the individual elements has taken place; as a consequence, the difference between the texts of the dream-content and the dream-thoughts makes its appearance. The process we are assuming here is *the* essential part of the dream-work; it has earned the name of *dream-displacement*. *Dream-displacement* and *dream-condensation* are the two foremen in charge of the dream-work, and we may put the shaping of our dreams down mainly to their activity.

*

So far we have been occupied with examining how the dream represents relations between the dream-thoughts, but in doing so we frequently returned to the broader topic of the general nature of the changes undergone by the dream-material for the purposes of dream-formation. Now we know that the dream-material, largely divested of its logical relations, undergoes a concentration, while at the same time displacements of intensity among its elements necessarily bring about a psychical transvaluation of this material. The displacements we were considering turned out to be substitutions of one particular idea by another somehow closely associated with it; and they were useful in condensation, for in this way, instead of two elements, an intermediate factor common to them both gained entry to the dream. We have not yet mentioned another kind of displacement. But we learn from our analyses that there is such a thing, and that it makes its presence known in a *transposition in the words used to express the thought concerned*. In both cases it is a matter of displacement along a chain of associations, but the same procedure takes place in different psychical spheres, and the result of this displacement is that in one case one element is replaced by another, while in the other one element exchanges its verbal formulation for another.

This second kind of displacement occurring in the formation of dreams is not only of great theoretical interest; it is also particularly well suited to explain the appearance of fantastic absurdity in which dreams disguise themselves. As a rule, the displacement follows the direction taken when a colourless and abstract expression of the dream-thought is exchanged for a pictorial and concrete one. The advantage, and thus the intention of the substitution, is obvious. For the dream, what is pictorial is *capable of representation*, can be integrated into a situation where an abstract expression would cause similar difficulties for the dream-representation to those a political leading article, say, would make for an illustrated news-magazine. But not only representability has to gain from this exchange; the several interests of condensation and the censorship are able to do so too. Once the abstract, unusable thought is transformed into a pictorial language, the contacts and identities which the dream-work requires – and will create where they are not present – come about between this new expression and the rest of the dream-material more easily than before, for language has developed in such a way that the concrete words of every language are far richer in associations than its conceptual terms. One can imagine that a good bit of the intermediary work in the process of dream-formation takes place in this way – by appropriate linguistic transformation of the individual thoughts – for it aims at reducing the separate dream-thoughts to the most economical and unified expression possible in the dream. [...]

NOTE

1. The psychical intensity, value, weight of interest, of an idea is of course to be kept separate from the sensory intensity of its representation.

PART TWO:

THEORIES OF IMAGES

3: IDEOLOGY CRITIQUE

INTRODUCTION

Karl Marx and Friedrich Engels (2.3) initiated a tradition of social analysis that sees ideology as pervading and distorting human relations and consciousness. In their initial critique of 'German ideology', the version of Hegelian thought popular in Germany in their time, they argued that the philosophers had an inverted vision of reality because they imagined that ideas change the world. Hence, the German ideologists' philosophical critique of the 'false conceptions' and 'chimeras' in the ruling ideas was useless, because it did not change the material conditions reflected by those ideas. Marx did not himself develop further the notion of ideology, the term 'false consciousness' being a later invention. But W.J.T. Mitchell (1986) and others argue that Marx's (2.4) analysis of the capitalist commodity as a mysterious fetish is, like ideology critique, part of Marx's iconoclastic critique of capitalist idolatry. Marx moves from the mental idolatry of the inverted ideas of the German idealist philosophers to the material idolatry of commodities. Mitchell (1986: 4) claims that 'the notion of ideology is rooted in the concept of imagery, and reenacts the ancient struggles of iconoclasm, idolatry, and fetishism'. Ideology critique thus entails the problems discussed in the introduction to Section 1.

Ideology critique is also an analysis of the power relations involved in the reproduction of capitalism, which legitimates itself by means of a set of ruling ideas. The critique unmasks those ideas as false, partial, mythical or imaginary images of capitalist society, which generally obscure the contradictions and exploitation in capitalist economics and class relations. Marx's idea of ideology has been developed in many ways, some of which do not regard ideological consciousness as false, or as an epistemological error (Žižek, 1994). Ideology critique has been a powerful tool for the critical analysis of contemporary 'image culture', particularly useful for unmasking images of society, subjectivity and human relations broadcast by the mass media (Nichols, 1981; Williams, 1974). Versions of ideology critique adopted in cultural and media studies often employ other concepts and methods of image analysis, such as semiotics and psychoanalysis (see introductions to Sections 5 and 7).

As with Marx's analysis of the commodity, critical theorists focused on the form of ideological representation in order to reveal its ideological function. Max Horkheimer and Theodor Adorno (1993) critiqued the capitalist structure of the 'culture industry' as a tool of 'mass deception', whose standardised products rob the audience of their faculties of imagination and reflection, turning leisure time into the work of consumption and conformism. Adorno's (3.1) analysis of the television image links this type of structural investigation with Freud's (2.8) language of psychoanalysis.

The harmonious 'manifest' content of the image masks a contradictory and harmful social reality – the 'latent' base out of which the image grows. The role of the critic is to describe the relationship between these two elements so that the audience can see the social truth behind the image.

If Horkeimer and Adorno had theorised the commodification of mass culture, Guy Debord (3.2) conceives the spectacle, of which the mass media are the most obvious manifestation, as the commodification of all social life. Analysing, unlike Marx, conditions of economic abundance rather than poverty, he considers how workers have become isolated consumers of illusions or pseudo-needs. He also refers back to Marx's key figures of ideology, conceiving the social relations of the spectacle as fetishistic. Yet, he regards the spectacle not as the inverse image of reality, but as an inversion or negation of 'real' life, a false reality that is the materialisation of ideology. There is also a clear resonance with Plato's (1.4) iconoclasm, in that the 'spectator's consciousness' is 'imprisoned ... by the *screen* of the spectacle' which 'is his "mirror image"' (Debord, 1983: §218).

Jean Baudrillard (3.3) concurs with Debord's analysis that ideological images have lost their illusionary character to become reality. But Baudrillard criticises Marxism and ideology critique for serving as alibis for the disappearance of reality into simulation and hyperreality. His basic argument is that both production and signification lose their connection with reality, such that referential value (in respect of use value or the referent) is annihilated and everything 'collapses into simulation' (Baudrillard, 1993: 8). The world that has been transformed into images is not a society of the spectacle, which is 'an extension of the commodity form' (Best, 1994: 51), but is a dematerialisation of everything into signs. Following the ramifications of Byzantine iconoclasm (1.8 to 1.10) to the limit, Baudrillard concludes that the hyperreal simulated image does not conceal anything, so ideology critique is redundant.

Fredric Jameson (3.4) adopts ideas from Horkheimer and Adorno, Debord and Baudrillard, among many other influences, while retaining a Marxist, historical materialist approach. He explicitly characterises contemporary spectacle or image culture, which he takes to be the cultural logic of a new, multinational or late stage of capitalism, as postmodern. In this mode of capitalism, that is more extensive and intrusive than earlier stages, the distinction between economic base and cultural superstructure is eclipsed, so that we seem obliged 'to talk about cultural phenomena ... in business terms' (Jameson, 1991: xxi). The commodified media are central to this identification, as the market merges with media into an image of social totality, legitimated by the consumption of consumption, of products as images.

The underlying approach of ideology critique in revealing that which is concealed by images has proved useful for cultural analysis that is not only or primarily concerned with unveiling capitalism. Other forms of oppression, such as racism and sexism, can be shown to be at work, often unconsciously, in images. Critical race analysis often highlights the visibility of race (Fanon, 1986). Paul Gilroy (3.5) provides an example of how ostensibly inclusive images of class, citizenship or nationality ideologically conceal racist exclusions. Feminist criticism has often been directed against demeaning and reductive representations of women that not only express or promote sexist attitudes to women (Dworkin, 1981; Mulvey, 7.3), but also shape women's sense of self. Susan Bordo (3.6) focuses on the normalising power of images of women's bodies, such that women embody images, like Baudrillard's simulacra that precede reality. Bordo invokes Plato's (1.4) scene of the power of images in the cave, but claims that cultural critics must remain in the cave of mystifying cultural images while trying to demystify them.

REFERENCES

Baudrillard, J. (1993) *Symbolic Exchange and Death*, tr. I.H. Grant. London: Sage.

Best, S. (1994) 'The commodification of reality and the reality of commodification: Baudrillard, Debord, and postmodern theory', in D. Kellner (ed.), *Baudrillard: A Critical Reader*. Oxford: Blackwell. pp. 41–67.

Debord, G. (1983) *Society of the Spectacle*. Detroit: Black & Red.

Dworkin, A. (1981) *Pornography*. New York: Perigree Books.

Fanon, F. (1986) *Black Skin, White Masks*, tr. C.L. Markmann. New York: Grove Press.

Horkheimer, M. and Adorno, T. (1993) *Dialectic of Enlightenment*, tr. J. Cumming. New York: Continuum.

Jameson, F. (1991) *Postmodernism, or, The Cultural Logic of Late Capitalism*. London: Verso.

Mitchell, W.J.T. (1986) *Iconology: Image, Text, Ideology*. Chicago: University of Chicago Press.

Nichols, B. (1981) *Ideology and the Image*. Bloomington, IN: Indiana University Press.

Williams, R. (1974) *Television: Technology and Cultural Form*. London: Fontana.

Žižek, S. (ed.) (1994) *Mapping Ideology*. London: Verso.

3:1 TELEVISION: MULTILAYERED STRUCTURE[1]
Theodor Adorno

A depth-psychological approach to television has to be focused on its multilayered structure. Mass media are not simply the sum total of the actions they portray or of the messages that radiate from these actions. Mass media also consist of various layers of meanings superimposed on one another, all of which contribute to the effect. True, due to their calculative nature, these rationalized products seem to be more clear-cut in their meaning than authentic works of art, which can never be boiled down to some unmistakable 'message'. But the heritage of polymorphic meaning has been taken over by cultural industry inasmuch as what it conveys becomes itself organized in order to enthral the spectators on various psychological levels simultaneously. As a matter of fact, the hidden message may be more important than the overt, since this hidden message will escape the controls of consciousness, will not be 'looked through', will not be warded off by sales resistance, but is likely to sink into the spectator's mind.

Probably all the various levels in mass media involve *all* the mechanisms of consciousness and unconsciousness stressed by psycho-analysis. The difference between the surface content, the overt message of televised material, and its hidden meaning is generally marked and rather clear-cut. The rigid superimposition of various layers probably is one of the features by which mass media are distinguishable from the integrated products of autonomous art, where the various layers are much more thoroughly fused. The full effect of the material on the spectator cannot be studied without consideration of the hidden meaning in conjunction with the overt one, and it is precisely this interplay of various layers which has hitherto been neglected and which will be our focus. This is in accordance with the assumption shared by numerous social scientists that certain political and social trends of our time, particularly those of a totalitarian nature, feed to a considerable extent on irrational and frequently unconscious motivations. Whether the conscious or the unconscious message of our material is more important is hard to predict and can be evaluated only after careful analysis. We do appreciate, however, that the overt message can be interpreted much more adequately in the light of psychodynamics – that is, in its relation to instinctual urges as well as control – than by looking at the overt in a naive way and by ignoring its implications and presuppositions.

The relation between overt and hidden message will prove highly complex in practice. Thus, the hidden message frequently aims at reinforcing conventionally rigid and 'pseudo-realistic' attitudes similar to the accepted ideas more rationalistically propagated by the surface message. Conversely, a number of repressed gratifications which play a large role on the hidden level

Theodor Adorno, from 'How to look at television', in *The Culture Industry*, ed. J. Bernstein. London: Routledge, 1991, pp. 164–8, 175–7. Reproduced with permission. Originally in: *The Quarterly Film, Radio and Television*, 8 (3), 1954, pp. 213–35, The Regents of the University of California.

are somehow allowed to manifest themselves on the surface in jests, off-colour remarks, suggestive situations, and similar devices. All this interaction of various levels, however, points in some definite direction: the tendency to channelize audience reaction. This falls in line with the suspicion widely shared, though hard to corroborate by exact data, that the majority of television shows today aim at producing, or at least reproducing, the very smugness, intellectual passivity and gullibility that seem to fit in with totalitarian creeds even if the explicit surface message of the shows may be anti-totalitarian.

With the means of modern psychology, we will try to determine the primary prerequisites of shows eliciting mature, adult, and responsible reactions – implying not only in content but in the very way things are being looked at, the idea of autonomous individuals in a free democratic society. We perfectly realize that any definition of such an individual will be hazardous; but we know quite well what a human being deserving of the appellation 'autonomous individual' should *not* be, and this 'not' is actually the focal point of our consideration.

When we speak of the multilayered structure of television shows, we are thinking of various superimposed layers of different degrees of manifestness or hiddenness that are utilized by mass culture as a technological means of 'handling' the audience. This was expressed felicitously by Leo Lowenthal when he coined the term 'psychoanalysis in reverse'. The implication is that somehow the psychoanalytic concept of a multilayered personality has been taken up by cultural industry, and that the concept is used in order to ensnare the consumer as completely as possible and in order to engage him psycho-dynamically in the service of premeditated effects. A clear-cut division into allowed gratifications, forbidden gratifications, and recurrence of the forbidden gratifications in a somewhat modified and deflected form is carried through.

To illustrate the concept of the multilayered structure: the heroine of an extremely light comedy of pranks is a young schoolteacher who is not only underpaid but is incessantly fined by the caricature of a pompous and authoritarian school principal. Thus, she has no money for her meals and is actually starving. The supposedly funny situations consist mostly of her trying to hustle a meal from various acquaintances, but regularly without success. The mention of food and eating seems to induce laughter – an observation that can frequently be made and invites a study of its own. Overtly, the play is just slight amusement mainly provided by the painful situations into which the heroine and her arch-opponent constantly run. The script does not try to 'sell' any idea. The 'hidden meaning' emerges simply by the way the story looks at human beings; thus the audience is invited to look at the characters in the same way without being made aware that indoctrination is present. The character of the underpaid, maltreated schoolteacher is an attempt to reach a compromise between prevailing scorn for the intellectual and the equally conventionalized respect for 'culture'. The heroine shows such an intellectual superiority and high-spiritedness that identification with her is invited, and compensation is offered for the inferiority of her position and that of her ilk in the social set-up. Not only is the central character supposed to be very charming, but she wisecracks constantly. In terms of a set pattern of identification, the script implies: 'If you are as humorous, good-natured, quick-witted, and charming as she is, do not worry about being paid a starvation wage. You can cope with your frustration in a humorous way; and your superior wit and cleverness put you not only above material privations, but also above the rest of mankind'. In other words, the script is a shrewd method of promoting adjustment to humiliating conditions by presenting them as objectively comical and by giving a picture of a person who experiences even her own inadequate position as an object of fun apparently free of any resentment.

Of course, this latent message cannot be considered as unconscious in the strict psychological sense, but rather as 'inobtrusive'; this message is hidden only by a style which does not pretend to touch anything serious and expects to be regarded as featherweight. Nevertheless, even such amusement tends to set patterns for the members of the audience without their being aware of it.

[...]

Here, an objection may be raised: is such a sinister effect of the hidden message of television known to those who control, plan, write and direct shows? Or it may even be asked: are those traits possible projections of the unconscious of the decision-makers' own minds according to the widespread assumption that works of art can be properly understood in terms of psychological projections of their authors? As a matter of fact, it is this kind of reasoning that has led to the suggestion that a special socio-psychological study of decision-makers in the field of television be made. We do not think that such a study would lead us very far. Even in the sphere of autonomous art, the idea of projection has been largely overrated. Although the authors' motivations certainly enter the artifact, they are by no means so all-determining as is often assumed. As soon as an artist has set himself his problem, it obtains some kind of impact of its own; and, in most cases, he has to follow the objective requirements of his product much more than his own urges of expression when he translates his primary conception into reality. To be sure, these objective requirements do not play a decisive role in mass media, which stress the effect on the spectator far beyond any artistic problem. However, the total set-up here tends to limit the chances of the artists' projections utterly. Those who produce the material follow, often grumblingly, innumerable requirements, rules of thumb, set patterns, and mechanisms of control which by necessity reduce to a minimum the range of any kind of artistic self-expression. The fact that most products of mass media are not produced by one individual but by collective collaboration – as happens to be true with most of the illustrations so far discussed – is only one contributing factor to this generally prevailing condition. To study television shows in terms of the psychology of the authors would almost be tantamount to studying Ford cars in terms of the psychoanalysis of the late Mr Ford.

*

We do not pretend that the individual illustrations and examples, or the theories by which they are interpreted, are basically new. But in view of the cultural and pedagogical problem presented by television, we do not think that the novelty of the specific findings should be a primary concern. We know from psychoanalysis that the reasoning, 'But we know all this!' is often a defence. This defence is made in order to dismiss insights as irrelevant because they are actually uncomfortable and make life more difficult for us than it already is by shaking our conscience when we are supposed to enjoy the 'simple pleasures of life'. The investigation of the television problems we have here indicated and illustrated by a few examples selected at random demands, most of all, taking seriously notions dimly familiar to most of us by putting them into their proper context and perspective and by checking them by pertinent material. We propose to concentrate on issues of which we are vaguely but uncomfortably aware, even at the expense of our discomfort's mounting, the further and the more systematically our studies proceed. The effort here required is of a moral nature itself: knowingly to face psychological mechanisms operating on various levels in order not to become blind and passive victims. We can change this medium of far-reaching potentialities only if we look at it in the same spirit which we hope will one day be expressed by its imagery.

NOTE

1. Footnotes removed.

SOCIETY OF THE SPECTACLE 3:2
Guy Debord

1. In societies where modern conditions of production prevail, all life presents itself as an immense accumulation of *spectacles*. Everything that was directly lived has moved away into a representation.

2. The images detached from every aspect of life fuse in a common stream in which the unity of this life can no longer be reestablished. Reality considered *partially* unfolds, in its own general unity, as a pseudo-world apart, an object of mere contemplation. The specialization of images of the world is completed in the world of the autonomous image, where the liar has lied to himself. The spectacle in general, as the concrete inversion of life, is the autonomous movement of the non-living.

3. The spectacle presents itself simultaneously as all of society, as part of society, and as *instrument of unification*. As a part of society it is specifically the sector which concentrates all gazing and all consciousness. Due to the very fact that this sector is *separate*, it is the common ground of the deceived gaze and of false consciousness, and the unification it achieves is nothing but an official language of generalized separation.

Guy Debord, from *Society of the Spectacle*. Detroit: Black & Red, 1983, Parts 1–5 and 215.

4. The spectacle is not a collection of images, but a social relation among people, mediated by images.

5. The spectacle cannot be understood as an abuse of the world of vision, as a product of the techniques of mass dissemination of images. It is, rather, a *Weltanschauung* which has become actual, materially translated. It is a world vision which has become objectified.

*

215. The spectacle is ideology par excellence, because it exposes and manifests in its fullness the essence of all ideological systems: the impoverishment, servitude and negation of real life. The spectacle is materially 'the expression of the separation and estrangement between man and man.' Through the 'new *power* of fraud,' concentrated at the base of the spectacle in this production, 'the new domain of alien beings to whom man is subservient ... grows coextensively with the mass of objects.' It is the highest stage of an expansion which has turned need against life. 'The need for money is thus the real need produced by political economy, and the only need it produces' (*Economic and Philosophical Manuscripts*). The spectacle extends to all social life the principle which Hegel (in the *Realphilosophie* of Jena) conceives as the principle of money: it is 'the life of what is dead, moving within itself.'

3:3 THE PRECESSION OF SIMULACRA[1]
JEAN BAUDRILLARD

> The simulacrum is never what hides the truth – it is truth that hides the fact that there is none.
> The simulacrum is true. – Ecclesiastes

If once we were able to view the Borges fable in which the cartographers of the Empire draw up a map so detailed that it ends up covering the territory exactly (the decline of the Empire witnesses the fraying of this map, little by little, and its fall into ruins, though some shreds are still discernible in the deserts – the metaphysical beauty of this ruined abstraction testifying to a pride equal to the Empire and rotting like a carcass, returning to the substance of the soil, a bit as the double ends by being confused with the real through aging) – as the most beautiful allegory of simulation, this fable has now come full circle for us, and possesses nothing but the discrete charm of second-order simulacra.

Today abstraction is no longer that of the map, the double, the mirror, or the concept. Simulation is no longer that of a territory, a referential being, or a

Jean Baudrillard, 'The precession of simulacra', from *Simulacra and Simulation*, tr. Sheila Faria Glaser. Ann Arbor, MI: University of Michigan Press, 1994, pp. 1 and 3–7. © The University of Michigan 1994. Reproduced with permission.

substance. It is the generation by models of a real without origin or reality: a hyperreal. The territory no longer precedes the map, nor does it survive it. It is nevertheless the map that precedes the territory – *precession of simulacra* – that engenders the territory, and if one must return to the fable, today it is the territory whose shreds slowly rot across the extent of the map. It is the real, and not the map, whose vestiges persist here and there in the deserts that are no longer those of the Empire, but ours. *The desert of the real itself.*

*

To dissimulate is to pretend not to have what one has. To simulate is to feign to have what one doesn't have. One implies a presence, the other an absence. But it is more complicated than that because simulating is not pretending: 'Whoever fakes an illness can simply stay in bed and make everyone believe he is ill. Whoever simulates an illness produces in himself some of the symptoms' (Littré). Therefore, pretending, or dissimulating, leaves the principle of reality intact: the difference is always clear, it is simply masked, whereas simulation threatens the difference between the 'true' and the 'false,' the 'real' and the 'imaginary.' Is the simulator sick or not, given that he produces 'true' symptoms? Objectively one cannot treat him as being either ill or not ill. Psychology and medicine stop at this point, forestalled by the illness's henceforth undiscoverable truth. For if any symptom can be 'produced,' and can no longer be taken as a fact of nature, then every illness can be considered as simulatable and simulated, and medicine loses its meaning since it only knows how to treat 'real' illnesses according to their objective causes. Psychosomatics evolves in a dubious manner at the borders of the principle of illness. As to psychoanalysis, it transfers the symptom of the organic order to the unconscious order: the latter is new and taken for 'real' more real than the other – but why would simulation be at the gates of the unconscious? Why couldn't the 'work' of the unconscious be 'produced' in the same way as any old symptom of classical medicine? Dreams already are.

Certainly, the psychiatrist purports that 'for every form of mental alienation there is a particular order in the succession of symptoms of which the simulator is ignorant and in the absence of which the psychiatrist would not be deceived.' This (which dates from 1865) in order to safeguard the principle of a truth at all costs and to escape the interrogation posed by simulation – the knowledge that truth, reference, objective cause have ceased to exist. Now, what can medicine do with what floats on either side of illness, on either side of health, with the duplication of illness in a discourse that is no longer either true or false? What can psychoanalysis do with the duplication of the discourse of the unconscious in the discourse of simulation that can never again be unmasked, since it is not false either?

What can the army do about simulators? Traditionally it unmasks them and punishes them, according to a clear principle of identification. Today it can discharge a very good simulator as exactly equivalent to a 'real' homosexual, a heart patient, or a madman. Even military psychology draws back from

Cartesian certainties and hesitates to make the distinction between true and false, between the 'produced' and the authentic symptom. 'If he is this good at acting crazy, it's because he is.' Nor is military psychology mistaken in this regard: in this sense, all crazy people simulate, and this lack of distinction is the worst kind of subversion. It is against this lack of distinction that classical reason armed itself in all its categories. But it is what today again outflanks them, submerging the principle of truth.

Beyond medicine and the army, favored terrains of simulation, the question returns to religion and the simulacrum of divinity: 'I forbade that there be any simulacra in the temples because the divinity that animates nature can never be represented.' Indeed it can be. But what becomes of the divinity when it reveals itself in icons, when it is multiplied in simulacra? Does it remain the supreme power that is simply incarnated in images as a visible theology? Or does it volatilize itself in the simulacra that, alone, deploy their power and pomp of fascination – the visible machinery of icons substituted for the pure and intelligible Idea of God? This is precisely what was feared by Iconoclasts, whose millennial quarrel is still with us today. This is precisely because they predicted this omnipotence of simulacra, the faculty simulacra have of effacing God from the conscience of man, and the destructive, annihilating truth that they allow to appear – that deep down God never existed, that only the simulacrum ever existed, even that God himself was never anything but his own simulacrum – from this came their urge to destroy the images. If they could have believed that these images only obfuscated or masked the Platonic Idea of God, there would have been no reason to destroy them. One can live with the idea of distorted truth. But their metaphysical despair came from the idea that the image didn't conceal anything at all, and that these images were in essence not images, such as an original model would have made them, but perfect simulacra, forever radiant with their own fascination. Thus this death of the divine referential must be exorcised at all costs.

One can see that the iconoclasts, whom one accuses of disdaining and negating images, were those who accorded them their true value, in contrast to the iconolaters who only saw reflections in them and were content to venerate a filigree God. On the other hand, one can say that the icon worshipers were the most modern minds, the most adventurous, because, in the guise of having God become apparent in the mirror of images, they were already enacting his death and his disappearance in the epiphany of his representations (which, perhaps, they already knew no longer represented anything, that they were purely a game, but that it was therein the great game lay – knowing also that it is dangerous to unmask images, since they dissimulate the fact that there is nothing behind them).

This was the approach of the Jesuits, who founded their politics on the virtual disappearance of God and on the worldly and spectacular manipulation of consciences – the evanescence of God in the epiphany of power – the end of transcendence, which now only serves as an alibi for a strategy altogether free of influences and signs. Behind the baroqueness of images hides the éminence grise of politics.

This way the stake will always have been the murderous power of images, murderers of the real, murderers of their own model, as the Byzantine icons could be those of divine identity. To this murderous power is opposed that of representations as a dialectical power, the visible and intelligible mediation of the Real. All Western faith and good faith became engaged in this wager on representation: that a sign could refer to the depth of meaning, that a sign could be exchanged for meaning and that something could guarantee this exchange – God of course. But what if God himself can be simulated, that is to say can be reduced to the signs that constitute faith? Then the whole system becomes weightless, it is no longer itself anything but a gigantic simulacrum – not unreal, but a simulacrum, that is to say never exchanged for the real, but exchanged for itself, in an uninterrupted circuit without reference or circumference.

Such is simulation, insofar as it is opposed to representation. Representation stems from the principle of the equivalence of the sign and of the real (even if this equivalence is utopian, it is a fundamental axiom). Simulation, on the contrary, stems from the utopia of the principle of equivalence, *from the radical negation of the sign as value*, from the sign as the reversion and death sentence of every reference. Whereas representation attempts to absorb simulation by interpreting it as a false representation, simulation envelops the whole edifice of representation itself as a simulacrum.

Such would be the successive phases of the image:

- It is the reflection of a profound reality;
- It masks and denatures a profound reality;
- It masks the *absence* of a profound reality;
- It has no relation to any reality whatsoever: it is its own pure simulacrum.

In the first case, the image is a *good* appearance – representation is of the sacramental order. In the second, it is an evil appearance – it is of the order of maleficence. In the third, it plays at being an appearance – it is of the order of sorcery. In the fourth, it is no longer of the order of appearances, but of simulation.

The transition from signs that dissimulate something to signs that dissimulate that there is nothing marks a decisive turning point. The first reflects a theology of truth and secrecy (to which the notion of ideology still belongs). The second inaugurates the era of simulacra and of simulation, in which there is no longer a God to recognize his own, no longer a Last Judgment to separate the false from the true, the real from its artificial resurrection, as everything is already dead and resurrected in advance.

When the real is no longer what it was, nostalgia assumes its full meaning. There is a plethora of myths of origin and of signs of reality – a plethora of truth, of secondary objectivity, and authenticity. Escalation of the true, of lived experience, resurrection of the figurative where the object and substance have disappeared. Panic-stricken production of the real and of the referential, parallel to and greater than the panic of material production: this is how simulation appears in the phase that concerns us – a strategy of the real, of the neoreal and the hyperreal that everywhere is the double of a strategy of deterrence.

NOTE

1. Footnotes removed.

3:4 IMAGE AS COMMODITY
FREDRIC JAMESON

Horkheimer and Adorno observed long ago, in the age of radio, the peculiarity of the structure of a commercial 'culture industry' in which the products were free.[1] The analogy between media and market is in fact cemented by this mechanism: it is not because the media is *like* a market that the two things are comparable; rather, it is because the 'market' is unlike its 'concept' (or Platonic idea) as the media is unlike its own concept that the two things are comparable. The media offers free programs in whose content and assortment the consumer has no choice whatsoever but whose selection is then rebaptized 'free choice.'

In the gradual disappearance of the physical marketplace, of course, and the tendential identification of the commodity with its image (or brand name or logo), another, more intimate, symbiosis between the market and the media is effectuated, in which boundaries are washed over (in ways profoundly characteristic of the postmodern) and an indifferentiation of levels gradually takes the place of an older separation between things and concept (or indeed, economics and culture, base and superstructure). For one thing, the products sold on the marketplace become the very content of the media image, so that, as it were, the same referent seems to maintain in both domains. [...] Today the products are, as it were, diffused throughout the space and time of the entertainment (or even news) segments, as part of that content, so that [...] it is sometimes not clear when the narrative segment has ended and the commercial has begun.

[...] [T]he products form a kind of hierarchy whose climax lies very precisely in the technology of reproduction itself, which now, of course, fans out well beyond the classical television set and has come in general to epitomize the new informational or computer technology of the third stage of capitalism. We must therefore also posit another type of consumption: consumption of the very process of consumption itself, above and beyond its content and the immediate commercial products. [...] Much of the euphoria of postmodernism derives from the celebration of the very process

Fredric Jameson, from *Postmodernism, or, The Cultural Logic of Late Capitalism*. Durham, NC: Duke University Press, 1991, pp. 275–7. Reproduced by permission.

of high-tech informatization (the prevalence of current theories of communication, language, or signs being an ideological spinoff of this more general 'worldview'). This is then [...] a second moment in which [...] the media 'in general' as a unified process is somehow foregrounded and experienced (as opposed to the content of individual media projections); and it would seem to be this 'totalization' that allows a bridge to be made to fantasy images of 'the market in general' or 'the market as a unified process.'

The third feature of the complex set of analogies between media and market that underlies the force of the latter's current rhetoric may then be located in the form itself. This is the place at which we need to return to the theory of the image, recalling Guy Debord's remarkable theoretical derivation (the image as the final form of commodity reification).[2] At this point the process is reversed, and it is not the commercial products of the market which in advertising become images but rather the very entertainment and narrative processes of commercial television, which are, in their turn, reified and turned into so many commodities: from the serial narrative itself, with its well-nigh formulaic and rigid temporal segments and breaks, to what the camera shots do to space, story, characters, and fashion, and very much including a new process of the production of stars and celebrities that seems distinct from the older and more familiar historical experiences of these matters and that now converges with the hitherto 'secular' phenomena of the former public sphere itself (real people and events in your nightly news broadcast, the transformation of names into something like news logos, etc.). Many analyses have shown how the news broadcasts are structured exactly like narrative serials; meanwhile, some of us in that other precinct of an official, or 'high,' culture, have tried to show the waning and obsolescence of categories like 'fiction' (in the sense of something that is opposed to either the 'literal' or the 'factual'). But here I think a profound modification of the public sphere needs to be theorized: the emergence of a new realm of image reality that is both fictional (narrative) and factual (even the characters in the serials are grasped as real 'named' stars with external histories to read about), and which now – like the former classical 'sphere of culture' – becomes semiautonomous and floats above reality, with this fundamental historical difference that in the classical period reality persisted independently of that sentimental and romantic 'cultural sphere,' whereas today it seems to have lost that separate mode of existence. Today, culture impacts back on reality in ways that make any independent and, as it were, non- or extracultural form of it problematical [...] so that finally the theorists unite their voice in the new doxa that the 'referent' no longer exists.

At any rate, in this third moment the contents of the media itself have now become commodities, which are then flung out on some wider version of the market with which they become affiliated until the two things are indistinguishable. Here, then, the media, as which the market was itself fantasized, now returns to the market and by becoming a part of it seals and certifies the formerly metaphorical or analogical identification as a 'literal' reality.

NOTES

1. Max Horkheimer and T.W. Adorno, *Dialectic of Enlightenment*, John Cumming, trans. (New York, 1972), pp. 161–67.
2. Guy Debord, *Society of the Spectacle* (Detroit, 1977), chapter 1.

3:5 'RACE' AND NATION
PAUL GILROY

[…] Britain's languages of 'race' and nation have been articulated together. The effect of their combination can be registered even where 'race' is not overtly referred to, or where it is discussed outside of crude notions of superiority and inferiority. The discourses of nation and people are saturated with racial connotations. […]

[…] The Conservatives appear to recognize this and seek to play with the ambiguities which this situation creates. […]

The Conservatives' ethnic election poster of 1983 provides further insight into the right's grasp of these complexities. The poster was presumably intended to exploit ambiguities between 'race' and nation and to salve the sense of exclusion experienced by the blacks who were its target. The poster appeared in the ethnic minority press during May 1983 and was attacked by black spokespeople for suggesting that the categories black and British were mutually exclusive. It set an image of a young black man, smartly dressed in a suit with wide lapels and flared trousers, above the caption 'Labour says he's black. Tories say he's British'. The text which followed set out to reassure readers that 'with Conservatives there are no "blacks" or "whites", just people'. A variant on the one nation theme emerged, entwined with criticism of Labour for treating blacks 'as a "special" case, as a group all on your own'. At one level, the poster states that the category of citizen and the formal belonging which it bestows on its black holders are essentially colourless, or at least colour-blind. Yet […] populist racism does not recognize the legal membership of the national community conferred by its legislation as a substantive guarantee of Britishness. 'Race' is, therefore, despite the text, being defined beyond these definitions in the sphere of culture. There is more to Britishness than a passport. Nationhood, as Alfred Sherman pointed out in 1976,

Paul Gilroy, from *There Ain't No Black in the Union Jack*. London: Routledge, 1992, pp. 56–9. Reproduced by permission of T&F Informa.

FIGURE 3.1:
Conservative Party election poster, 1978. Courtesy of The Conservative Party.

With the Conservatives, there are no 'blacks', no 'whites', just people.

Conservatives believe that treating minorities as equals encourages the majority to treat them as equals.

Yet the Labour Party aim to treat you as a 'special case', as a group all on your own.

Is setting you apart from the rest of society a sensible way to overcome racial prejudice and social inequality?

The question is, should we really divide the British people instead of uniting them?

WHOSE PROMISES ARE YOU TO BELIEVE?

When Labour were in government, they promised to repeal Immigration Acts passed in 1962 and 1971. Both promises were broken.

This time, they are promising to throw out the British Nationality Act, which gives full and equal citizenship to everyone permanently settled in Britain.

But how do the Conservatives' promises compare?

We said that we'd abolish the 'SUS' law.

We kept our promise.

We said we'd recruit more coloured policemen, get the police back into the community, and train them for a better understanding of your needs.

We kept our promise.

PUTTING THE ECONOMY BACK ON ITS FEET.

The Conservatives have always said that the only long term answer to our economic problems was to conquer inflation.

Inflation is now lower than it's been for over a decade, keeping all prices stable, with the price of food now hardly rising at all.

Meanwhile, many businesses throughout Britain are recovering, leading to thousands of new jobs.

Firstly, in our traditional industries, but just as importantly in new technology areas such as microelectronics.

In other words, the medicine is working.

Yet Labour want to change everything, and put us back to square one.

They intend to increase taxation. They intend to increase the National Debt.

They promise import and export controls.

Cast your mind back to the last Labour government. Labour's methods didn't work then.

They won't work now.

A BETTER BRITAIN FOR ALL OF US.

The Conservatives believe that everyone wants to work hard and be rewarded for it.

Those rewards will only come about by creating a mood of equal opportunity for everyone in Britain, regardless of their race, creed or colour.

The difference you're voting for is this:

To the Labour Party, you're a black person.

To the Conservatives, you're a British Citizen.

Vote Conservative, and you vote for a more equal, more prosperous Britain.

LABOUR SAYS HE'S BLACK. TORIES SAY HE'S BRITISH.

CONSERVATIVE ☒

Remains … man's main focus of identity, his link with the wider world, the past and future, 'a partnership with those who are living, those who are dead and those who are to be born' … It includes national character reflected in the way of life … a passport or residence permit does not automatically implant national values or patriotism.[1]

At this point the slightly too large suit worn by the young man, with its unfashionable cut and connotations of a job interview, becomes a key signifier. It conveys what is being asked of the black readers as the price of admission to the colour-blind form of citizenship promised by the text. Blacks are being invited to forsake all that marks them out as culturally distinct before real Britishness can be guaranteed. National culture is present in the young man's clothing. Isolated and shorn of the mugger's icons – a tea-cosy hat and the dreadlocks of Rastafari – he is redeemed by his suit, the signifier of British civilization. The image of black youth as a problem is thus contained and rendered assimilable. The wolf is transformed by his sheep's clothing. The solitary maleness of the figure is also highly significant. It avoids the hidden threat of excessive fertility which is a constant presence in the representation of Black women (Parmar, 1984). This lone young man is incapable of swamping 'us'. He is alone because the logics of racist discourse militate against the possibility of making British blackness visible in a family or an inter-generational group.[2] The black family is presented as incomplete, deviant and ruptured.

REFERENCE
Parmar, P. (1984) 'Hateful Contraries' *Ten 8*, no. 16.

NOTES
1. *Sunday Telegraph*, 8.9.76.
2. Footnote removed.

3:6 NEVER JUST PICTURES
SUSAN BORDO

In *The Republic* Plato presents a parable well known to students in introductory philosophy classes. He asks us to imagine our usual condition as knowers as comparable to life in a dark cave, where we have been confined since childhood, cut off from the world outside. In that cave we are chained by the leg and neck in such a way that we are unable to see in any position but straight ahead, at a wall in front of us, on which is projected a procession of shadow figures cast by artificial puppets manipulated by hidden puppeteers. In such a condition, Plato asks us, would not these shadow images, these illusions, seem to be 'reality' to us? They would be the only world we knew; we would not even be aware that they were artificially created by other human beings. If suddenly forced outside the cave, we would surely be confused and even scornful of anyone who tried to tell us that this, not the cave, was the real world, that we had been living inside an illusion, deceived into believing that artificial images were the real thing. But our enlightenment would require this recognition.

Never has Plato's allegory about the seductiveness of appearances been more apt than today, but note the contemporary twist. For Plato, the artificial images cast on the wall of the cave are a metaphor for the world of sense perception. The illusion of the cave is in mistaking that world – what we see, hear, taste, feel – for the Reality of enduring ideas, which can only be 'seen' with the mind's eye. For us, bedazzlement by created images is no metaphor; it is the actual condition of our lives. If we do not wish to remain prisoners of these images, we must recognize that they are not reality. But instead of moving closer to this recognition, we seem to be moving farther away from it, going deeper and deeper into the cave of illusion.

[...]

Unless one recognizes one's own enmeshment in culture, one is in no position to theorize about that culture or its effects on others. But unless one strives to develop critical distance on that enmeshment, one is apt to simply embody and perpetuate the illusions and mystifications of the culture (for example, communicating anxiety about body weight and height to one's children). So, for me, the work of cultural criticism is not exactly like that of Plato's philosopher, whose enlightenment requires that he transcend his experience of *this* world and ascend to another, purer realm. (Actually, I'm not so sure Plato believed that, either, but it is certainly the way his ideas have been dominantly interpreted.) Cultural criticism does not so much ask that we leave the cave as turn a light on *in* it.

*

Although [the organisation *Boycott Anorexic Marketing*] and the fashion industry seem to be standing on opposite sides of the fence in the debate about cultural images and eating disorders, they (and *People* and therapists Mead and Strober) share an important and defective assumption about the way we interact with media imagery of slenderness. Because these images use bodies to sell surface adornments (such as clothing, jewelry, footwear), the images are taken to be advertising, at most, a certain 'look' or style of appearance. What that 'look' or style might project (intelligence, sophistication, childlikeness) is unacknowledged and unexplored, along with the values that the viewer might bring to the experience of looking. Throughout the literature on eating disorders, whether 'fashion' is being let off the hook or condemned, it appears as a whimsical, capricious, and socially disembodied force in our lives.

This trivializing of fashion reflects a more general failure to recognize that looks are more than skin deep, that bodies *speak* to us. The notion that bodies are mere bodies, empty of meaning, devoid of mind, just material stuff occupying space, goes back to the philosopher Descartes. But do we ever interact with or experience 'mere' bodies? People who are attracted to certain sizes and shapes of bodies or to a particular color of hair or eyes are mistaken if they think their preference is only about particular body parts. Whether we are conscious of it or not, whether our preferences have their origins in (positive or negative) infant memories, culturally learned associations, or accidents of our histories, we are drawn to what the desired body *evokes* for us and in us. I have always found certain kinds of male hands – sturdy, stocky hands, the kind one might find on a physical laborer or a peasant – to be sexually attractive, even strangely moving. My father had hands like this, and I am convinced my 'aesthetic' preferences here derive from a very early time when my attitudes toward my father's masculinity were not yet ambivalent, when he existed in my life simply as the strong, omnipotent, secure hands that held me snugly against harm.

Once we recognize that we never respond *only* to particular body parts or their configuration but *always* to the meanings they carry for us, the old feminist charge of 'objectification' seems inadequate to describe what is going on when women's bodies are depicted in sexualized or aestheticized ways. The notion of women-as-objects suggests the reduction of women to 'mere' bodies, when actually what's going on is often far more disturbing than that, involving the depiction of regressive ideals of feminine behavior and attitude that go much deeper than appearance. I remember Julia Roberts in *Mystic Pizza* when she was still swinging her (then much ampler) hips and throwing sassy wisecracks, not yet typecast as the perpetually startled, emotional teeter-totter of later films. In order for Roberts to project the vulnerability that became her trademark, those hips just had to go. They suggested too much physical stability, too much sexual assertiveness, too much womanliness. Today the camera fastens on the coltlike legs of a much skinnier Roberts, often wobbly and off balance, not because she has 'great legs' in some absolute aesthetic sense (actually, when they do aestheticized close-ups of her legs, as in *Pretty Woman*, they use a body double!) but because her legs convey the qualities of fragility that directors – no doubt responding to their sense of the cultural zeitgeist as well as their own preferences – have chosen to emphasize in her.

The criticism of 'objectification' came naturally to feminism because of the continual cultural fetishization of women's bodies and body parts – breasts and legs and butts, for example. But these fetishes are not mere body parts. Often, features of women's bodies are arranged in representations precisely in order to suggest a particular attitude – dependence or seductiveness or vulnerability, for example. Heterosexual pornography, which has been accused of being the worst perpetrator of a view of women as mute 'meat,' in fact seems more interested than fashion layouts in animating women's bodies with fantasies of what's going on inside their minds. Even the pornographic motif of spread legs – arguably the worst offender in reducing the woman to the status of mere receptacle – seems to me to use the body to 'speak' in this way. 'Here I am,' spread legs declare, 'utterly available to you, ready to be and do whatever you desire.'

Many women may not like what this fetish, as I have interpreted it, projects – the woman's willing collapsing of her own desire into pleasing the male. Clearly, my interpretation won't make pornography less of a concern to many feminists. But it situates the problem differently, so we're not talking about the reduction of women to mere bodies but about what those bodies *express*. This resituating also opens up the possibility of a non-polarizing conversation between men and women, one that avoids unnuanced talk of 'male dominance' and control in favor of an exploration of images of masculinity and femininity and the 'subjectivities' they embody and encourage. Men and women may have very different interpretations of those images, differences that need to be brought out into the open and disinfected of sin, guilt, and blame.

Some feminists, for example, might interpret a scene of a man ejaculating on a woman's face as a quintessential expression of the male need to degrade and dominate. Many men, however, experience such motifs as fantasies of unconditional acceptance. 'From a male point of view,' writes Scott MacDonald, 'the desire is not to see women harmed, but to momentarily identify with men who – despite their personal unattractiveness by conventional cultural definition, despite the unwieldy size of their erections, and despite their aggressiveness with their semen – are adored by the women they encounter sexually.'[1] From this point of view, then, what much (soft) heterosexual porn provides for men is a fantasy world in which they are never judged or rejected, never made to feel guilty or embarrassed. I think that all of us, male and female alike, can identify with the desire to be unconditionally adored, our most shame-haunted body parts and body fluids worshipped, our fears about personal excess and ugliness soothed and calmed.

From the perspective of many women, however, the female attitudes that provide reassurance to MacDonald – although he may, as he says, 'mean no harm' by them – *are* demeaning. They are demeaning not because they reduce women to *bodies* but because they *embody* and promulgate images of feminine subjectivity that idealize passivity, compliance, even masochism. Just as women need to understand why men – in a culture that has required them to be sexual initiators while not permitting them the 'weakness' of feeling hurt when they are rejected – might crave uncomplicated adoration, so men need to understand why women might find the depiction of female bodies in utterly compliant poses to be problematic. In our gender history, after all, being unstintingly obliging – which in an ideal world would be a sexual 'position' that all of us could joyfully adopt with each other – has been intertwined with social subordination. When bodies get together in sex, a whole history, cultural as well as personal, comes along with them.[2]

NOTES

1. Scott MacDonald, 'Confessions of a Feminist Porn Watcher,' in Michael Kimmel, ed., *Men Confront Pornography* (New York: Meridian, 1990), p. 41.
2. Footnote removed.

4: ART HISTORY

INTRODUCTION

Art history is the longest standing academic discipline to be concerned with the study of visual artefacts. In recent years, it has become a highly contested discipline, particularly in relation to the emergent field of visual culture (see Sections 11 and 12; and Buck-Morss, 4.4). Giorgio Vasari's (1511–74) *Lives of the Artists* is widely considered to provide the first coherent history of art in which Vasari assesses the quality, style and technical achievements of artists from antiquity to his contemporary present. Until the end of the nineteenth century, art history was concerned primarily with objects of fine art – drawings, paintings and works of sculpture – and most practitioners wrote only about the art of the past. In that sense, the discipline at least had a coherent field of investigation as its object, even if the concept of history that influenced thinkers in the subject underwent radical transformations. The emergence of modern art at the turn of the nineteenth century was seen by many critics as a radical break with the past. As Eric Fernie (1995: 15–16) has said: 'Since the Renaissance the representation of the visible world constituted one of the underlying principles of painting and sculpture, but with the development of expressionism and abstraction in the early years of the twentieth century this ceased to be the case'. While art historians such as Ernst Gombrich (4.2) emphasised aspects of historical continuity in artworks and other images, the fact that artists began to question the definition of art is well-documented (Foster et al., 2004). Art historians began writing more about contemporary images and about the nature of the relationship between art and images.

One of the key methods in art history is the detailed description of individual artworks and the effects that they have on the viewer. This entails paying close attention to the way particular images look that takes account of the content of the work, the way that this content is presented and the materials out of which the artefacts are made. The cultivation of a way of seeing that is sensitive to an image's pictorial elements is a practice that can be learnt by comparing the appearance of a great number of images from many historical periods (Acton, 1997). One of the aims of this form of visual connoisseurship has been to attribute paintings, for example, to specific artists and to categorise them into stylistic schools and historical periods – as well as judging their quality and place in the historical canon (Fernie, 1995). The diagrams of Alfred Barr can be seen as part of this tradition (Figure 4.2).

Art historians supplement this attention to images with knowledge about particular artists and the historical circumstances in which they worked. In that sense, art history is a highly empirical practice, but it has been criticised for its relatively unreflective approach to its theoretical presuppositions. For example, James Elkins (1988) has argued that this lack of reflection is one of the characteristics of this form of cultural analysis that gives it its particular appeal, whereas writers such as Keith Moxley (1994) have aimed to make debates about the inherently political nature of images that have arisen from post-structuralism more central to the field. In addition, T.J. Clark (1985) has developed a Marxist, historical ideological critique of art images, while Griselda Pollock (1988) is one example of feminist criticism in art history.

Erwin Panofsky's (4.1) iconography could be seen as one attempt to map how the various pictorial elements in artworks are to be interpreted and considered. His ambitious three-tiered scheme aims to synthesise the different factors that are at play in our understanding of images, from basic psychological processes to highly complex cultural influences that operate at a symbolic level. This interplay between the science of vision and the cultural construction of vision has been considered as highly problematic by later writers such as Jonathan Crary (1992 and 12.1). For Panofsky, only the correct analysis of images at the level of detail and the identification of 'motifs' can give rise to the 'synthesis' of understanding needed to make sense of all of the different threads of meaning that we attach to the image. Ernst Gombrich (4.2), in the piece chosen here, compares visual innovation in art to the development of knowledge in the natural sciences. In suggesting that art arises from an inductive process of experimentation that has as its materials both the technologies of production – canvas, oils, etc. – and the stock of previous efforts by past artists, Gombrich shifts the emphasis of interpretation from viewing and the observer, to making and the artist.

While both Panofsky and Gombrich wrote on a wide variety of subjects and from a range of perspectives, they were among those theorists criticised for a narrowness of view by the New Art Historians in the 1970s and 1980s, such as Clark and Pollock. For example, Svetlana Alpers (4.3) suggests that neither Panofsky nor Gombrich pay sufficient attention to those compositional elements of pictures that enable us to understand pictures *as* representations of real social relations in the world. She draws attention to the differences between reality and imaging, differences that she accuses the earlier writers of overlooking even though they can be discerned in the pictures themselves. While Alpers holds on to the techniques of art historical analysis by praising the virtues of paying close attention to the image (see also Bal, 5.4), she emphasises the social and political implications of particular techniques of representation using theoretical methods pioneered by Michel Foucault (1973).

Buck-Morss (4.4) also draws attention to the social context of images when she questions the pertinence not only of art history but also of the traditional concept of fine art in contemporary visual culture, in which capitalist consumerism coincides with the advent and pervasiveness of modern imaging technologies. What is the place of art in a culture and economy dominated by an imaging industry? The perceived shortcomings of art history and its future as an academic discipline are also a central concern for those trying to define a field of image studies, such as James Elkins (13.2) and Barbara Maria Stafford (13.3). But they and other critics have suggested that while art history's primary focus has been limited to describing and making value judgements on the appearance and quality of particular images – rather than engaging with the social and cultural practices that make those images possible – its practice of detailed image analysis makes it an essential starting point for any form of visual research (Rose, 2001).

REFERENCES

Acton, M. (1997) *Learning to Look at Paintings*. London: Routledge.

Clark, T.J. (1985) *The Painting of Modern Life: Paris in the Art of Manet and his Followers*. London: Thames & Hudson.

Crary, J. (1990) *Techniques of the Observer: On Vision and Modernity in the Nineteenth Century*. Cambridge, MA: MIT Press.

Elkins, J. (1988) 'Art history without theory', *Critical Inquiry*, 14: 354–78.

Fernie, E. (1995) *Art History and its Methods: A Critical Anthology*. London: Phaidon Press.

Foster, H., Krauss, R., Bois, Y.-A. and Buchloh, B.H.D. (2004) *Art since 1900: Modernism, AntiModernism, PostModernism*. London: Thames & Hudson.

Foucault, M. (1973) *The Order of Things*, tr. unidentified collective. New York: Vintage.

Moxley, K. (1994) *The Practice of Theory: Poststructuralism, Cultural Politics and Art History*. Ithaca, NY: Cornell University Press.

Pollock, G. (1988) *Vision and Difference: Femininity, Feminism and the Histories of Art*. London: Routledge.

Rose, G. (2001) *Visual Methodologies*. London: Sage.

Vasari, G. (1987) *Lives of the Artists: Volumes 1 and 2*. London: Penguin Books.

4:1 STUDIES IN ICONOLOGY
ERWIN PANOFSKY

Iconography is that branch of the history of art which concerns itself with the subject matter or meaning of works of art, as opposed to their form. Let us, then, try to define the distinction between *subject matter* or *meaning* on the one hand, and *form* on the other.

When an acquaintance greets me on the street by removing his hat, what I see from a *formal* point of view is nothing but the change of certain details within a configuration forming part of the general pattern of colour, lines and volumes which constitutes my world of vision. When I identify, as I automatically do, this configuration as an *object* (gentleman), and the change of detail as an *event* (hat-removing), I have already overstepped the limits of purely *formal* perception and entered a first sphere of *subject matter* or *meaning*. The meaning thus perceived is of an elementary and easily understandable nature, and we shall call it the *factual meaning*; it is apprehended by simply identifying certain visible forms with certain objects known to me from practical experience, and by identifying the change in their relations with certain actions or events.

Now the objects and events thus identified will naturally produce a certain reaction within myself. From the way my acquaintance performs his action I may be able to sense whether he is in a good or bad humour, and whether his feelings towards me are indifferent, friendly or hostile. These psychological nuances will invest the gestures of my acquaintance with a further meaning which we shall call *expressional*. It differs from the *factual* one in that it is apprehended, not by simple identification, but by 'empathy.' To understand it, I need a certain sensitivity, but this sensitivity is still part of my practical experience, that is, of my every-day familiarity with objects and events. Therefore both the *factual* and the *expressional meaning* may be classified together: they constitute the class of *primary* or *natural* meanings.

However, my realization that the lifting of the hat stands for a greeting belongs in an altogether different realm of interpretation. This form of salute is peculiar to the western world and is a residue of mediaeval chivalry: armed men used to remove their helmets to make clear their peaceful intentions and their confidence in the peaceful intentions of others. Neither an Australian bushman nor an ancient Greek could be expected to realize that the lifting of a hat is not only a practical event with certain expressional connotations, but also a sign of politeness. To understand this significance of the gentleman's action I must not only be familiar with the practical world of objects and events, but also with the more-than-practical world of customs and cultural traditions peculiar to a certain civilization. Conversely, my acquaintance could not feel impelled to greet me by removing his hat were he not conscious of the significance of this feat. As for the expressional connotations which accompany his action, he may or may not be conscious of them. Therefore, when I

Erwin Panofsky, from 'Introductory', in *Studies in Iconology: Humanistic Themes in the Art of the Renaissance*. New York: Harper Torchbooks, 1962, pp. 3–17. © 1972, The Perseus Book Group. Reprinted with permission of Westview Press, a member of Perseus Books, LLC.

Object of Interpretation	Act of Interpretation	Equipment for Interpretation	Controlling Principle of Interpretation
I. *Primary or natural subject matter –* (A) factual, (B) expressional –, constituting the world of *artistic motifs.*	*Pre-iconographical description* (and pseudo-formal analysis).	*Practical experience* (familiarity with *objects and events*).	History of *style* (insight into the manner in which, under varying historical conditions, *objects* and *events* were expressed by *forms*).
II. *Secondary or conventional subject matter,* constituting the world of *images, stories* and *allegories.*	*Iconographical analysis* in the narrower sense of the word.	*Knowledge of literary sources* (familiarity with specific *themes and concepts*).	History of *types* (insight into the manner in which, under varying historical conditions, specific *themes or concepts* were expressed by *objects and events*).
III. *Intrinsic meaning* or *content,* constituting the world of 'symbolical' values.	*Iconographical interpretation* in a deeper sense (*Iconographical synthesis*).	*Synthetic intuition* (familiarity with the essential tendencies of the human mind), conditioned by personal psychology and '*Weltanschauung*'.	History of *cultural symptoms* or '*symbols*' in general (insight into the manner in which, under varying historical conditions, *essential tendencies of the human mind* were expressed by specific *themes and concepts*).

FIGURE 4.1
Three strata of subject matter or meaning

interpret the removal of a hat as a polite greeting, I recognize in it a meaning which may be called *secondary* or *conventional*; it differs from the *primary* or *natural* one in that it is intelligible instead of being sensible, and in that it has been consciously imparted to the practical action by which it is conveyed.

And finally: besides constituting a natural event in space and time, besides naturally indicating moods or feelings, besides conveying a conventional greeting, the action of my acquaintance can reveal to an experienced observer all that goes to make up his 'personality.' This personality is conditioned by his being a man of the twentieth century, by his national, social and educational background, by the previous history of his life and by his present surroundings, but it is also distinguished by an individual manner of viewing things and reacting to the world which, if rationalized, would have to be called a philosophy. In the isolated action of a polite greeting all these factors do not manifest themselves comprehensively, but nevertheless symptomatically. We could not construct a mental portrait of the man on the basis of this single action, but only by co-ordinating a large number of similar observations and by interpreting them in connection with our general information as to the gentleman's period, nationality, class, intellectual traditions and so forth. Yet all the qualities which this mental portrait would show explicitly are implicitly inherent in every single action, so that, conversely, every single action can be interpreted in the light of those qualities.

The meaning thus discovered may be called the *intrinsic meaning* or *content*; it is essential where the two other kinds of meaning, the *primary* or *natural* and the *secondary* or *conventional*, are phenomenal. It may be defined as a unifying principle which underlies and explains both the visible event and its intelligible significance, and which determines even the form in which the visible event takes shape. This *intrinsic meaning* or *content* is, of course, as much above the sphere of conscious volitions as the *expressional* meaning is beneath this sphere.

Transferring the results of this analysis from every-day life to a work of art, we can distinguish in its subject matter or meaning the same three strata:

1. PRIMARY OR NATURAL SUBJECT MATTER, subdivided into FACTUAL and EXPRESSIONAL. It is apprehended by identifying pure *forms*, that is: certain configurations of line and colour, or certain peculiarly shaped lumps of bronze or stone, as representations of natural *objects* such as human beings, animals, plants, houses, tools and so forth; by identifying their mutual relations as *events*; and by perceiving such *expressional* qualities as the mournful character of a pose or gesture, or the homelike and peaceful atmosphere of an interior. The world of pure *forms* thus recognized as carriers of *primary* or

FIGURE 4.2

Alfred H. Barr, Jr, 'The Development of Abstract Art', a chart prepared for the dust-jacket of the exhibition catalogue, *Cubism and Abstract Art*, Museum of Modern Art, New York, 1936. Reproduced by permission of the Museum of Modern Art, New York. Digital Image © 2006, The Museum of Modern Art/Scala, Florence.

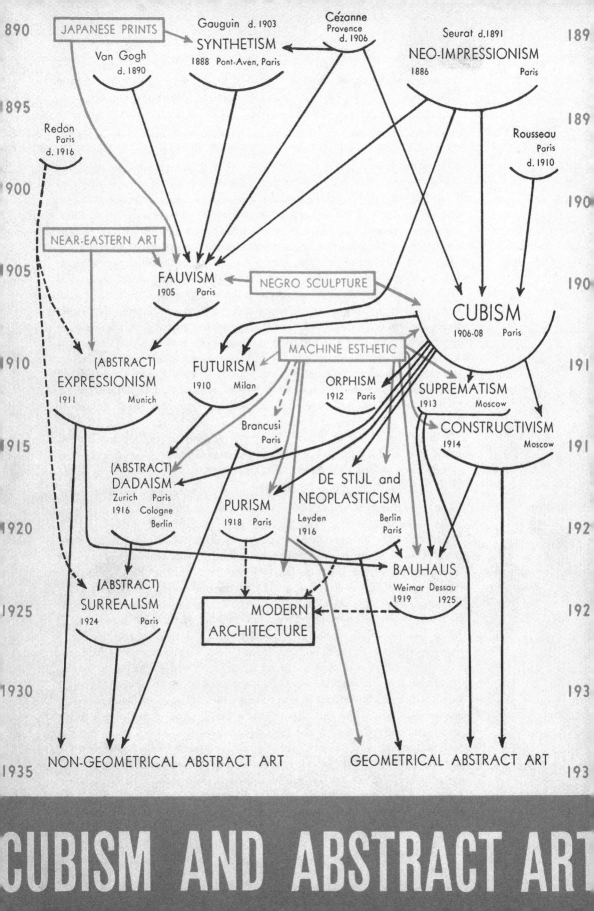

CUBISM AND ABSTRACT ART

natural meanings may be called the world of artistic *motifs*. An enumeration of these motifs would be a *pre-iconographical* description of the work of art.

2. SECONDARY OR CONVENTIONAL SUBJECT MATTER. It is apprehended by realizing that a male figure with a knife represents St. Bartholomew, that a female figure with a peach in her hand is a personification of Veracity, that a group of figures seated at a dinner table in a certain arrangement and in certain poses represents the Last Supper, or that two figures fighting each other in a certain manner represent the Combat of Vice and Virtue. In doing this we connect artistic *motifs* and combinations of artistic *motifs* (*compositions*) with *themes* or *concepts*. *Motifs* thus recognized as carriers of a *secondary* or *conventional* meaning may be called *images*, and combinations of images are what the ancient theorists of art called '*invenzioni*;' we are wont to call them *stories* and *allegories*.[1] The identification of such *images*, *stories* and *allegories* is the domain of iconography in the narrower sense of the word. In fact, when we loosely speak of '*subject matter* as opposed to *form*' we chiefly mean the sphere of *secondary* or *conventional* subject matter, viz. the world of specific *themes* or *concepts* manifested in *images*, *stories* and *allegories*, as opposed to the sphere of *primary* or *natural subject matter* manifested in artistic *motifs*. 'Formal analysis' in Wölfflin's sense is largely an analysis of motifs and combinations of motifs (compositions); for a formal analysis in the strict sense of the word would even have to avoid such expressions as 'man,' 'horse,' or 'column,' let alone such evaluations as 'the ugly triangle between the legs of Michelangelo's David' or 'the admirable clarification of the joints in a human body.' It is obvious that a correct *iconographical analysis in the narrower sense* presupposes a correct identification of the motifs. [...]

3. INTRINSIC MEANING OR CONTENT. It is apprehended by ascertaining those underlying principles which reveal the basic attitude of a nation, a period, a class, a religious or philosophical persuasion – unconsciously qualified by one personality and condensed into one work. Needless to say, these principles are manifested by, and therefore throw light on, both 'compositional methods' and 'iconographical significance.' In the 14th and 15th centuries for instance (the earliest example can be dated around 1310), the traditional type of the Nativity with the Virgin Mary reclining in bed or on a couch was frequently replaced by a new one which shows the Virgin kneeling before the Child in adoration. From a compositional point of view this change means, roughly speaking, the substitution of a triangular scheme for a rectangular one; from an iconographical point of view in the narrower sense of the term, it means the introduction of a new theme textually formulated by such writers as Pseudo-Bonaventura and St. Bridget. But at the same time it reveals a new emotional attitude peculiar to the later phases of the Middle Ages. A really exhaustive interpretation of the intrinsic meaning or content might even show that the technical procedures characteristic of a certain country, period, or artist, for instance Michelangelo's preference for sculpture in stone instead of in bronze, or the peculiar use of hatchings in his drawings, are symptomatic of the same basic attitude that is discernible in all the other specific qualities of his style. In thus conceiving of pure forms, motifs, images, stories and allegories as manifestations of underlying principles, we interpret all these elements as what

Ernst Cassirer has called *'symbolical' values*. [...] The discovery and interpretation of these *'symbolical' values* (which are generally unknown to the artist himself and may even emphatically differ from what he consciously intended to express) is the object of what we may call *iconography in a deeper sense*: of a method of interpretation which arises as a synthesis rather than as an analysis. And as the correct identification of the *motifs* is the prerequisite of a correct *iconographical analysis in the narrower sense*, the correct analysis of *images, stories* and *allegories* is the prerequisite of a correct *iconographical interpretation in a deeper sense,* – unless we deal with such works of art in which the whole sphere of secondary or conventional subject matter is eliminated, and a direct transition from *motifs* to *content* is striven for, as is the case with European landscape painting, still-life and genre; that is, on the whole, with exceptional phenomena, which mark the later, over-sophisticated phases of a long development.

NOTE
1. Footnote removed.

INVENTION AND DISCOVERY[1]
ERNST GOMBRICH

4:2

The revision I advocate in the story of visual discoveries, in fact, can be paralleled with the revision that has been demanded for the history of science. Here, too, the nineteenth century believed in passive recording, in unbiased observation of uninterpreted facts. The technical term for this outlook is the belief in induction, the belief that the patient collection of one instance after the other will gradually build up into a correct image of nature, provided always that no observation is ever colored by subjective bias. In this view nothing is more harmful to the scientist than a preconceived notion, a hypothesis, or an expectation which may adulterate his results. Science is a record of facts, and all knowledge is trustworthy only in so far as it stems directly from sensory data.

This inductivist ideal of pure observation has proved a mirage in science no less than in art. The very idea that it should be possible to observe without expectation, that you can make your mind an innocent blank on which nature will record its secrets, has come in for strong criticism. Every observation, as Karl Popper has stressed, is a result of a question we ask nature, and every question implies a tentative hypothesis. We look for something because our hypothesis makes us expect certain results. Let us see if they follow. If not, we must revise our hypothesis and try again to test it against observation as rigorously as we can; we do that by trying to disprove it, and the hypothesis that

Ernst Gombrich, from 'Invention and discovery', in *Art and Illusion*. Princeton, NJ: Princeton University Press, 2000, pp. 320–4. *Gombrich, E.H.; Art and Illusion*. © 1960 Princeton University Press, 1988, renewed PUP, 2000 paperback edition. Reprinted by permission of Princeton University Press.

survives that winnowing process is the one we feel entitled to hold, pro tempore.

This description of the way science works is eminently applicable to the story of visual discoveries in art. Our formula of schema and correction, in fact, illustrates this very procedure. You must have a starting point, a standard of comparison, in order to begin that process of making and matching and remaking which finally becomes embodied in the finished image. The artist cannot start from scratch but he can criticize his forerunners.

There is an interesting pamphlet by a minor painter called Henry Richter, published in 1817 – the year Constable exhibited Wivenhoe Park – which well illustrates the spirit of creative research that animated the young painters of the nineteenth century. It is called *Daylight: A Recent Discovery in the Art of Painting*. In this amusing dialogue the painter challenges the Dutch seventeenth-century masters, or rather their ghosts assembled at an exhibition, with the question: 'Was there no clear sky in your day, and did not the broad blue light of the atmosphere shine then, as it does now ... ? I find it is this which gives the chief splendour of sunshine by contrasting the golden with the azure lights. ...'

Like Constable, Richter scrutinized the traditional formula handed down in the science of painting and found that if you tested pictures painted in that way they did not look like scenes in daylight. He therefore advocated the addition of more blue in contrast to yellow in order to achieve that equivalence to daylight which had hitherto eluded art.

Richter's criticism was right, but he does not appear to have succeeded in producing a satisfactory alternative. Perhaps he was not inventive enough to put his hypothesis to the test of a successful painting, perhaps he lacked the stamina for trying again and again, and so he disappeared into the oblivion of a tame and uninspired Victorian illustrator while Constable went on experimenting till he found those brighter and cooler harmonies which, indeed, took painting nearer to the *plein air*.

But the evidence of history suggests that all such discoveries involve the systematic comparison of past achievements and present motifs, in other words, the tentative projection of works of art into nature, experiments as to how far nature can in fact be seen in such terms. One of the most influential teachers of art in nineteenth-century France, Lecoq de Boisbaudran, who was an ardent reformer and advocate of memory training, provides another instance of this interaction. Critical of accepted life-class routines and eager to guide the student toward 'the immense field, almost unexplored, of living action, of changing, fugitive effects,' he obtained permission to let models pose in the open air and made them move freely, as Rodin was to do: 'Once our admiration rose to the height of enthusiasm. One of our models, a man of splendid stature with a great sweeping beard, lay at rest upon the bank of the pond, close to a group of rushes, in an attitude at once easy and beautiful. The illusion was complete – mythology made true lived before our eyes, for there, before us was a river god of old, ruling in quiet dignity over the course of his waters. ... '

What an opportunity, we may infer, to test tradition and improve upon it. It is examples such as these which explain the gradual nature of all artistic changes, for variations can be controlled and checked only against a set of invariants.

Does not the experience of Lecoq de Boisbaudran suggest the revolutionary work of a much greater innovator, Manet's *Déjeuner sur l'herbe*? It is well known that this daring exploit of naturalism was based, not on an incident in the environs of Paris as the scandalized public believed, but on a print from Raphael's circle which none other than Fréart de Chambray had extolled as a masterpiece of composition. Seen from our point of view this borrowing loses much of its puzzling nature. The systematic explorer can afford less than any one else to rely on random actions. He cannot just splash colors about to see what happens, for even if he should like the effect he could never repeat it. The naturalistic image, as we have seen, is a very closely knit configuration of relationships which cannot be varied beyond certain limits without becoming unintelligible to artist and public alike. Manet's action in modifying a compositional schema of Raphael's shows that he knew the value of the adage 'One thing at a time.' Language grows by introducing new words, but a language consisting only of new words and a new syntax would be indistinguishable from gibberish.

These considerations must surely increase our respect for the achievement of the successful innovator. More is needed than a rejection of tradition, more also than an 'innocent eye.' Art itself becomes the innovator's instrument for probing reality. He cannot simply battle down that mental set which makes him see the motif in terms of known pictures; he must actively try that interpretation, but try it critically, varying here and there to see whether a better match could not be achieved. He must step back from the canvas and be his own merciless critic, intolerant of all easy effects and all short-cut methods. And his reward might easily be the public's finding his equivalent hard to read and hard to accept because it has not yet been trained to interpret these new combinations in terms of the visible world.

No wonder the boldest of these experiments led to the conviction that the artist's vision is entirely subjective. With impressionism the popular notion of the painter became that of the man who paints blue trees and red lawns and who answers every criticism with a proud 'That is how I see it.' This is one part of the story but not, I believe, the whole. This assertion of subjectivity can also be overdone. There is such a thing as a real visual discovery, and there is a way of testing it despite the fact we may never know what the artist himself saw at a certain moment. Whatever the initial resistance to impressionist paintings, when the first shock had worn off, people learned to read them. And having learned this language, they went into the fields and woods, or looked out of their window onto the Paris boulevards, and found to their delight that the visible world *could* after all be seen in terms of these bright patches and dabs of paint. The transposition worked. The impressionists had taught them, not, indeed, to see nature with an innocent eye, but to explore an unexpected alternative that turned out to fit certain experiences better than did any earlier paintings. The artists convinced art lovers so thoroughly that the bon mot 'nature imitates art' became current. As Oscar Wilde said, there was no fog in London before Whistler painted it.

NOTE

1. Images removed.

4:3 INTERPRETATION WITHOUT REPRESENTATION, OR, THE VIEWING OF *LAS MENINAS*
Svetlana Alpers

Along with Vermeer's *Art of Painting* and Courbet's *Studio*, Velázquez's *Las Meninas* (Figure 4.3) is surely one of the greatest representations of pictorial representation in all of Western painting. Why has this work eluded full and satisfactory discussion by art historians? Why should it be that the major study, the most serious and sustained piece of writing on this work in our time, is by Michel Foucault?[1] There is, I shall argue, a structural explanation built into the interpretive procedures of the discipline itself that has made a picture such as *Las Meninas* literally unthinkable under the rubric of art history. Before considering the work, as I propose to do, in representational terms, let us consider why this should be so.

Historically, we can trace two lines of argument about *Las Meninas*: the first, most elegantly encapsulated in Théophile Gautier's 'Où est donc le tableau?' has been concerned with the extraordinarily real presence of the painted world.[2] The frame appears to intersect a room whose ceiling, floor, and window bays extend, so it is suggested, to include the viewer. The light and shadow-filled space is not only intended for the viewer's eyes — as in the case of its much smaller predecessor hung at the Spanish court, Van Eyck's *Arnolfini Wedding*. Given the great size of the canvas, it is intended also for the viewer's body. The size of the figures is a match for our own. This appeal at once to eye and to body is a remarkable pictorial performance which contradictorily presents powerful human figures by means of illusionary surfaces. In the nineteenth century it was a commonplace for travellers to Madrid to refer to it in what we can call photographic terms. Continuing a tradition started in the eighteenth century about such works as Vermeer's *View of Delft*, it was compared to nature seen in a *camera obscura*, and Stirling-Maxwell, an early writer, noted that *Las Meninas* anticipated Daguerre. The pictorial quality of presence is sustained in the apparently casual deportment of the figures that is distinguished, as so often in the works of Velázquez, by a particular feature: the fact that we are looked at by those at whom we are looking. To twentieth century eyes at least, this gives it the appearance of a snapshot being taken. In the foreground, the little princess turns to us from her entourage, as does one

FIGURE 4.3
Diego Velázquez, *Las Meninas*,
1656, Museo del Prado. Madrid

of her maids, and a dwarf, and of course Velázquez himself who has stepped back from his canvas for this very purpose.

The gaze out of the canvas is a consistent feature in Velázquez's works. […] It does not initiate or attend to some occurrence; empty of expression, it is not, in short, narrative in nature. The gaze, rather, signals from within the picture that the viewer outside the picture is seen and in turn it acknowledges the state of being seen. Though not invented for the occasion of *Las Meninas*, the device is heightened here because it is thematized by the situation, or possibly the situations at hand.

Just what the situation is – hence what the subject of the work is – has been the concern of the second line of argument about *Las Meninas*. The problem is not one of identification – an early commentator identified each participant in the scene (even including the figure pausing in the light of the distant doorway whose role of marshal in the queen's entourage significantly matches Velázquez's role in service to the king). However the presence of the king and queen marked by their reflection in the prominent mirror at the center of the far wall, and the large picture seen from the back on its stretcher, which intrudes at the left, raise problems. Where are the king and queen or what is the source of their reflections, and what is the subject being painted on the unseen canvas? The impulse in recent studies has been to answer these questions by attempting to supply the plot – a little playlet as one scholar calls it – of which this picture is a scene. The little Infanta, so this account goes, has dropped in to see Velázquez at work, stops to ask her maid of honor for a drink of water and looks up when surprised by the unexpected entrance of her parents, the king and queen.

It is characteristic of art historical practice that it is the question of plot to which the notion of the meaning of the work is appended, rather than to the question of the nature of the pictorial representation [...]. And it is on this basis that the meaning of *Las Meninas* is today interpreted as a claim for the nobility of painting as a liberal art and as a personal claim for nobility on the part of Velázquez himself. In short, *Las Meninas* is now understood as a visual statement of the social rank desired by the painter.

[...]

In order to reduce *Las Meninas* to its current meaning two moves are necessary: first, against the evidence of the picture it is argued that artist and king are represented together and their proximity is seen as the central feature of the work; second, art historians separate what they claim to be the seventeenth century meaning of the work from its *appearance*, which is put in its place as merely the concern of modern viewers.

It is this insistence on the separation of questions of meaning from questions of representation that makes *Las Meninas* unthinkable within the established rubric of art history. The problem is endemic to the field. [...] What is missing is a notion of representation or a concern with what it is to picture something. [...]

Why should art history find itself in this fix? The answer lies, paradoxically, in a great strength of the discipline particularly as it has been viewed and used by literary scholarship. The cornerstone of the art historical notion of meaning is iconography – so named by Panofsky who was its founding father in our time. Its great achievement was to demonstrate that representational pictures are not intended solely for perception, but can be read as having a secondary or deeper level of meaning. What then do we make of the pictorial surface itself? In his seminal essay on iconography and iconology, Panofsky clearly evades this question. He introduces his subject with the simple example of meeting a friend on the street who lifts his hat in greeting. The blur of shapes and colors identified as a man and the sense that he is in a certain humor are called by Panofsky the primary or natural meanings, but the understanding that to raise the hat is a greeting is a secondary or conventional meaning. So far we have been dealing only with life. Panofsky's strategy is then to simply recommend transferring the results of this analysis from everyday life to a work of art. So now we have a *picture* of a man lifting his hat. What Panofsky chooses to ignore is that the man is not present but is *re*-presented in the picture. In what manner, under what conditions is the man represented in paint on the surface of a canvas?

Art historians answer this question in stylistic terms. Gombrich, quite consciously taking up where Panofsky left off, made it his major task to define style. Encapsulated in the brilliant phrase 'making comes before matching,' the ruling insight of Gombrich's *Art and Illusion* has provided a generation of literary critics with the touchstone for their analyses of literary convention. But they have ignored the fact that in the process of replacing an expressive notion of style with a representational one, Gombrich effectively eliminates just what he sets out to define. Despite his emphasis on 'making' or convention, he is far from the structuralist that he is sometimes taken to be. Gombrich treats representation as a matter of skill – skill in rendering and skill in perception. Pictorial conventions in Western art, he argues, serve the perfection of naturalistic representation which Gombrich significantly chooses to call 'illusion.' Basing himself on the irrefutable evidence offered by the study of perception, Gombrich concludes by defining a perfect representation as indistinguishable to our eyes from nature. Like the current commentators on *Las Meninas*, Gombrich effectively credits the perfect representation with making pictures disappear: the question of representation retreats before the perfect illusion Velázquez produces of the painter, the princess, and her entourage. Any meaning must clearly lie elsewhere – beyond or beneath the surface of the picture.

It is here that the strength of Foucault's commentary on *Las Meninas* lies. Beginning, as he does, with a determinate and determining notion of classical representation, he finds in this painting *its* representation. Foucault's exposition of this point proceeds through a careful viewing of the work which is impressive for its attentiveness. His interest in representation gives him the motive for looking which is lost to those who seek meaning in signs of a claim to social status. Foucault finely evokes the theme of reciprocity between an absent viewer (before the painting) and the world in view. He argues that the absence of a subject-viewer is essential to classical representation. This seems to me wrong. For the reciprocity between absent viewer and world in view is produced not by the *absence* of a conscious human subject, as Foucault argues, but rather by Velázquez's ambition to embrace two conflicting modes of representation, each of which constitutes the relationship between the viewer and the picturing of the world differently. It is the tension between these two – as between the opposing poles of two magnets that one might attempt to bring together with one's hands – that informs this picture.

Imagine two different kinds of pictures – the first is conceived to be like a window on the perceived world. The artist positions himself on the viewer's side of the picture surface and looks through the frame to the world, which he then reconstructs on the surface of the picture by means of the geometric convention of linear perspective. [...]

The second mode is not a window but rather a surface onto which an image of the world casts itself, just as light focussed through a lens forms a picture on the retina of the eye. In place of an artist who frames the world to picture it, the world produces its own image without a necessary frame. This replicative image is just there for the looking, without the intervention of a human maker. The world so seen is conceived of as existing prior to the artist-viewer. [...] The artist of the first kind claims that 'I see the world' while that of the second shows rather that the world is 'being seen.'

I am not just imagining two kinds of pictures, but describing two modes of representation that are central in Western art. [...] In Velázquez's *Las Meninas* we find the two as it were compounded in a dazzling, but fundamentally unresolvable way. While in the Albertian picture the artist presumes himself to stand with the viewer *before* the pictured world in both a physical and epistemological sense, in the descriptive mode he is accounted for, if at all, *within* that world. A pictorial device signalling this is the artist mirrored in the work (as in Van Eyck's *Arnolfini*) or a figure situated as a looker within, rather like a surveyor situated within the very world he maps. In Dutch paintings of this type the looker within the picture does not look out. That would indeed be a contradiction since a picture of this sort does not assume the existence of viewers prior to and external to it, as does the Albertian mode.

In *Las Meninas* the looker within the picture – the one whose view it is – not only looks out, but is suitably none other than the artist himself. What is extraordinary about this picture as a representation is that we must take it at once as a replication of the world *and* as a reconstruction of the world that we view through the window frame. The world seen has priority, but so also do we, the viewers on this side of the picture surface. Let me explain. Paradoxically, the world seen that is prior to us is precisely what, by looking out (and here the artist is joined by the princess and part of her retinue), confirms or acknowledges us. But if *we* had not arrived to stand before this world to look at it, the priority of the world seen would not have been defined in the first place. Indeed, to come full circle, the world seen is before us because we (along with the king and queen as noted in the distant mirror) are what commanded its presence.

Las Meninas is produced not out of a single, classical notion of representation as Foucault suggests, but rather out of specific pictorial traditions of representation. It confounds a stable reading, not because of the absence of the viewer-subject, but because the painting holds in suspension two contradictory (and to Velázquez's sense of things, inseparable) modes of picturing the relationship of viewer, and picture, to world. One assumes the priority of a viewer before the picture who is the measure of the world and the other assumes that the world is prior to any human presence and is thus essentially immeasurable.

NOTES

1. Michel Foucault, *The Order of Things,* English Translation, New York: Random House, Vintage Books, 1973, pp. 3–16.
2. This footnote and all subsequent footnotes have been removed.

TOWARDS A VISUAL CRITICAL THEORY
SUSAN BUCK-MORSS

4:4

The production of a discourse of visual culture entails the liquidation of art as we have known it. There is no way within such a discourse for art to sustain a separate existence, not as a practice, not as a phenomenon, not as an experience, not as a discipline. Museums would then need to become double encasings, preserving art objects, and preserving the art-idea. Art history departments would be moved in with archaeology. And what of 'artists'? In the recently expired socialist societies, they printed up calling cards with their profession listed confidently after their name and phone number. In recently restructured capitalist societies, they became caught in a dialectical cul-de-sac, attempting to rescue the autonomy of art as a reflective, critical practice by attacking the museum, the very institution that sustains the illusion that art exists. Artists as a social class demand sponsors: the state, private patrons, corporations. Their products enter the market through a dealer-critic system that manipulates value and is mediated by galleries, museums, and private collections. Tomorrow's artists may opt to go underground, much like freemasons of the eighteenth century. They may choose to do their work esoterically, while employed as producers of visual culture.

Their work is to sustain the critical moment of aesthetic experience. Our work as critics is to recognize it. Can this be done best, or done at all, within a new interdisciplinary field of visual studies? What would be the *episteme*, or theoretical frame, of such a field? Twice at Cornell over the past decade we have had meetings to discuss the creation of a visual studies program. Both times, it was painfully clear that institutionalization cannot by itself produce such a frame, and the discussions – among a disparate group of art historians, anthropologists, computer designers, social historians, and scholars of cinema, literature, and architecture – did not coalesce into a program. Still, visual culture has become a presence on campus. It has worked its way into many of the traditional disciplines and lives there in suspended isolation, encapsulated within theoretical bubbles. The psychoanalytic bubble is the biggest, but there are others. One could list a common set of readings, a canon of texts by Barthes, Benjamin, Foucault, Lacan, as well as a precanon of texts by a long list of contemporary writers. Certain themes are standard: the reproduction of the image, the society of the spectacle, envisioning the Other, scopic regimes, the simulacrum, the fetish, the (male) gaze, the machine eye. Today the phrase 'visual studies' calls up 202 entries in a keyword search at the Cornell University Libraries. There is a media library, a cinema program, an art museum, a theater arts center, two slide libraries, and a half dozen possessively guarded, department-owned videocassette players. If the theoretical bubbles burst, there remains this infrastructure of technological reproduction. Visual culture, once a foreigner to the academy, has gotten its green card and is here to stay.

Susan Buck-Morss, from 'Visual culture questionnaire', in *October* 77, Summer 1996, pp. 29–31. © 1996 Susan Buck-Morss. Reproduced with permission of the author.

Silent movies at the beginning of the century initiated the utopian idea of a universal language of images, one that could glide over political and ethnic borders, and set to right the Tower of Babel. Action films and MTV at the end of the century have realized this idea in secularized, instrumentalized form, producing subjects for the next stage of global capitalism. In this way, visual culture becomes the concern of the social sciences. 'Images in the mind motivate the will,' wrote Benjamin, alluding to the political power of images claimed by Surrealism. But his words could provide the motto as well for the advertising industry, product sponsoring, and political campaigning, whereas today the freedom of expression of artists is defended on formal grounds that stress the virtuality of the representation. The images of art, it is argued, have no effect in the realm of deeds.

A critical analysis of the image as a social object is needed more urgently than a program that legitimates its 'culture.' We need to be able to read images emblematically and symptomatically, in terms of the most fundamental questions of social life. This means that critical theories are needed, theories that are themselves visual, that show rather than argue. Such conceptual constellations convince by their power to illuminate the world, bringing to consciousness what was before only dimly perceived, so that it becomes available for critical reflection. I do not understand the description of 'anthropological' models and 'socio-historical' models as antithetical poles of this theoretical project. Any interpretation worth its salt demands both. It needs to provide a socio-historical and biographical story of origins that estranges the object from us and shows us that its truth is not immediately accessible (the object's prehistory), and a story of deferred action (its afterhistory) that comes to terms with the potency of the object within our own horizon of concerns.

While the Internet is the topic and the medium for new courses in digital culture, it is striking to anyone who has visited the Internet how visually impoverished a home-page can be. Cyberdigits reproduce the moving image haltingly, and the static image unimpressively. The possibility of computer screens replacing television screens may mean a great deal to stockholders of telephone companies, but it will not shake the world of the visual image. Aesthetic experience (sensory experience) is not reducible to information. Is it old-fashioned to say so? Perhaps the era of images that are more than information is already behind us. Perhaps discussions about visual culture as a field have come too late. It is with nostalgia that we boycott the videostore and insist upon seeing movies on the big screen.

The producers of the visual culture of tomorrow are the camera-women, video/film editors, city planners, set designers for rock stars, tourism packagers, marketing consultants, political consultants, television producers, commodity designers, layout persons, and cosmetic surgeons. They are the students who sit in our classes today. What is it they need to know? What will be gained, and by whom, in offering them a program in visual studies?

5: Semiotics

INTRODUCTION

Semiotics – or the 'study of signs' – is concerned with meaning-making and representation in many forms. It has been applied widely in the analysis of images in media, communication and cultural studies, as well as in art history, as a method of 'taking an image apart and tracing how it works in relation to broader systems of meaning' (Rose, 2001: 68). Semiotics, often in conjunction with psychoanalysis (Silverman, 1983), came to prominence at the height of French structuralist thought in the 1950s and 1960s (Hawkes, 1977). Since this time, various semiotic approaches – exemplified by the journal *Applied Semiotics* – have been adopted and adapted across a whole range of disciplines outside of the arts and humanities, including, for example, medicine, law, business studies, engineering and the cognitive sciences.

There are two main traditions recognised in semiotics. The first stems from the work of the Swiss linguist Ferdinand de Saussure and the second from the American philosopher and logician Charles Sanders Peirce. Saussure's (5.1) structuralist, dyadic model of semiotics focuses on the linguistic sign, which he argues does not correspond to its object or referent. Rather, there is an arbitrary relation between the signifier, meaning a sign that is the acoustic image of a sound, and the signified, meaning the concept corresponding to the signifier. The meaning of language comes from the differential relations between signs, or the place of a sign in a whole structure of interrelated signifying units. The impact of Saussure's work relates directly to what Rorty (1979: 263) terms 'the linguistic turn', whereby all of social and cultural life is critically examined in terms of 'texts' and 'textuality'. In light of debates about contemporary image culture, W.J.T. Mitchell (1994: 16) suggests there has been a further 'pictorial turn', marked by a 'postlinguistic, postsemiotic rediscovery of the picture'; which arguably might entail a *visual* semiotics.

Peirce's (5.2) semiotics, which expressly engages with visual as well as linguistic signs, involves a triadic model along with a series of layered and at times quite opaque taxonomies (Elkins, 2003). Similar to Saussure's signifier and signified respectively, Peirce describes the interaction between a *representamen* (the form the sign takes) and an *interpretant* (the sense made of the sign), but also includes an *object* (to which the sign refers). However, Peirce was no naïve realist, arguing that all experience is mediated by signs. Overall, Peirce's notion of 'semiosis' – in contrast to Saussure's synchronic emphasis upon structure – describes a semiotic *process*. His much adopted classification of iconic, indexical and symbolic signs, for example, depends primarily upon the *use* of the sign, thereby emphasising the 'role of the reader' in semiotic analysis (Eco, 1984).

The cultural and literary critic Roland Barthes (1972) initially combined Saussure's semiotics with Marxist ideology critique to uncover the myths of contemporary society and politics. Applying semiotics to political and advertising images, Barthes distinguished between that which a picture actually signifies, or denotes (such as a Black French soldier saluting) and its broader cultural and ideological meaning, connotation or signified (the civilising role of French imperialism). Barthes claimed that the ideological 'rhetoric of the image' is underwritten by the seeming naturalness of photographic denotation (1977: 32–51). But Barthes (5.3) became dissatisfied with the quasi-scientific nature of structuralist semiotics, moving towards poststructuralism and more open systems of meaning and criticism. He identifies in images a 'third' level of meaning, which, following Julia Kristeva (1984), he refers to as *signifiying* – a signifier without a signified. The third meaning, as a supplementary signifier, is indifferent to, or free from, the narrative or codes that surround it. The third meaning can structure a film differently to established codes and connotations, without subverting the story, leading Barthes to suggest that '[t]he filmic is what, in the film, cannot be described' (see also Eisenstein, 10.2).

Art historian Mieke Bal (5.4) takes inspiration both from Barthes and Peirce, as well as drawing on psychoanalysis, feminism and narratology. She deploys two new terms: sub- and suprasemiotic, which, respectively, refer to the smallest, technical aspects of a picture (in themselves *not* signs as such) and the overarching, holistic interaction of signs. Her analysis of the relationship between these two extremes leads her to see something akin to Barthes' third, obtuse meaning in painting. In conceiving of the sign not as a thing, but as an *event*, which brings to mind Peirce's semiotic process, Bal acknowledges that pictures do not stand alone, but 'move' because of the viewer. Her use of narratology as an aspect of visual semiotics accords with her critical move beyond a word-image opposition (Bal, 1991; Bal and Bryson, 1991). But it has also, along with her notion of non-semiotic elements, sparked a controversy about the general appropriateness of semiotics for the analysis of visual images and whether or not a properly visual semiotics can be established (Elkins, 1995, 1996, 2003; Bal, 1996; see also Section 8, Images and Words).

Gunter Kress and Theo van Leeuwen (5.5) have no qualms about applying 'social semiotics' (Halliday, 1978; van Leeuwen, 2005) across a broad social terrain of communication, which they refer to as the 'semiotic landscape'. Noting the increasing reliance on visual as opposed to linguistic modalities of communication, which reflects the shift to a more visual than literary culture (see Sections 11 and 12), they call for new forms of visual literacy that have hitherto been suppressed. The clear distinction they draw between visual and linguistic modes of communication, similar to Romanyshyn (8.4) and Debray (13.4), also draws attention to the multi-modality of signs (Kress and van Leeuwen, 2001). Kress and van Leeuwen develop a critical discourse analysis of the conventions or grammar of contemporary visual communication, drawing attention to the motives and interests behind, as well as the effects of, dominant forms of visual communication, as they seek to change the 'semiotic landscape' at the same time as interpreting it.

REFERENCES

Bal, M. (1991) *On Story-Telling: Essays in Narratology*, ed. D. Jobling. Sonoma, CA: Polebridge Press.
Bal, M. (1996) 'Semiotic elements in academic practices', *Critical Inquiry*, 22 (3): 573–89.

Bal, M. and Bryson, N. (1991) 'Semiotics and art history', *Art Bulletin*, LXXIII (2): 174–208.

Barthes, R. (1972) *Mythologies,* tr. A. Lavers. London: Jonathan Cape.

Barthes, R. (1977) *Image, Music, Text,* tr. S. Heath. Glasgow: Fontana.

Eco, U. (1984) *The Role of the Reader.* Bloomington, IN: Indiana University Press.

Elkins, J. (1995) 'Marks, traces, *traits,* contours, *orli,* and *splendores*: nonsemiotic elements in pictures', *Critical Inquiry,* 21 (Summer): 822–60.

Elkins, J. (1996) 'What do we want pictures to be? Reply to Mieke Bal', *Critical Inquiry,* 22 (3): 590–602.

Elkins, J. (2003) 'What does Peirce's sign theory have to say to art history?', *Culture, Theory and Critique,* 44 (1): 5–22.

Halliday, M.A.K. (1978) *Language as Social Semiotic.* London: Arnold.

Hawkes, T. (1977) *Structuralism and Semiotics.* London: Routledge.

Kress, G. and van Leeuwen, T. (2001) *Multimodal Discourse: The Modes and Media of Contemporary Communication.* London: Arnold.

Kristeva, J. (1984) *Revolution in Poetic Language,* tr. M. Waller. New York: Columbia University Press.

Mitchell, W.J.T. (1994) *Picture Theory: Essays on Verbal and Visual Representation.* Chicago: University of Chicago Press.

Rorty, R. (1979) *Philosophy and the Mirror of Nature.* Princeton, NJ: Princeton University Press.

Rose, G. (2001) *Visual Methodologies: An Introduction to the Interpretation of Visual Materials.* London: Sage.

Silverman, K. (1983) *The Subject of Semiotics.* New York: Oxford University Press.

van Leeuwen, T. (2005) *Introducing Social Semiotics.* London: Routledge.

NATURE OF THE LINGUISTIC SIGN
FERDINAND DE SAUSSURE

Some people regard language, when reduced to its elements, as a naming-process only – a list of words, each corresponding to the thing that it names. For example:

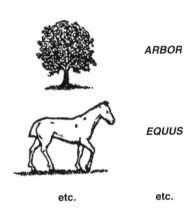

ARBOR

EQUUS

etc.   etc.

This conception is open to criticism at several points. It assumes that ready-made ideas exist before words [...]; it does not tell us whether a name is vocal or psychological in nature (*arbor*, for instance, can be considered from either viewpoint); finally, it lets us assume that the linking of a name and a thing is a very simple operation – an assumption that is anything but true. But this rather naive approach can bring us near the truth by showing us that the linguistic unit is a double entity, one formed by the associating of two terms.

[...]

The linguistic sign unites, not a thing and a name, but a concept and a sound-image. The latter is not the material sound, a purely physical thing, but the psychological imprint of the sound, the impression that it makes on our senses. The sound-image is sensory, and if I happen to call it 'material,' it is only in that sense, and by way of opposing it to the other term of the association, the concept, which is generally more abstract.

The psychological character of our sound-images becomes apparent when we observe our own speech. Without moving our lips or tongue, we can talk to ourselves or recite mentally a selection of verse. Because we regard the words of our language as sound-images, we must avoid speaking of the 'phonemes' that make up the words. This term, which suggests vocal

Ferdinand de Saussure, from *Course in General Linguistics*. New York: McGraw Hill, 1966, pp. 65–8, 120, tr. Roy Harris. © 1983 Roy Harris, English translation and editorial matter. Reproduced with permission of The McGraw-Hill Companies.

activity, is applicable to the spoken word only, to the realization of the inner image in discourse. We can avoid that misunderstanding by speaking of the *sounds* and *syllables* of a word provided we remember that the names refer to the sound-image.

The linguistic sign is then a two-sided psychological entity that can be represented by the drawing:

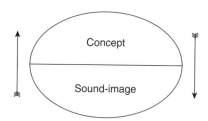

The two elements are intimately united, and each recalls the other. Whether we try to find the meaning of the Latin word *arbor* or the word that Latin uses to designate the concept 'tree,' it is clear that only the associations sanctioned by that language appear to us to conform to reality, and we disregard whatever others might be imagined.

Our definition of the linguistic sign poses an important question of terminology. I call the combination of a concept and a sound-image a *sign*, but in current usage the term generally designates only a sound-image, a word, for example (*arbor*, etc.). One tends to forget that *arbor* is called a sign only because it carries the concept 'tree,' with the result that the idea of the sensory part implies the idea of the whole.

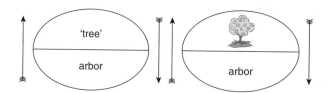

Ambiguity would disappear if the three notions involved here were designated by three names, each suggesting and opposing the others. I propose to retain the word *sign* [*signe*] to designate the whole and to replace *concept* and *sound-image* respectively by signified [*signifié*] and signifier [*signifiant*]; the last two terms have the advantage of indicating the opposition that separates them from each other and from the whole of which they are parts. As regards *sign*, if I am satisfied with it, this is simply because I do not know of any word to replace it, the ordinary language suggesting no other.

[...]

The bond between the signifier and the signified is arbitrary. Since I mean by sign the whole that results from the associating of the signifier with the signified, I can simply say: *the linguistic sign is arbitrary*.

[... In] language there are only differences. Even more important: a difference generally implies positive terms between which the difference is set up; but in language there are only differences *without positive terms*. Whether we take the signified or the signifier, language has neither ideas nor sounds that existed before the linguistic system, but only conceptual and phonic differences that have issued from the system. The idea [signified] or phonic substance [signifier] that a sign contains is of less importance than the other signs that surround it.

[...]

But the statement that everything in language is negative is true only if the signified and signifier are considered separately; when we consider the sign in its totality, we have something that is positive in it own class. A linguistic system is a series of differences of sound combined with a series of differences of ideas; but the pairing of a certain number of acoustical signs with as many cuts made from the mass of thought engenders a system of values; and this system serves as the effective link between the phonic and psychological elements within each sign.

THE SIGN: ICON, INDEX, AND SYMBOL[1] 5:2
CHARLES SANDERS PEIRCE

A sign, or *representamen*, is something which stands to somebody for something in some respect or capacity. It addresses somebody, that is, creates in the mind of that person an equivalent sign, or perhaps a more developed sign. That sign which it creates I call the *interpretant* of the first sign. The sign stands for something, its *object*. It stands for that object, not in all respects, but in reference to a sort of idea, which I have sometimes called the *ground* of the representamen. 'Idea' is here to be understood in a sort of Platonic sense, very familiar in everyday talk; I mean in that sense in which we say that one man catches another man's idea, in which we say that when a man recalls what he was thinking of at some previous time, he recalls the same idea, and in which when a man continues to think anything, say for a tenth of a second, in so far as the thought continues to agree with itself during that time, that is to have a *like* content, it is the same idea, and is not at each instant of the interval a new idea.

Reprinted by permission of the publisher from *The Collected Papers of Charles Sanders Peirce: Vol. II*, ed. Charles Hartshorne and Paul Weiss, pp. 135, 143–4, 169–73. Cambridge, MA: The Belknap Press of Harvard University Press. Copyright © 1932, 1960, by the President and Fellows of Harvard College.

[...]

A sign is either an *icon,* an *index,* or a *symbol.* An *icon* is a sign which would possess the character which renders it significant, even though its object had no existence; such as a lead-pencil streak as representing a geometrical line. An *index* is a sign which would, at once, lose the character which makes it a sign if its object were removed, but would not lose that character if there were no interpretant. Such, for instance, is a piece of mould with a bullet-hole in it as sign of a shot; for without the shot there would have been no hole; but there is a hole there, whether anybody has the sense to attribute it to a shot or not. A symbol is a sign which would lose the character which renders it a sign if there were no interpretant. Such is any utterance of speech which signifies what it does only by virtue of its being understood to have that signification.

[...]

ICON: A sign which refers to the Object that it denotes merely by virtue of characters of its own, and which it possesses, just the same, whether any such Object actually exists or not. It is true that unless there really is such an Object, the Icon does not act as a sign; but this has nothing to do with its character as a sign. Anything whatever, be it quality, existent individual, or law, is an Icon of anything, in so far as it is like that thing and used as a sign of it.

[...]

INDEX: A sign, or representation, which refers to its object not so much because of any similarity or analogy with it, nor because it is associated with general characters which that object happens to possess, as because it is in dynamical (including spatial) connection both with the individual object, on the one hand, and with the senses or memory of the person for whom it serves as a sign, on the other hand.

No matter of fact can be stated without the use of some sign serving as an index. If A says to B, 'There is a fire,' B will ask, 'Where?' Thereupon A is forced to resort to an index, even if he only means somewhere in the real universe, past and future. Otherwise, he has only said that there is such an idea as fire, which would give no information, since unless it were known already, the word 'fire' would be unintelligible. If A points his finger to the fire, his finger is dynamically connected with the fire, as much as if a self-acting fire alarm had directly turned it in that direction; while it also forces the eyes of B to turn that way, his attention to be riveted upon it, and his understanding to recognize that his question is answered. If A's reply is, 'Within a thousand yards of here,' the word 'here' is an index; for it has precisely the same force as if he had pointed energetically to the ground between him and B.

[...]

Indices may be distinguished from other signs, or representations, by three characteristic marks: first, that they have no significant resemblance to their objects; second, that they refer to individuals, single units, single collections of units or single continua; third, that they direct the attention to their objects by blind compulsion. But it would be difficult if not impossible, to instance an absolutely pure index, or to find any sign absolutely devoid of the indexical quality. Psychologically, the action of indices depends upon association by contiguity, and not upon association by resemblance or upon intellectual operations.

SYMBOL: A Sign which is constituted a sign merely or mainly by the fact that it is used and understood as such, whether the habit is natural or conventional, and without regard to the motives which originally governed its selection. [...]

It is of the nature of a sign, and in particular of a sign which is rendered significant by a character which lies in the fact that it will be interpreted as a sign. Of course, nothing is a sign unless it is interpreted as a sign; but the character which causes it to be interpreted as referring to its object may be one which might belong to it irrespective of its object and though that object had never existed, or it may be in a relation to its object which it would have just the same whether it were interpreted as a sign or not. But the *thema* of Burgersdicius seems to be a sign which, like a word, is connected with its object by a convention that it shall be so understood, or else by a natural instinct or intellectual act which takes it as a representative of its object without any action necessarily taking place which could establish a factual connection between sign and object. If this was the meaning of Burgersdicius, his thema is the same as the present writer's 'symbol.'[2]

NOTES

1. *Editor's note*: For the sake of clarity and brevity the order of the text from the original has been altered slightly. Also, the original numbering of the paragraphs has been removed.
2. *Editor's note*: Peirce is referring here to Burgersdicius' *Logic* (I., ii., §1), of 1635, in which the word 'thema' is coined. The meaning of which, Peirce suggests, is equivalent to what Aristotle sometimes expresses by λόγος (logos), being the immediate object of a thought or meaning.

THE THIRD MEANING
ROLAND BARTHES

5:3

Here is an image from [Eisenstein's] *Ivan the Terrible* (Figure 5.1): two courtiers, confederates, or supernumeraries (it doesn't matter whether or not I recall the story's details exactly) are showering the young tsar's head with gold. I believe I can distinguish three levels of meaning in this scene:

From *The Responsibility of Forms*, New York: Farrar, Straus & Giroux (Hill & Wang), 1985, pp. 41–4, 47–8, 51, 54–9. Reprinted by permission of Blackwell Publishing.

FIGURE 5.1
From Eisenstein's *Ivan the Terrible*. Source: British Film Institute.

1. An informational level: everything I can learn from the setting, the costumes, the characters, their relationships, their insertion in an anecdote familiar to me (however vaguely). This level is that of *communication*. If I had to find a mode of analysis for it, I should resort to a primary semiotics (that of the 'message'), though I shall not deal with this level and this semiotics here.

2. A symbolic level: the shower of gold. This level is itself stratified. There is a referential symbolism: the imperial ritual of baptism by gold. Then there is a diegetic symbolism: the theme of gold, of wealth (assuming it exists) in *Ivan the Terrible*, which in this image would make a significant intervention. There is also an Eisensteinian symbolism – if, say, a critic decided to show that gold, or a shower of gold, or the curtain constituted by this shower, or the disfigurement it produces, can participate in a system of displacements and substitutions characteristic of Eisenstein. Finally, there is a historical symbolism, if it can be shown, in a manner even more generalized than the preceding, that gold introduces a (theatrical) function, a scenography of exchange which we can locate both psychoanalytically and economically, i.e., semiologically. This second level, in its totality, is that of *signification*. Its mode of analysis would be a more highly elaborated semiotics than the first, a second or neo-semiotics no longer accessible to a science of the message but to sciences of the symbol (psychoanalysis, economics, dramaturgy).

Is this all? No, for I cannot yet detach myself from the image. I read, I receive (probably straight off, in fact) a third meaning, erratic yet evident and persistent.[1] I do not know what its signified is, at least I cannot give it a name, but I can clearly see the features – the signifying accidents of which this heretofore incomplete sign is composed. There is a certain density of the courtiers' makeup, in one case thick and emphatic, in the other smooth and 'distinguished;' there is the 'stupid' nose on one and the delicate line of the eyelids on the other, his dull blond hair, his wan complexion, the affected smoothness of his hairstyle which suggests a wig, the connection with chalky skin tints, with rice powder. I am not certain whether my reading of this third meaning is justified – if it can be generalized – but already it seems to me that its signifier (the features I have just attempted to express, if not to describe) possesses a theoretical individuality. For, on the one hand, this signifier cannot be identified with the simple *Dasein* of the scene; it exceeds the copy of the referential motif, it compels an interrogative reading – an interrogation bearing precisely on the signifier, not on the signified, on the reading, not on intellection: it is a 'poetic' apprehension. On the other hand, it cannot be identified with the episode's dramatic meaning. To say that these features refer to a significant 'expression' of the courtiers, here remote and bored, there diligent ('*They are simply doing their job as courtiers*'), does not altogether satisfy me. Something in these two faces transcends psychology, anecdote, function, and, in short, meaning, though without being reduced to the persistence which any human body exerts by merely being present. In opposition to the first two levels, that of communication and that of signification, this third level – even if my reading of it is still uncertain – is that of *signifying* [*signifiance*], a word that has the advantage of referring to the field of the signifier (and not of signification) and of approaching, along the trail blazed by Julia Kristeva, who proposed the term, a semiotics of the text.

[...] The symbolic meaning (the shower of gold, power, wealth, the imperial rite) compels my recognition by a double determination. It is intentional (it is what the author has meant) and it is selected from a kind of general, common lexicon of symbols; it is a meaning which seeks me out – me, the recipient of the message, the subject of the reading – a meaning which proceeds from Eisenstein and moves *ahead of me*. It is evident, of course (as is the other meaning, too), but evident in a *closed* sense, participating in a complete system of destination. I propose to call this complete sign *the obvious meaning*. [...] In theology, we are told, the obvious meaning is the one 'which presents itself quite naturally to the mind,' and this, too, is the case: to me the symbolics of a shower of gold has always seemed endowed with a 'natural' clarity. As for the other, the third meaning, the one which appears 'in excess,' as a supplement my intellection cannot quite absorb, a meaning both persistent and fugitive, apparent and evasive, I propose calling it *the obtuse meaning*. This word readily comes to my mind, and miraculously, upon exploring its etymology, I find it already yields a theory of the supplementary meaning; *obtusus* means *blunted, rounded*. Now, the features I have indicated – makeup, whiteness, false hair, etc. – are they not a kind of blunting of a too evident meaning, a too violent meaning? Do they not give the obvious signified a kind of ineffable roundness, do they not cause my reading to *skid*? An obtuse angle is greater than a right angle: *an obtuse angle of 100°*, says the dictionary; the third meaning, too, seems to me greater than the pure perpendicular, the trenchant, legal upright of the narrative.

FIGURE 5.2
From *Ordinary Fascism*.
Source: British Film
Institute.

It seems to me to open the field of meaning totally, i.e., infinitely. I even accept, for this obtuse meaning, the word's pejorative connotation: the obtuse meaning seems to extend beyond culture, knowledge, information. Analytically, there is something ridiculous about it; because it opens onto the infinity of language, it can seem limited in the eyes of analytic reason. It belongs to the family of puns, jokes, useless exertions; indifferent to moral or aesthetic categories (the trivial, the futile, the artificial, the parodic), it sides with the carnival aspect of things. *Obtuse* therefore suits my purpose well.

*

In this documentary image (Figure 5.2) from *Ordinary Fascism* I readily read an obvious meaning, that of fascism (an aesthetic and symbolics of strength, the theatrical hunt), but I also read an obtuse supplement; the (again) disguised blond stupidity of the youth carrying the arrows, the slackness of his hands and his mouth (I am not describing, I cannot manage that, I am merely designating a site), Goering's coarse nails, his trashy ring (here we are already at the limit of the mean obvious meaning, like the vapid smile of the man in glasses in the background, obviously an ass-kisser). In other words, the obtuse meaning is not structurally situated, a semantologist would not acknowledge its objective existence (but what is an objective reading?). [... T]he obtuse meaning is a signifier without signified; whence the difficulty of naming it: my reading remains suspended between the image and its description, between definition and approximation. If we cannot describe the obtuse meaning, this is because, unlike the obvious meaning, it copies nothing: how describe what represents nothing? Here the pictorial 'rendering' of words is impossible. Consequently, if we remain, you and I, on the level of articulated language in the presence of these images – that is, on the level of my own text – the obtuse meaning will not come into being, will not enter into the critic's metalanguage. Which means that the obtuse meaning is outside (articulated) language, but still within interlocution. For if you look at these images I am talking about, you will see the meaning: we can understand each other about it 'over the shoulder' or 'on the back' of articulated language: thanks, to the image [...], indeed thanks to what in the image is purely image (and which, to tell the truth, is very little indeed), we do without speech yet continue to understand each other.

In short, what the obtuse meaning disturbs, sterilizes, is metalanguage (criticism). We can offer several reasons for this. First of all, the obtuse meaning is discontinuous, *indifferent* to the story and to the obvious meaning (as signification of the story); this dissociation has a *contra naturam* or at least a distancing effect with regard to the referent (to 'reality' as nature, a realist instance). Eisenstein would probably have acknowledged and accepted this incongruity, this im-pertinence of the signifier, for it is he who remarks, apropos of sound and colour: 'Art begins the moment the creaking of a boot (on the sound track) accompanies a different visual shot and thereby provokes corresponding associations. The same is true of colour: colour begins where it no longer corresponds to natural coloration ...'. Thereupon, the signifier (the third meaning) is not filled; it is in a permanent state of *depletion* (a term from linguistics which designates the empty, all-purpose verbs – for example, the French verb *faire*); we might also say, on the other hand – and this would be quite as true – that this same signifier is not emptied (cannot be emptied); it maintains itself in a state of perpetual erethism; in it desire does not attain that spasm of the signified which usually causes the subject to sink voluptuously into the peace of nomination. Ultimately the obtuse meaning can be seen as an *accent,* the very form of an emergence, of a fold (even a crease) marking the heavy layer of information and signification. If it could be described (a contradiction in terms), it would have exactly the being of the Japanese haiku: an anaphoric gesture without significant content, a kind of gash from which meaning (the desire for meaning) is expunged. [...]

[...]

[... T]he supplementary signifier's *indifference,* or freedom of position with respect to narrative, permits locating Eisenstein's historical, political, theoretical achievements quite precisely. In his work, the story, the anecdotal, diegetic representation, is not destroyed; quite the contrary: what finer story than that of *Ivan,* that of *Potemkin?* This stature of narrative is necessary *in order to be understood* in a society which, unable to resolve the contradictions of history without a long political process, draws support (provisionally?) from mythic (narrative) solutions. The *present* problem is not to destroy narrative but to subvert it; to dissociate subversion from destruction is today's task. Eisenstein makes, it seems to me, just this distinction. The presence of a supplementary, obtuse, third meaning – even if only in a few images, but then as an imperishable signature, like a seal which endorses the entire work – and the entire oeuvre – this presence profoundly alters the theoretical status of the anecdote. The story (diegesis) is no longer merely a powerful system (an age-old narrative system), but also and contradictorily a simple space, a field of permanences and permutations; it becomes that configuration, that stage whose false limits multiply the signifier's permutative play; it is that vast outline which, by difference, compels a *vertical* reading (Eisenstein's word); it is that *false* order which permits us to avoid pure series, aleatory combination (chance is only a crude, a cheap signifier), and to achieve a structuration which *leaks from inside*. Hence we can say that with Eisenstein we have to reverse the cliché which holds that the more gratuitous the meaning the more it appears to be simply parasitic on the story told: on the contrary, it is this story which becomes somehow parametric to the signifier, of which it is no more than the field of displacement, the constitutive negativity, or again: the fellow traveller.

In short, the third meaning structures the film *differently,* without subverting the story (at least in Eisenstein), and for this reason, perhaps, it is at this level, and only here, that the 'filmic' at last appears. The filmic is what, in the film, cannot be described, it is the representation that cannot be represented. The filmic begins only where language and articulated metalanguage cease. Everything we can *say* about *Ivan* or *Potemkin* can be said about a written text (which would be called *Ivan the Terrible* or *The Battleship Potemkin*), except this – which is the obtuse meaning; [...] hence the filmic is precisely here, at this point where articulated language is no more than approximative and where another language begins (a language whose 'science' cannot therefore be linguistics, soon discarded like a booster rocket). The third meaning, which we can locate theoretically but not describe, then appears as the transition from language to *signifying* [*significance*] and as the founding act of the filmic itself. Obliged to emerge from a civilization of the signified, it is not surprising that the filmic (despite the incalculable quantity of films in the world) should still be rare (a few flashes in Eisenstein; perhaps elsewhere?), to the point where we might assert that the film, like the text, does not yet exist: there is only 'cinema,' i.e., there is language, narrative, poetry, sometimes very 'modern,' 'translated' into 'images' said to be 'animated.' Nor is it surprising that we can perceive the filmic only after having traversed – analytically – the 'essential,' the 'depth,' and the 'complexity' of the cinematic work – all riches belonging only to articulated language, out of which we constitute that work and believe we exhaust it. For the filmic is different from the film: the filmic is as far from the film as the novelistic is from the novel (I can write novelistically without ever writing novels).

NOTE

1. Footnote removed.

FROM SUB- TO SUPRASEMIOTIC: THE SIGN AS EVENT[1]
Mieke Bal

5:4

If we want to assess to what extent we can circumscribe the signifying units called signs and understand our dealings with them, we must delimit the field of signs and meanings in two directions. At one extreme there are the subsemiotic technical aspects of the works of art. Although they all contribute to the construction of signs, stylistic variation, light and dark, composition, or more technical aspects like brushstrokes, paint thickness, and lines are not, a priori, signs in themselves; not any more than in a literary text sheer ink on the page, mere punctuation marks, and syntactic structures are. Although they are part of what make us interpret the work, we do not give them meaning in themselves, except in some truly special cases. [...]

At the other extreme, there are the suprasemiotic holistic aspects of the works. Although there has been a tendency to conflate the concepts of 'text' and 'sign,' and, by extension, of 'work' and 'sign,' I think such a conflation only displaces the problem of what kinds of encounters signs and meanings are. [...] The consequence of such a position is that the compound sign will be subdivided into discrete units, and this division will become a gesture at best either of articulation or of slicing up, delimiting, what supposedly adds up in the whole. This subdivision is held more acceptable for verbal than for visual art; indeed, the distinction between the two is often based on the very assumption that verbal works are composed of discrete units whereas visual works are 'dense.' The distinction is deceptively self-evident and can be deconstructed only by reversing it and arguing that to some extent verbal texts are dense – the sign of the effect of the real cannot be distinguished from the work as a whole on which it sheds a specific meaning – and that visual texts are discrete, which sometimes, and in some respects, they are. The distinction is untenable, but it nevertheless reflects different attitudes of reading that operate conventionally for each art. [...]

*

Vermeer's *Woman Holding a Balance* (Figure 5.3), housed in the National Gallery in Washington, represents a woman in a blue dress, holding a balance above a table; on the wall, in the background, is a painting of the *Last Judgment*. Light streams in from a stained-glass window at the upper left. It is a strikingly still painting. It avoids narrative – both the anecdotal and the dynamic. Instead it presents an image in terms of visual rhythm, equilibrium, balanced contrasts, and subtle lighting. [...]

Svetlana Alpers, I assume from her *Art of Describing* (1985), would call this a descriptive painting. It is a painting that appeals to visuality if ever there was one, a case for Alpers' opposition to Italian infatuation with narrativity. Any

From *Reading "Rembrandt": Beyond the Word-Image Opposition*. Cambridge: Cambridge University Press, 1991, pp. 1, 3, 12–15; © Mieke Bal, reproduced with permission of the author.

FIGURE 5.3
Vermeer, *Woman Holding a Balance*
c. 1662–4. Source: National Gallery,
Washington, DC. **See colour Plate 1**

attempt to read the painting as a narrative can only misread it. It is a surface carefully balanced for visual experience, where the appeal to visuality is worked out in the tiniest details. On the upper left part of the painting, in the white wall near the represented *Last Judgment*, is a nail, and near that nail, a hole in the wall. The minutely detailed work of painting is so highly emphasized in these tiny details that both inside the hole and next to the nail we can see a shadow. The soft, warm light streaming in from the window on the upper left touches these two irregularities in the wall, as if to demonstrate that realistic description of the world seen knows no limits. [...]

For me it was the nail and the hole that the light made visible, produced; that instigated a burst of speculative fertility. When I saw this nail, the hole, and the shadows, I was fascinated: I could not keep my eyes off them. Why are they there? I asked myself, Are these merely meaningless details that Roland Barthes would chalk up to an 'effect of the real'? Are these the signs that make a connotation of realism shift to the place of denotation because there is no denotative meaning available? Or do they point to a change in the significance of the *Last Judgment*? Do they suggest that the represented painting which [...]

is there to balance the work, to foreground the similarity, the rhyme, between God and this woman, has been displaced from an earlier, 'original' position to a better, visually more convincing balance, leaving only the telltale trace of a nail hole? As it is, the woman stands right below God, a position that emphasizes the similarity between judging and weighing. Also, the separation between the blessed and the doomed is obliterated by her position, suggesting, perhaps, that the line between good and evil is a fine one. But in the midst of this speculative flourish, I am caught up short by the remembrance that we are looking at a painting of this balance, not at a real room. The painter surely did not need to *paint* the nail and the hole, even if, in setting up his studio, he actually may have displaced the *Last Judgment*.

[…]

In the painting, narrativity so blatantly absent on first – and even second – glance is found to have been inserted by means of a sign that makes a statement on visuality. The visual experience that encodes the iconic association between woman and God is not displaced but, on the contrary, underscored by this narrative aspect. We imagine someone trying to hang the painting in exactly the right place. We are suddenly aware of the woman's artificial pose: Instead of changing the painting's position, the artist arranging his studio could simply have changed the woman's place, or his own angle of vision. All of a sudden something is happening, the still scene begins to move, and the spell of stillness is broken.

The nail and the hole, both visual elements to which no iconographic meaning is attached, unsettle the poetic description and the passively admiring gaze that it triggered, and dynamize the activity of the viewer. Whereas before the discovery of these details the viewer could gaze at the work in wonder, now he or she is aware of his or her imaginative addition in the very act of looking. The work no longer stands alone; now the viewer must acknowledge that he or she makes it work, and that the surface is no longer still but tells the story of its making.

[…]

[…] Whenever a literary scholar, moved by the commendable intention of putting an end to the current proliferation of interpretation, stands up to claim that some details in realistic texts have no narrative function, that they merely serve to produce an 'effect of the real' (Barthes, 1968) or an effect of verisimilitude (*vraisemblance;* Genette, 1969), someone else responds that the examples given do have a narrative function after all, if only one looks hard enough. There seems to be a resistance to meaninglessness that invariably looks convincing. As a consequence, we continue to assume that everything in a work of art contributes to, and modifies, the meaning of the work.

But if everything in a work of art participates equally in the production of meaning, then how do we know what texts and images are 'about' and why? In other words, which signs convey, or trigger, which meanings? One answer is that there is no answer because texts and images do nothing, the interpreter invents the meaning. Putting the question differently, we may ask, On what basis do we process verbal and visual signs? The debate is particularly troublesome in literary theory because the question interferes with the apparent obviousness of the answer. We assume we know what signs are and which signs we process because we know what a letter, a word, and a sentence are, and we assume that words are the units we call signs in verbal works.

Here, visual poetics reminds us of this assumption's untenability, by forcing us to ask what the visual counterpart of a word is: Is it an image, as the phrase 'word and image' too easily suggests? Mulling over this difficult equation, we become less sure that words are, in fact, the 'stuff' of verbal signification.

The problem of delimiting signs and delineating interpretation – of distinguishing interpretation from description – is related. Since readers and viewers bring to the texts and images their own cultural and personal baggage, there can be no such thing as a fixed, predetermined meaning, and the very attempt to summarize meanings, as we do in encyclopaedias and textbooks, is by definition reductive. Yet as soon as we are forced to draw from these views the inevitable conclusion that 'anything goes' and that interpretation is a futile scholarly activity since it all depends on the individual interpreter, we draw back. We then turn around, trying to locate, in the text or image, not a meaning, but the 'occasion' of meaning, the thing that triggers meaning; not fixity, but a justification for our flexibility.

[…]

The view of signs to which I [adhere…] posits the basic density of both verbal and visual texts. I use the term 'density' in Goodman's (1976) sense: as conveying the fundamental inseparability of individual signs, as the opposite of discreteness. This view eliminates at least one difference between discourse and image. Resisting the early Wittgenstein's anguish about, and sympathizing with his later happy endorsement of, the cloudiness of language, I contend that the same density that characterizes visual texts obstructs the propositional clarity of verbal texts.[2] Thus, separate words cannot be taken to rule interpretation, and the ideal of 'pure' propositional content longed for in the *Tractatus* is untenable: the elements of a proposition cannot have independent meaning. This recognition means that the difference between verbal and visual texts is no longer one of the status and delimitation of the signs that constitute them. And the visual model, apparently predominant, overwhelms the concrete particularity of the signifier, giving rise to 'cloudiness' in each medium. Hence, the Wittgenstein of the *Tractatus* mourns the fact that there is no nondense language, whereas later, in the *Investigations*, Wittgenstein denounces the positivistic illusion that makes visuality the basis of interpretation, sacrificing both the signifier and the activity of semiosis. In this later work he endorses the view he earlier regretted, that language is as dense as pictures. This may not make language visual, but it does displace the difference between the two media.

Yet the density of both visual and linguistic signs is not really the issue. Rather, it is the dynamism of signs that the recognition of their density makes possible that is at issue. The perception of signs as static can be traced to the atomistic view of verbal signs, itself a relic of early structuralism which, in its turn, had inherited it from more explicitly positivistic schools of cultural scholarship.[3] The problem and source of this atomistic view are the semiotic positivism that claims ontological status for the sign. If the sign is a 'real thing,' then signs must be numerable, hence discrete and intrinsically static. A radically dynamic view, however, would conceive the sign not as a thing but as an event, the issue being not to delimit and isolate the one sign from other signs, but to trace the possible emergence of the sign in a concrete situation of work–reader interaction. Wittgenstein's concept of language games posits a dynamic view of the sign, which makes signs as *active*, and requires them to be both deployed *according to rules* and *public. A sign, then, is not a thing but an event*. Hence the meaning of a sign is neither preestablished and fixed, nor purely subjective and idiosyncratic.

Although this view seems to open the discussion to a paralyzing infinitude of phenomena, this apparent problem disappears as soon as we acknowledge that sign events occur in specific circumstances and according to a finite number of culturally valid, conventional, yet not unalterable rules, which semioticians call 'codes.' The selection of those rules and their combination leads to specific interpretive behaviour.

NOTES

1. *Editor's note*: The opening paragraphs of this selection outlining the concepts of sub- and suprasemiotic marks appear in Bal's original text as a lengthy footnote. It has been included here as a theoretical supplement to the main text.
2. Footnote removed.
3. Footnote removed.

WORKS CITED

Alpers, S. (1983) *Art of Describing: Dutch Art in the Seventeenth Century*. Chicago: University of Chicago Press.
Barthes, R. (1968) 'L'Effet de réel', in *Communications*, 4: 84–9. [English: 'The reality effect', in Roland Barthes, *The Rustle of Language*, tr. Richard Howard. New York: Hill & Wang. pp. 141–54.
Genette, G. (1969) 'Vraisemblance et motivation', *Figures II*, 71–100. Paris: Editions du Seuil.
Goodman, N. (1976) *Languages of Art: An Approach to a Theory of Symbols*. Indianapolis: Hackett.
Wittgenstein, L. (1958) *Philosophical Investigations*, tr. G.E.M. Anscombe. New York: Macmillan.
Wittgenstein, L. (1961) *Tractatus Logico-Philosophicus*, tr. B.F. McGuiness. New York: Humanities Press.

THE SEMIOTIC LANDSCAPE
GUNTER KRESS AND THEO VAN LEEUWEN

5:5

The place of visual communication in a given society can only be understood in the context of, on the one hand, the range of forms or modes of public

From *Reading Images: The Grammar of Visual Design*, by Gunter Kress and Theo van Leeuwen. London: Routledge, 1996, pp. 33–4, 37–40. Reproduced with permission.

communication available in that society, and, on the other hand, their uses and valuations. We refer to this as 'the semiotic landscape.' The metaphor is worth exploring a little, as is its etymology. Just as the features of a landscape (a field, a wood, a clump of trees, a house, a group of buildings) only make sense in the context of their whole environment [...] so particular modes of communication should be seen in *their* environment, in the environment of all the other modes of communication which surround them, and of their functions. The use of the visual mode is not the same now as it was even fifty years ago in Western societies, it is not the same from one society to another; and it is not the same from one social group or institution to another.

[...]

The new realities of the semiotic landscape are [...] primarily brought about by social and cultural factors: by the intensification of linguistic and cultural diversity within the boundaries of nation states, and by the weakening of these boundaries, due to multiculturalism, electronic media of communication, technologies of transport and global economic developments. Global flows of capital and information dissolve not only cultural and political boundaries but also semiotic boundaries. This is already beginning to have the most far-reaching effects on the characteristics of English (and Englishes), globally, and even within the national boundaries of England.

The place of language in public forms of communication is changing. Language is moving from its former, unchallenged role as *the* medium of communication, to a role as *one* medium of communication, and perhaps to the role of the medium of comment, albeit more so in some domains than in others, and more rapidly in some areas than in others. Although this is a relatively new phenomenon in public communication, children do this quite 'naturally.'

*

Figure 5.5 comes from a science textbook for children in the early to middle years of secondary schooling in England. Two questions can be asked. The first: 'What is the effect of the mode of representation on the epistemology of science?,' 'Do different modes of representation facilitate, or rule out, different accounts of natural phenomena?' The second question is, again, the question of subjectivity: the implied reader of this page is a fundamentally different reader from that of the older textbook shown in Figure 5.4. Readers who have become habituated to the contemporary textbook page (Figure 5.5) not only have a different conception of what science is, but also of what (being) a scientist is. They have different notions of authority relations, of the status of science as a discipline, of epistemological positions, and so on – just as the designers of this page have different conceptions of these questions to those of the page shown in Figure 5.4.

[...What] is the status of written language in these pages? In Figure 5.4 it is the central medium, the medium of information. Images have the function of illustrating an argument carried by the written word, that is, of presenting ('translating') the contents of the written language in a different

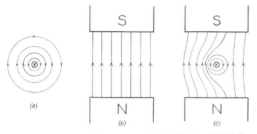

76   MAGNETISM AND ELECTRICITY

the magnetic poles. Fig. 62 (c) shows the combined field of (a) and (b) when the wire is placed between the poles.

Note that, in Fig. 62 (a) and (b), the lines of force on the left of the wire are in the same direction as those of the external field, while those on the right of the wire are in the opposite direction. Consequently in the combined field of Fig. 62 (c) the field to the left of the wire is strong—there are a large number of lines, while the field to the right is weak.

If we assume, with Faraday, that the lines of force are in tension and trying to shorten (see p. 13), we should expect the wire to be urged to the right. This is precisely what we find by experiment.

Fig. 62. (a) Magnetic field due to current in straight wire. (b) Field due to magnetic poles. (c) Combined field of (a) and (b).

The principle of the electric motor.

The simple electric motor consists of a coil pivoted between the poles of a permanent magnet (see Fig. 63). When a current is passed through the coil in the direction indicated in the figure we can show, by applying Fleming's left-hand rule, that the left-hand side of the coil will tend to move down and the right-hand side to move up. (Remember that the direction of the field due to the permanent magnet is from the N. to the S. pole.) Thus the coil will rotate in a counter-clockwise direction to a vertical position.

FIGURE 5.4

Early twentieth-century science textbook.
McKenzie, 1938, Cambridge University Press.

medium. The subjectivity of the reader is here formed in, and implied by, the hierarchic organization of the mode of (scientific) writing. It is a subjectivity which treats language naturally as the medium of information, the medium of truth, and of truth transmitted relatively transparently in the syntax of the writing; and it is a subjectivity habituated to sustained, concentrated analysis, attention, reflection. In Figure 5.5, images are the central medium of information, and the role of language has become that of a medium of commentary. Images (and this includes the layout of the page) carry the argument. The subjectivity of the reader is formed in a mix of semiotic modes in which the visual is clearly dominant. It is a subjectivity which relies on the visual rather than on the verbal, as a medium of entertainment as much as a medium of information; information in fact becomes relatively marginal as an aim, both on the part of the student and on the part of the textbook designer, though for different reasons. It is also a subjectivity habituated to the more ready apprehension of the transparently presented visual. The apprehension of facts displaces the concern with truth, and the emphasis is not on sustained, concentrated analysis, but on the quick apprehension of facts and information.

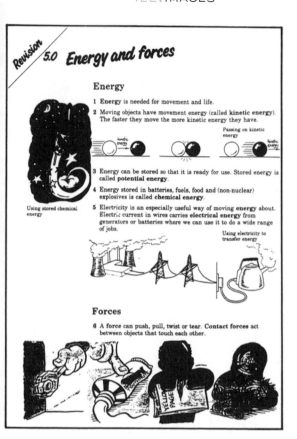

FIGURE 5.5
Science textbook (Suffolk Coordinated
Science, 1978, Longman Educational).

The shift is based on changed relations of power in two distinct areas: in the area of social valuations of scientific knowledge, where the authority of science can no longer be taken for granted; and in the area of education, where the authority of the transmitters of social values can no longer be taken for granted, but has to be *achieved*. In this set of relations the subjectivity of the student readers in relation to power and authority is changed. They no longer accept the social valuations of science and education accepted by most earlier students, even if many of them turned away from internalizing them as their own.

[...]

These changes in the semiotic landscape ... reveal what has in fact always been the case: language, whether in speech or writing, has always existed as just one mode in the totality of modes involved in the production of any text, spoken or written. A spoken text is not just verbal but also visual, combining with 'non-verbal' modes of communication such as facial expression, gesture, posture and other forms of self-presentation. A written text, similarly, involves more than language: it is written *on* something, on some *material* (paper, wood, vellum, stone, metal, rock, etc.) and it is written *with* something (gold, ink, (en)gravings, dots of ink, etc.); with letters formed in systems influenced by aesthetic, psychological, pragmatic and other considerations; and with a layout imposed on the material substance, whether on the page, the computer screen or a polished brass plaque. The multimodality of written texts has, by and large, been ignored, whether in educational contexts, in linguistic theorizing or in popular common sense. Today, in the age of 'multimedia,' it can suddenly be perceived again.

We can summarize this discussion in the form of a set of hypotheses: (a) human societies use a variety of modes of representation; (b) each mode has, inherently, a different representational potential, a different potential for meaning-making; (c) each mode has a specific social valuation in particular social contexts; (d) different potential for meaning-making may imply different potentials for the formation of subjectivities; (e) individuals use a range of representational modes, and therefore have available a range of means of meaning-making, each affecting the formation of their subjectivity; (f) the different modes of representation are not held discretely, separately, as autonomous domains in the brain, or as autonomous communicational resources in a culture, nor are they deployed discretely, either in representation or in communication; rather, they intermesh and interact at all times; (g) affective aspects of human behaviour and being are not discrete from other cognitive activity, and therefore never separate from representational and communicative behaviour; (h) each mode of representation has a continuously evolving history, in which its semantic reach can contract or expand or move into different areas as a result of the uses to which it is put.

As modes of representation are made and remade, they contribute to the making and remaking of human societies and of the subjectivities of their members. None of these hypotheses would, we imagine, attract significant disagreement, especially when put singly. Together, however, they represent a challenge to the existing common sense on the relations between language and thought, and on mainstream theories and practices in all areas of public communication. This is a crucial feature of the new semiotic landscape.

6: PHENOMENOLOGY

INTRODUCTION

Phenomenology is primarily concerned with the structure of experience and, in particular, how things appear to us in the way that they do. Art images and artefacts have occupied a central role in phenomenological thinking because each type of object in the world is thought to foster a particular kind of consciousness. Writers such as Martin Heidegger (6.1) have held that artworks have the potential to emancipate consciousness because they elicit an imaginative and creative response to living in a world constrained by convention.

The key to understanding the phenomenological approach to images is the concept of 'intentionality', first outlined by its founder Edmund Husserl in his seminal work *Logical Investigations* (1970a). Husserl's basic insight, which drew on the psychology of Franz Brentano, is that consciousness and the world are co-constituting. In particular, each individual experience involves a particular type of intentional relation between consciousness and the world – so the experience of a remembered image, a loved image and a perceived image can be understood as each having their own particular, defining characteristics. One task of phenomenology is to describe the structure, or 'essence', of such experiences by enumerating those characteristics. For example, Husserl's (2005) fine-grained analysis of 'image-consciousness' aims to describe how we are able to see representational paintings as both three-dimensional objects and as canvas and paint at the same time.

Since phenomenology attempts to deal with individual experiences, it often begins with a detailed analysis of a particular image, or type of image, in a similar way to art history. For example, Martin Heidegger describes a painting of peasant shoes by Van Gogh in order to point out the perceptual interplay between the oil and canvas of the painting as a thing and its representation of a pair of shoes (Pattison, 2000). In a similar vein, Gaston Bachelard (1969) has dealt with the images of architecture and the spaces of the home. However, phenomenology also focuses on the role of images in constituting subjectivities and, in that respect, is perhaps closer to psychoanalysis than traditional art history. For example, Heidegger's distinction between a piece of equipment and a work of art is intended to demonstrate not only that an art object is not used in the same way as, say, a carpenter's hammer or a sack of coal, but that it engenders a particular type of consciousness. Equipment fosters a utilitarian view of a world that is passive before the technological forces at work in society, whereas artworks emphasise the ability of people to create a world of meaning in harmony with nature. Heidegger (1977) developed this romanticised view of artwork and its potential for social liberation into a fully-fledged critique of modern technology.

In opposition to iconoclastic views of images that also pay close attention to individual artefacts, such as ideological critique and semiotics, phenomenology broadly understands images positively and as having a high degree of cognitive content. However, this cognitive content is not necessarily associated with conscious thought. Building on Husserl's (1989) work on the body as a lived phenomenon, Merleau-Ponty (6.2) explained how meaning is created by the pre-conscious, bodily activity of the artist as a social being in which art becomes a form of 'figured philosophy'. Images and the consciousnesses that accompany them are social products refracted through the medium of the artist and his or her equipment.

The 'phenomenon' of phenomenology can be either a physical object, such as a painting or a film (Ingarden, 1989), or an object of consciousness, such as a dream, sensation, feeling or mental image. Phenomenologists such as Jean-Paul Sartre (6.3) and Mikel Dufrenne (6.4) have, therefore, also turned their attention to what psychologists have variously called mental images, qualia, or the contents of consciousness. In doing so, they have applied the same descriptive techniques used to analyse artworks and images of science to reveal the structure, or essence, of cognition. Both Sartre and Dufrenne criticise the empiricist notion of David Hume and John Locke (1.14) that mental images are somehow 'in' consciousness, suggesting, instead, that consciousness is made up of intentional acts. For Dufrenne, as with Kant (2.1), imagination is the organising principle that makes the process of synthesising the mind's representative faculties and empirical sense-data possible. In one respect, this phenomenological practice is intended as a supplement to psychology and cognitive science because it is argued that by paying close attention to the details of conscious experience scientists are better able to discriminate the phenomena they wish to investigate (Petitot et al., 1999).

While most texts of classical phenomenology tend to focus on either traditional art objects and aesthetic theory, or different aspects of cognition, more recently writers have turned their attention to non-art images – a subject that has become central to such art critics as James Elkins (13.2). For example, Don Ihde (6.5) argues that the scientific way of understanding the world is predominantly visual and the way that its images are constructed by technology helps determine what can be accepted as knowledge in that field. Ihde shows that the 'lifeworld' (Husserl, 1970b) of institutional practices and technologies, such as those deployed in science, do not produce neutral ways of seeing, but come with a sedimented, cognitive content that phenomenology can uncover. Others have suggested combining such 'lifeworld' analyses with a close attention to particular images and the perceptual vision those foster to both art images (Brough, 2001) and non-art images (Piper, 2006).

REFERENCES

Bachelard, G. (1969) *The Poetics of Space*, tr. M. Jolas. Boston, MA: Beacon Press.

Brough, J. (2001) 'Art and non-art: a millennial puzzle', in S. Crowell, L. Embree and S. J. Julian (eds), *The Reach of Reflection: Issues for Phenomenology's Second Century*. Electronically published by the Center for Advanced Research in Phenomenology at www.electronpress.com pp. 1–16.

Heidegger, M. (1977) *Question Concerning Technology and Other Essays*, tr. W. Lovitt. New York: Harper & Row.

Husserl, E. (1970a) *Logical Investigations*, tr. J.N. Findlay. London: Routledge & Kegan Paul; Atlantic Highlands, NJ: Humanities Press.

Husserl, E. (1970b) *The Crisis of European Sciences and Transcendental Phenomenology*, tr. D. Carr. Evanston, IL: Northwestern University Press.

Husserl, E. (1989) *Ideas Pertaining to a Pure Phenomenology and a Phenomenological Philosophy, Second Book*, tr. R. Rojcewicz and A. Schuwer. Dordrecht: Kluwer Academic.

Husserl, E. (2005) *Phantasy, Image Consciousness, and Memory (1898–1925)*, tr. J.B. Brough. Dordrecht: Kluwer Academic.

Ingarden, R. (1989) *Ontology of the Work of Art: The Musical Work, The Picture, The Architectural Work and The Film*, tr. R. Meyer and J.T. Goldwait. Athens, OH: Ohio University Press.

Pattison, G. (2000) *The Later Heidegger*. London: Routledge.

Petitot, J., Varela, F.J., Pachoud, B. and Roy, J.-M. (eds) (1999) *Naturalizing Phenomenology: Issues in Contemporary Phenomenology and Cognitive Science*. Stanford, CA: Stanford University Press.

Piper, A. (2006) 'Sensible models in cognitive neuroscience', in *Logos of Phenomenology and Phenomenology of the Logos, Book Four: The Logos of Scientific Interrogation. Analecta Husserliana*, Vol. 91. Berlin: Springer. pp. 105–18.

6:1

THING AND WORK
MARTIN HEIDEGGER

We choose as example a common sort of equipment – a pair of peasant shoes. We do not even need to exhibit actual pieces of this sort of useful article in order to describe them. Everyone is acquainted with them. But since it is a matter here of direct description, it may be well to facilitate the visual realization of them. For this purpose a pictorial representation suffices. We shall choose a well-known painting by Van Gogh, who painted such shoes several times. But what is there to see here? Everyone knows what shoes consist of. If they are not wooden or bast shoes, there will be leather soles and uppers, joined together by thread and nails. Such gear serves to clothe the feet. Depending on the use to which the shoes are to be put, whether for work in the field or for dancing, matter and form will differ.

Such statements, no doubt correct, only explicate what we already know. The equipmental quality of equipment consists in its usefulness. But what about this usefulness itself? In conceiving it, do we already conceive along with it the equipmental character of equipment? In order to succeed in

FIGURE 6.1
Vincent Van Gogh,
A Pair of Shoes: 1887.
Source: Van Gogh
Museum, Amsterdam.

Martin Heidegger, from 'The origin of the work of art', in *Basic Writings: Revised and Expanded Edition*. London: Routledge, 1993, pp. 158–64. Reproduced with permission of Taylor & Francis Books. Copyright © 1977, 1993 by David Farrell Krell. Reprinted by permission of HarperCollins Publishers.

doing this, must we not look out for useful equipment in its use? The peasant woman wears her shoes in the field. Only here are they what they are. They are all the more genuinely so, the less the peasant woman thinks about the shoes while she is at work, or looks at them at all, or is even aware of them. She stands and walks in them. That is how shoes actually serve. It is in this process of the use of equipment that we must actually encounter the character of equipment.

As long as we only imagine a pair of shoes in general, or simply look at the empty, unused shoes as they merely stand there in the picture, we shall never discover what the equipmental being of the equipment in truth is. From Van Gogh's painting we cannot even tell where these shoes stand. There is nothing surrounding this pair of peasant shoes in or to which they might belong – only an undefined space. There are not even clods of soil from the field or the field-path sticking to them, which would at least hint at their use. A pair of peasant shoes and nothing more. And yet.

From the dark opening of the worn insides of the shoes the toilsome tread of the worker stares forth. In the stiffly rugged heaviness of the shoes there is the accumulated tenacity of her slow trudge through the far-spreading and ever-uniform furrows of the field swept by a raw wind. On the leather lie the dampness and richness of the soil. Under the soles stretches the loneliness of the field-path as evening falls. In the shoes vibrates the silent call of the earth, its quiet gift of the ripening grain and its unexplained self-refusal in the fallow desolation of the wintry field. This equipment is pervaded by uncomplaining worry as to the certainty of bread, the wordless joy of having once more withstood want, the trembling before the impending childbed and shivering at the surrounding menace of death. This equipment belongs to the *earth*, and it is protected in the *world* of the peasant woman. From out of this protected belonging the equipment itself rises to its resting-within-itself.

But perhaps it is only in the picture that we notice all this about the shoes. The peasant woman, on the other hand, simply wears them. If only this simple wearing were so simple. When she takes off her shoes late in the evening, in deep but healthy fatigue, and reaches out for them again in the still dim dawn, or passes them by on the day of rest, she knows all this without noticing or reflecting. The equipmental being of the equipment consists indeed in its usefulness. But this usefulness itself rests in the abundance of an essential Being of the equipment. We call it reliability. By virtue of this reliability the peasant woman is made privy to the silent call of the earth; by virtue of the reliability of the equipment she is sure of her world. World and earth exist for her, and for those who are with her in her mode of being, only thus – in the equipment. We say 'only' and therewith fall into error; for the reliability of the equipment first gives to the simple world its security and assures to the earth the freedom of its steady thrust.

The equipmental being of equipment, reliability, keeps gathered within itself all things according to their manner and extent. The usefulness of equipment is nevertheless only the essential consequence of reliability. The former vibrates in the latter and would be nothing without it. A single piece of equipment is worn out and used up; but at the same time the use itself also falls into disuse, wears away, and becomes usual. Thus equipmentality wastes away, sinks into mere stuff. In such wasting, reliability vanishes. This dwindling, however, to which use-things owe their boringly obtrusive usualness, is only one more testimony to the original essence of equipmental being. The worn-out usualness of the equipment then obtrudes itself as the sole mode of being, apparently peculiar to it exclusively. Only blank usefulness now remains visible. It awakens the impression that the origin of equipment lies in a mere fabricating that impresses a form upon some matter. Nevertheless, in its genuinely equipmental being, equipment stems from a more distant source. Matter and form and their distinction have a deeper origin.

The repose of equipment resting within itself consists in its reliability. Only in this reliability do we discern what equipment in truth is. But we still know nothing of what we first sought: the thing's thingly character. And we know nothing at all of what we really and solely seek: the workly character of the work in the sense of the work of art.

Or have we already learned something unwittingly – in passing, so to speak – about the work-being of the work?

The equipmental quality of equipment was discovered. But how? Not by a description and explanation of a pair of shoes actually present; not by a report about the process of making shoes; and also not by the observation of the actual use of shoes occurring here and there; but only by bringing ourselves before Van Gogh's painting. This painting spoke. In the nearness of the work we were suddenly somewhere else than we usually tend to be.

The artwork lets us know what shoes are in truth. It would be the worst self-deception to think that our description, as a subjective action, had first depicted everything thus and then projected it into the painting. If anything is questionable here, it is rather that we experienced too little in the nearness of the work and that we expressed the experience too crudely and too literally. But above all, the work did not, as it might seem at first, serve merely for a better visualizing of what a piece of equipment is. Rather, the equipmentality of equipment first expressly comes to the fore through the work and only in the work.

What happens here? What is at work in the work? Van Gogh's painting is the disclosure of what the equipment, the pair of peasant shoes, *is* in truth. This being emerges into the unconcealment of its Being. The Greeks called the unconcealment of beings *alētheia*. We say 'truth' and think little enough in using this word. If there occurs in the work a disclosure of a particular being, disclosing what and how it is, then there is here an occurring, a happening of truth at work.

In the work of art the truth of beings has set itself to work. 'To set' means here 'to bring to stand.' Some particular being, a pair of peasant shoes, comes in the work to stand in the light of its Being. The Being of beings comes into the steadiness of its shining.

The essence of art would then be this: the truth of beings setting itself to work. But until now art presumably has had to do with the beautiful and beauty, and not with truth. The arts that produce such works are called the fine arts, in contrast with the applied or industrial arts that manufacture equipment. In fine art the art itself is not beautiful, but is called so because it produces the beautiful. Truth, in contrast, belongs to logic. Beauty, however, is reserved for aesthetics.

[…]

The work, therefore, is not the reproduction of some particular entity that happens to be at hand at any given time; it is, on the contrary, the reproduction of things' general essence. […]

EYE AND MIND
MAURICE MERLEAU-PONTY

6:2

The painter 'takes his body with him,' says Valéry. Indeed we cannot imagine how a *mind* could paint. It is by lending his body to the world that the artist changes the world into paintings. To understand these transubstantiations we must go back to the working, actual body – not the body as a chunk of space or a bundle of functions but that body which is an intertwining of vision and movement.

I have only to see something to know how to reach it and deal with it, even if I do not know how this happens in the nervous machine. My mobile body makes a difference in the visible world, being a part of it; that is why I can steer it through the visible. Conversely, it is just as true that vision is attached to movement. We see only what we look at. What would vision be without eye movement? And how could the movement of the eyes bring things together if the movement were blind? If it were only a reflex? If it did not have its antennae, its clairvoyance? If vision were not prefigured in it?

In principle all my changes of place figure in a corner of my landscape; they are recorded on the map of the visible. Everything I see is in principle within my reach, at least within reach of my sight, and is marked upon the map of the 'I can.' Each of the two maps is complete. The visible world and the world of my motor projects are each total parts of the same Being.

This extraordinary overlapping, which we never think about sufficiently, forbids us to conceive of vision as an operation of thought that would set up

Maurice Merleau-Ponty, *The Primacy of Perception*, Northwestern University Studies in Phenomenology and Existential Philosophy. Evanston, IL: Northwestern University Press, 1964, pp. 162–9. Copyright © 1964 by Northwestern University Press. Reproduced with permission of Northwestern University Press. Originally *L'oeil et l'esprit* © Editions Gallimard, Paris. Reproduced with permission.

before the mind a picture or a representation of the world, a world of immanence and of ideality. Immersed in the visible by his body, itself visible, the see-er does not appropriate what he sees; he merely approaches it by looking, he opens himself to the world. And on its side, this world of which he is a part is not *in itself*, or matter. My movement is not a decision made by the mind, an absolute doing which would decree, from the depths of a subjective retreat, some change of place miraculously executed in extended space. It is the natural consequence and the maturation of my vision. I say of a thing that it is moved; but my body moves itself, my movement deploys itself. It is not ignorant of itself; it is not blind for itself; it radiates from a self. . . .

The enigma is that my body simultaneously sees and is seen. That which looks at all things can also look at itself and recognize, in what it sees, the 'other side' of its power of looking. [...]

[...]

[...] Since things and my body are made of the same stuff, vision must somehow take place in them; their manifest visibility must be repeated in the body by a secret visibility. 'Nature is on the inside,' says Cézanne. Quality, light, color, depth, which are there before us, are there only because they awaken an echo in our body and because the body welcomes them.

Things have an internal equivalent in me; they arouse in me a carnal formula of their presence. Why shouldn't these [correspondences] in their turn give rise to some [external] visible shape in which anyone else would recognize those motifs which support his own inspection of the world?[1] Thus there appears a 'visible' of the second power, a carnal essence or icon of the first. It is not a faded copy, a *trompe l'oeil*, or another *thing*. The animals painted on the walls of Lascaux are not there in the same way as the fissures and limestone formations. But they are not *elsewhere*. Pushed forward here, held back there, held up by the wall's mass they use so adroitly, they spread around the wall without ever breaking from their elusive moorings in it. I would be at great pains to say *where* is the painting I am looking at. For I do not look at it as I do at a thing; I do not fix it in its place. My gaze wanders in it as in the halos of Being. It is more accurate to say that I see according to it, or with it, than that I *see it*.

The word 'image' is in bad repute because we have thoughtlessly believed that a design was a tracing, a copy, a second thing, and that the mental image was such a design, belonging among our private bric-a-brac. But if in fact it is nothing of the kind, then neither the design nor the painting belongs to the in-itself any more than the image does. They are the inside of the outside and the outside of the inside, which the duplicity of feeling [*le sentir*] makes possible and without which we would never understand the quasi presence and imminent visibility which make up the whole problem of the imaginary. The picture and the actor's mimicry are not devices to be borrowed from the real world in order to signify prosaic things which are absent. For the imaginary is much nearer to, and much farther away from, the actual — nearer because it is in my body as a diagram of the life of the actual, with all its pulp and carnal obverse [*son envers charnel*] exposed to view for the first time. In this sense, Giacometti[2] says energetically, 'What interests me in all paintings is resemblance – that is, what is resemblance for me: something which makes me discover more of the world.' And the imaginary is much farther away from the actual because the painting is an analogue or likeness only according to the body; because it does *not* present the *mind* with an occasion to rethink the constitutive relations of things; because, rather, it offers to our *sight* [*regard*], so that it might join with them, the inward traces of vision, and because it offers to vision its inward tapestries, the imaginary texture of the real.[3]

[...]

In paintings themselves we could seek a figured philosophy[4] of vision – its iconography, perhaps. It is no accident, for example, that frequently in Dutch paintings (as in many others) an empty interior is 'digested' by the 'round eye of the mirror.'[5] This prehuman way of seeing things is the painter's way. More completely than lights, shadows, and reflections, the mirror image anticipates, within things, the labor of vision. Like all other technical objects, such as signs and tools, the mirror arises upon the open circuit [that goes] from seeing body to visible body. Every technique is a 'technique of the body.' A technique outlines and amplifies the metaphysical structure of our flesh. The mirror appears because I am seeing-visible [*voyant-visible*], because there is a reflexivity of the sensible; the mirror translates and reproduces that reflexivity. My outside completes itself in and through the sensible. Everything I have that is most secret goes into this *visage*, this face, this flat and closed entity about which my reflection in the water has already made me puzzle. Schilder[6] observes that, smoking a pipe before a mirror, I feel the sleek, burning surface of the wood not only where my fingers are but also in those ghostlike fingers, those merely visible fingers inside the mirror. The mirror's ghost lies outside my body, and by the same token my own body's 'invisibility' can invest the other bodies I see.[7] Hence my body can assume segments derived from the body of another, just as my substance passes into them; man is mirror for man. The mirror itself is the instrument of a universal magic that changes things into a spectacle, spectacles into things, myself into another, and another into myself. [...] Where in the realm of the understanding can we place these occult operations, together with the potions and idols they concoct? What can we call them? Consider, as Sartre did in *Nausea*, the smile of a long-dead king which continues to exist and to reproduce itself [*de se produire et de se reproduire*] on the surface of a canvas. It is too little to say that it is there as an image or essence; it is there as itself, as that which was always most alive about it, even now as I look at the painting. The 'world's instant' that Cézanne wanted to paint, an instant long since passed away, is still thrown at us by his paintings.[8] His Mount Saint Victor is made and remade from one end of the world to the other in a way that is different from, but no less energetic than, that of the hard rock above Aix. Essence and existence, imaginary and real, visible and invisible – a painting mixes up all our categories in laying out its oneiric universe of carnal essences, of effective likenesses, of mute meanings.

NOTES

1. Footnote removed.
2. G. Charbonnier, *Le monologue du peintre* (Paris, 1959), p. 172.
3. Footnote removed.
4. '... une philosophie figurée...'.
5. P. Claudel, *Introduction à la peinture hollandaise* (Paris, 1935).
6. P. Schilder, *The Image and Appearance of the Human Body* (London, 1935; New York, 1950), pp. 223–24). [...]
7. Cf. Schilder, *Image,* pp. 281–82 – Trans.
8. Footnote removed.

6:3 DESCRIPTION
JEAN-PAUL SARTRE

Despite several preconceptions, to which we shall return shortly, it is certain that when I produce the image of Peter, it is Peter who is the object of my actual consciousness. As long as that consciousness remains unaltered, I could give a description of the object as it appears to me in the form of an image but not of the image as such. To determine the properties of the image as image I must turn to a new act of consciousness: I must *reflect*. Thus the image as image is describable only by an act of the second degree in which attention is turned away from the object and directed to the manner in which the object is given. It is this reflective act which permits the judgment 'I have an image.'

It is necessary to repeat at this point what has been known since Descartes: that a reflective consciousness gives us knowledge of absolute certainty; that he who becomes aware 'of having an image' by an act of reflection cannot deceive himself. There have been psychologists, no doubt, who maintained that a vivid image could not be distinguished from a faint perception. Titchener even cites some experiments in support of this view. But we shall see further on that such claims rest on an error. In fact, the confusion is impossible; what has come to be known as an 'image' occurs immediately as such to reflection. But it is not a metaphysical and ineffable revelation that concerns us here. If this consciousness is immediately distinguishable from all others, it is because it presents itself to reflection with certain traits, certain characteristics, which at once determine the judgment 'I have an image.' The act of reflection thus has a content of immediate certainty which we shall call the *essence* of the image. This essence is the same for everyone; and the first task of psychology is to explain this essence, to describe it, to fix it.

Why, then, should there be so many different theories concerning this immediate knowledge on which all psychologists should certainly be of one

Jean-Paul Sartre, from *The Psychology of the Imagination*. New York: Philosophical Library, 1948, pp. 3–8. Reproduced with permission of Taylor & Francis.

mind? Our answer is that the majority of psychologists ignore this primary knowledge and prefer to build explanatory hypotheses concerning the nature of the image.[1] These like all other scientific hypotheses, never possess more than a certain probability: the data of reflection are certain.

All new studies of the image should therefore begin with a basic distinction: that it is one thing to *describe* the image and quite another to draw *conclusions* regarding its nature. In going from one to the other we pass from certainty to probability. The first duty of the psychologist is obviously to formulate into concepts the knowledge that is immediate and certain.

So we shall ignore theories. We want to know nothing about the image but what reflection can teach us. Later on we shall attempt, as do other psychologists, to classify the consciousness of the image among the other types of consciousness, to find a 'family' for it, and we shall form hypotheses concerning its inherent nature. For the present we only wish to attempt a 'phenomenology' of the image. The method is simple: we shall produce images, reflect upon them, describe them; that is, attempt to determine and to classify their distinctive characteristics.

*

The very first reflective glimpse shows us that up to now we have been guilty of a double error. We believed, without giving the matter any thought, that the image was *in* consciousness and that the object of the image was *in* the image. We pictured consciousness as a place peopled with small likenesses and these likenesses were the images. No doubt but that this misconception arises from our habit of thinking in space and in terms of space. This we shall call: *the illusion of immanence*. The clearest expression of this illusion is found in Hume, where he draws a distinction between impressions and ideas:

> Those perceptions, which enter with most force and violence, we may name *impressions*. . . By *ideas* I mean the faint images of these in thinking and reasoning. ...[2]

These ideas are none other than what we called *images*. Now Hume adds several pages further on:

> But to form the idea of an object, and to form an idea simply is the same thing; the reference of the idea to an object being an extraneous denomination, of which in itself it bears no mark or character. Now as 'tis impossible to form an idea of an object, that is possest of quantity and quality, and yet is possest of no precise degree of either; it follows, that there is an equal impossibility of forming an idea, that is not limited and confined in both these particulars.[3]

According to this view my actual idea of chair has but an extraneous relation to an existing chair. It is not the chair of the external world, the chair I just perceived; it is not the chair of straw and wood by which I am able to distinguish my idea from the idea of a table or an inkwell. But, my actual idea is nevertheless an idea *of* chair. What can this mean but that, for Hume, the idea of chair and the chair as an idea are one and the same thing. To have an idea of chair is to have a chair in consciousness. That this is so is shown by the fact that what is true of the object is also true of the idea. If the object must have a determined quantity and quality, so must the idea.

Psychologists and philosophers have in the main adopted this point of view. It is also the point of view of common sense. When I say that 'I have an image' of Peter, it is believed that I now have a certain picture of Peter in my consciousness. The object of my actual consciousness is just this picture, while Peter, the man of flesh and bone, is reached but very indirectly, in an 'extrinsic' manner, because of the fact that it is he whom the picture represents. Likewise, in an exhibition, I can look at a portrait for its own sake for a long time without noticing the inscription at the bottom of the picture 'Portrait of Peter Z. . . .' In other words, an image is inherently like the material object it represents.

What is surprising is that the radical incongruity between consciousness and this conception of the image has never been felt. It is doubtless due to the fact that the illusion of immanence has always been taken for granted. Otherwise it would have been noticed that it was impossible to slip these material portraits into a conscious synthetic structure without destroying the structure, without breaking the contacts, arresting the flow, breaking the continuity. Consciousness would cease being transparent to itself; its unity would be broken in every direction by unassimilable, opaque screens. The works of men like Spaier, Buhler and Flach, in which the image is shown to be supple by being full of life, suffused with feeling and knowledge are useless; for by turning the image into an organism they did not make it any the less unassimilable by consciousness. It is for this reason that certain logical minds, like F. Moutier,[4] have felt that the existence of mental images must be denied if the integrity of the mental synthesis is to be saved. Such a radical solution is contradicted by the data of introspection. I can, at will, think of an image of a horse, tree or house. But if we accept the illusion of immanence, we are necessarily led to construct the world of the mind out of objects entirely like those of the external world, but which simply obey different laws.

Let us ignore these theories and see what reflection teaches us, so that we may rid ourselves of the illusion of immanence.

When I perceive a chair it would be absurd to say that the chair is in my perception. According to the terminology we have adopted, my perception is a certain consciousness and the chair is the object of that consciousness. Now I shut my eyes and I produce an image of the chair I have just perceived. The chair, now occurring as an image, can no more enter into consciousness than it could do so as an object. An image of a chair is not, and cannot be a chair. In fact, whether I perceive or imagine that chair of straw on which I am seated, it always remains outside of consciousness. In both cases it is there, in space, in that room, in front of the desk. Now — and this is what reflection teaches us above all — whether I see or imagine that chair, the object of my perception and that of my image are identical: it is that chair of straw on which I am seated. Only consciousness is *related* in two different ways to the same chair. The chair is envisioned in both cases in its concrete individuality, its corporeality. Only, in one of the cases, the chair is 'encountered' by consciousness; in the other, it is not. But the chair is not in consciousness; not even as an image. What we find here is not a semblance of the chair which suddenly worked its way into consciousness and which has but an 'extrinsic' relation to the existing chair, but a certain type of consciousness, a synthetic organization, which has a direct relation to the existing chair and whose very essence consists precisely of being related in this or that manner to the existing chair.

And what exactly is the image? Evidently it is not the chair: in general, the object of the image is not itself an image. Shall we say then that the image is the total synthetic organization, consciousness? But this consciousness is an actual and concrete nature, which exists in and for itself and which can always occur to reflection without any intermediary. The word image can therefore only indicate the relation of consciousness to the object; in other words, it means a certain manner in which the object makes its appearance to consciousness, or, if one prefers, a certain way in which consciousness presents an object to itself. The fact of the matter is that the expression 'mental image' is confusing. It would be better to say 'the consciousness of Peter as an image' or 'the imaginative consciousness of Peter.' But since the word image is of long standing we cannot reject it completely. However, in order to avoid all ambiguity, we must repeat at this point that an image is nothing else than a relationship. The imaginative consciousness I have of Peter is not a consciousness of the image of Peter: Peter is directly reached, my attention is not directed on an image, but on an object.[5]

Thus, in the woof of the synthetic acts of Consciousness there appear at times certain structures which we shall call imaginative consciousness. They are born, develop and disappear in accordance with laws proper to them and which we shall try to ascertain. And it would be a grave error to confuse this life of the imaginative consciousness, which lasts, becomes organized, and disintegrates, with the object of this consciousness which in the meantime can well remain immutable.

NOTES

1. Cf. our critical study *L'Imagination,* Alcan, 1936.
2. *A Treatise of Human Nature.* Oxford, 1941, p. 1.
3. *Ibid,* p. 20.
4. F. Moutier, *L'aphasie de Broca.* Thèse de Paris. Steinheil, 1908. Cf. p. 244: 'We absolutely deny the existence of images.'
5. Cases may be cited in which I produce an image of an object which has no real existence outside myself. But the chimera does not exist 'as an image.' It exists neither as such nor otherwise.

6:4

IMAGINATION
MIKEL DUFRENNE

The advent of representation occurs with the upsurge of space and time. In agreement with Heidegger's interpretation of Kant, we shall attribute this upsurge to the transcendental imagination. The empirical imagination prolongs this movement, converting appearance into object. The transcendental imagination prefigures the empirical, making the empirical possible. Transcendental imagination expresses the possibility of representation, while empirical imagination accounts for a given representation's meaningfulness and its integration into a total representation of a world. As transcendental, the imagination sees to it that there is a given; as empirical, imagination makes certain that this given, enriched by possibles, possesses a meaning.

What is the source of these possibles? How do they intervene in the form of an image? That which imagination actually contributes to perception by way of extending and animating appearances is not created *ex nihilo*. Imagination nourishes representation with modes of implicit knowledge [*les savoirs*] previously constituted in lived experience. More precisely, imagination plays a dual role. It mobilizes such knowledge, and it converts what is acquired by experience [*l'acquis*] into something visible. In the former case, we must consider knowledge as an aspect of imagination. For knowledge is a virtual state of the image, whose intentional correlate is the possible. Imagination mobilizes the knowledge which it furnishes to representation. Hume's analysis is relevant here. Imagination constitutes the associations which form the indispensable commentary on present impressions and which enable us to know an object. The only problem is that Hume's analysis is warped by the sensationalist prejudice which inspired it. Associations appear as a mechanical miracle, because they are effected between ideas that are the residues of heterogeneous impressions. Synthesis is achieved through habit, which, even though natural (not premeditated or organized by a transcendental activity), still remains somewhat artificial. To avoid this artificiality, we must look to the experience of presence, in which what Husserl calls 'passive synthesis' operates naturally by means of the body.[1] Thus, through our body, we are on an even level with the object, though without fully realizing it. We acquire a familiarity with the object which no act of thought can supplant and which is indispensable for all knowledge by acquaintance [*connaissance*]. In affirming this, we are only taking Hume at his word. But we refuse to interpret habit as a mechanical means of associating ideas. Rather, we envisage habit as the organ of an inner condition and, in accordance with its etymology, of a mastery of

Mikel Dufrenne, from 'Representation and imagination', in *The Phenomenology of Aesthetic Experience*, tr. Edward S. Casey, Northwestern University Studies in Phenomenology and Existential Philosophy. Evanston, IL: Northwestern University Press, 1973, pp. 345–53. Copyright © 1973 by Northwestern University Press. Reproduced with permission of Northwestern University Press. Originally *Phénoménologie de l'expérience esthétique*, Presses Universitaires de France, 1953. Reproduced with permission.

the corporeal object. Therefore, if imagination mobilizes modes of implicit knowledge, it does so not so much by taking the initiative in an unpredictable outburst as by following the course of a previous experience undergone by the body on the plane of presence.

As a result, the essential function of imagination is to convert this experience into something visible, giving it the status of representation. We could say that representation is that which makes us think *of*, but we should place the emphasis on the evocative capacity suggested by the 'think,' not on the connective capacity suggested by the 'of' (a capacity belonging to the body). The crucial matter is always the transition from presence to representation. On both the empirical and the transcendental levels, imagination is a force which strives for visibility. The transcendental imagination having opened up the area in which something given can appear, the empirical imagination fills out this field. This is done without multiplying the given. Instead, images are elicited to form a quasi given. These images are not, strictly speaking, images of the visible. However, they put us en route toward the visible by continually appealing to perception for decisive confirmation. For we must realize that the modes of implicit knowledge with which imagination seeks to dominate appearances are neither perceptual nor conceptual. They exist in a prior form in which they can be annexed to a representation.

When we perceive, these modes of knowledge are not evoked *as* knowledge, that is, as supplementary information added to the perceived from the outside, or as a gloss adjoined to a text. They are there as the very meaning of the perceived object, given with it and in it. This proximity of knowledge to the perceived is the work of imagination, for knowledge thus integrated should be termed an 'image.' If I *know* that snow is cold, I can actualize the memory of experiences that I have had of this coldness; but when I see snow, it appears cold to me without my effecting this actualization. This means, first, that the cold is not known by an influence which would summon up a previously constituted knowledge of cold. Yet it is not felt in the way that white is seen (though we may, instructed by painters, doubt that white itself is seen, and it could be shown that white is not itself seen without the aid of imagination). This sort of immediate presence, nonconceptual and yet nonsensuous, is the 'image' of cold which accompanies the perception of snow and renders it eloquent. My implicit knowledge is converted into an abstract and yet real presence *of* something sensuous which is adumbrated but not wholly given. The same holds for the symbolic images in which comprehension is occasionally made determinate. In Sartre's example, the tumultuous and endless sea is an image of the proletariat; it gives neither a true nor an objective comprehension of the object designated by it.[2] Comprehension in the form of an image is an image of comprehension, just as the cold of unfelt snow or the flavor of a roast evoked by a famished man is the image of an unsensed sensuousness [*un sensible non senti*].[3] Second, the cold can be anticipated only because it has already been known. When memory takes the form of an image, anticipation becomes reminiscence. Finally, the image adheres to perception in constituting the object. It is not a piece of mental equipment in consciousness but a way in which consciousness opens itself to the object, prefiguring it from deep within itself as a function of its implicit knowledge.

Therefore, the world is present to us in flesh and blood only because it is at the same time implicitly present in images. To unfold the empirical content of these images, we must appeal to the modes of implicit knowledge which constitute experience. However, in perception such modes of knowledge remain in a latent state of 'empty intentions.' Consequently, we cannot assert that perception is composed of sensations to which judgment adds modes of knowledge. Modes of implicit knowledge are not *known* [*connu*] as such. Rather, as latent in the form of images, they are incarnate in objects. In this manner, imagination comes to the aid of perception. There *is* an irrecusable given which elicits and directs the imagination: perception is not wholly imagination. But this given is only appearance, since it is contemplated and not lived. Under its transcendental aspect, the imagination allows the given to arise, but as empirical, it restores on the plane of representation a degree of the density and warmth of presence. Thus, instead of saying that the imaginary *is* a quasi present, we prefer to say that the imagination *furnishes* a quasi present, the equivalent of lived significations at the level of representation. It is in this fashion that, for example, the word *flower* designates 'l'absente de tout bouquet.'[4] But the designatum is nevertheless a flower whose look, fragrance, jocund spontaneity, or naïve pride exists in the margin of our consciousness. Imagination, guided by the text, creates a possible flower which blossoms forth from the word which names it. Similarly, the imagination makes the stone of a monument appear in its hardness, obstinacy, and coldness. These qualities are present as a halo around what I see, enriching my perception without encumbering or altering it.

We can now verify the ultimate unity of the transcendental and empirical imagination. The empirical imagination, which exploits the concrete knowledge [*le savoir concret*] that structures perception, can be clarified only in terms of the transcendental, which founds the possibility of seeing. The unity of the two makes the ambiguity of imagination evident – an ambiguity which is finally that of the human condition itself. In fact, imagination appears to possess at once the two faces of nature and mind [*esprit*]. It belongs to the body to the degree that it animates the modes of implicit knowledge inherited from the experience of presence, while opening up reflection to the degree that it allows us to substitute the perceived for the lived. In this latter role, imagination interrupts the intimacy of presence by introducing not so much an absence as the distance within presence which constitutes representation, in terms of which the object confronts us at a distance, open to a look or to judgment.

NOTES

1. See Edmund Husserl, *Analysen zur passiven Synthesis*, ed. M. Fleischer (The Hague: Nijhoff, 1966), passim. (Translator's note).

2. See Jean-Paul Sartre, *The Psychology of Imagination*, trans. B. Frechtman (New York: Washington Square Press, 1966), pp. 133 ff.

3. We shall, perhaps, be criticized for juxtaposing the examples of a man who perceives cold in the whiteness of snow and of a famished man who dreams of food. But it is incorrect to restrict imagination to the second case. Insofar as the snow is not in contact with my skin, its coldness is as absent as food is to the famished. The whiteness alone is given to me. Of course, it is the whiteness *of snow*, for perception goes immediately to the object, and its coldness is then given with the object. Yet the coldness is not given in the same way as the whiteness: it is implicit, i.e., a manner of being absent in presence. In contrast, the food which obsesses the famished man is radically absent. Nevertheless, it is present enough to make his mouth water. Without being deluded, he at least realizes the implicit savor and taste of meat and thus enters the universe of food. In the first case, we have an absent presence; in the second, a present absence. It is the context provided by the world which determines whether the image is illusory or valid. All depends on the extent to which the image adheres to perception. In both cases, however, the image is something implicit which blossoms forth on the basis of the real – whether to confirm or to betray it.

4. This is a well-known phrase of Mallarmé, the French symbolist poet. (Translator's note).

SCIENTIFIC VISUALISM
Don Ihde

6:5

It has frequently been noted that scientific 'seeing' is highly visualistic. This is, in part, because of historical origins … arising in early Modern times in the Renaissance. Leonardo da Vinci played an important bridge role here, with the invention of what can be called the 'engineering paradigm' of vision.[1] His depictions of human anatomy, particularly those of autopsies which display musculature, organs, tendons, and the like – 'exploded' to show parts and interrelationships – were identical with the same style when he depicted imagined machines in his technical diaries. In short, his was not only a way of seeing which anticipated modern anatomies (later copied and improved upon by Vesalius) and modern draughtsmanship, but an approach which thus visualized both exteriors and interiors (the exploded style). Leonardo was a 'handcraft imagist.'

The move, first to an almost exclusively visualist emphasis, and second to a kind of 'analytic' depiction, was faster to occur in some sciences than in others. In astronomy, analytic drawing of telescopic sightings was accurate

Don Ihde, from *Expanding Hermeneutics, Visualism in Science*. Northwestern University Studies in Phenomenology and Existential Philosophy. Evanston, IL: Northwestern University Press, 1998, pp. 159–63. Copyright © 1998 by Northwestern University Press. Reproduced with permission of Northwestern University Press.

early on and is being rediscovered as such today. The 'red spot' on Jupiter was already depicted in the seventeenth century. But here, visual observations and depictions were almost the only sensory dimension which could be utilized. Celestial phenomena were at first open only to visual inspection, at most magnified through optical instrumentation. It would be much later – the middle of the twentieth century – that astronomy would expand beyond the optical and reach beyond the Earth with instruments other than optical ones.

Medicine, by the time of Vesalius, shifted its earlier tactile and even olfactory observations in autopsy to the visualizations à la da Vincian style, but continued to use diagnostics which included palpitations, oscultations, and other tactile, kinesthetic, and olfactory observations. In the medical sciences, the shift to the predominantly visual mode for analysis began much later. The invention of both photography and X-rays in the nineteenth century helped these sciences become more like their other natural science peers.

Hermeneutically, in the perceptualist style of interpretation emphasized here – the progress of 'hermeneutic sensory translation devices' as they might be called – *imaging technologies* have become dominantly visualist. These devices make nonvisual sources into visual ones. This, through new visual probes of interiors, from X-rays, to MRI scans, to ultrasound (in visual form) and PET processes, has allowed medical science to deal with bodies become transparent.[2]

More abstract and semiotic-like visualizations also are part of science's sight. Graphs, oscillographic, spectrographic, and other uses of visual hermeneutic devices give Latour reason to claim that such instrumentation is simply a complex *inscription-making device* for a visualizable result. This vector toward forms of 'writing' is related to, but different from, the various isomorphic depictions of imaging. [...]

While all this instrumentation designed to turn all phenomena into visualizable form for a 'reading' illustrates what I take to be one of science's deeply entrenched 'hermeneutic practices,' it also poses something of a problem and a tension for a stricter phenomenological understanding of perception.

Although I shall outline a more complete notion of perception below, here I want to underline the features of perception which are the source of a possible tension with scientific 'seeing' as just described. Full human perception, following Merleau-Ponty, is always *multidimensional* and *synesthetic*. In short, we *never just see something* but always experience it within the complex of sensory fields. Thus the 'reduction' of perception to a monodimension – the visual – is already an abstraction from the lived experience of active perception within a world.

Does this visualizing practice within science thus reopen the way to a division of science from the lifeworld? Does it make of science an essentially reductive practice? I shall argue against this by way of attempting to show that visualization in the scientific sense is a deeply *hermeneutic practice* which plays a special role. Latour's insight that experiments deliver inscriptions helps suggest the hermeneutic analogy, which works well here. Writing is language through 'technology' in that written language is inscribed by some technologically embodied means. I am suggesting that the sophisticated ways in which science *visualizes* its phenomena is another mode by which understanding or interpretive activity is embodied. Whether the technologies are translation technologies (transforming nonvisual dimensions into visual ones), or more isomorphically visual from the outset, the visualization processes through technologies are science's particular hermeneutic means.

First, what are the epistemological advantages of visualization? The traditional answer, often given within science as well, is that vision is the 'clearest' of the senses, that it delivers greater distinctions and clarities, and this seems to fit into the histories of perception tracing all the way back to the Greeks. But this is simply *wrong*. My own earlier researches into auditory phenomena showed that even measurable on physiological bases, hearing delivers within its dimension distinctions and clarities which equal and in some cases exceed those of visual acuity. [...] It is simply a cultural prejudice to hold that vision is ipso facto the 'best' sense.

I argue, rather, that what gives scientific visualization an advantage are its *repeatable Gestalt features* which occur within a technologically produced visible form, and which lead to the rise and importance of *imaging* in both its ordinary visual and specific hermeneutic visual displays. And, here, a phenomenological understanding of perception can actually enhance the hermeneutic process which defines this science practice.

Let us begin with one of the simplest of these Gestalt features, the appearance of a figure against a ground. Presented with a visual display, humans can 'pick out' some feature which, once chosen, is seen against the variable constant of a field or ground. It is not the 'object' which presents this figure itself – rather, it is the interaction of visual intentionality that a figure can appear against a ground.

In astronomy, for example, sighting comets is one such activity. Whether sighted with the naked eye, telescopic observation, or tertiary observations of telescopic photographs, the sighting of a comet comes about by noting the movement of a single object against a field which remains relatively more constant. Here is a determined and trained figure/ground perceptual activity. This is also an *interest-determined* figure/ground observation. While, empirically, a comet may be accidently discovered, to recognize it as a comet is to have sedimented a great deal of previous informed perception.

These phenomenological features of comet discovery stand out by noting that the very structure of figure/ground is not something simply 'given' but is *constituted* by its context and field of significations. To vary our set of observables, one could have 'fixed' upon any single (or small group) of stars and attended to these instead. Figures 'stand out' relative to interest, attention, and even history of perceivability *which includes cultural or macroperceptual features* as well. [...]

When one adds to this mix the variability and changeability of instruments or technologies, the process can rapidly change. As Kuhn has pointed out, with increased magnifications in later Modern telescopes, there was an explosion of planet discoveries due to the availability of detectable 'disc size,' which differentiated planets from stars much more easily.[3]

[...]

If laboratories (and other controlled observational practices) are where one prepares inscriptions, they are also the place where objects are made 'scientific,' or, in this context, *made readable*. Things, the ultimate referential objects of science, are never just naively or simply observed or taken, they must be *prepared* or *constituted*. And, in late Modern science, this constitutive process is increasingly pervaded by technologies.

But, I shall also argue that the results are often not so much 'textlike,' but are more like repeatable, variable *perceptual Gestalts*. These are sometimes called 'images' or even pictures, but because of the vestigial remains of modernist epistemology, I shall call them *depictions*. This occurs with increasing sophistication in the realm of *imaging technologies* which often dominate contemporary scientific hermeneutics.

To produce the best results, the now technoconstituted objects need to stand forth with the greatest possible clarity and within a context of variability and repeatability. For this to occur, the conditions of instrumental transparency need to be enhanced as well. This is to say that the instrumentation, in operation, must 'withdraw' or itself become transparent so the thing may stand out (with chosen or multiple features). The means by which the depiction becomes 'clear' is constituted by the 'absence' or invisibility of the instrumentation.

Of course, the instrumentation can never *totally* disappear. Its 'echo effect' will always remain within the mediation. The mallet (brass, wood, or rubber) makes a difference in the sound produced. In part, this becomes a reason in late Modern science for the deliberate introduction of *multivariant* instrumentation or measurements. These *instrumental phenomenological variations* as I have called them also function as a kind of multiperspectival equivalent in scientific vision (which drives it, not unlike other cultural practices, toward a more postmodern visual model).

NOTES

1. Footnote removed.
2. Footnote removed.
3. Thomas Kuhn, *Structure of Scientific Revolutions*, 1962, Chicago: University of Chicago Press. pp. 115–16.

7 : PSYCHOANALYSIS

INTRODUCTION

Psychoanalysis has always had a special relationship with images because of the role of images in the unconscious. Freud (2.8) found evidence of the primary psychic processes, meaning the repressed, unconscious mind in the mental imagery of dreams. (See Section 9, Image as Thought.) In his 'return to Freud', Jacques Lacan (7.1) reworked the form of the psyche along structuralist terms, claiming that it consists of an imaginary, symbolic and real order. Very simply put, 'imaginary' refers to a psychic register or realm of images, 'symbolic' to language and the law-like ordering of society, and the 'real' to the unobtainable sense of fullness that escapes symbolisation. The form of the self corresponds not to the Cartesian subject, the unified and self-aware *cogito* (1.12, 1.13), but is radically split between the three orders, and hence is an ex-centric subject. In an effort to become a unified self, the subject attempts, always unsuccessfully, to make itself whole by means of 'acts of identification' with images or discourses (Stavrakakis, 2004: 23). Significantly, Lacan defines identification as 'the transformation that takes place in the subject when he assumes an image' (Lacan, 1977: 4). The primary, pre-Oedipal, imaginary identification with an image is both fictional and optical. In the 'mirror-stage' the infant 'misrecognises' its uncoordinated, undifferentiated self in its reflection, taking itself to be a coherent whole. Imaginary identifications are thus key to the subject's failed attempts to overcome its ex-centricity, or alienation from itself.

Christian Metz (7.2) works from Lacan's approach to posit that there is a particular act of identification that occurs in cinema spectatorship, on the basis of the 'already constituted ego' that allows the viewers to identify with themselves. His view contrasts with the common-sense notion that viewers identify primarily with characters. The gaze itself, the act of looking, is an object of desire for the scopic drive, or urge to look, the source of which is the biological visual system (Aumont, 1997: 90). The scopic drive is one of several human drives, which gains partial satisfaction in spectatorship. Lacan first discussed the scopic drive in relation to painting, but the point has been taken up subsequently, primarily in relation to film.

In Lacanian terms, cinema viewers' identification with the gaze is another attempt to occlude the 'splitness' of the subject, as they are actually identifying with only one of the many drives of the psyche. In that sense, cinematic identification is one of the many fantasises, which may consist of images or discourse, in which the subject hopes, vainly, to achieve fullness. Psychoanalysis blends with ideology critique as a 'hermeneutics of suspicion', when it becomes a tool to analyse the fantastic identifications of subjects, such as with the false fullness promised by advertising images (Williamson, 1978) and as substantiated in the work of Slavoj Žižek (1989).

As well as the unconscious containing imagery, 'the image "contains" unconsciousness, primary processes that can be analysed', such that images can be treated as symptoms of individual and social psychic processes (Aumont, 1997: 84). Žižek and others use cinema to illustrate psychoanalytic theory, in addition to using psychoanalytic theory to illuminate the meaning of film (1992). Freud (1995) analysed Leonardo da Vinci's paintings as traces of the latter's neurosis, but more commonly cultural images such as films are analysed as symptoms of social conditions. Psychoanalysis has had a great influence on feminist film scholarship (Cowie, 1997; Silverman, 1988), which among other issues has examined how the implication of viewers in the gaze is differentiated by gender. Laura Mulvey (7.3) differs from Metz in arguing that cinema does invite the viewer to identify with the active male protagonist who moves the narrative along, but not with woman, who appears passively, as spectacle. Mulvey's analysis of classical narrative film exposes it as a site in which male scopophilia ('the perversion linked to the exacerbation of the scopic drive' (Aumont, 1997: 91)) turns women into fetishes and objects of sadistic voyeurism in order to assuage male castration anxieties. Cinema is symptomatic of gender inequality. Her iconoclastic attitude to cinema, even in its revised form (Mulvey, 1981), has certainly been challenged within psychoanalytic feminism (Stacey, 1988). Yet it does express a consistent feminist concern that media images not only misrepresent women (Friedan, 1963: 28-31) but also shape them into something other than they are, as male fantasies of femininity: 'Hold still, we are going to do your portrait, so that you can begin looking like it right away' (Cixous, 1981: 263).

Cindy Sherman's photographic self-portraits seem to comment directly on the social construction of femininity through media images. Joan Copjec's (7.4) analysis of them, however, indirectly undermines Mulvey's attack on cinema. Copjec concurs with Mulvey's view that the close-up of the woman's face stands apart from the film's representation of time and space, but not that her face simply becomes a fetish for the male gaze. Nor does she accept that the photographs represent the splitting of the female subject's identification between her actual place in the masculine or phallic symbolic order of the film and another imagined identity, as a 'real' woman. Rather, the photographs affirm that femininity exists only as image, appearance or masquerade (Riviere, 1986). At the same, time, though, they affirm the value of Sherman's love for herself as a woman and the cinematic image of herself as an Other, as an object of desire. On this reading, the cinematic image is not symptomatic of misrepresentation and oppression but illustrative of the possibility of the split subject finding love by recognising that wholeness (as woman, as subject) is unobtainable.

From a non-Lacanian perspective, Anton Ehrenzweig (7.5) does not read art as a symptom but examines the unconscious structures that organise artworks. Ehrenzweig was both influenced by modern artists such as Paul Klee (10.1) who tried to allow unconscious processes to emerge in their work, and also influenced artists such as Robert Morris and Robert Smithson to do the same. The viewer of a painting should, like the modern artist and the analyst, allow the primary processes of the unconscious to come to the fore in order to appreciate its full aesthetic effect. Ehrenzweig's psychoanalytic approach to images, his 'polyphonic', 'unconscious scanning' becomes a hermeneutics of appreciation rather than suspicion.

REFERENCES

Aumont, J. (1997) *The Image*, tr. C. Pajackowska. London: British Film Institute.

Cixous, H. (1981) 'The laugh of the Medusa', in E. Marks and I. de Courtivron (eds), *New French Feminisms*, tr. K. Cohen and P. Cohen. New York: Schocken. pp. 245–64.

Cowie, E. (1997) *Representing the Woman: Cinema and Psychoanalysis*. London: Macmillan.

Freud, S. (1995) 'Leonardo da Vinci and a memory of his childhood', in P. Gay (ed.), *The Freud Reader*. New York: W.W. Norton. pp. 443–80.

Friedan, B. (1963) *The Feminine Mystique*. New York: Dell Publishing.

Lacan, J. (1977) *Écrits: A Selection*, tr. A. Sheridan. London: Routledge.

Mulvey, L. (1981) 'Afterthoughts on "Visual Pleasure and Narrative Cinema" inspired by *Duel in the Sun*', *Framework*, 15/16/17: 12–15.

Riviere, J. (1986) 'Womanliness as a masquerade', in V. Burgin, J. Donald and C. Kaplan (eds), *Formations of Fantasy*. London: Methuen. pp. 35–44.

Silverman, K. (1988) *The Acoustic Mirror: The Female Voice in Psychoanalysis and Cinema*. Bloomington, IN: Indiana University Press.

Stacey, J. (1988) 'Desperately seeking difference', in L. Gamman and M. Marshment (eds), *The Female Gaze*. London: Woman's Press. pp. 112–200.

Stavrakakis, Y. (2004) 'Jacques Lacan', in J. Simons (ed.), *Contemporary Critical Theory: From Lacan to Said*. Edinburgh: Edinburgh University Press. pp. 18–33.

Williamson, J. (1978) *Decoding Advertising: Ideology and Meaning in Advertising*. London: Marion Boyars.

Žižek, S. (1989) *The Sublime Object of Ideology*. London: Verso.

Žižek, S. (ed.) (1992) *Everything You Always Wanted to Know About Lacan (But Were Too Afraid to Ask Hitchcock)*. London: Verso.

THE GAZE
JACQUES LACAN

But what is the gaze?

I shall set out from this first point of annihilation in which is marked, in the field of the reduction of *the subject*, a break – which warns us of the need to introduce another reference, that which analysis assumes in reducing the privileges of the consciousness.

Psycho-analysis regards the consciousness as irremediably limited, and institutes it as a principle, not only of idealization, but of *méconnaissance,* as – using a term that takes on new value by being referred to a visible domain – *scotoma.* The term was introduced into the psycho-analytic vocabulary by the French School. Is it simply a metaphor? We find here once again the ambiguity that affects anything that is inscribed in the register of the scopic drive.

For us, consciousness matters only in its relation to what, for propaedeutic reasons, I have tried to show you in the fiction of the incomplete text – on the basis of which it is a question of recentring the subject as speaking in the very lacunae of that in which, at first sight, it presents itself as speaking. But I am stating here only the relation of the preconscious to the unconscious. The dynamic that is attached to the consciousness as such, the attention the subject brings to his own text, remains up to this point, as Freud has stressed, outside theory and, strictly speaking, not yet articulated.

It is here that I propose that the interest the subject takes in his own split is bound up with that which determines it – namely, a privileged object, which

FIGURE 7.1
Hans Holbein: *The Ambassadors,* 1533.
Source: The National Gallery, London.

Jacques Lacan, from *The Four Fundamental Concepts of Psycho-Analysis,* tr. Alan Sheridan. London: Vintage, 1998, edited from pp. 82–8, 92. Used by permission of W.W. Norton and Company Inc, © 1973 by Editions du Sevil. English translation © Alan Sheridan.

has emerged from some primal separation, from some self-mutilation induced by the very approach of the real, whose name, in our algebra, is the *objet a*.

In the scopic relation, the object on which depends the phantasy from which the subject is suspended in an essential vacillation is the gaze. Its privilege – and also that by which the subject for so long has been misunderstood as being in its dependence – derives from its very structure.

Let us schematize at once what we mean. From the moment that this gaze appears, the subject tries to adapt himself to it, he becomes that punctiform object, that point of vanishing being with which the subject confuses his own failure. Furthermore, of all the objects in which the subject may recognize his dependence in the register of desire, the gaze is specified as unapprehensible. That is why it is, more than any other object, misunderstood (*méconnu*), and it is perhaps for this reason, too, that the subject manages, fortunately, to symbolize his own vanishing and punctiform bar (*trait*) in the illusion of the consciousness of *seeing oneself see oneself*, in which the gaze is elided.

If, then, the gaze is that underside of consciousness, how shall we try to imagine it?

[...]

We can apprehend this privilege of the gaze in the function of desire, by pouring ourselves, as it were, along the veins through which the domain of vision has been integrated into the field of desire.

It is not for nothing that it was at the very period when the Cartesian meditation inaugurated in all its purity the function of the subject that the dimension of optics that I shall distinguish here by calling 'geometral' or 'flat' (as opposed to perspective) optics was developed.

*

In my seminar, I have made great use of the function of anamorphosis, in so far as it is an exemplary structure. What does a simple, non-cylindrical anamorphosis consist of? Suppose there is a portrait on this flat piece of paper that I am holding. By chance, you see the blackboard, in an oblique position in relation to the piece of paper. Suppose that, by means of a series of ideal threads or lines, I reproduce on the oblique surface each point of the image drawn on my sheet of paper. You can easily imagine what the result would be – you would obtain a figure enlarged and distorted according to the lines of what may be called a perspective. One supposes that – if I take away that which has helped in the construction, namely, the image placed in my own visual field – the impression I will retain, while remaining in that place, will be more or less the same. At least, I will recognize the general outlines of the image – at best, I will have an identical impression.

I will now pass around something that dates from a hundred years earlier, from 1533, a reproduction of a painting that, I think, you all know – Hans Holbein's *The Ambassadors*. It will serve to refresh the memories of those who know the picture well. Those who do not should examine it attentively. I shall come back to it shortly.

Vision is ordered according to a mode that may generally be called the function of images. This function is defined by a point-by-point correspondence of two unities in space. Whatever optical intermediaries may be used to establish their relation, whether their image is virtual, or real, the point-by-point correspondence is essential. That which is of the mode of the image in the field of vision is therefore reducible to the simple schema that enables us to establish anamorphosis, that is to say, to the relation of an image, in so far as it is linked to a surface, with a certain point that we shall call the 'geometral' point. Anything that is determined by this method, in which the straight line plays its role of being the path of light, can be called an image.

Art is mingled with science here. Leonardo da Vinci is both a scientist, on account of his dioptric constructions, and an artist. Vitruvius's treatise on architecture is not far away. It is in Vignola and in Alberti that we find the progressive interrogation of the geometral laws of perspective, and it is around research on perspective that is centred a privileged interest for the domain of vision – whose relation with the institution of the Cartesian subject, which is itself a sort of geometral point, a point of perspective, we cannot fail to see. And, around the geometral perspective, the picture – this is a very important function to which we shall return – is organized in a way that is quite new in the history of painting.

[...]

Now, in *The Ambassadors* – I hope everyone has had time now to look at the reproduction – what do you see? What is this strange, suspended, oblique object in the foreground in front of these two figures?

The two figures are frozen, stiffened in their showy adornments. Between them is a series of objects that represent in the painting of the period the symbols of *vanitas*. At the same period, Cornelius Agrippa wrote his *De Vanitate Scientiarum*, aimed as much at the arts as the sciences, and these objects are all symbolic of the sciences and arts as they were grouped at the time in the *trivium* and *quadrivium*. What, then, before this display of the domain of appearance in all its most fascinating forms is this object, which from some angles appears to be flying through the air, at others to be tilted? You cannot know – for you turn away, thus escaping the fascination of the picture.

Begin by walking out of the room in which no doubt it has long held your attention. It is then that, turning round as you leave – as the author of the *Anamorphoses* describes it – you apprehend in this form . . . What? A skull.

This is not how it is presented at first – that figure, which the author compares to a cuttlebone and which for me suggests rather that loaf composed of two books which Dali was once pleased to place on the head of an old woman, chosen deliberately for her wretched, filthy appearance and, indeed, because she seems to be unaware of the fact, or, again, Dali's soft watches, whose signification is obviously less phallic than that of the object depicted in a flying position in the foreground of this picture.

All this shows that at the very heart of the period in which the subject emerged and geometral optics was an object of research, Holbein makes visible for us here something that is simply the subject as annihilated – annihilated in the form that is, strictly speaking, the imaged embodiment of the *minus-phi* $[(-\Phi)]$ of castration, which for us, centres the whole organization of the desires through the framework of the fundamental drives.

But it is further still that we must seek the function of vision. We shall then see emerging on the basis of vision, not the phallic symbol, the anamorphic ghost, but the gaze as such, in its pulsatile, dazzling and spread out function, as it is in this picture.

This picture is simply what any picture is, a trap for the gaze.

*

In Holbein's picture I showed you at once – without hiding any more than usual – the singular object floating in the foreground, which is there to be looked at, in order to catch, I would almost say, *to catch in its trap,* the observer, that is to say, us. It is, in short, an obvious way, no doubt an exceptional one, and one due to some moment of reflection on the part of the painter, of showing us that, as subjects, we are literally called into the picture, and represented here as caught. For the secret of this picture, whose implications I have pointed out to you, the kinships with the *vanitas,* the way this fascinating picture presents, between the two splendidly dressed and immobile figures, everything that recalls, in the perspective of the period, the vanity of the arts and sciences – the secret of this picture is given at the moment when, moving slightly away, little by little, to the left, then turning around, we see what the magical floating object signifies. It reflects our own nothingness, in the figure of the death's head. It is a use, therefore, of the geometral dimension of vision in order to capture the subject, an obvious relation with desire which, nevertheless, remains enigmatic.

[...]

7:2   THE ALL-PERCEIVING SUBJECT
CHRISTIAN METZ

[F]ilm is like the mirror. But it differs from the primordial mirror in one essential point: although, as in the latter, everything may come to be projected, there is one thing and one thing only that is never reflected in it: the spectator's own body. In a certain emplacement, the mirror suddenly becomes clear glass.

In the mirror the child perceives the familiar household objects, and also its object par excellence, its mother, who holds it up in her arms to the glass. But above all it perceives its own image. This is where primary identification

Christian Metz, from *Psychoanalysis and Cinema,* tr. Celia Britton, Annwyl Williams, Ben Brewster and Alfred Guzzetti. London: Macmillan, 1982, pp. 45–9. Reproduced with permission.

(the formation of the ego) gets certain of its main characteristics: the child sees itself as an other, and beside an other. This other other is its guarantee that the first is really it: by her authority, her sanction, in the register of the symbolic, subsequently by the resemblance between her mirror image and the child's (both have a human form). Thus the child's ego is formed by identification with its like, and this in two senses simultaneously, metonymically and metaphorically: the other human being who is in the glass, the own reflection which is and is not the body, which is like it. The child identifies with itself as an object.

In the cinema, the object remains: fiction or no, there is always something on the screen. But the reflection of the own body has disappeared. The cinema spectator is not a child and the child really at the mirror stage (from around six to around eighteen months) would certainly be incapable of 'following' the simplest of films. Thus, what *makes possible* the spectator's absence from the screen – or rather the intelligible unfolding of the film despite that absence – is the fact that the spectator has already known the experience of the mirror (of the true mirror), and is thus able to constitute a world of objects without having first to recognise himself within it. In this respect, the cinema is already on the side of the symbolic (which is only to be expected): the spectator knows that objects exist, that he himself exists as a subject, that he becomes an object for others: he knows himself and he knows his like: it is no longer necessary that this similarity be literally *depicted* for him on the screen, as it was in the mirror of his childhood. Like every other broadly 'secondary' activity, the practice of the cinema presupposes that the primitive undifferentiation of the ego and the non-ego has been overcome.

But *with what,* then, does the spectator identify during the projection of the film? For he certainly has to identify: identification in its primal form has ceased to be a current necessity for him, but he continues, in the cinema – if he did not the film would become incomprehensible, considerably more incomprehensible than the most incomprehensible films – to depend on that permanent play of identification without which there would be no social life (thus, the simplest conversation presupposes the alternation of the *I* and the *you,* hence the aptitude of the two interlocutors for a mutual and reversible identification). What form does this *continued* identification, whose essential role Lacan has demonstrated even in the most abstract reasoning[1] and which constituted the 'social sentiment' for Freud[2] (= the sublimation of a homosexual libido, itself a reaction to the aggressive rivalry of the members of a single generation after the murder of the father), take in the special case of one social practice among others, cinematic projection?

Obviously the spectator has the opportunity to identify with the *character* of the fiction. But there still has to be one. This is thus only valid for the narrative-representational film, and not for the psychoanalytic constitution of the signifier of the cinema as such. The spectator can also identify with the actor, in more or less 'a-fictional' films in which the latter is represented as an actor, not a character, but is still offered thereby as a human being (as a perceived human being) and thus allows identification. However this factor (even added to the previous one and thus covering a very large number of films) cannot suffice. It only designates secondary identification in certain of its forms (secondary in the cinematic process itself, since in any other sense all identification except that of the mirror can be regarded as secondary).

An insufficient explanation, and for two reasons, the first of which is only the intermittent, anecdotal and superficial consequence of the second (but for that reason more visible, and that is why I call it the first). The cinema deviates from the theatre on an important point that has often been emphasised: it often presents us with long sequences that can (literally) be called 'inhuman' – the familiar theme of cinematic 'cosmomorphism' developed by many film theorists – sequences in which only inanimate objects, landscapes, etc. appear and which for minutes at a time offer no human form for spectator identification: yet the latter must be supposed to remain intact in its deep structure, since at such moments the film *works* just as well as it does at others, and whole films (geographical documentaries, for example) unfold intelligibly in such conditions. The second, more radical reason is that identification with the human form appearing on the screen, even when it occurs, still tells us nothing about the *place of the spectator's ego* in the inauguration of the signifier. As I have just pointed out, this ego is already formed. But since it exists, the question arises precisely of *where it is* during the projection of the film (the true primary identification, that of the mirror, forms the ego, but all other identifications presuppose, on the contrary, that it has been formed and can be 'exchanged' for the object or the fellow subject). Thus when I 'recognise' my like on the screen, and even more when I do not recognise it, where am I? Where is that someone who is capable of self-recognition when need be?

It is not enough to answer that the cinema, like every social practice, demands that the psychical apparatus of its participants be fully constituted, and that the question is thus the concern of general psychoanalytic theory and not that of the cinema proper. For my *where is it?* does not claim to go so far, or more precisely tries to go slightly further: it is a question of the *point* occupied by this already constituted ego, occupied during the cinema showing and not in social life in general.

The spectator is absent from the screen: contrary to the child in the mirror, he cannot identify with himself as an object, but only with objects which are there without him. In this sense the screen is not a mirror. The perceived, this time, is entirely on the side of the object, and there is no longer any equivalent of the own image, of that unique mix of perceived and subject (of other and I) which was precisely the figure necessary to disengage the one from the other. At the cinema, it is always the other who is on the screen; as for me, I am there to look at him. I take no part in the perceived, on the contrary, I am *all-perceiving*. All-perceiving as one says all-powerful (this is the famous gift of 'ubiquity' the film makes its spectator); all-perceiving, too, because I am entirely on the side of the perceiving instance: absent from the screen, but certainly present in the auditorium, a great eye and ear without which the perceived would have no one to perceive it, the instance, in other words, which *constitutes* the cinema signifier (it is I who make the film). If the most extravagant spectacles and sounds or the most unlikely combination of them, the combination furthest removed from any real experience, do not prevent the constitution of meaning (and to begin with do not *astonish* the spectator, do not really astonish him, not intellectually: he simply judges the film as strange), that is because he knows he is at the cinema.

In the cinema the *subject's knowledge* takes a very precise form without which no film would be possible. This knowledge is dual (but unique). I know I am perceiving something imaginary (and that is why its absurdities, even if they are extreme, do not seriously disturb me), and I know that it is I who am perceiving it. This second knowledge divides in turn: I know that I am really perceiving, that my sense organs are physically affected, that I am not phantasising, that the fourth wall of the auditorium (the screen) is really different from the other three, that there is a projector facing it (and thus it is not I who am projecting, or at least not all alone), and I also know that it is I who am perceiving all this, that this perceived-imaginary material is deposited in me as if on a second screen, that it is in me that it forms up into an organised sequence, that therefore I am myself the place where this really perceived imaginary accedes to the symbolic by its inauguration as the signifier of a certain type of institutionalised social activity called the 'cinema'.

In other words, the spectator *identifies with himself,* with himself as a pure act of perception (as wakefulness, alertness): as the condition of possibility of the perceived and hence as a kind of transcendental subject, which comes before every *there is.*

A strange mirror, then, very like that of childhood. Very like [...] because during the showing we are, like the child, in a sub-motor and hyper-perceptive state; because, like the child again, we are prey to the imaginary, the double, and are so paradoxically through a real perception. Very different, because this mirror returns us everything but ourselves, because we are wholly outside it, whereas the child is both in it and in front of it. As an arrangement (and in a very topographical sense of the word), the cinema is more involved on the flank of the symbolic, and hence of secondariness, than is the mirror of childhood.

NOTES

1. 'Le temps logique et l'assertion de certitude anticipée,' *Ecrits*, pp. 197–213.
2. 'The Ego and the Id' (vol. XIX) pp. 26 and 30 (on 'desexualised social sentiment'); see also (on the subject of paranoia) 'On Narcissism: an Introduction' (vol. XIV) pp. 95–6, 101–2.

7:3 WOMAN AS IMAGE (MAN AS BEARER OF THE LOOK)
LAURA MULVEY

In a world ordered by sexual imbalance, pleasure in looking has been split between active/male and passive/female. The determining male gaze projects its fantasy onto the female figure, which is styled accordingly. In their traditional exhibitionist role women are simultaneously looked at and displayed, with their appearance coded for strong visual and erotic impact so that they can be said to connote *to-be-looked-at-ness*.

[...]

[In mainstream narrative film] the woman displayed has functioned on two levels: as erotic object for the characters within the screen story, and as erotic object for the spectator within the auditorium, with a shifting tension between the looks on either side of the screen. For instance, the device of the show-girl allows the two looks to be unified technically without any apparent break in the diegesis. A woman performs within the narrative; the gaze of the spectator and that of the male characters in the film are neatly combined without breaking narrative verisimilitude. For a moment the sexual impact of the performing woman takes the film into a no man's land outside its own time and space. Thus Marilyn Monroe's first appearance in *The River of No Return* and Lauren Bacall's songs in *To Have and Have Not*. Similarly, conventional close-ups of legs (Dietrich, for instance) or a face (Garbo) integrate into the narrative a different mode of eroticism. One part of a fragmented body destroys the Renaissance space, the illusion of depth demanded by the narrative; it gives flatness, the quality of a cut-out or icon, rather than verisimilitude, to the screen.

An active/passive heterosexual division of labour has similarly controlled narrative structure. According to the principles of the ruling ideology, and the psychical structures that back it up, the male figure cannot bear the burden of sexual objectification. Man is reluctant to gaze at his exhibitionist like. Hence the split between spectacle and narrative supports the man's role as the active one of advancing the story, making things happen. The man controls the film fantasy and also emerges as the representative of power in a further sense: as the bearer of the look of the spectator, transferring it behind the screen to neutralise the extra diegetic tendencies represented by woman as spectacle. This is made through the processes set in motion by structuring the film around a main controlling figure with whom the spectator can identify. As the spectator identifies with the main male protagonist, he projects his look onto that of his like, his screen surrogate, so that the power of the male protagonist as he controls events coincides with the active power of the erotic look, both giving a satisfying sense of omnipotence. A male movie star's glamorous characteristics are thus not those of the erotic object of the gaze, but those of the more perfect, more complete, more powerful ideal ego conceived in the original moment of recognition in front of the mirror. The character in the story can make things happen and control events better than the subject/spectator, just as the image in the mirror was more in control of motor co-ordination.

In contrast to woman as icon, the active male figure (the ego ideal of the identification process) demands a three-dimensional space corresponding to that of the mirror recognition, in which the alienated subject internalised his own representation of his imaginary existence. He is a figure in a landscape. Here the function of film is to reproduce as accurately as possible the so-called natural conditions of human perception. Camera technology (as exemplified by deep focus in particular) and camera movements (determined by the action of the protagonist), combined with invisible editing (demanded by realism), all tend to blur the limits of screen space. The male protagonist is free to command the stage, a stage of spatial illusion in which he articulates the look and creates the action.

[…]

[… In] psychoanalytic terms, the female figure poses a deeper problem. She also connotes something that the look continually circles around but disavows: her lack of a penis, implying a threat of castration and hence unpleasure. Ultimately, the meaning of woman is sexual difference, the visually ascertainable absence of the penis, the material evidence on which is based the castration complex essential for the organisation of entrance to the symbolic order and the law of the father. Thus the woman as icon, displayed for the gaze and enjoyment of men, the active controllers of the look, always threatens to evoke the anxiety it originally signified. The male unconscious has two avenues of escape from this castration anxiety: preoccupation with the re-enactment of the original trauma (investigating the woman, demystifying her mystery), counterbalanced by the devaluation, punishment or saving of the guilty object (an avenue typified by the concerns of the *film noir*); or else complete disavowal of castration by the substitution of fetish object or turning the represented figure itself into a fetish so that it becomes reassuring rather than dangerous (hence over-valuation, the cult of the female star).

This second avenue, fetishistic scopophilia, builds up the physical beauty of the object, transforming it into something satisfying in itself. The first avenue, voyeurism, on the contrary, has associations with sadism: pleasure lies in ascertaining guilt (immediately associated with castration), asserting control and subjugating the guilty person through punishment or forgiveness. This sadistic side fits in well with narrative. Sadism demands a story, depends on making something happen, forcing a change in another person, a battle of will and strength, victory/defeat, all occurring in a linear time with a beginning and an end. Fetishistic scopophilia, on the other hand, can exist outside linear time as the erotic instinct is focused on the look alone. […]

Sternberg once said he would welcome his films being projected upside-down so that story and character involvement would not interfere with the spectator's undiluted appreciation of the screen image. [...] Sternberg, produces the ultimate fetish, taking it to the point where the powerful look of the male protagonist (characteristic of traditional narrative film) is broken in favour of the image in direct erotic rapport with the spectator. The beauty of the woman as object and the screen space coalesce; she is no longer the bearer of guilt but a perfect product, whose body, stylised and fragmented by close-ups, is the content of the film and the direct recipient of the spectator's look.

[...]

In Hitchcock, by contrast, the male hero does see precisely what the audience sees. However, although fascination with an image through scopophilic eroticism can be the subject of the film, it is the role of the hero to portray the contradictions and tensions experienced by the spectator. In *Vertigo* in particular, but also in *Marnie* and *Rear Window*, the look is central to the plot, oscillating between voyeurism and fetishistic fascination. [...] His heroes are exemplary of the symbolic order and the law – a policeman (*Vertigo*), a dominant male possessing money and power (*Marnie*) – but their erotic drives lead them into compromised situations. The power to subject another person to the will sadistically or to the gaze voyeuristically is turned onto the woman as the object of both. [...] Hitchcock's skilful use of identification processes and liberal use of subjective camera from the point of view of the male protagonist draw the spectators deeply into his position, making them share his uneasy gaze. The spectator is absorbed into a voyeuristic situation within the screen scene and diegesis, which parodies his own in the cinema.

In an analysis of *Rear Window*, Douchet takes the film as a metaphor for the cinema. Jeffries is the audience, the events in the apartment block opposite correspond to the screen. As he watches, an erotic dimension is added to his look, a central image to the drama. His girlfriend Lisa had been of little sexual interest to him, more or less a drag, so long as she remained on the spectator side. When she crosses the barrier between his room and the block opposite, their relationship is reborn erotically. He does not merely watch her through his lens, as a distant meaningful image, he also sees her as a guilty intruder exposed by a dangerous man threatening her with punishment, and thus finally giving him the opportunity to save her. Lisa's exhibitionism has already been established by her obsessive interest in dress and style, in being a passive image of visual perfection; Jeffries' voyeurism and activity have also been established through his work as a photo-journalist, a maker of stories and captor of images. However, his enforced inactivity, binding him to his seat as a spectator, puts him squarely in the fantasy position of the cinema audience.

*

[...The] voyeuristic-scopophilic look that is a crucial part of traditional filmic pleasure can itself be broken down. There are three different looks associated with cinema: that of the camera as it records the pro-filmic event, that of the audience as it watches the final product, and that of the characters at each other within the screen illusion. The conventions of narrative film deny the first two and subordinate them to the third, the conscious aim being always to eliminate intrusive camera presence and prevent a distancing awareness in the audience. Without these two absences (the material existence of the recording process, the critical reading of the spectator), fictional drama cannot achieve reality, obviousness and truth. Nevertheless, the structure of looking in narrative fiction film contains a contradiction in its own premises: the female image as a castration threat constantly endangers the unity of the diegesis and bursts through the world of illusion as an intrusive, static, one-dimensional fetish. Thus the two looks materially present in time and space are obsessively subordinated to the neurotic needs of the male ego. The camera becomes the mechanism for producing an illusion of Renaissance space, flowing movements compatible with the human eye, an ideology of representation that revolves around the perception of the subject; the camera's look is disavowed in order to create a convincing world in which the spectator's surrogate can perform with verisimilitude. Simultaneously, the look of the audience is denied an intrinsic force: as soon as fetishistic representation of the female image threatens to break the spell of illusion, and the erotic image on the screen appears directly (without mediation) to the spectator, the fact of fetishisation, concealing as it does castration fear, freezes the look, fixates the spectator and prevents him from achieving any distance from the image in front of him.

This complex interaction of looks is specific to film. The first blow against the monolithic accumulation of traditional film conventions (already undertaken by radical film-makers) is to free the look of the camera into its materiality in time and space and the look of the audience into dialectics and passionate detachment. There is no doubt that this destroys the satisfaction, pleasure and privilege of the 'invisible guest', and highlights the way film has depended on voyeuristic active/passive mechanisms. Women, whose image has continually been stolen and used for this end, cannot view the decline of the traditional film form with anything much more than sentimental regret.

CINDY SHERMAN'S *UNTITLED FILM STILLS*
Joan Copjec

7:4

In these photographs [*Untitled Film Stills*, produced between 1977 and 1980], Sherman masquerades in a wardrobe to match the various background settings she has designed to evoke some Hollywood period, genre, or directorial style. In an early article, Judith Williamson put her

Joan Copjec, from *Imagine There's No Woman: Ethics and Sublimation*. Cambridge, MA: MIT Press, 2002, pp. 67, 73–7, 79–80. Copyright © 2002 Massachusetts Institute of Technology. Reproduced with permission.

finger on what would become in subsequent criticism the central issue of the photographs: 'What comes out of the imagined narratives is, specifically, femininity. It is not just a range of feminine expressions that are shown but the process of the "feminine" as an effect, something acted upon.'[1] The passivity of the feminine refers to the fact that in the culture evoked by the photographs woman is not allowed to become the 'bearer of the look,' but is condemned to be its object. She is forced to see herself – more so than men – in the images culture produces of her. She must compose herself in their terms, compose herself for the gaze they presuppose.

Accordingly, Sherman's photographs are almost always read as images of women attempting to see themselves in a number of culturally approved forms, as women attempting to adapt themselves to stereotypes. These are women who want to be loved. Sometimes a critical effort is made to pull these women away from the image that informs her self-presentation by drawing attention to the photograph's exposure of its own 'con-structedness.' Ideology may construct the woman but the photograph or critic can deconstruct the ideology. Another strategy points out that the aspirations of these women are tripped up by the bodies that strive after them. The photographs open a gap between the ideal images the women emulate and the noncompliant fact of what they corporeally are, their real bodily circumstances: this one's arms are a bit heavy, her ankles too thick, that one's tawdry dress ill-fits the romantic scenario she is fanticizing. The body of the woman is always in these readings 'finite' in the cultural theory sense of that term, in the first case because it, like the photograph, is simply constructed, a simple realization of conditions existing elsewhere. In the second, the body is doubly finite, a mere object exposed to the look of the spectator or any diegetically conceivable passer-by *and* a simple opacity resisting the woman's hopeful look, an inert unyielding to her idealizing demand.

I argue, however, that one can locate in the *Untitled Film Stills* a gap between the women and their immediate surroundings without giving in to the pre-emptive narrativization of that gap that generally follows. The rush to narrativize, to compose the background story that landed these women in the places where they now find themselves, is problematic on a number of counts. First, linking woman to her concrete milieu, this reading strategy proceeds as if each photograph contained a *different* woman; that is, it fully diegeticizes each woman. It asks us to focus on the relations that bind the particular situation to the particular woman contained in it, without recognizing that the very process of constructing this narrative produces the particularity it finds, or to say it better, reduces what it finds to particularity. No, there are not several different women in these photographs, there is only one, the *same* woman, Cindy Sherman, who appears over and over again, and one of the profound questions posed by the photographs – 'How can someone be the same if all her appearances are different?' – is slighted if we do not privilege in our analysis the fact that it is she who reappears again and again in her photographs. This is the question raised by feminine being as such, by femininity, which is, to reinvoke Badiou's term, 'multiple being' or multiple *appearings/masqueradings*. The implication here is not that the masquerade of femininity is only a semblance that hides a being which is beneath, but that semblance or appearance is what feminine being is. On the other hand, however, the fact that Sherman is the subject of all her images, that she has consistently chosen to place herself on display in them, has hardly gone unnoticed. In fact, her supposed narcissism is a constant of the critical literature. The problem is that the notion of narcissism sustaining this evaluation is so thin that it seems to require repeating just to create an echo: Sherman so loves being looked at that she herself takes pleasure in looking only at herself. Moreover, the issue of Sherman's narcissism is never integrated into the analysis of the relation of the women (who remain pluralized) to their surroundings in the photographs, except to suggest that 'they,' too, nourish themselves on the meager diet of their own self-regard.

The second major difficulty with the narrative – and (it must be said) *psychologizing* – reading of the photographs is a corollary of the first: it drains from the woman's face all expression but that which is able to feed the narrative. It is not that a certain determinate ambiguity of expression, a hovering between fear and defiance, for example, or longing and resignation, has escaped these readings. But it is always assumed that *the situation imprints itself*, however ambiguously, *on the woman's face*. She is stamped by her setting.

[…]

Basically I am arguing that the images of Cindy Sherman's face function as close-ups in the *Untitled Film Stills* even before they actually become close-ups, in the purely technical sense, in Sherman's later work. Included, then, in the various diegetic spaces of this photographic series, the face of Sherman does not belong to them.

The face of Sherman, in short, does not play the ordinary role of the face, which […] displays the features of the individual's *particularity* as it is defined differentially, through one's relations to other people and objects, or to a situation; the face relates the person to its milieu. In the close-up, however, the normal role of the face is suspended; it no longer individuates the person, but serves, on the contrary, to de-individuate or impersonalize her. The close-up discloses a depredication of the subject, an emptying out of personality.

[…]

This antinomic relation between the space of the close-up and the diegetic space of the film is echoed in Lacan's account of the antinomic relation between the gaze and the represented space. The antinomy defines the difference between two levels of representation: the level of enunciation, marked by the appearance of the gaze, and the level of the statement or represented space. That is, a surplus object appears in the field while announcing itself as *not* part of the represented, as being of a different order than the one in which it shows itself. Lacan links the manner of identifying this split between enunciation and statement, gaze and representation, to Descartes's procedure of radical doubt, in which the entire content of the represented is effectively negated by being thrown into question. At the end

FIGURE 7.2
Cindy Sherman, *Untitled Film Still # 2* (1977).
Courtesy of Metro Pictures.

of this procedure, however, something is left standing, something resists the erosion by doubt: the cogito or the instance of enunciation. The fact that it escapes the annihilating gesture that demolishes all else is proof that the cogito is not identical to the represented or thought.

The theory of this split sets a trap, however, which the *Untitled Film Stills* will help us evade. [...] [L]et us consider a reading of the photographs obviously suggested by this argument. One can detect in the face of Sherman a certain distractedness, as though she were lost in reverie and thus not actually present to her current situation, in some way untouched by it. The sole figure in all the photographs, the lonely one in each, she interacts with no one and is absorbed in no activity but that of her silent musings. The [...] much remarked solitude of women who want nothing more than a room of their own, even the already mentioned role as 'ironists of community,' all leap to mind in support of this reading, giving it resonance and credibility. The only difficulty is that the photographs themselves do not yield to it. They resist, we might say, the analogical impulse to attribute to woman the same charming inaccessibility one finds in small children, cats, and large beasts of prey. For, the look of reverie on the face of the woman in these photographs – a familiar topos of painting and film alike (think of the countless images you have seen of women peering dreamily out of windows

FIGURE 7.3
Cindy Sherman, *Untitled Film Still # 35* (1979).
Courtesy of Metro Pictures.

or simply out of frame) – does not lift her from the space that surrounds her. Why? Because she happens to be represented in the very sort of imagined elsewhere, the cinematic or screen space, we imagine her to be fantasizing, the melodramatic spaces of 'female fantasy.' It is as if these photographs were endorsing the thesis of film theorists regarding the closeness of the woman to the screen image. Inseparable from the image, from appearance, woman is theorized as incapable of distancing herself from it, of occupying a position beyond. She remains instead immersed in the world of appearances. But where film theorists condemned this theoretical and cinematic conflation of the woman with the image, the *Untitled Film Stills* does not. It accepts that there is 'no exit' for woman from the level of appearance, that 'womanliness' *is* always but masquerade.

[…]

The close-up or face of the woman does not transport her, we noted, out of the space in which she finds herself, despite the dreaminess of her expression. Her blank or objectless look of longing, directed out of frame, is filled by the scenes that surround her. Blocking or filling the blankness of the woman's look, the photographs shift attention away from an imagined elsewhere onto the object they actually represent. What is that object? Film, cinema, represented in a series of scenes that reproduce a variety of periods and styles. The *Untitled Film Stills* represent film as an object of amorous fascination.

What prevents the love of cinema from being a banal subject for a series of photographs is the series' brilliant demonstration of the truth of Freud's thesis that love, any love, is always and fundamentally narcissistic. Again: when one loves something, one loves something in it that is more than itself, its nonidentity to itself. But a new point can now be made, one that was only inadequately expressed before. To say that what we love in the object is something more than that object is not to say only that we love that real point in the object from where it can cease being what it was to become something different from itself, but also that *what we love in the object is ourselves.* [...]

When Lacan makes the claim that in love there are not two ones, but a One and an Other, or One plus a, we must understand the One to be not the lover, but the beloved object. This is at least the way Freud's theory of narcissism demands we understand Lacan's statement. The lover, on the contrary, is locatable only in the object a, the partial object or indivisible remainder of the act of love. Indivisible (because irreducible to spatio-temporal coordinates) *and* the product of no division, part of no whole. We should not be surprised, then, to find the face of Cindy Sherman returning consistently *as* close-up (in Deleuze's sense) or as object a in all her photographs, the perennial *residue of* her love for the cinematic–photographic image. We should rather take to heart the lesson her photographs teach us: genuine love is never selfless – nor, for that matter, is sublimation. This lesson is the very opposite of a cynicism.

NOTE

1. Judith Williamson, "Images of 'Woman' – the Photographs of Cindy Sherman," in *Screen*, vol. 24, no. 6 (Nov.–Dec. 1983), p. 104. Despite my contrary views, still a very useful essay.

7:5 TWO KINDS OF ATTENTION
Anton Ehrenzweig

The conscious gestalt compulsion makes us bisect the visual field into significant 'figure' and insignificant 'ground'. Yet bisecting the picture plane into significant and insignificant areas is precisely what the artist cannot afford to do. Only a bad artist will concentrate his attention exclusively on the large-scale composition and treat less articulate form elements like textures or the scribbles of artistic 'handwriting' as decorative additions that have no structural significance. A true artist will agree with the psychoanalyst that nothing can be deemed insignificant or accidental in a product of the human spirit and that – at least on an unconscious level – the usual evaluation has to be reversed. Superficially insignificant or accidental

Anton Ehrenzweig, from *The Hidden Order of Art*. London: Weidenfeld & Nicolson, a division of The Orion Publishing Group, 1967, pp. 21–5, 30–1. Reproduced with permission.

looking detail may well carry the most important unconscious symbolism. Indeed the great emotional power of spontaneous handwriting testifies to its hidden meaning and symbolism [...]. A great work of painting stripped of its original brush work by a bad restorer will lose almost all of its substance. There was little point in restoring Leonardo's *Last Supper*.

[...]

Paul Klee[1] spoke of two kinds of attention practised by the artist. The normal type of attention focuses on the positive figure which a line encloses, or else – with an effort – on the negative shape which the figure cuts out from the ground. Klee speaks of the endotopic (inside) area and the exotopic (outside) area of the picture plane. He says that the artist can either emphasize the boundary contrast produced by the bisection of the picture plane; in which case he will keep his attention on one (endotopic or exotopic) side of the line he draws; or else he can scatter his attention and watch the simultaneous shaping of inside and outside areas on either side of the line, a feat which the gestalt psychologists would consider impossible. According to the gestalt theory, we have to make a choice; we can choose either to see the figure; then the shape of the around becomes invisible, or else – with an effort – to scrutinize the negative shape cut from the ground; then the original figure disappears from view. We can never see both at the same time. [...] Somehow – as Paul Klee postulates – a good artist must be able to hold the entire picture plane in a single undivided focus. He will, as he draws a single line, automatically give aesthetic shape to the negative which his line cuts out from the ground.

[...]

A flexible scattering of attention comes quite easily to the artist, if only because of his need for holding all elements of the picture in a single undivided act of attention. He cannot afford the fatal bisection into figure and ground imposed by the conscious gestalt principle. How often have we not observed how an artist suddenly stops in his tracks without apparent reason, steps back from his canvas and looks at it with a curiously vacant stare? What happens is that the conscious gestalt is prevented from crystallizing. Nothing seems to come into his mind. Perhaps one or another detail lights up for a moment only to sink back into the emptiness. During this absence of mind an unconscious scanning seems to go on. Suddenly as from nowhere some offending detail hitherto ignored will come into view. It had somehow upset the balance of the picture, but had gone undetected. With relief the painter will end his apparent inactivity. He returns to his canvas and carries out the necessary retouching. This 'full' emptiness of unconscious scanning occurs in many other examples of creative work. Paul Klee's scattered attention that can attend to figure and ground on both sides of a line is of this kind. As far as consciousness is concerned, it is empty. For the gestalt principle ruling conscious perception cannot relinquish its hold on the figure.

The 'full' emptiness of attention also exists in hearing. Paul Klee himself makes the link between painting and music. He calls his dispersed attention that can attend to the entire picture plane 'multi-dimensional' (this expression happily stresses its irrational structure) and also 'polyphonic'.

This too is a good name. Polyphonic hearing also overcomes the conscious division between figure and ground. In music the figure is represented by the melody standing out against an indistinct ground of the harmonic accompaniment. Musicians are loath to call the polyphonic strands of a well-constructed harmonic progression a mere accompaniment. Often the accompanying voices form parallel melodic phrases expressive in themselves. Yet the usual description fits the ordinary naive way of enjoying music well enough. Moreover, it corresponds to the demands of the gestalt principle which exalts the melody as the figure to which the accompaniment serves as a background. In our memory a piece of music is remembered only as the sound of a melody. But as we have come to appreciate, artistic perception is neither ordinary, nor is it bound to the narrow limits of everyday attention, nor confined to its precise focus which can only attend to a single melody at a time. The musician like the painter has to train himself to scatter his attention over the entire musical structure so that he can grasp the polyphonic fabric hidden in the accompaniment.

[...]

[...] This total integration can only be controlled by the empty stare of unconscious scanning which alone is capable of overcoming the fragmentation in art's surface structure. The relative smallness of micro-elements defies conscious articulation; so do the macro-elements of art owing to their excessive breadth. This applies for instance to the macro-structure of a symphony as distinct from its single movements. The much-vaunted grasp of a symphony's total structure is well beyond the capacities even of many well-known conductors. Most are content to shape their phrases only in their immediate context and this procedure emphasizes the fragmentation of the whole. On the surface the overall structure of a sonata or symphony seems to go out of its way to evade a total grasp. The single movements are tightly organized and form good gestalt structures in themselves. These are then sharply contrasted in rhythm, harmony and form. More than ever an undifferentiated empty stare is needed to transcend such sharp divisions and forge the total work into a single indivisible whole. It seems that art, almost perversely, creates tasks that cannot be mastered by our normal faculties. Chaos is precariously near.

We arrive back at our central problem, the role which the unconscious plays in controlling the vast substructure of art. Its contribution appears chaotic and altogether accidental, but only as long as we rely on the gestalt-bound discipline of conscious perception. In spite of the caution built into the foundations of psycho-analytic thinking, which makes it beware of superficial impressions of chaos and accidentality, psycho-analytic aesthetics have so far faltered and succumbed to the chaotic impression which the substructure of art so seductively presents. Once we have overcome the deception, the eminently constructive role of the primary process in art can no longer be ignored.

NOTE

1. Footnote removed.

PART THREE:

IMAGE CULTURE

8: IMAGES AND WORDS

INTRODUCTION

A key issue in the emerging field of image studies is the fraught and complex relation between images and words, as indicated by a journal dedicated to the topic, *Word & Image*. Visual images and words might be considered simply as different kinds of signs used to communicate and to represent. In this case, some tools of signification seem better at some purposes than at others, as in the adage 'a picture paints a thousand words'. The making, perception and interpreting of visual and verbal signs might be thought to involve different faculties and cognitive functions (Zeki, 12.5). In art history, for example, there has been a heated debate about whether semiotics is an appropriate method for interpreting visual images (Bal, 5.4; Manghani, 2003). Efforts to classify words and images, language and pictures, as different kinds of signification tend to break down. Words and language may be spoken or written, heard or seen, so some words are visual as well as verbal. Jacques Derrida (1976) takes spoken language to depend on writing and other forms of graphic marking. The growing interest in semiotics (see Section 5, Semiotics) amongst artists led to a direct fusion between words and images, photography and narratives (see Berger, 9.7; Burgin, 1986; Lomax, 2000).

Writing is generally regarded as formal and conventional signification of the sounds of language. In the classical understanding, the written sign points beyond itself to the referent or thing. The conventional link between sign and referent was disrupted by the structuralist linguist Ferdinand de Saussure (5.1, see also introduction to Section 5, Semiotics) who argued for the arbitrariness of the sign. But Ernest Fenollosa (8.1) upheld the idea, contrary to most other scholars of Chinese language, that the Chinese written character remains an ideogram, an actual picture of its referent. His opinion proved influential among early twentieth-century imagist poets, such as Ezra Pound, who defined an image as 'that which presents an intellectual and emotional complex in an instant of time' (1935: 4). The imagists sought to convey through poetry the vividness that Fenollosa found in Chinese script.

If the imagists were interested in the poetic function of metaphor, Paul Ricoeur (8.2) analysed metaphor as the process through which linguistic imagination creates and recreates meaning. In the book from which this extract is taken, Ricoeur works from a rhetorical analysis of the word, through a semantic analysis of the sentence, to a phenomenological, hermeneutic analysis of discourse. Significantly, the semantic analysis of metaphor finds its limit when it comes up against imagery, which Ricoeur characterises as non-verbal and quasi-visual. Yet, in a way that brings to mind both Kant's role of the imagination in constructing schema (2.1) and the later Wittgenstein's conception of language (1958), Ricoeur claims that the poetic image is at the heart of human language and being. It will not then be surprising to find that metaphor is central, rather than incidental, to philosophical discourse (Le Doeuff, 9.4).

Metaphorical language, or verbal images, are often considered to be images only in 'some extended, figurative, or improper' sense of the term, but that assumes we already know which are the proper, literal images and that they represent transparently (Mitchell, 13.1). Similarly, nothing should be taken for granted in the relationships between words and images: 'The history of culture is in part the story of a protracted struggle for dominance between pictorial and linguistic signs' (Mitchell, 1986: 43). Scholarship can establish historically and contextually what is at stake in various contests between words and images, but any particular theory about the proper relation between words and images is likely to serve certain powers and interests. Thus, Lessing's (2.2) insistence on the distinct formal natures of poetry and painting turns out to be also an ideological opposition to the adulteration of political and social distinctions of gender and nationality (Mitchell, 1986: 109).

Similar ideological stakes and value judgements are at work in the selections in this section. Foucault (8.3) engaged with Magritte's paintings that explicitly explore the relation between words and things. For Foucault, Magritte's calligrams, in which both words and images signify objects, disturb 'all the traditional bounds of language and image' (Foucault, 1983: 22). Magritte demonstrates visually a critique of language that Foucault develops historically, pointing to the absent foundation of language that is unable to represent things through words, just as the picture is not identical with its object. Magritte's unravelled calligrams are transgressive moments for Foucault, which expose the limits of the rules of representation at work in successive epistemes, or systems of knowledge, that characterise different epochs. Such moments, when 'the relation of language to painting is … infinite' (Foucault, 1973: 9), exemplify for Foucault the reflexive, critical ethos of modernity that reveals the contingency of all 'orders of things' (Simons, 2000).

For Robert Romanyshyn (8.4), what is at stake between book consciousness and contemporary media image consciousness, epitomised by television, is also an epochal difference between modernity and postmodernity. Walter Benjamin claimed that, 'During long periods of history, the mode of human sense perception changes with humanity's entire mode of existence' (1968: 222). Romanyshyn similarly holds that human consciousness changes according to the media in which we are immersed (see also Debray, 13.4). Critics of contemporary image culture such as Neil Postman (1986) remain attuned to a modernist, typographic culture that is bound up with Cartesian mind–body dualism, objectivism and individualism (1.12, 1.13) as well as visual conventions of linear perspective (Panofsky, 1997). In Romanyshyn's view, such critics overlook the potential of televisual consciousness to access the paradox of metaphor (Ricoeur, 8.2) and the unconscious of dream states (Freud, 2.8; Ehrenzweig, 7.5), which can address the pathologies of modern consciousness.

Kevin DeLuca (8.5) also sees more critical potential in contemporary image culture than ideology critique and its liberal counterparts allow for (Boorstin, 1992). Challenging Debord's iconoclasm (3.2), he writes: 'Critique through spectacle, not critique versus spectacle' (DeLuca, 1999: 22). His work is an example of a contemporary emphasis on the visual aspects of rhetoric (Hariman and Lucaites, 2001; see also Kress and van Leeuwen, 5.5) which are generally overlooked in models that focus on its verbal aspects. At the same time, DeLuca also challenges Jürgen Habermas' (1989) influential, normative concept of the public sphere as a space in which politics is conducted as discursive argumentation. Instead, he focuses on activist politics as 'imagefare' waged on 'the public screen' (DeLuca and Peebles, 2002).

REFERENCES

Benjamin, W. (1968) *Iluminations*, tr. H. Zohn. New York: Schocken Books.

Boorstin, D. (1992) *The Image*. New York: Vintage Books.

Burgin, V. (1986) *The End of Art Theory: Criticism and Postmodernity*. London: Macmillan.

DeLuca, K. (1999) *Image Politics: The New Rhetoric of Environmental Activism*. New York: Guilford Press.

DeLuca, K. and Peebles, J. (2002) 'From public sphere to public screen: democracy, activism, and the "violence" of Seattle', *Critical Studies in Media Communication,* 19 (2): 125–51.

Derrida, J. (1976) *Of Grammatology*, tr. G. C. Spivak. Baltimore, MD: Johns Hopkins University Press.

Foucault, M. (1973) *The Order of Things*, tr. unidentified collective. New York: Vintage Books.

Foucault, M. (1983) *This Is Not a Pipe*, tr. J. Harkness. Berkeley, CA: University of California Press.

Habermas, J. (1989) *The Structural Transformation of the Public Sphere*, tr. T. Burger. Cambridge: Polity Press.

Hariman, R. and Lucaites, J. (2001) 'Visual rhetoric, photojournalism and democratic public culture', *Rhetoric Review*, 20: 37–42.

Lomax, Y. (2000) *Writing the Image: An Adventure with Theory and Art*. London: I.B. Tauris.

Manghani, S. (2003) 'Adventures in subsemiotics: towards a new "object" and writing of visual culture', *Culture, Theory and Critique*, 44 (1): 23–36.

Mitchell, W.J.T. (1986) *Iconology: Image, Text, Ideology*. Chicago: University of Chicago Press.

Panofsky, E. (1997) *Perspective as Symbolic Form*, tr. C. Wood. New York: Zone Books.

Postman, N. (1986) *Amusing Ourselves to Death*. New York: Penguin.

Pound, E. (1935) 'A retrospect', in T.S. Eliot (ed.), *Literary Essays of Ezra Pound*. New York: New Directions. pp. 3–14.

Simons, J. (2000) 'Modernist misapprehensions of Foucault's aesthetics', *Cultural Values*, 4 (1): 40–57.

Wittgenstein, L. (1958) *Philosophical Investigations*, tr. G.E.M. Anscombe. New York: Macmillan.

8:1 THE ROOTS OF POETRY
ERNEST FENOLLOSA

In what sense can verse, written in terms of visible hieroglyphics, be reckoned true poetry? It might seem that poetry, which like music is a *time art,* weaving its unities out of successive impressions of sound, could with difficulty assimilate a verbal medium consisting largely of semi-pictorial appeals to the eye.

Contrast, for example, Gray's line:

The curfew tolls the knell of parting day

with the Chinese line:

| Moon | Rays | Like | Pure | Snow |

Unless the sound of the latter be given, what have they in common? It is not enough to adduce that each contains a certain body of prosaic meaning; for the question is, how can the Chinese line imply, as *form,* the very element that distinguishes poetry from prose?

On second glance, it is seen that the Chinese words, though visible, occur in just as necessary an order as the phonetic symbols of Gray. All that poetic form requires is a regular and flexible sequence, as plastic as thought itself. The characters may be seen and read, silently by the eye, one after the other:

Moon rays like pure snow.

Perhaps we do not always sufficiently consider that thought is successive, not through some accident or weakness of our subjective operations but because the operations of nature are successive. The transferences of force from agent to object, which constitute natural phenomena, occupy time. Therefore, a reproduction of them in imagination requires the same temporal order.[1]

Suppose that we look out of a window and watch a man. Suddenly he turns his head and actively fixes his attention upon something. We look ourselves and see that his vision has been focused upon a horse. We saw, first, the man before he acted; second, while he acted; third, the object toward which

Ernest Fenollosa, from *The Chinese Written Character as a Medium for Poetry*, ed. Ezra Pound. San Francisco: City Lights Books, 1936, pp. 6–10.

his action was directed. In speech we split up the rapid continuity of this action and of its picture into its three essential parts or joints in the right order, and say:

Man sees horse.

It is clear that these three joints, or words, are only three phonetic symbols, which stand for the three terms of a natural process. But we could quite as easily denote these three stages of our thought by symbols equally arbitrary, *which had no basis in sound*; for example, by three Chinese characters:

Man   Sees   Horse

If we all knew *what division* of this mental horse-picture each of these signs stood for, we could communicate continuous thought to one another as easily by drawing them as by speaking words. We habitually employ the visible language of gesture in much this same manner.

But Chinese notation is something much more than arbitrary symbols. It is based upon a vivid shorthand picture of the operations of nature. In the algebraic figure and in the spoken word there is no natural connection between thing and sign: all depends upon sheer convention. But the Chinese method follows natural suggestion. First stands the man on his two legs. Second, his eye moves through space: a bold figure represented by running legs under an eye, a modified picture of an eye, a modified picture of running legs, but unforgettable once you have seen it. Third stands the horse on his four legs.

The thought-picture is not only called up by these signs as well as by words, but far more vividly and concretely. Legs belong to all three characters: they are *alive*. The group holds something of the quality of a continuous moving picture.

The untruth of a painting or a photograph is that, in spite of its concreteness, it drops the element of natural succession.

Contrast the Laocoön statue with Browning's lines:

'*I sprang to the stirrup, and Joris, and he*

…

And into the midnight we galloped abreast.'

One superiority of verbal poetry as an art rests in its getting back to the fundamental reality of *time*. Chinese poetry has the unique advantage of combining both elements. It speaks at once with the vividness of painting, and with the mobility of sounds. It is, in some sense, more objective than either, more dramatic. In reading Chinese we do not seem to be juggling mental counters, but to be watching *things* work out their own fate.

Leaving for a moment the form of the sentence, let us look more closely at this quality of vividness in the structure of detached Chinese words. The earlier forms of these characters were pictorial, and their hold upon the imagination is little shaken, even in later conventional modifications. It is not so well known, perhaps, that the great number of these ideographic roots carry in them a *verbal idea of action*. It might be thought that a picture is naturally the picture of a *thing*, and that therefore the root ideas of Chinese are what grammar calls nouns.

But examination shows that a large number of the primitive Chinese characters, even the so-called radicals, are shorthand pictures of actions or processes.

For example, the ideograph meaning 'to speak' is a mouth with two words and a flame coming out of it [...] (*vide* Figure 8.1 [...]). But this concrete *verb* quality, both in nature and in the Chinese signs, becomes far more striking and poetic when we pass from such simple, original pictures to compounds. In this process of compounding, two things added together do not produce a third thing but suggest some fundamental relation between

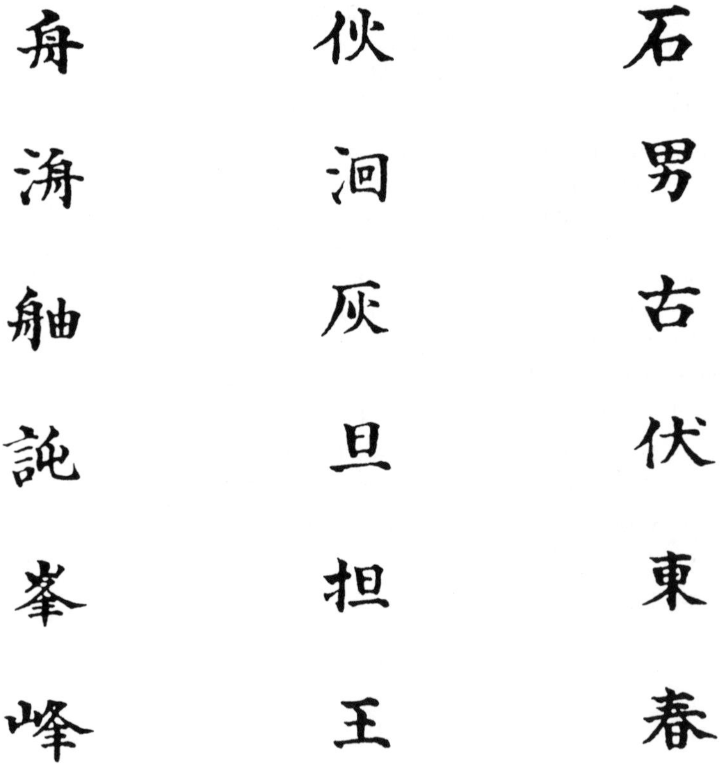

舟　　　伙　　　石

湁　　　洄　　　男

舳　　　灰　　　古

詑　　　旦　　　伏

峯　　　担　　　東

峰　　　王　　　春

FIGURE 8.1

Note on Figure 8.1,
COLUMN 2

1. Man + fire = messmate.
2. Water + revolve within a circle = eddy.
3. Hand + fire = fire that can be taken in the hand = cinder, ashes.
4. Sun above line of horizon = dawn.
5. Earth (sign not very well drawn – left lower stroke should be at bottom) + the foregoing = level plain, wide horizon.
6. One who binds three planes: heaven, earth and man = ruler, to rule.

COLUMN 3

4. Man + dog (dog beside man) = dog lying at man's feet or crawling to man's feet; hence, to lie down.

them. For example, the ideograph for a 'messmate' is a man and a fire (*vide* Figure 8.1, col. 2).

A true noun, an isolated thing, does not exist in nature. Things are only the terminal points, or rather the meeting points, of actions, cross-sections cut through actions, snapshots. Neither can a pure verb, an abstract motion, be possible in nature. The eye sees noun and verb as one: things in motion, motion in things, and so the Chinese conception tends to represent them.[2]

NOTES

1. Footnote removed.
2. Dog *attending* man = dogs him [*vide* Figure 8.1, col. 3].

ICON AND IMAGE 8:2
PAUL RICOEUR

Is a psycholinguistics of imaginative illusion possible? If [...] semantics goes no further than the verbal aspects of imagination, could psycholinguistics perhaps cross over this line and join the properly *sensual* aspect of the image to a semantic theory of metaphor?

[...]

The fundamental question posed by the introduction of image or imagery (Hester[1] uses the two terms interchangeably) into a theory of metaphor concerns the status of a sensible, thus non-verbal, factor inside a semantic theory. The difficulty is amplified by the fact that image, as opposed to perception, cannot be related to any 'public' realities, and seems to reintroduce the sort of 'private' mental experience condemned by Wittgenstein, Hester's chosen master. So the problem is to bring to light a liaison between sense and sensa that can be reconciled with semantic theory.

A first trait of the iconicity of meaning seems to facilitate this accord. Images evoked or aroused in this way are not the 'free' images that a simple association of ideas would join to meaning. Rather, to return to an expression of Richards in *The Principles of Literary Criticism*[2], they are 'tied' images, that is, connected to poetic diction. In contrast to mere association, iconicity involves meaning controlling imagery. In other words, this is imagery involved in language itself; it is part of the game of language itself.[3]

Paul Ricoeur, from *The Rule of Metaphor*. London: Routledge, 1977, pp. 207–14. Reproduced with permission.

It seems to me that this notion of imagery tied by meaning is in accord with Kant's idea that the schema is a method for constructing images. The verbal icon in Hester's sense is also a method for constructing images. The poet, in effect, is that artisan who sustains and shapes imagery using no means other than language.

Does this concept of 'tied' image entirely escape the objection of psychologism? That can be doubted. The manner of Hester's detailed explanation of the fusion of sense and sensa, even when understood as tied images rather than as real sounds, leaves the sensible moment very much outside the verbal moment. [...] All these explanations remain more psychological than semantic.

The most satisfying explanation, and in any case the only one that can be reconciled with semantic theory, is the one that Hester links to the notion of 'seeing as' (which is Wittgensteinian in origin). *This theme constitutes Hester's positive contribution to the iconic theory of metaphor.*

What is 'seeing as'?

The factor of 'seeing as' is exposed through the act of reading, even to the extent that this is 'the mode in which such imagery is realized'[4]. The 'seeing as' is the positive link between vehicle and tenor. In poetic metaphor, the metaphorical vehicle is *as* the tenor – from one point of view, not from all points of view. To explicate a metaphor is to enumerate all the appropriate senses in which the vehicle is 'seen as' the tenor. The 'seeing as' is the intuitive relationship that makes the sense and image hold together.

With Wittgenstein,[5] the 'seeing as' concerns neither metaphor nor even imagination, at least in its relationship to language. Considering ambiguous figures (like the one that can be seen as a duck or a rabbit), Wittgenstein remarks that it is one thing to say 'I see this . . .' and another to say 'I see this as . . .'; and he adds: 'seeing it as . . .' is 'having *this* image.' The link between 'seeing as' and imagining appears more clearly when we go to the imperative mood, where, for example, one might say 'Imagine this,' 'Now, see the figure as this.' Will this be regarded as a question of interpretation? No, says Wittgenstein, because to interpret is to form a hypothesis which one can verify. There is no hypothesis here, nor any verification; one says quite directly, 'It's a rabbit.' The 'seeing as,' therefore, is half thought and half experience. And is this not the same sort of mixture that the iconicity of meaning presents?[6]

Following Virgil C. Aldrich,[7] Hester proposes to have the 'seeing as' and the imaging function of language in poetry clarify each other. The 'seeing as' of Wittgenstein lends itself to this transposition because of its imaginative side; conversely, as Aldrich puts it, thinking in poetry is a picture-thinking. Now this 'pictorial' capacity of language consists also in 'seeing an aspect.' In the case of metaphor, to depict time in terms of the characteristics of a beggar is to see time as a beggar. This is what we do when we read the metaphor; to read is to establish a relationship such that X is like Y in some senses, but not in all.

It is true that the transfer from Wittgenstein's analysis to metaphor introduces an important change. In the case of the ambiguous figure, there is a *Gestalt* (B) that allows a figure A or another figure C to be seen. Thus the problem is, given B, to construct A or C. In the case of metaphor, A and C are given in reading – they are the tenor and vehicle. What must be constructed is the common element B, the *Gestalt,* namely, the point of view in which A and C are similar.

Whatever the case with this reversal, 'seeing as' proffers the missing link in the chain of explanation. 'Seeing as' is the sensible aspect of poetic language. Half thought, half experience, 'seeing as' is the intuitive relationship that holds sense and image together. How? Essentially through its selective character: '*Seeing as is an intuitive experience-act by which one selects from the quasi-sensory mass of imagery one has on reading metaphor the relevant aspects of such imagery*'.[8] This definition contains the essential points. 'Seeing as' is an experience and an act at one and the same time. On the one hand, the mass of images is beyond all voluntary control; the image arises, occurs, and there is no rule to be learned for 'having images.' One sees, or one does not see. The intuitive talent for 'seeing as'[9] cannot be taught; at most, it can be assisted, as when one is helped to see the rabbit's eye in the ambiguous figure. On the other hand, 'seeing as' is an act. To understand is to do something. As we said earlier, the image is not free but tied; and, in effect, 'seeing as' orders the flux and governs iconic deployment. In this way, the experience-act of 'seeing as' ensures that imagery is implicated in metaphorical signification: 'The same imagery which *occurs* also *means*'.[10]

Thus, the 'seeing as' activated in reading ensures the joining of verbal meaning with imagistic fullness. And this conjunction is no longer something outside language, since it can be reflected as a relationship. 'Seeing as' contains a ground, a foundation, that is, precisely, resemblance – no longer the resemblance between two ideas, but that very resemblance the 'seeing as' establishes. Hester claims emphatically that similarity is what results from the experience-act of 'seeing as.' '*Seeing as*' defines the resemblance, and not the reverse. This priority of 'seeing as' over the resemblance relationship is proper to the language-game in which meaning functions in an iconic manner. That is why the 'seeing as' can succeed or fail. It can fail as in forced metaphors, because they are inconsistent or fortuitous, or on the contrary, as in banal and commonplace metaphors; and succeed, as in those that fashion the surprise of discovery.

Thus, 'seeing as' quite precisely plays the role of the schema that unites the *empty* concept and the *blind* impression; thanks to its character as half thought and half experience, it joins the light of sense with the fullness of the image. In this way, the non-verbal and the verbal are firmly united at the core of the image-ing function of language.

Besides this role of bridging the verbal and the quasi-visual, 'seeing as' ensures another mediative service. Semantic theory, as we remember, puts the accent on the tension between the terms of the statement, a tension grounded in contradiction at the literal level. In the case of banal, even dead, metaphor, the tension with the body of our knowledge disappears. [...] In living metaphor, on the other hand, this tension is essential. When Hopkins says 'Oh! The mind has mountains,' the reader knows that, literally, the mind does not have mountains; the literal *is not* accompanies the metaphorical *is*. [...] Now, a theory of fusion of sense and the sensible, adopted prior to the revision proposed by Hester, appears to be incompatible with this characteristic, of tension between metaphorical meaning and literal meaning. On the other hand, once it is re-interpreted on the basis of 'seeing as,' the theory of fusion is perfectly compatible with interaction and tension theory. 'Seeing X *as* Y' encompasses 'X is *not* Y'; seeing time *as* a beggar is, precisely, to know also that time is *not* a beggar. The borders of meaning are transgressed but not abolished. Barfield[11] pictures metaphor well as 'a deliberate yoking of unlikes by an individual artificer.' Hester therefore is justified in saying that '*seeing as*' permits harmonization of a tension theory and a fusion theory. I should personally go further; I should say that fusion of sense and the imaginary, which is characteristic of 'iconized meaning,' is the necessary counterpart of a theory of interaction.

Metaphorical meaning, as we saw, is not the enigma itself, the semantic clash pure and simple, but the solution of the enigma, the inauguration of the new semantic pertinence. In this connection, the interaction designates only the *diaphora*; the *epiphora* properly speaking is something else. It cannot take place without fusion, without intuitive passage. The secret of *epiphora* then appears truly to reside in the iconic nature of intuitive passage. Metaphorical meaning as such feeds on the density of imagery released by the poem.

If this is how things really stand, then 'seeing as' designates the *non-verbal* mediation of the metaphorical statement. With this acknowledgment, semantics finds its frontier; and, in so doing, it accomplishes its task.

If semantics meets its limit here, a *phenomenology of imagination*, like that of Gaston Bachelard,[12] could perhaps take over from psycholinguistics and extend its functioning to realms where the verbal is vassal to the non-verbal. Yet it is still the semantics of the poetic verb that is to be heard in these depths. Bachelard has taught us that the image is not a residue of impression, but an aura surrounding speech: 'The poetic image places us at the origin of the speaking being'.[13] The poem gives birth to the image; the poetic image 'becomes a new being in our language, expressing us by making us what it expresses; in other words, it is at once a becoming of expression, and a becoming of our being. Here expression created being ... one would not be able to mediate in a zone that preceded language.'[14]

If then the phenomenology of imagination does extend beyond psycholinguistics and even beyond the description of 'seeing-as,' this is because it follows the path of the 'reverberation'[15] of the poetic image into the depths of existence. The poetic image becomes 'a source of psychic activity.' What was 'a new being in language' becomes an 'increment to consciousness,' or better, a 'growth of being.'[16] Even in 'psychological poetics,' even in 'reveries on reverie,' psychism continues to be directed by the poetic verb. And so, one must attest: 'Yes, words do really dream.'[17]

NOTES

1. Marcus B. Hester *The Meaning of Poetic Metaphor*. The Hague: Mouton, 1967.

2. Ivor A. Richards *Principles of Literacy Criticism*. New York: Harcourt Brace, 1925, pp. 118–19.

3. Footnote removed.

4. *The Meaning of Poetric Metaphor*, 21.

5. Ludwig Wittgenstein *Philosophical Investigations*. Trans. G.E.M. Anscombe. Oxford: Blackwell, 1953, 37th edition 1968, II, xi.

6. Footnote removed.

7. Virgil C. Aldrich 'Image-Mongering and Image-Management,' *Philosophy and Phenomenological Research* 23 (September 1962) and 'Pictorial Meaning, Picture-Thinking and Wittgenstein's Theory of Aspects' *Mind* 67 (January 1958), pp. 75–6.

8. *The Meaning of Poetic Metaphor*, 180.

9. *The Meaning of Poetic Metaphor*, 182.

10. *The Meaning of Poetic Metaphor*, 188.

11. Owen Barfield *Poetic Diction: A Study in Meaning*. Quoted in Hester *Poetic Metaphor* New York: McGraw Hill, 1928, 2nd edition, 1964, 27.

12. Gaston Bachelard *The Poetics of Space* trans. Maria Jolas. Boston, MA: Beacon, 1969, introduction xi–xxxv; and *The Poetics of Reverie* trans. Daniel Russell. New York: Orion, 1969, introduction 1–26.

13. *The Poetics of Space* xix.

14. Ibid. […]

15. The term and theme are taken from Eugène Minkowski *Vers une Cosmologie: Fragments philosophiques*, Chapter 9. Paris: Aubier, 1936.

16. Bachelard *Poetics of Reverie* 3–6.

17. Ibid. 18.

THIS IS NOT A PIPE
MICHEL FOUCAULT

8:3

The first version, that of 1926 I believe: a carefully drawn pipe, and underneath it (handwritten in a steady, painstaking, artificial script, a script from the convent, like that found heading the notebooks of schoolboys, or on a blackboard after an object lesson[1]), this note: 'This is not a pipe.'

The other version – the last, I assume – can be found in *Aube à l'Antipodes*.[2] The same pipe, same statement, same handwriting. But instead of being juxtaposed in a neutral, limitless, unspecified space, the text and the figure are set within a frame. The frame itself is placed upon an easel, and the latter in turn upon the clearly visible slats of the floor. Above everything, a pipe exactly like the one in the picture, but much larger.

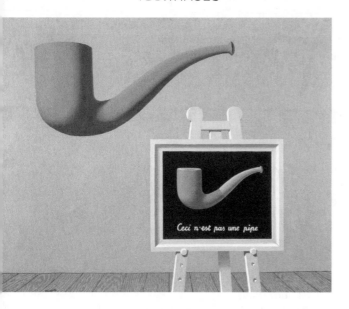

FIGURE 8.2
Les Deux Mystères, 1966 (oil on panel)
by René Magritte. Source: Private
Collection/James Goodman Gallery,
New York/The Bridgeman Art Library ©
DACS London.

The first version disconcerts us by its very simplicity. The second multiplies intentional ambiguities before our eyes. Standing upright against the easel and resting on wooden pegs, the frame indicates that this is an artist's painting: a finished work, exhibited and bearing for an eventual viewer the statement that comments upon or explains it. And yet this naïve handwriting, neither precisely the work's title nor one of its pictorial elements; the absence of any other trace of the artist's presence; the roughness of the ensemble; the wide slats of the floor – everything suggests a blackboard in a classroom. Perhaps a swipe of the rag will soon erase the drawing and the text. Perhaps it will erase only one or the other, in order to correct the 'error' (drawing something that will truly not be a pipe, or else writing a sentence affirming that this indeed is a pipe). A temporary slip (a 'mis-writing' suggesting a misunderstanding) that one gesture will dissipate in white dust?

But this is still only the least of the ambiguities; here are some others. There are two pipes. Or rather must we not say, two drawings of the same pipe? Or yet a pipe and the drawing of that pipe, or yet again two drawings each representing a different pipe? Or two drawings, one representing a pipe and the other not, or two more drawings yet, of which neither the one nor the other are or represent pipes? Or yet again, a drawing representing not a pipe at all but another drawing, itself representing a pipe so well that I must ask myself. To what does the sentence written in the painting relate? 'See these lines assembled on the blackboard – vainly do they resemble, without the least digression or infidelity, what is displayed above them. Make no mistake; the pipe is overhead, not in this childish scrawl.'

Yet perhaps the sentence refers precisely to the disproportionate, floating, ideal pipe – simple notion or fantasy of a pipe. Then we should have to read,

'Do not look overhead for a true pipe. That is a pipe dream. It is the drawing within the painting, firmly and rigorously outlined, that must be accepted as a manifest truth.'

[…]

About even this ambiguity, however, I am ambiguous. Or rather what appears to me very dubious is the simple opposition between the higher pipe's dislocated buoyancy and the stability of the lower one. Looking a bit more closely, we easily discern that the feet of the easel, supporting the frame where the canvas is held and where the drawing is lodged – these feet, resting upon a floor made safe and visible by its own coarseness, are in fact beveled. They touch only by three tiny points, robbing the ensemble, itself somewhat ponderous, of all stability. An impending fall? The collapse of easel, frame, canvas or panel, drawing, text? Splintered wood, fragmented shapes, letters scattered one from another until words can perhaps no longer be reconstituted? All this litter on the ground, while above, the large pipe without measure or reference point will linger in its inaccessible, balloon-like immobility?

*

The exteriority of written and figurative elements, so obvious in Magritte, is symbolized by the non-relation – or in any case by the very complex and problematic relation – between the painting and its title. This gulf, which prevents us from being both the reader and the viewer at the same time, brings the image into abrupt relief above the horizontal line of words. 'The titles are chosen in such a way as to keep anyone from assigning my paintings to the familiar region that habitual thought appeals to in order to escape perplexity.' A little like the anonymous hand that designated the pipe by the statement, 'This is not a pipe,' Magritte names his paintings in order to focus attention upon the very act of naming. And yet in this split and drifting space, strange bonds are knit, there occur intrusions, brusque and destructive invasions, avalanches of images into the milieu of words, and verbal lightning flashes that streak and shatter the drawings. […] Magritte secretly mines a space he seems to maintain in the old arrangement. But he excavates it with words: And the old pyramid of perspective is no more than a molehill about to cave in.

[…]

Between the two extremes, Magritte's work deploys the play of words and images. Often invented after the fact and by other people, the titles intrude into the figures where their applicability was if not indicated at least authorized in advance, and where they play an ambiguous role: supporting pegs and yet termites that gnaw and weaken. […]

Moreover, listen to Magritte: 'Between words and objects one can create new relations and specify characteristics of language and objects generally ignored in everyday life.' Or again: 'Sometimes the name of an object takes the place of an image. A word can take the place of an object in reality. An image can take the place of a word in a proposition.' And the following statement, conveying no contradiction but referring to the inextricable tangle of words and images and to the absence of a common ground to sustain them: 'In a painting, words are of the same cloth as images. Rather one sees images and words differently in a painting.'[3]

[…]

Make no mistake: In a space where every element seems to obey the sole principle of resemblance and plastic representation, linguistic signs (which had an excluded aura, which prowled far around the image, which the title's arbitrariness seemed to have banished forever) have surreptitiously reapproached. Into the solidity of the image, into its meticulous resemblance, they have introduced a disorder – an order pertaining to the eyes alone. They have routed the object, revealing its filmy thinness.

[…] Magritte allows the old space of representation to rule, but only at the surface, no more than a polished stone, bearing words and shapes: beneath, nothing. It is a gravestone: The incisions that drew figures and those that marked letters communicate only by void, the non-place hidden beneath marble solidity. I will note that this absence reascends to the surface and impinges upon the painting itself. […]

*

Separation between linguistic signs and plastic elements; equivalence of resemblance and affirmation. These two principles constituted the tension in classical painting, because the second reintroduced discourse (affirmation exists only where there is speech) into an art from which the linguistic element was rigorously excluded. Hence the fact that classical painting spoke – and spoke constantly – while constituting itself entirely outside language; hence the fact that it rested silently in a discursive space, hence the fact that it provided, beneath itself, a kind of common ground where it could restore the bonds of signs and the image.

Magritte knits verbal signs and plastic elements together, but without referring them to a prior isotopism. He skirts the base of affirmative discourse on which resemblance calmly reposes, and he brings pure similitudes and nonaffirmative verbal statements into play within the instability of a disoriented volume and an unmapped space. A process whose formulation is in some sense given by *Ceci n'est pas une pipe.*

1. To employ a calligram where are found, simultaneously present and visible, image, text, resemblance, affirmation, and their common ground.
2. Then suddenly to open it up, so that the calligram immediately decomposes and disappears, leaving as a trace only its own absence.
3. To allow discourse to collapse of its own weight and to acquire the visible shape of letters. Letters which, insofar as they are drawn, enter into an uncertain, indefinite relation, confused with the drawing itself – but minus any area to serve as a common ground.

4. To allow similitudes, on the other hand, to multiply of themselves, to be born from their own vapor and to rise endlessly into an ether where they refer to nothing more than themselves.
5. To verify clearly, at the end of the operation, that the precipitate has changed color, that it has gone from black to white, that the 'This is a pipe' silently hidden in mimetic representation has become the 'This is not a pipe' of circulating similitudes.

A day will come when, by means of similitude relayed indefinitely along the length of a series, the image itself, along with the name it bears, will lose its identity. Campbell, Campbell, Campbell, Campbell.[4]

NOTES

1. Translator's Note: *Leçon de choses,* literally 'lesson of things.' An allusion to the title of a 1947 Magritte canvas, as well as a 1960 film about Magritte made by Luc de Heusch. Magritte also wrote an essay to which he gave the title.
2. Translator's Note: 'Dawn at the Ends of the Earth,' the title of a book with illustrations by Magritte. Actually, Magritte's pipe and its wry subscript appear in a whole series of paintings and drawings. There is also a pun on the word *aube,* which can mean either 'dawn' or 'float.'
3. I cite all these quotations from P. Waldberg's *Magritte.* They illustrated a series of drawings in the twelfth issue of *Revolution Surrealiste.*
4. Translator's Note: Foucault's reference is not to Magritte but to Andy Warhol, whose various series of soup cans, celebrity portraits, and so on Foucault apparently sees as undermining any sense of the unique, indivisible identity of their 'models.' [...]

THE DESPOTIC EYE AND ITS SHADOW: MEDIA IMAGE IN THE AGE OF LITERACY
ROBERT D. ROMANYSHYN

8:4

[T]his essay [...] is an experiment in cultural therapeutics which begins not with the past but with how the past is present in the present as symptom. [...] [W]e must eschew the primarily modern and mostly negative idea of the symptom, an idea which would invite us to evaluate the symptom in order to 'cure' it, that is, dismiss it. In place of that idea we need to embrace the more difficult notion that the symptom *is* a vocation, a call to listen and give voice to what would otherwise remain silenced.

The experiment in this essay is to demonstrate media image consciousness, illustrated here via TV consciousness, as the symptomatic ending of

Robert D. Romanyshyn, from *Modernity and the Hegemony of Vision,* ed. David Levin. Berkeley, CA: University of California Press, 1993, pp. 339–59. Copyright © 1993, The Regents of the University of California. Reproduced by permission of The Regents of the University of California and the author.

modernity. Such an experiment, however, initially needs some justification, because the media image industry in general, and television in particular, seems so much to be an expression of modernity, and even the epitome of its values. [...] Television is the intensification of many of the values of modernity; indeed it is the incarnation of these values in the extreme. But that is precisely the sense of television as symptom. As exaggeration and caricature of the values of modernity, it brings those values to our attention, inviting us not to call them into question but to wonder about them, perhaps in some instances for the first time. As symptom, then, television asks for a hearing, not a judgment.

The hypothesis of this experiment is that television is the cultural unconscious of the book. It is the other side, the shadow side, of a book consciousness whose origins coincide with modernity. [...] [T]he ocularcentrism of modernity, the hegemony of vision, the installation of the reign of the despotic eye, is also a verbocentrism, the consciousness of the book, and an egocentrism, the consciousness of a separated, detached atom of individuality.

[...] [T]he sense of modernity is presented in this essay as ego-ocular-verbocentrism. It is this gestalt out of which many of the unquestioned values of modernity arise. Television as the shadow of the book makes visible the pathology of verbo-ocular-ego consciousness by challenging its values of linear rationality, contextual coherence, narrative continuity, focused concentration, infinite progress, individual privacy, productive efficiency, detached comprehensiveness, and neutral objectivity. The challenge, of course, is not for the sake of negating these values. On the contrary, the challenge is for the sake of pointing up their symptomatic character, of remembering their genesis at those cultural-historical moments when things could have been otherwise. That these values have not been otherwise attests to the fact that these moments of genesis were also moments of forgetfulness, in which these values were transformed from perspectives into unquestioned cultural conventions, sedimented habits of mind. [...] That television seems intent upon the destruction of the verbo-ocular-ego values of modernity invites from us not an unthinking, even self-righteous defense of those values, but an attentive response to our participation in the creation of those values. It is not safe simply to defend the book against television. On the contrary, we need to attend to how television, as the shadow of the book, as its symptomatic expression, calls us to become responsible by remembering what we have made.

In this essay, television as symbolic of the ending of modernity is presented as the symptomatic breakdown of modernity. [...]

The television experience can be a breakthrough to a postmodern style insofar as it breaks the gestalt of verbo-ocular-egocentrism, and in so doing redefines the ocularcentrism of modernity. If television is ocularcentric – and in many ways it is – it nevertheless revisions the eye. The eye of ego consciousness, the eye of the reader of the book, arises within a cultural-historical moment in which the ego as disembodied spectator is invited to keep his or her eye, singular, fixed, and distant, upon the world. The double anamnesis of this spectator eye makes these features quite clear. The television eye, the ocularcentrism of the television experience, is of a quite different sort. [...] [T]he eye of television consciousness is *re-minded* of the body. Seduced by images, a seduction which to be sure is not without its problems, the eye of the television body is an emotional vision, a vision that is moved at a bodily level.

As emotional-rationality, the television body is not verbocentric. In place of a literate consciousness, the television body is an image consciousness. Drawing upon psychoanalysis, the television body is said to be more like the dream body than the waking body. Drawing also upon the preliterate body of poetic performance in Homeric Greece, the television body is said to be more akin to this body of orality, where knowing is emotional, participatory, and sensuous, rather than rational, detached, and logical, and where waking and dreaming are less clearly distinguished and are more confused. In these respects, the postmodernism of the television body is presented as a postliterate orality, a surreal reality in which the values of literacy are confused with a new, technologically produced orality.

Finally, television body consciousness can be postmodern insofar as it is the decentering of the ego. Just as the dream in psychoanalysis decentered the ego, television can move the ego out of its privacy and isolation into a kind of group – even tribal – consciousness, where the tension between fusion with the other and distance from the other is refigured. The figure of the borderline patient is offered as an illustration of this decentering of ego consciousness which the television experience brings. It is suggested that working with a borderline is more like watching television than it is like reading a book. The symptomatic value of television, then, might very well lie in its invitation toward another kind of consciousness now visible in our culture only as the pathology of the borderline.

*

[T]elevision as a medium, along with film, is an evolution in human consciousness, a new style of consciousness, that is imprisoned in the heady eye of mind. The problem with television is that we treat it like a book, that we measure it by the book, by those patterns of consciousness appropriate to the isolated atom of individuality ensconced within the room of ego subjectivity. TV, however, is a challenge to ego consciousness, as much as it is a challenge to the political counterpart of ego consciousness, the individual nation-state. [...] TV as a medium brings out such strong criticism because it is the *breakdown* of literate, linear, ego consciousness, the consciousness of the book. The evolution is a revolution, akin in its implications to that earlier transformation in Platonic times from mythic to literate consciousness.

[...]

[T]he media image poses also for the postliterate mind a challenge to Descartes's difference between waking and dreaming. [...]

The nuclear family in front of its television set is neither sleeping nor insane. It is awake and it is dreaming. Television consciousness today haunts book consciousness because it eclipses those boundaries between waking and sleeping (reason and madness; fact and fiction) which ego literate consciousness so firmly established at the foundation of modernity. In doing so, it exposes the modern ego to a new sense of time, disrupting the familiar pattern of narrative and replacing it with the episodic pattern of the dream. [...] [W]atching television is akin to interpreting dreams, making sense of them, while dreaming. [...] [C]overage of the Persian Gulf War [in 1991] is [a good] [...] example , since the illusion of being informed was continually broken. Coverage of that event did demonstrate that the accounts of the war were allusions to what remained frustratingly elusive. [...] [T]he frustration in this experience is built into the relation between the medium, with its multi-perspectival, collage type of consciousness, and the viewer, with his or her still relatively intact linear perspectival consciousness. The frustration belongs to the surreal quality of the reality which con-fuses or blends together episodic and story line time. And it is generated by the effort to dismiss this play of levels between a collage of images and the story line by forcing the former into the latter.

[...]

The television experience is a radical separation of body and mind. On the one hand, the headless *body* of the *cogito* seems fused with the emotional appeals of the media image, moved by these images with either judgment or reflection. On the other hand, the very absence of these capacities, so visible in the iconographic display of the *headless* body in front of its TV, betrays a distance between the person watching television and his or her emotionally infected body already fused with the television.

*

The kind of consciousness which characterizes the media image, television consciousness for example, is a breakdown of the kind of consciousness which characterizes ego, literate consciousness, book consciousness for example. [...] [B]reakdown can also be breakthrough. [...]

The dream, however, is an invitation which asks to be played with by a wakeful consciousness aware of its continuous and reciprocal relation of making the dream while being made by it. In doing so, the dream infects the seriousness of cogito consciousness with play, even as it undermines the idea of an origin outside that process which in searching for origins simultaneously creates the origins that are discovered. The dream, then, breaks through to a consciousness which in its playfulness is participatory, and which in its sense of participation accepts its oxymoronic character of created-discoveries, of serious-play, of constructed-origins. It breaks through to a consciousness which in its acceptance of paradox is radically metaphorical.[1]

Television consciousness certainly partakes of these features of the dream. It is no less participatory, especially at the level of the emotional body, working upon it in much the same fashion that the dream works upon the body. It is also oxymoronic insofar as it continuously presents us with those juxtapositions of experience – the news story followed by the commercial, for example – which to the serious eye of ego, literate consciousness seem only like an opposition. And it is finally radically metaphorical insofar as its images, like Magritte's pipe, are not what they appear to be and yet are. Or at least television consciousness might break through to these features which characterize much of postmodern consciousness, if its symptomatic character is attended as a vocation.

To call media image consciousness postmodern is not, however, sufficiently descriptive, for its postmodernism is a postliterate orality. The television body, like the dreaming body, is in many respects a re-presentation of the preliterate body of orality, of that body of speaking and listening which is always prior to the body of the text. [...] It is a body which culturally and historically spirals out of the body of the book, out of the literate ego, a body which is not a repetition of preliterate orality but a re-membrance of that body, a re-play of it after the reign of the despotic eye. Like the body of poetic performance, the television body is emotional-rationality, drawn out of itself and into the world aesthetically, sensibly, as a matter of sense. It is also a body of group consciousness, a body already wedded via the sensuous and even erotic experience of the image to other bodies – a tribal body, then, immersed in a landscape that is more mythical than it is logical, and invited into action that is more ritual in texture than moral in outlook. That this kind of bodily presence to reality is open to exploitation and manipulation is obvious. Television has been manipulated, primarily by submitting to the industry of capitalism the potential of the medium to be a breakthrough to another kind of experience. But it need not do so. The use of television during the Vietnam War demonstrated its power to de-isolate the ego of literate consciousness and to create a coherent tribal identity, held together with a powerful myth of its place in history and prepared to act in such fashion that its emotional thought, contained within the space of dramatic ritual, was an important catalyst to stop that war.

[...] The very same features of television consciousness described above were sufficient for Plato to ban the poet-singer from the polis. The danger was that in becoming enmeshed in the poet's song one would be diffused, distracted, unfocused, and without fixed moral direction. The danger was that one would become plural in place of the unified, self-contained, self-organized, and autonomous individual. [...]

The history of the Western psyche shows the results of the exclusion of the poets from the polis. [...] It is a history of a radical shift from ear to eye, and particularly to that eye of detached, spectator distance, a history of the despotic eye. Media image consciousness, especially the television, seems to be the shadow and the symptom of that eye, and in this respect a retuning of it. The images of television are no mere spectacles. They are spoken images, oracular insights, emotional visions. Perhaps with the television the poetic returns, or at least might do so. [...] [T]elevision might be the means by which the poet is restored to the polis. Such a restoration would bring in its wake a re-membrance of the body's participation in vision, a re-minder which would restore a sense of limits to a vision which, detached from the body, developed a singular, fixed devotion to the infinite, pursued in a linear, active, willful fashion. [...] [C]riticisms of television as fostering distraction, passivity, and the trivial might then be reimagined. Distraction might be revalued as an appreciation for what lies off to the side, an attention to the oblique, an openness to allusion. Passivity might be restored as a balance to the hyperactivity of willful consciousness, an antidote to the ego as will to power, the development of an attitude of receptivity. And the trivial might be recovered as a sensitivity for the detail, a refound sense of the local so easily lost sight of in the big picture achieved with distance. Each and all might be rescued from the current negative condition assigned to them by an ego consciousness in its headlong pursuit of separating its vision of life from living.

NOTE

1. For a discussion of the metaphorical character of psychological consciousness, see my earlier book, *Psychological Life: From Science to Metaphor* (Austin: University of Texas Press, 1982). In that work the hidden metaphoric character of modern scientific consciousness is indicated, suggesting that ego, literate consciousness already harboured within itself the seed of its own symptomatic undoing.

8:5 IMAGES, AUDIENCES, AND READINGS
KEVIN DELUCA

In studying media that employ a mix of words and images, critics in rhetoric and cultural studies have tended to emphasize words and narrative form. A famous example is Hall's discussion (1973) of how words anchor the meanings of news photographs. [...] Gitlin 1980 goes so far as to deride television's reputation as a visual medium and instead concludes that television news is typically an 'illustrated lecture' controlled by the verbal narrative (1980, pp. 264–265). This is an egregious error, especially with respect to the study of television, which is an imagistic discourse driven by associative logic or what Barthes terms 'myth' (1972 [...]).

For decades, quantitative media research, whatever its weaknesses, has pointed to the dominance of images over words, the visual over the verbal.[1] Recently, Kathleen Jamieson (1994) and Justin Lewis (1991), working out of the traditions of rhetoric and cultural studies, respectively, have reconfirmed the primacy of images in televisual discourse. Their audience

Kevin DeLuca, from *Image Politics: The New Rhetoric of Environmental Activism*. New York: The Guilford Press, 1999, pp. 119–38. Reprinted by permission of The Guilford Press.

research studies are telling because both scholars, working out of traditions that value the word, were surprised by the power of images in the sense-making process of audiences.

[...]

Lewis's conclusions shed light on why hegemonic framing of the news often fails to lead to closure, why, in other words, the broadcasting of Earth First!'s image events is politically potent in spite of the framing. First, people forget almost everything they watch on the news (1991, pp. 124–5). [...]

Benjamin fruitfully suggests that distraction be considered a mode of perception: 'Reception in a state of distraction, which is increasing noticeably in all fields of art and is symptomatic of profound changes in apperception, finds in the film its true means of exercise' (1968, p. 240). Instead of being condemned as the negative of concentration, distraction is an appropriate form of attention in a culture operating at the speed of technology and immersed in fleeting images. Lewis suggests that this habit of distraction is further encouraged by the lack of classical narrative structure in television news.

*

The previous chapter offered a standard rhetorical criticism of the ABC News report on Earth First!. That criticism found that while there were some positive (or at least ambiguous) portrayals of Earth First! in the report, the preferred reading or dominant meaning worked to construct Earth First! as a terrorist organization that must be stopped by the forces of law and order. Further, this construction is typical of other representations of Earth First! in the national public sphere. Yet radical environmental groups and their causes remain popular. In the midst of a double-barrel corporate media atrocity drive[2] on many fronts (television, radio, newspapers, magazines) and a corporate and congressional legal assault in the name of progress and patriotism on environmentalists and environmental protection, most Americans (91%) believe that protecting the environment should be a top or important priority (Public Agenda, 1999). [...]

[...] [A] rhetorical reading of news coverage of radical environmental image events cued in to the insights of audience research will not dismiss environmental image events as quixotic assaults on an impervious corporate industrial system, but will instead read such image events as possibly appropriate and effective tactics in a heteroglossic public sphere.

*

An analysis of ABC's report on Earth First! in light of audience research leads to a radically different reading that points to the potential rhetorical force of the practice of image events. Following is such a possible reading.

Considering the dominance of images over words, the eye over the ear, the first step is to focus on images to the near exclusion of words. This radically alters our earlier reading of the news report, for in that analysis words were the driving force in the mutation of Earth First! from a bunch of civil disobedience protesters to a terrorist organization. Clearly, the reporter is using words to attempt to determine the meaning of the images. This is similar to Hall's argument regarding the use of words to determine the meaning of photographs. The distinction I want to make here is that, yes, news organizations attempt to construct a hegemonic frame through the strategic use of words to delimit possible interpretations of images, but this is only a strategy, and one whose efficacy is thrown into doubt by audience research.

Lewis's work suggests not only that we focus on images, but also that we concentrate on action images:

> The powerful moment in the news discourse is the portrayal of the "event" – or at least the part of the story audiences perceive as the event. Just as newspaper readers will skim the opening paragraphs for the main gist of the news story, so viewers will focus their attention upon its televisual equivalent. The equivalent moment, perhaps surprisingly, does not appear to be the anchor's introduction but the first main *action sequence* in the report. (1991, p. 149)

In the example of the ABC News story 'War in the Woods,' the first three action sequences [...] are of Earth First! activists performing image events: machine-chaining, tree-sitting, and road-blocking. The images are largely positive and are clearly of nonviolent civil disobedience. In addition, the voiceover (though of secondary importance) is simply descriptive and two of the protesters are allowed to explain what they are doing and why. In short, through the synecdochical tactic of image events, Earth First! is able to present itself and its causes in an extremely favorable light during powerful moments of the news story.

Also, importantly, the extended segment of the report devoted to constructing Earth First! as a terrorist organization is bereft of action images of Earth First!ers performing ecotage. Indeed, in all the action images throughout the report, the Earth First! protesters are non-violent and twice [...] they peacefully submit to being arrested. In fact, the only action sequence that hints at violence is when the one-armed logger (a victim of industrial violence) speeds toward a group of activists blocking a road and then gets out of his pickup and angrily confronts them.

If the audience is using these action sequences to make sense of Earth First!, what sort of sense are they likely to make? Since these action sequences are ahistoricized fragments, meaning will depend on associations made with larger social discourses, on the discourses to which viewers link these fragments. Clearly, the reporter attempts to associate Earth First! with terrorism, but it is an association based on inference and devoid of action images. Still, the proffered reading of Earth First! image events in the 'War in the Woods' places them in a context constructed by the discourses of terrorism and law and order. That this is a compelling link and context for the audience is doubtful.

Earth First! simply does not fit these discourses. These are powerful discourses that have been clearly defined. Terrorist acts involve bombings, mass destruction, and shattered bodies. Violations of law and order involve violent crimes: murder, assault, armed robbery, carjacking, kidnapping, and rape. Tree-sitting and burying oneself in a road do not make sense within these discourses. Indeed, the only likely victims are the 'perpetrators.' Similarly, ecotage, which is never shown, does not resonate with these discourses. It is difficult to equate putting a nail in a tree with blowing up the World Trade Center or a 747.

Of equal significance, Earth First! activists do not fit the most prevalent images of villains in either the discourses of terrorism or of law and order. Conventionally, terrorists are Middle Eastern Muslims. [...]

[...] Similarly, in law and order discourse the monsters to be exterminated are often African-American.

[...]

Another discursive context floated in the report is that of the economic discourse asserting that protecting the environment costs jobs – environment versus jobs. [...] [U]rban and suburban viewers are more likely to understand nature not as a source of money and work but as a place to spend money and leisure time. [...] Put in this context, the image of a protester buried in a road saying 'Defending what's left of the wilderness' makes sense as a courageous act. The protester is a hero, not a nutcase or someone costing people jobs. He is the defender not merely of wilderness but also of the values of a cultural formation.

The actions and images of Earth First! are easier to link to a discourse of social protest and civil disobedience that gained prominence and respect through the civil rights struggle and the anti-war protests of the 1960s and 1970s. The image events of the early action sequences in the report show Earth First!ers acting in the best tradition of civil disobedience. They are acting peacefully while putting themselves at great personal risk in the cause of interests that transcend narrow self-interests. Further, many of their looks are reminiscent of the student protesters against the Vietnam War.

The tradition of protest points to one final discourse that may affect how viewers make sense of 'War in the Woods.' Encapsulated discursively on bumper stickers as [...] a prevalent distrust of authority, of law and order, across the political spectrum that has manifested itself in a range of acts [...]. From the context of this discourse of distrusting authority, the arrests of Earth First! activists may be read as another example of excessive government repression (often for corporate interests at the expense of 'the people,' i.e., ordinary citizens). Why is the government arresting a bunch of hippies sitting in the woods (on public lands)?

Which one of these discourses does the audience use? The only thing that can be said with certainty is 'not just one.' Indeed, probably all these discourses and more come into play as people work to make sense of the image events. My purpose is not to provide the correct alternative reading but to open up the possibilities and provide an example of what it means to say that audiences (we) function in a heteroglossic public sphere composed of competing discourses. [...]

NOTES

1. Footnote removed.
2. Footnote removed.

WORKS CITED

Barthes, R. (1972) *Mythologies*. New York: Hill and Wang.

Benjamin, W. (1968) 'The Work of Art in the Age of Mechanical Reproduction', in H. Arendt (Ed.), *Illuminations* (pp. 217–252). New York: Schocken Books.

Gitlin, T. (1980) *The Whole World is Watching*. Berkeley and Los Angeles: University of California Press.

Hall, S. (1973) 'The determination of news photographs', in S. Cohen and J. Young (Eds.), *The Manufacture of News*. London: Constable.

Jamieson, K. H. (1994, September 28) 'Political Ads, the Press, and Lessons in Psychology', in *The Chronicle of Higher Education*, p. A56.

Lewis, J. (1991) *The Ideological Octopus: An Exploration of Television and Its Audience*. New York: Routledge.

Public Agenda Online (1999, May 25) 'Environment: People's chief concerns.' In www.publicagenda.org.issues

9: IMAGE AS THOUGHT

INTRODUCTION

Since Aristotle's claim that the soul never thinks without a mental image (1.7) there has been an ongoing dispute about the currency of consciousness or the medium of thought, in particular whether humans think in pictorial images or language. Stephen Kosslyn (1980) and Howard Gardner (1985) point out that on the basis of a philosophical tradition covered in Part One of this volume, the study of mental imagery was central to early, pre-behaviourist psychology. When the topic returned to the agenda as part of the cognitive revolution, the question was whether 'there were two separate and equally valid forms of representation' of thoughts in the mind, one pictorial and the other propositional (Gardner, 1985: 326). Kosslyn subsequently claimed to have resolved the imagery debates by presenting 'a theory of imagery piggybacked upon a theory of high level visual perception' (1996: 406). But his attempt to narrow images 'seen' in the mind's eye and regarded as the 'mother of all internal representations' down to a 'functional form' in some visual thought processes (1980: 455) has not stopped the debate about whether mental images are best thought of as representations or pictures – or whether any talk of images is really necessary (Rorty, 1980).

Ludwig Wittgenstein's early philosophy of language (9.1) nicely complicates the choice between thought as pictures or propositions by considering mental images as both. He famously later rejected his 'picture theory' of language when he realised that the depiction of reality is only one of many 'language games' or functions of language (Wittgenstein, 1958). According to W.J.T. Mitchell, he also wanted to correct the misreading of his 'pictures' as 'unmediated copies' of reality, rather than as 'artificial, conventional signs', 'very much like Peirce's icons' (5.2) that are 'not to be confused with graphic images in the narrow sense' (1986: 21, 26). On this account, thinking is an activity of working with verbal and pictorial signs.

Neuroscientist Antonio Damasio (9.2) proposes an ambitious theory that takes images in a broad sense to refer not only to interior representations of the exterior world but also to interior representations or maps of the state of the body in relation to the environment. '*Thought* is an acceptable word to denote such a flow of images … images are the currency of our minds' (Damasio, 1999: 318, 319). He seems to take us back to both Aristotle and Bergson (2.7). But for Kosslyn, the absence, acknowledged by Damasio, of 'a theory that specifies exactly how an image is represented and processed … allows one to postulate an image for *everything*' (1980: 452). According to a neuroscientist and philosopher pairing, M.R. Bennett and P.M.S. Hacker: 'Mental images … are a major source of conceptual confusion. For it is deeply tempting to conceive of mental images as species of the genus *image*' (2003: 181). They would not even allow mental images to be included in

W.J.T. Mitchell's family of images (13.1). No wonder that Gardner characterises mental imagery as among the most 'vexing issues' of cognitive science (1985: 339).

The selection from Damasio also introduces a key problem for contemporary neuroscience and the study of consciousness, namely, how physical, observable events in the embodied brain are also subjectively available for reflection. One of the ways in which cognitive scientists have tried to come to grips with mental imagery is by considering certain types of thought, such as memory. Marcel Proust (9.3) provides a wonderful literary example of a first-person reflection on a childhood memory as an extended image, that is, in Damasio's terms, sparked by a gustatory image charged with positive emotion. Proust's vivid verbal representation of both his childhood and the process of remembering bring to mind the verbal imagery and metaphoric language discussed by Nietzsche (2.6) and Ricoeur (8.2). Philosopher Michèle Le Doeuff (9.4) argues that such imagistic language is intrinsic and necessary to philosophy as a specialised way of thinking and writing. Her view contrasts sharply with the early Wittgenstein's complaint that colloquial 'language disguises the thought', giving rise to philosophical nonsense that can be eradicated by philosophy as 'the logical clarification of thoughts' (1922: §4.002, §4.112). That is the self-understanding of much analytical philosophy.

Gilles Deleuze (9.5) conceives of philosophy as a specialised practice of working with concepts that arise from other practices, such as cinema. In the first of his two-volume study on cinema, Deleuze focused on the nature of film as moving images, a medium that brought together 'movement, as physical reality in the external world, and the image, as psychic reality in consciousness', a combination that Bergson (2.7) had contemplated (1992: xiv). Following Peirce (5.2), Deleuze classified movement-images according to three forms, categorising time-images similarly in his second volume. Here Deleuze explores how certain post-war cinema responds to the disjuncture between situation and action, 'a shattering of the sensory-motor schema' (Deleuze, 1992: ix). Cinema not only implies the passage of time through movement, but 'almost allows us to *perceive* time' through different time-images (Aumont, 1997: 130). Rather than philosophy providing the logical concepts to think about cinema, the visual practice of cinema and philosophy are 'intercut' together into a new assemblage in which concepts, like sound and colour 'are the images of thought' (Deleuze, 1992: xi; see also Barthes (5.3) and Eisenstein (10.2)).

Walter Benjamin's (9.6) difficult notion of the dialectic image also concerns how a practice gives rise to different ways of thinking about time by means of an image, but his practice is writing in montage. Rather than leaving a method to emulate, Benjamin's unfinished *Arcades project* (1999) offers an inspiration for others to devise their own approach (Buck-Morss, 1989). He attempts to refashion the iconoclastic mode of Marxist historical materialism (see the introduction to Section 3, Ideology Critique) by presenting history as an image that juxtaposes past and present and in which the contradictions of capitalism, the simultaneity of progress and catastrophe, appear in a flash, like Proust's moment of awakening (9.3).

John Berger (9.7) holds, in contrast to Benjamin, that historical meaning makes sense of the capitalist present through narrative. His famous analysis of advertising images follows the model of ideology critique by exposing the 'false standard' of desire generated by what Benjamin called the 'phantasmagoria' of consumer images (Berger, 1972: 154; Benjamin, 1999: 8). Berger understands the significance of photographs for personal and especially family memories, proposing that such images can be invested with a critical consciousness that is not unlike Benjamin's notion. Berger considers each image to be 'man-made' in that it 'is a sight which has been recreated or reproduced, ... detached from the place and time in which it first made its appearance (1972: 9–10). To raise consciousness of a better future, he suggests that photographs should be attached to contexts that connect personal memories to social experiences, recent examples of which might be the work of W. G. Sebald (1998) and Stephen Poliakoff (2004).

REFERENCES

Aumont, J. (1997) *The Image*, tr. C. Pajackowska. London: British Film Institute.

Benjamin, W. (1999) *The Arcades Project*, tr. H. Eiland and K. McLaughlin. Cambridge, MA: Harvard University Press.

Bennett, M.R. and Hacker, P.M.S. (2003) *Philosophical Foundations of Neuroscience*. Oxford: Blackwell.

Berger, J. (1972) *Ways of Seeing*. London: Penguin.

Buck-Morss, S. (1989) *The Dialectics of Seeing: Walter Benjamin and the Arcades Project*. Cambridge, MA: MIT Press.

Damasio, A. (1999) *The Feeling of What Happens: Body, Emotion and the Making of Consciousness*. London: Heinemann.

Deleuze, G. (1992) *Cinema 1: The Movement-Image*, tr. H. Tomlinson and B. Habberjam. London: Athlone Press.

Gardner, H. (1985) *The Mind's New Science: A History of the Cognitive Revolution*. New York: Basic Books.

Kosslyn, S.M. (1980) *Image and Mind*. Cambridge, MA: Harvard University Press.

Kosslyn, S.M. (1996) *Image and Brain: The Resolution of the Imagery Debate*. Cambridge, MA: MIT Press.

Mitchell, W.J.T. (1986) *Iconology: Image, Text, Ideology*. Chicago: University of Chicago Press.

Poliakoff, S. (2004) *Shooting the Past* (DVD). London: BBC Worldwide Ltd.

Rorty, R. (1980) *Philosophy and the Mirror of Nature*. Oxford: Blackwell.

Sebald, W.G. (1998) *Rings of Saturn,* tr. M. Hulse. London: Harvill Press.

Wittgenstein, L. (1922) *Tractatus Logico-Philosophicus*, tr. C.K. Ogden. London: Routledge & Kegan Paul.

Wittgenstein, L. (1958) *Philosophical Investigations*, tr. G.E.M. Anscombe. New York: Macmillan.

PICTURE THEORY OF LANGUAGE
LUDWIG WITTGENSTEIN

9:1

1	The world is everything that is the case.
1.1	The world is the totality of facts, not of things.
[...]	
1.13	The facts in logical space are the world.
1.2	The world divides into facts.
[...]	
2.1	We make to ourselves pictures of facts.
2.11	The picture presents the facts in logical space, the existence and non-existence of atomic facts.
2.12	The picture is a model of reality.
[...]	
2.141	The picture is a fact.
[...]	
2.1511	Thus the picture is linked with reality; it reaches up to it.
2.1512	It is like a scale applied to reality.
[...]	
2. 16	In order to be a picture a fact must have some thing in common with what it pictures.
2.161	In the picture and the pictured there must be something identical in order that the one can be a picture of the other at all.
2.17	What the picture must have in common with reality in order to be able to represent it after its manner – rightly or falsely – is its form of representation.
[...]	
2.18	What every picture, of whatever form, must have in common with reality in order to be able to represent it at all – rightly or falsely – is the logical form, that is, the form of reality.
[...]	
2.19	The logical picture can depict the world.
[...]	
2.201	The picture depicts reality by representing a possibility of the existence and non-existence of atomic facts.
[...]	

Ludwig Wittgenstein, from *Tractatus Logico-Philosophicus, 1–4.06*. London: Routledge & Kegan Paul, 1922, pp. 29–49. Reproduced by permission.

2.21   The picture agrees with reality or not; it is right or wrong, true or false.

2.222   In the agreement or disagreement of its sense with reality, its truth or falsity consists.

2.223   In order to discover whether the picture is true or false we must compare it with reality.

[...]

3   The logical picture of the facts is the thought.

[...]

3.01   The totality of true thoughts is a picture of the world.

[...]

3.03   We cannot think anything unlogical, for otherwise we should have to think unlogically.

3.032   To present in language anything which 'contradicts logic' is [...] impossible [...].

3.1   In the proposition the thought is expressed perceptibly through the senses.

3.11   We use the sensibly perceptible sign (sound or written sign, etc.) of the proposition as a projection of the possible state of affairs [...].

3.12   The sign through which we express the thought I call the propositional sign [...].

3.14   [...] The propositional sign is a fact.

[...]

3.322   [...] the sign is arbitrary [...]

4   Thought is the significant proposition.

4.001   The totality of propositions is the language.

[...]

4.01   The proposition is a picture of reality.

        The proposition is a model of the reality as we think it is.

4.011   At the first glance the proposition – say as it stands printed on paper – does not seem to be a picture of the reality of which it treats. But nor does the musical score appear at first sight to be a picture of a musical piece; nor does our phonetic spelling (letters) seem to be a picture of our spoken language. And yet these symbolisms prove to be pictures – even in the ordinary sense of the word – of what they represent.

[...]

4.014   The gramophone record, the musical thought, the score, the waves of sound, all stand to one another in that pictorial internal relation, which holds between language and the world.

To all of them the logical structure is common.

[...]

4.015 The possibility of similes, of all the imagery of our language, rests on the logic of representation.

4.016 In order to understand the essence of the proposition, consider hieroglyphic writing, which pictures the facts it describes.

And from it came the alphabet without the essence of the representation being lost.

[...]

4.0312 The possibility of propositions is based upon the principle of the representation of objects by signs [...]

4.06 Propositions can be true or false only by being pictures of the reality.

BODY IMAGES 9:2
ANTONIO DAMASIO

[... In brief, my] theoretical account specifies the following:

- That the body (the body-proper) and the brain form an integrated organism and interact fully and mutually via chemical and neural pathways.
- That brain activity is aimed primarily at assisting with the regulation of the organism's life processes both by coordinating internal body-proper operations, and by coordinating the interactions between the organism as a whole and the physical and social aspects of the environment.
- That brain activity is aimed primarily at survival with well-being; a brain equipped for such a primary aim can engage in anything else secondarily from writing poetry to designing spaceships.
- That in complex organisms such as ours, the brain's regulatory operations depend on the creation and manipulation of mental images (ideas or thoughts) in the process we call mind.
- That the ability to perceive objects and events, external to the organism or internal to it, requires images. Examples of images related to the exterior include visual, auditory, tactile, olfactory, and gustatory images. Pain and nausea are examples of images of the interior. The execution of both automatic and deliberated responses requires images. The anticipation and planning of future responses also require images.
- That the critical interface between body-proper activities and the mental patterns we call images consists of specific brain regions employing

From *Looking for Spinoza* by Antonio Damasio. London: Harvill Press, 2003, pp. 194–8. Reprinted by permission of The Random House Group Ltd.

circuits of neurons to construct continual, dynamic neural patterns corresponding to different activities in the body – in effect, mapping those activities as they occur.

- That the mapping is not necessarily a passive process. The structures in which the maps are formed have their own say on the mapping and are influenced by other brain structures.

Because the mind arises in a brain that is integral to the organism, the mind is part of that well-woven apparatus. In other words, body, brain, and mind are manifestations of a single organism. Although we can dissect them under the microscope for scientific purposes, they are in effect inseparable under normal operating circumstances.

*

From my perspective the brain produces two kinds of images of the body. The first I call *images from the flesh*. It comprises images of the body's interior, drawn, for example, from the sketchy neural patterns that map the structure and state of viscera such as the heart, the gut, and the muscles, along with the state of numerous chemical parameters in the organism's interior.

The second kind of body image concerns particular parts of the body, such as the retina in the back of the eye and the cochlea in the inner ear. I call these *images from special sensory probes*. They are images based on the state of activity in those particular body parts when they are modified by objects that physically impinge upon those devices from outside the body. That physical impingement takes many forms. In the case of the retina and cochlea, respectively, the objects perturb the patterns of light and sound waves, and the altered pattern is captured in the sensory devices. In the case of touch, the actual mechanical contact of an object against the body boundary will change the activity of nerve endings distributed in the boundary itself – the skin. Shape and texture images are derivatives of this process.

The range of body changes that can be mapped in the brain is very wide. It includes the microscopic changes that occur at the level of chemical and electrical phenomena (for example, in the specialized cells of the retina that respond to patterns of photons carried in light rays). It also includes macroscopic changes that can be seen by the naked eye (a limb moving) or sensed at the tip of a finger (a bump in the skin).

In either body image, from the flesh or from the special sensory probes, the mechanism of production is the same. First, the activity in body structures results in momentary structural body changes. Second, the brain constructs maps of those body changes in a number of appropriate regions with the help of chemical signals conveyed in the bloodstream, and electrochemical signals conveyed in nerve pathways. Finally, the neural maps become mental images.

In the first kind of body images, the images from the flesh, the changes occur all over our interior landscape and are signaled to the body-sensing regions of the central nervous system by chemical molecules and nerve activity. In the second kind of body image, the images from special sensory probes, the changes occur within highly specialized body parts such as the retina. The resulting signals are relayed by neuronal connections to regions dedicated to mapping the state of that specialized body receptor. The regions are made of collections of neurons whose state of activity or inactivity forms a pattern that can be conceived as a map or representation of whatever event caused the activity to occur at a given time in a certain group of neurons and not in another. In the case of the retina, for example, those vision-related structures include the geniculate nucleus (part of the thalamus), the superior colliculus (part of the brain stem), and the visual cortices (part of the cerebral hemispheres). The list of specialized parts of the body includes: the cochlea in the inner ear (related to sound); the semicircular canals of the vestibule, also within the inner ear, where the vestibular nerve begins (the vestibule is related to the mapping of the body's position in space; our sense of balance depends on it): the olfactory nerve endings in the nasal mucosae (for the sense of smell); the gustatory papillae in the back of the tongue (for taste); and the nerve endings distributed in the superficial layers of the skin (for touch).

I believe that the foundational images in the stream of mind are images of some kind of body event, whether the event happens in the depth of the body or in some specialized sensory device near its periphery. The basis for those foundational images is a collection of brain maps, that is, a collection of patterns of neuron activity and inactivity (neural patterns, for short) in a variety of sensory regions. Those brain maps represent, comprehensively, the structure and state of the body at any given time. Some maps relate to the world within, the organism's interior. Other maps relate to the world outside, the physical world of objects that interact with the organism at specific regions of its shell. In either case, what ends up being mapped in the sensory regions of the brain and what emerges in the mind, in the form of an idea, corresponds to some structure of the body, in a particular state and set of circumstances.[1]

*

It is important that I qualify these statements, especially the last. There is a major gap in our current understanding of how neural patterns become mental images. The presence in the brain of dynamic neural patterns (or maps) related to an object or event is a *necessary* but not sufficient basis to explain the mental images of the said object or event. We can describe neural patterns – with the tools of neuroanatomy, neurophysiology, and neurochemistry – and we can describe images with the tools of introspection. How we get from the former to the latter is known only in part, although the current ignorance neither contradicts the assumption that images are biological processes nor denies their physicality. Many recent studies on the neurobiology of consciousness address this issue. Most consciousness studies are actually centered on this issue of the making of the mind, the part of the consciousness puzzle that consists of having the brain make images that are synchronized and edited into what I have called the 'movie-in-the-brain.' But those studies do not provide an answer to the puzzle yet, and I wish to make clear that I am not providing an answer either. [...] At the level of systems, I can explain the process up to the organization of neural patterns on the basis of which mental images will arise. But I fall short of suggesting, let alone explaining, how the last steps of the image-making process are carried out.[2]

NOTES
1. Footnote removed.
2. Footnote removed.

9:3 INVOLUNTARY MEMORY
MARCEL PROUST

For many years already, everything about Combray that was not the theatre and drama of my bedtime had ceased to exist for me, when one day in winter, as I came home, my mother, seeing that I was cold, suggested that, contrary to my habit, I have a little tea. I refused at first and then, I do not know why, changed my mind. She sent for one of those squat, plump cakes called *petites madeleines* that look as though they have been moulded in the grooved valve of a scallop-shell. And soon, mechanically, oppressed by the gloomy day and the prospect of a sad future, I carried to my lips a spoonful of the tea in which I had let soften a piece of madeleine. But at the very instant when the mouthful of tea mixed with cake-crumbs touched my palate, I quivered, attentive to the extraordinary thing that was happening in me. A delicious pleasure had invaded me, isolated me, without my having any notion as to its cause. It had immediately made the vicissitudes of life unimportant to me, its disasters innocuous, its brevity illusory, acting in the same way that love acts, by filling me with a precious essence: or rather this essence was not in me, it was me. I had ceased to feel I was mediocre, contingent, mortal. Where could it have come to me from – this powerful joy? I sensed that it was connected to the taste of the tea and the cake, but that it went infinitely far beyond it, could not be of the same nature. Where did it come from? What did it mean? How could I grasp it? I drink a second mouthful, in which I find nothing more than in the first, a third that gives me a little less than the second. It is time for me to stop, the virtue of the drink seems to be diminishing. It is clear that the truth I am seeking is not in the drink, but in me. The drink has awoken it in me, but does not know that truth, and cannot do more than repeat indefinitely, with less and less force, this same testimony which I do not know how to interpret and which I want at least to be able to

From *In Search of Lost Time: Volume I: The Way By Swann's* by Marcel Proust, translated with an Introduction and Notes by Lydia Davis. (London: Allen Lane, The Penguin Press, 2002). Translation and editorial matter copyright © Lydia Davis, 2002.

ask of it again and find again, intact, available to me, soon, for a decisive clarification. I put down the cup and turn to my mind. It is up to my mind to find the truth. But how? What grave uncertainty, whenever the mind feels overtaken by itself; when it, the seeker, is also the obscure country where it must seek and where all its baggage will be nothing to it. Seek? Not only that: create. It is face to face with something that does not yet exist and that only it can accomplish, then bring into its light.

And I begin asking myself again what it could be, this unknown state which brought with it no logical proof, but only the evidence of its felicity, its reality, and in whose presence the other states of consciousness faded away. I want to try to make it reappear. I go back in my thoughts to the moment when I took the first spoonful of tea. I find the same state, without any new clarity. I ask my mind to make another effort, to bring back once more the sensation that is slipping away. And, so that nothing may break the thrust with which it will try to grasp it again, I remove every obstacle, every foreign idea, I protect my ears and my attention from the noises in the next room. But feeling my mind grow tired without succeeding, I now force it to accept the very distraction I was denying it, to think of something else, to recuperate before a supreme attempt. Then for a second time I create an empty space before it, I confront it again with the still recent taste of that first mouthful and I feel something quiver in me, shift, try to rise, something that seems to have been unanchored at a great depth; I do not know what it is, but it comes up slowly; I feel the resistance and I hear the murmur of the distances traversed.

Undoubtedly what is fluttering this way deep inside me must be the image, the visual memory which is attached to this taste and is trying to follow it to me. But it is struggling too far away, too confusedly; I can just barely perceive the neutral glimmer in which is blended the elusive eddying of stirred-up colours; but I cannot distinguish the form, cannot ask it, as the one possible interpreter, to translate for me the evidence of its contemporary, its inseparable companion, the taste, ask it to tell me what particular circumstance is involved, what period of the past.

Will it reach the surface of my limpid consciousness – this memory, this old moment which the attraction of an identical moment has come so far to summon, to move, to raise up from my very depths? I don't know. Now I no longer feel anything, it has stopped, gone back down perhaps; who knows if it will ever rise up from its darkness again? Ten times I must begin again, lean down towards it. And each time, the timidity that deters us from every difficult task, from every important piece of work, has counselled me to leave it, to drink my tea and think only about my worries of today, my desires for tomorrow, which may be pondered painlessly.

And suddenly the memory appeared. That taste was the taste of the little piece of madeleine which on Sunday mornings at Combray (because that day I did not go out before it was time for Mass), when I went to say good morning to her in her bedroom, my Aunt Léonie would give me after dipping it in her infusion of tea or lime-blossom. The sight of the little madeleine had not recalled anything to me before I tasted it; perhaps because I had often seen them since, without eating them, on the pastry-cooks' shelves, and their image had therefore left those days of Combray and attached itself to others more recent; perhaps because, of these recollections abandoned so long outside my memory, nothing survived, everything had come apart; the forms and the form, too, of the little shell made of cake, so fatly sensual within its severe and pious pleating – had been destroyed, or, still half asleep, had lost the force of expansion that would have allowed them to rejoin my consciousness. But, when nothing subsists of an old past, after the death of people, after the destruction of things, alone, frailer but more enduring, more immaterial, more persistent, more faithful, smell and taste still remain for a long time, like souls, remembering, waiting, hoping, on the ruin of all the rest, bearing without giving way, on their almost impalpable droplet, the immense edifice of memory.

And as soon as I had recognized the taste of the piece of madeleine dipped in lime-blossom tea that my aunt used to give me (though I did not yet know and had to put off to much later discovering why this memory made me so happy), immediately, the old grey house on the street, where her bedroom was, came like a stage-set to attach itself to the little wing opening on to the garden that had been built for my parents behind it (that truncated section which was all I had seen before then); and with the house the town, from morning to night and in all weathers, the Square, where they sent me before lunch, the streets where I went to do errands, the paths we took if the weather was fine. And as in that game in which the Japanese amuse themselves by filling a porcelain bowl with water and steeping in it little pieces of paper until then indistinct, which, the moment they are immersed in it, stretch and shape themselves, colour and differentiate, become flowers, houses, human figures, firm and recognizable, so now all the flowers in our garden and in M. Swann's park, and the water-lilies on the Vivonne, and the good people of the village and their little dwellings and the church and all of Combray and its surroundings, all of this which is assuming form and substance, emerged, town and gardens alike, from my cup of tea.

9:4 THE PHILOSOPHICAL IMAGINARY
MICHÈLE LE DOEUFF

Whether one looks for a characterization of philosophical discourse to Plato, to Hegel or to Bréhier, one always meets with a reference to the rational, the concept, the argued, the logical, the abstract. Even when a certain coyness leads some authorities to pretend that they do not know what philosophy is, no agnosticism remains about what philosophy is not. Philosophy is not a story, not a pictorial description, not a work of pure

Michèle Le Doeuff, from *The Philosophical Imaginary*, tr. Colin Gordon. London: Athlone Press, 1989, pp. 1–19. Reprinted by permission of The Continuum International Publishing Group and Stanford University Press.

Plate 1 (Figure 5.3)

Plate 2 (Figure 11.1)

Plate 3 (Figure 12.4)

Plate 4 (Figure 11.2)

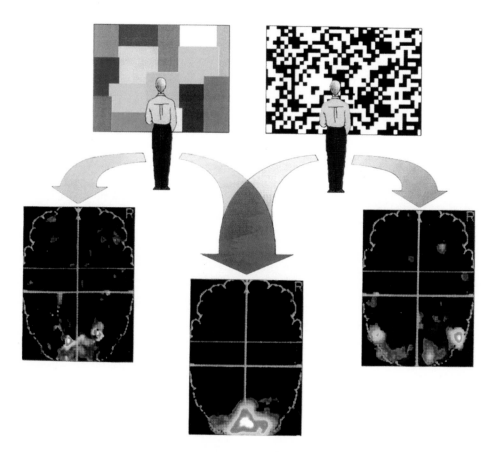

Plate 5 (Figure 12.5)

literature. Philosophical discourse is inscribed and declares its status as philosophy through a break with myth, fable, the poetic, the domain of the image. Hegel says, in effect, that the form of thought is the sole form of philosophy, after first remarking that 'opposition and struggle between philosophy and so-called popular notions conveyed through mythology is an old phenomenon.'[1] It is, indeed, a very old commonplace to associate philosophy with a certain *logos* thought of as defining itself through opposition to other types of discourse.

If, however, one goes looking for this philosophy in the texts which are meant to embody it, the least that can be said is that it is not to be found there in a pure state. We shall also find statues that breathe the scent of roses, comedies, tragedies, architects, foundations, dwellings, doors and windows, sand, navigators, various musical instruments, islands, clocks, horses, donkeys and even a lion, representatives of every craft and trade, scenes of sea and storm, forests and trees: in short, a whole pictorial world sufficient to decorate even the dryest 'History of Philosophy'.

But only to decorate, nothing more. If someone set out to write a history of philosophical imagery, would such a study ever be as much an accepted part of the historiography of philosophy as histories of philosophical concepts, procedures or systems? If one further argued that existing histories of philosophy are at the very least incomplete, not to say mutilating, in that they never present us with any individual philosopher's image-album, would such a reproach be deemed worthy of serious consideration? The images that appear in theoretical texts are normally viewed as extrinsic to the theoretical work, so that to interest oneself in them seems like a merely anecdotal approach to philosophy.

[...] Philosophy has always arrogated to itself the right or task of speaking about itself, or having a discourse about its own discourse and its (legitimate or other) modes, writing a commentary on its own texts.[2] This metadiscourse regularly affirms the non-philosophical character of thought in images. But this attempted exclusion always fails, for 'in fact, Socrates talks about laden asses, blacksmiths, cobblers, tanners.'[3] Various strategies have been pursued to exorcize this inner scandal. One of them consists in projecting the shameful side of philosophy on to an Other. This denegation (in which the writing subject disavows what he himself writes) is simple in its mechanism and variable in its forms. In rough terms one can say that the occurrence of a discourse in images can be despatched either upstream or downstream.

The upstream hypothesis is the resurgence of a primitive soul, of archaic or infantile thought, of an uneducated or ineducable part of the mind. Paradigms of this projected Other are the child (in that we have all been one, before becoming ... a man!), nursery stories, the people (irrational by nature), old wives' tales, folklore, etc. As Couturat puts it,[4] we rock the child who is still within us, even in the philosopher; and as this child is none other than the irrational part of the soul which Plato compares to the common crowd, myths will always serve 'to enchant what there is of the common people in us'. [...]

In the downstream variant of the idea, recourse (here termed didactic or pedagogic) to imagery is seen more in terms of an adaptation to the intended recipient of a discourse. Imagery speaks directly, with intuitive clarity, to a destined interlocutor who is still uncultivated by concepts and ignorant of philosophy, or at any rate of this philosophy. The image is a gangway, a mediation between two theoretical situations: the speaker's and the recipient's.

Here then are two possible *alibis,* two in fact diametrically opposite conceptions of the meaning within theoretical texts of thought in images, which nevertheless lead to the same result. Either one maximizes the image's heterogeneity [...] or one absorbs the image completely into the conceptualized problematic, its meaning being considered as congruent with the theoretical results which it simply translates or illustrates. A dross coming from elsewhere, or a duplicate, serviceable to the reader's deficient culture yet dispensable, if philosophers were left free to speak only to other philosophers! In each case there is a common failure of recognition: whether the image is seen as radically heterogeneous to, or completely isomorphous with, the corpus of concepts it translates into the Other's language, the status of an element within philosophical work is denied it. It is not part of the enterprise. [. . .]

*

Let us stress once more that imagery and knowledge form, dialectically, a common system. Between these two terms there is a play of feedbacks which maintains the particular regime of the discursive formation. Philosophical texts offer images through which subjectivity can be structured and given a marking which is that of the corporate body. In turn, the affectivity which is thus moulded sustains the effort of philosophic production and the system of presuppositions which govern the distinction between the thinkable and the unthinkable for a consciousness attached to settled loves. But since the relationship between the content of these two modes of writing is always marked by negativity, there can be no question of reducing one term to the other. Philosophical work is not the mechanical prolongation of fantasy – nor vice versa. [...] The idea of a dialectical solidarity between reverie and theoretical work must, in my view, necessarily lead to a study of the particularism of a social minority and its problematic encounter with other thought and other discourses – and also to an appreciation of the tension between what one would like to believe, what it is necessary to think and what it is possible to give logical form. There is no closure of discourse, discourse only ever being a compromise – or bricolage – between what it is legitimate to say, what one would like to contend or argue, and what one is forced to recognize.

[...]

NOTES

1. Hegel, *Lectures on the Philosophy of History*, Introduction.
2. Footnote removed.
3. Plato, *Symposium* 221e.
4. *Revue de Métaphysique et de Morale*, July 1896, Supplement, p. 16.

THOUGHT AND CINEMA:
THE TIME-IMAGE
GILLES DELEUZE

9:5

Over several centuries, from the Greeks to Kant, a revolution took place in philosophy; the subordination of time to movement was reversed, time ceases to be the measurement of normal movement, it increasingly appears for itself and created paradoxical movements. Time is out of joint: Hamlet's words signify that time is no longer subordinated to movement, but rather movement to time. It could be said that, in its own sphere, cinema has repeated the same experience, the same reversal, in more fast-moving circumstances. The movement-image of the so-called classical cinema gave way, in the post war period, to a direct time-image. Such a general idea must of course be qualified, corrected, adapted to concrete examples.

Why is the Second World War taken as a break? The fact is that, in Europe, the post-war period has greatly increased the situations which we no longer know how to react to, in spaces which we no longer know how to describe. These were 'any spaces whatever', deserted but inhabited, disused warehouses, waste ground, cities in the course of demolition or reconstruction. And in these any-spaces-whatever a new race of characters was stirring, kind of mutant: they saw rather than acted, they were seers. Hence Rosselini's great trio, *Europe 51*, *Stromboli*, *Germany Year 0*: a child in the destroyed city, a foreign woman on the island, a bourgeois woman who starts to 'see' what is around her. Situations would be extremes, or, on the contrary, those of everyday banality, or both at once: what tends to collapse, or at least lose its position, is the sensory-motor schema which constituted the action-image of the old cinema. And thanks to this loosening of the sensory-motor linkage, it is time, 'a little time in the pure state', which rises up to the surface of the screen. Time ceases to be derived from the movement, it appears in itself and itself gives rise to *false movements*. Hence the importance of *false continuity* in modern cinema: the images are no longer linked by rational cuts and continuity, but are relinked by means of false continuity and irrational cuts. Even the body is no longer exactly what moves; subject of movement or the instrument of action, it becomes rather the developer [*révélateur*] of time, it shows time through its tiredness and waitings (Antonioni).

It is not quite right to say that the cinematographic image is in the present. What is in the present is what the image 'represents', but not the image itself, which, in cinema as in painting, is never to be confused with what it represents. The image itself is the system of the relationships between its

Cinema 2: The Time-Image, by Gilles Deleuze, tr. Hugh Tomlinson and Robert Galeta. London: Athlone Press, 1989, pp. xi–xiii, 276–80. Translation © The Athlone Press, 1989. Originally published in France as *Cinema 2, l'Image-Temps* © Les Editions de Minuit, 1985. Reprinted by permission of The Continuum International Publishing Group and The University of Minnesota Press.

elements, that is, a set of relationships of time from which the variable present only flows. It is in this sense, I think, that Tarkovsky challenges the distinction between montage and shot when he defines cinema by the 'pressure of time' in the shot. What is specific to the image, as soon as it is creative, is to make perceptible, to make visible, relationships of time which cannot be seen in the represented object and do not allow themselves to be reduced to the present. Take, for example, a depth of field in Welles, a tracking shot in Visconti: we are plunged into time rather than crossing space. Sandra's car, at the beginning of Visconti's film,[1] is already moving in time, and Welles's characters occupy a giant-sized place in time rather than changing place in space.

This is to say that the time-image has nothing to with a flashback, or even with a recollection. Recollection is only a former present, whilst the characters who have lost their memories in modern cinema literally sink back into the past, or emerge from it, to make visible what is concealed even from recollection. Flashback is only a signpost, and, when it is used by great authors, it is there only to show much more complex temporal structures (for example, in Mankiewicz, 'forking' time: recapturing the moment when time could have taken a different course ...) In any case, what we call temporal structure, or direct time-image, clearly goes beyond the purely empirical succession of time – past-present-future. It is, for example, a coexistence of distinct durations, or of levels of duration; a single event can belong to several levels: the sheets of past coexist in a non-chronological order. We see this in Welles with his powerful intuition of the earth, then in Resnais with his characters who return from the land of the dead.

There are yet more temporal structures: [my ...] whole aim ... is to release those that the cinematographic image has been able to grasp and reveal, and which can echo the teachings of science, what the other arts can uncover for us, or what philosophy makes understandable for us, each in their respective ways. It is foolish to talk about the death of cinema because cinema is still at the beginning of its investigations: making visible these relationships of time which can only appear in a creation of the image. It is not cinema which needs television – whose image remains so regrettably in the present unless it is enriched by the art of cinema. The relations and disjunctions between visual and sound, between what is seen and what is said, revitalize the problem and endow cinema with new powers for capturing time in the image. [...]

*

The so-called classical image had to be considered on two axes. These two axes were the co-ordinates of the brain: on the one hand, the images were linked or extended according to laws of association, of continuity, resemblance, contrast, or opposition; on the other hand, associated images were internalized in a whole as concept (integration), which was in turn continually externalized in associable or extendable images (differentiation). This is why the whole remained open and changing, at the same time as a set of images was always taken from a larger set. This was the double aspect of the movement-image, defining the out-of-field: in the first place it was in touch with an exterior, in the second place it expressed a whole which changes. Movement in its extension was the immediate given, and the whole which changes, that is, time, was indirect or mediate representation. But there was a continual circulation of the two here, internalization in the whole, externalization in the image, circle or spiral which constituted for cinema, no less than for philosophy, the model of the True as totalization. This model inspired the noosigns of the classical image, and there were necessarily two kinds of noosign.[2] In the first kind, the images were linked by rational cuts, and formed under this condition an extendable world; between two images or sequences of images, the limit as interval is included as the end of the one *or* as the beginning of the other, as the last image of the first sequence or as the first of the second. The other kind of noosign marked the integration of the sequences into a whole (self-awareness as the internal representation), but also the differentiation of the whole into extended sequences (belief in the external world). And, from one to the other, the whole was constantly changing at the same time as the images were moving. Time as measure of movement thus ensured a general system of commensurability, in this double form of the interval and the whole. This was the splendour of the classical image.

The modern image initiates the reign of 'incommensurables' or irrational cuts: this is to say that the cut no longer forms part of one or the other image, of one or the other sequence that it separates and divided. It is on this condition that the succession or sequence becomes a series [...] The interval is set free, the interstice becomes irreducible and stands on its own. The first consequence is that images are no longer linked by rational cuts, but are relinked on to irrational cuts. [...] By relinkage must be understood, not a second linkage which would come and add itself on, but a mode of original and specific linkage, or rather a specific connection between the de-linked images. There are no longer grounds for talking about a real or possible extension capable of constituting an external world: we have ceased to believe in it, and the image is cut off from the external world. But the internalization or integration of self-awareness in a whole has no less disappeared: the relinkage takes place through a parcelling, whether it is a matter of the construction of series in Godard, or of the transformation of sheets in Resnais (relinked parcelings). This is why thought, as power which has not always existed, is born from an outside more distant than any external world, and, as power which does not yet exist, confronts an inside, an unthinkable or unthought, deeper than any internal world. In the second place, there is no longer any movement of internalization or externalization, integration or differentiation, but a confrontation of an outside and an inside independent of distance, this thought outside itself and this un-thought within thought. [...] The brain has lost its Euclidean co-ordinates, and now emits other signs. The direct time-image effectively has as noosigns the irrational cut between non-linked (but always relinked) images, and the absolute contact between non-totalizable, asymmetrical outside and inside. We move with ease from one to the other, because the outside and the inside are the two sides of the limit as irrational cut, and because the latter, no longer forming part of any sequence, itself appears as an autonomous outside which necessarily provides itself with an inside.

The limit or interstice, the irrational cut, pass especially between the visual image and the sound image. This implies several novelties or changes. The sound must itself become image instead of being a component of the visual image; the creation of a sound framing is thus necessary, so that the cut passes between the two framings, sound and visual; hence even if the out-of-field survives in fact [en fait], it must lose all power by right [de droit] because the visual image ceases to extend beyond its own frame, in order to enter into a specific relation with the sound image which is itself framed (the interstice between the two framings replaces the out-of-field); the voice-off must also disappear, because there is no more out-of-field to inhabit, but two heautonomous[3] images to be confronted, that of voices and those of views, each in itself, each for itself and in its frame. [...] And yet there is a relation between them, a free indirect or incommensurable relation, for incommensurability denotes a new relation not an absence. [...] This will be the contact independent of distance, between an outside where the speech-act rises, and an inside where the event is buried in the ground; a complementarity of the sound image, the speech-act as creative story-telling, and the visual image, stratigraphic or archaeological burying. And the irrational cut between the two, which forms the non-totalizable relation, the broken ring of their junction, the asymmetrical faces of their contact. This is a perpetual relinkage. Speech reaches its own limit which separates it from the visual; but the visual reaches its own limit which separates it from sound. [...] These new signs are lectosigns,[4] which show the final aspect of the direct time-image, the common limit: the visual image become stratigraphic is for its part all the more readable in that the speech-act becomes an autonomous creator. [...] From classical to modern cinema, from the movement-image to the time-image, what changes are not only the chronosigns,[5] but the noosigns and lectosigns, having said that it is always possible to multiply the passages from one regime to the other, just as to accentuate their irreducible differences.

[...] For many people, philosophy is something which is not 'made', but is pre-existent, ready-made in a prefabricated sky. However, philosophical theory is itself a practice, just as much as its object. It is no more abstract than its object. It is a practice of concepts, and it must be judged in the light of the other practices with which it interferes. A theory of cinema is not 'about' cinema, but about the concepts that cinema gives rise to and which are themselves related to other concepts corresponding to other practices, the practice of concepts in general having no privilege over others, any more than one object has over others. It is at the level of the interference of many practices that things happen, beings, images, concepts, all kinds of events. The theory of cinema does not bear on the cinema, but on the concepts of cinema, which are no less practical, effective or existent than cinema itself. The great cinema authors are like the great painters or musicians: it is they who talk best about what they do. But, in talking, they become something else, they become philosophers or theoreticians – even Hawks who wanted no theories, even Godard when he pretends to distrust them. Cinema's concepts are not given in cinema. And yet they are cinema's concepts, not theories about cinema. So there is always a time, midday–midnight, when we must no longer ask ourselves: 'What is cinema?' but 'What is philosophy?' Cinema itself is a new practice of images and signs, whose theory philosophy must produce as conceptual practice. For no technical determination, whether applied (psychoanalysis, linguistics) or reflexive, is sufficient to constitute the concepts of cinema itself.

NOTES

1. Editors' Note: Deleuze refers to *Sandra of a Thousand Delights* (1965).
2. [From the translators' glossary:] NOOSIGN: an image which goes beyond itself towards something which can only be thought.
3. Editors' Note: Heautonomy, a term used by Kant, means disjunctive synthesis, or the paradoxical conjoining of actively differentiating elements into a transformational synthetic whole.
4. [From the translators' glossary:] LECTOSIGN: a visual image which must be 'read' as much as seen.
5. [From the translators' glossary:] CHRONOSIGN (point and sheet): an image where time ceases to be subordinate to movement and appears for itself.

THE DIALECTICAL IMAGE
WALTER BENJAMIN

9:6

Mein Flügel ist zum Schwung bereit,
Ich kehrte gern zurück,
Denn bleib ich auch lebendige Zeit,
Ich hätte wenig Glück.
– Gerhard Scholem,
'Gruss vom Angelus'

A Klee painting named 'Angelus Novus' shows an angel looking as though he is about to move away from something he is fixedly contemplating. His eyes are staring, his mouth is open, his wings are spread. This is how one pictures the angel of history. His face is turned towards the past. Where we

Opening paragraph from 'Theses on the Philosophy of History', no. IX in *Illuminations*. New York: Schocken Books, 1968. The remainder from *The Arcades Project*, convolute 'N', 'The Theory of Knowledge, Theory of Progress', trans. Howard Eiland and Kevin McLaughlin, pp. 456, 461, 462–3, 464, 476, Cambridge, MA: Belknap Press of Harvard University Press, © 1999 by the President and Fellows of Harvard College.

perceive a chain of events, he sees one single catastrophe which keeps piling wreckage upon wreckage and hurls it in front of his feet. The angel would like to stay, awaken the dead, and make whole what has been smashed. But a storm is blowing from Paradise; it has got caught in his wings with such violence that the angel can no longer close them. This storm irresistibly propels him into the future to which his back is turned, while the pile of debris before him grows skyward. This storm is what we call progress.

*

In the fields with which we are concerned, knowledge comes only in lightning flashes. The text is the long roll of thunder that follows.

[N1,1]

*

A central problem of historical materialism that ought to be seen in the end: Must the Marxist understanding of history necessarily be acquired at the expense of the perceptibility of history? Or: in what way is it possible to cojoin a heightened graphicness <Anschaulichkeit> to the realization of the Marxist method? The first stage in this undertaking will be to carry over the principle of montage into history. That is, to assemble large-scale constructions out of the smallest and precisely cut components. Indeed, to discover in the analysis of the small, individual moment the crystal of the total event. And, therefore, to break with vulgar historical materialism. To grasp the construction of history as such. In the structure of the commentary. [] Refuse of history []

[N2,6]

*

It's not that what is past casts its light on what is present, or what is present its light on what is past; rather, image is that wherein what has been comes together in a flash with the now to form a constellation. In other words, image is dialectics at a standstill. For while the relation of the present to the past is a purely temporal, continuous one, the relation of what-has-been to the now is dialectical: is not progression but image, suddenly emergent. – Only dialectical images are genuine images (that is, not archaic); and the place where one encounters them is language. [] Awakening []

[N2a,3]

What distinguishes images from the "essences" of phenomenology is their historical index. (Heidegger seeks in vain to rescue history for phenomenology abstractly through "historicity.") These images are to be thought of entirely apart from the categories of the "human sciences", from so-called habitus, from style, and the like. For the historical index of the images not only says that they belong to a particular time; it says, above all, that they attain to legibility only at a particular time. And, indeed, this acceding "to legibility" constitutes a specific critical point in the movement at their interior. Every present day is determined by the images that are synchronic with it: each "now" is the now of a particular recognizability. In it, truth is charged to the bursting point with time. (This point of explosion, and nothing else, is the death of the *intentio*, which thus coincides with the birth of authentic historical time, the time of truth.) It is not that what is past casts its light on what is present, or what is present its light on what is past; rather, image is that wherein what has been comes together in a flash with the now to form a constellation. In other words: image is dialectics at a standstill. For while the relation of the present to the past is purely temporal, the relation of what-has-been to the now is dialectical: not temporal in nature but figural <*bildlich*>. Only dialectical images are genuinely historical - that is, not archaic images. The image that is read – which is to say, the image in the now of its recognizability – bears to the highest degree the imprint of the perilous critical moment on which all reading is founded.

[N3,1]

*

Is awakening perhaps the synthesis of dream consciousness (as thesis) and waking consciousness (as antithesis)? Then the moment of awakening would be identical with the "now of recognizability," in which things put on their true – surrealist – face. Thus, in Proust, the importance of staking an entire life on life's supremely dialectical point of rupture: awakening. Proust begins with an evocation of the space of someone waking up.

[N3a,3]

In the dialectical image, what has been within a particular epoch is always, simultaneously, "what has been from time immemorial." As such, however, it is manifest, on each occasion, only to a quite specific epoch – namely, the one in which humanity, rubbing its eyes, recognizes just this particular dream image as such. It is at this moment that the historian takes up, with regard to that image, the task of dream interpretation.

[N4,1]

*

To thinking belongs the movement as well as the arrest of thoughts. Where thinking comes to a standstill in a constellation saturated with tensions – there the dialectical image appears. It is the caesura in the movement of thought. Its position is naturally not an arbitrary one. It is to be found, in a word, where the tension between dialectical opposites is greatest. Hence, the object constructed in the materialist presentation of history is itself the dialectical image. The latter is identical with the historical object; it justifies its violent expulsion from the continuum of historical process.

[N10a,3]

*

[...] History decays into images, not into stories [...]

[N 11, 4]

*

9:7 WAYS OF REMEMBERING
JOHN BERGER

[T]here are two distinct uses of photography: the private and the public. The private, that is to say the photographs one has of the people one loves, one's friends, the class one was in at school, etc.; in private use a photograph is read in a context which is still continuous with that from which it was taken. Take a photograph of your Mother. There's still that prising away of an instant. But there remains a continuity between you and your experience and your Mother. The private context creates a continuity which is parallel to the continuity from which the photograph was originally taken.

Private photographs are nearly always of something which you have known. By contrast public photographs are usually images of the unknown or, at best, they are images of things which are known only through other photographs. The public photograph has been severed from life when it was taken, and it remains, as an isolated image, separate from your experience. The public photograph is like the memory of a total stranger, a total stranger who has shouted 'Look' at the event recorded.

There is something about every photograph which is intimate. It's bound to be so because it goes in, it isolates and it frames. You are always in a situation of intimacy towards what has been photographed. That is another reason why I talk about memory. At the same time because the public photograph is divorced from all first-hand experience, it represents the memory of a total stranger. Who is this stranger? One could answer that it is all the photographers. Yet the photographers are only the agents of this memory. They do not construct the system.

There is a cartoon that Daumier made of Nadar in a balloon over Paris. His hat is blowing off in the wind, and he has this very large clumsy camera with which he is photographing the whole of Paris below. This cartoon offers us a clue. Perhaps the eye of the total stranger is the eye of God, but the eye of a totally secularised, totally estranged God. A God of nothingness.

The faculty of memory allows us to preserve certain events from oblivion. Because of their experience of this faculty, women and men in nearly all cultures have assumed that there was somewhere an all-seeing eye. They accredited this eye to spirits, ancestors, Gods or a single God. Such an all-seeing eye recorded all events, and the idea of this eye was connected with the idea of justice, to be remembered was to be redeemed; to be forgotten was to be condemned. The all-seeing eye saw in order to judge. The all-seeing eye recorded all events and in that recording was implicit a kind of judgement.

Reproduced from *The Camerawork Essays: Context and Meaning in Photography*, ed. Jessica Evans, London: Rivers Oram Press, 1997, pp. 44–7. Reproduced by permission of Rivers Oram/Pandora Publishers.

Nineteenth-century capitalism elided the judgement of God into the judgement of history. Today we live in a culture which denies history, which cuts itself off from history, a culture of pure opportunism. So we have the systematic use of photographs, used as an all-seeing eye, recording events. But this all-seeing eye judges nothing: it uses neither the judgement of history, nor the judgement of God, it is totally without judgement. *It is an eye which records in order to forget.*

Is an alternative use of photography conceivable? Is it possible to use photography addressing such a use to the hope of an alternative future?

The immediate answer to that is yes. You can use photography in all kinds of agitprop ways, you can make propaganda with photographs – you can make anti-capitalist propaganda, anti-imperialist propaganda. I wouldn't deny the usefulness of this, but at the same time I think the answer is incomplete. It's like taking a cannon and turning it round and firing it in the opposite direction. You haven't actually changed the practice, you've simply changed the aim.

How is it possible to use photography so that it doesn't function like the eye of a totally estranged God? We have to go back to the distinction I made between the private and public uses of photography. In the private use of photography, the photograph does not lend itself to any use, it does not become a completely value-free object because the use reconstitutes the continuity from which it was taken. Maybe one has to consider how the private use of photography could be extended, could be enlarged so that it might cease to be private and become public.

[...] If the camera is not to be used as if it were the eye of a totally estranged God, we can say that photography awaits a world historical consciousness which has yet to be achieved. It awaits a social memory which will transcend the distinction between public and private.

How in practice can we use photographs, so that, even though we are using them publicly, they are replaced in a context which is comparable to that of private photographs? [...]

The problem is to construct a context for a photograph, to construct it with words, to construct it with other photographs, to construct it by its place in an ongoing text of photographs and images. How? Normally photographs are used in a very unilinear way – they are used to illustrate an argument, or to demonstrate a thought which goes like this:

Very frequently also they are used tautologically so that the photograph merely repeats what is being said in words. Memory is not unilinear at all. Memory works radially, that is to say with an enormous number of associations all leading to the same event. The diagram is like this:

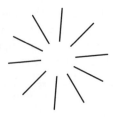

If we want to put a photograph back into the context of experience, social experience, social memory, we have to respect the laws of memory. We have to situate the printed photograph so that it acquires something of the surprising conclusiveness of that which was and is. There are a few great photographs which practically achieve this by themselves. Any photograph may become such a 'Now' if an adequate context is created for it. In general the better the photograph, the fuller the context which can be created.

[…]

Such a context replaces the photograph in time – not its own original time for that is impossible – but in narrated time. Narrated time becomes historic time when it is assumed by social memory and social action. The constructed narrated time needs to respect the process of memory which it hopes to stimulate.

There is never a single approach to something remembered. The remembered is not like a terminus at the end of a line. Numerous approaches or stimuli converge upon it and lead to it. Words, comparisons, signs need to create a context for a printed photograph in a comparable way: that is to say, they must mark and leave open diverse approaches. A radial system has to be constructed around the photograph so that it may be seen in terms which are simultaneously personal, political, economic, dramatic, everyday and historic.

10: Fabrication

INTRODUCTION

The notion of image studies suggests a practice of analysing and interpreting images, understanding their significance and their place in historical, cultural, political and economic environments. Yet, an equally important aspect of image studies is the practical matter of making and manipulating images. Different processes, materials and forms define different image-types, while cultural practices in one field, such as scientific experimentation, can influence image-making practices in another (Gombrich, 4.2). For the painter, the process of making an image is usually considered a creative experimentation or study of forms and qualities as they attest to various figurative or abstract concerns. For a radiologist, however, image production is about securing a precise form of visual knowledge. Yet, in both cases the results can lead to complex and beautiful images, which might equally be at home on a gallery wall. Similarly, a wide variety of materials and equipment are used in image making. Both the film-maker and astrophysicist, for example, need to use increasingly sophisticated visual technologies in order to carry out their work. In one case this might be to create a virtual environment in which to stage a science-fiction drama, or in another, to visualise far-flung dimensions of our universe, which normally remain invisible to the naked eye.

There is a clear danger – especially in the confines of a book such as this – for image studies to further institutionalise a distance between image making and image analysis. Art historian James Elkins (2003: 157–9) urges us to find ways 'of bringing image-making into the classroom – not just in theory but in actual practice'. Furthermore, he makes the point that the making of images (from drawing and painting to video editing) ought to be practised in the *same* seminar rooms where historical and interpretative work takes place. Otherwise, there will always remain a gulf between making and thinking about images; at worst, '[image] theory will be able to consolidate the notion that study is sufficient to the understanding of images, and independent of actual making' (Elkins, 2003: 159). This section has been devised not to fill the gulf, but to bridge it in part by focusing on the ways in which the processes, techniques and materials of image making impact not only on the appreciation and interpretation of images, but on the range of image-making practices.

In the first two entries, image-practitioners write about their own art forms as a way of both exploring their practice as well as seeking – in a quite didactic manner – to shape our understanding of new conceptual and aesthetic boundaries. Paul Klee (10.1) vividly demonstrates the productive tension between thinking about and doing art. Klee begins with nothing but the point of his pencil and a need to set it in motion. Klee is perhaps most well-known for how he turns nascent formations into whole new vocabularies, his approach resembling both the 'automatic writing' of the Surrealists and abstraction. His idea that lines and colours have an energy or charge is evident in the abstract works he inspired, such as Bridget Riley's black and white paintings that use strict geometric forms in tessellating patterns to create the optical illusion of movement. She understands Klee's method 'not [as] an end, but the beginning. Every painter starts with elements – lines, colours, forms – which are essentially abstract in relation to the pictorial experience that can be created with them' (Riley in Kudielka, 2002: 15). This attention to lines, colours, forms and even apparently random marks informs not only art practice but also appreciation, and also needs to be extended to non-art images, including, for example, scientific and informational images (see Bal, 5.4; Elkins, 1999).

The Soviet constructivist film-maker Sergei Eisenstein (10.2) – working around the same time as Klee – appears to have held a similar belief in the 'charged' materiality of his medium. Eisenstein sought to facilitate or 'construct' intellectual engagement, not in order to tell stories but to convey abstract, political, ideas. The foundational principle of his work is montage, the breaking up of 'reality' (in its filmed elements), to be recomposed for new psychological effect and ideational synthesis. For Eisenstein (like Benjamin, 9.6), montage meant more than the mere editing of one shot with another. Instead, his method was to break-up reality into usable blocks or units, equivalent to the palette of the musician's harmonic scale. He acknowledged the existence of a dominant meaning (such as narrative), but urged the film-maker to work 'with the overtones as much as the dominant in order to create the equivalent of the "impressionism" of Debussy or Scriabin' (Andrew, 1976: 59). Eisenstein identifies film's own specific aesthetic, which he called its 'filmic' fourth dimension, on this non-dominant level of meaning (see Barthes, 5.3). As with Klee, form and process appear to matter more than content.

The remaining three entries concern the historicising of images and image making (see also Crary, 12.1). William J. Mitchell (10.3) focuses on the technology of image making and the effect of new digital methods on both the nature of images and human relationships to images. The 'pixel' as the building block of all digital imaging, like Saussure's signifier (5.1), has meaning not because it corresponds visually to a reality that has been filtered into data, but in relation to the other pixels. Though pixels are not themselves signs, like Bal's (5.4) subsemiotic elements, they contribute to the overall meaning. The virtuality of the digital image enables an expansion of human relations with images, from looking to active interaction. Mitchell's tone emphasises the possibilities of digital images that bring to mind both Marshall McLuhan's (1964) optimistic notion of media as extensions of humankind, and critiques of McLuhan's technological utopianism that emphasise the constraints of media and image forms on human relations (Baudrillard, 1988). This raises the question of a possible overlap between technophobia and iconophobia, and technophilia and iconophilia (see the introduction to Section 1).

Renowned contemporary artist David Hockney (10.4) provides an interesting, controversial example of the application of specialist knowledge to art history, as well as an appreciation of how technologies shape the fabrication and appreciation of images (Ihde, 6.5; see also Section 12, Vision and Visuality). He claims that the Old Masters relied on contemporary optical devices to achieve the visual accuracy, but also occasional distortions, of their masterpieces. Susan Sontag is reported to have responded by saying: 'If David Hockney's thesis is correct, it would be a bit like finding out that all the great lovers of history have been using Viagra' (*Los Angeles Times*, 03.12.01, p. A1). At stake is the idea that the appreciation of great paintings must somehow depend on the 'true' ability of artists to produce them without technical mediation, which leads us to question how we appreciate figurative art since the invention of photography and new digital technologies.

Peter Galison (10.5) charts the oscillation between iconoclasm and iconophilia of attitudes towards imaging in astro- and microphysics. Returning to a scene set by Plato (1.4), Galison reviews debates about whether the nature of scientific knowledge is essentially imagistic and pictorial or abstract and logical. His sense that the debate cannot simply be settled but should be understood in its different contexts resonates with Mitchell's view (1986). Science images do not simply present non-visual data visually for convenience or pleasure, as images not only represent but also constitute scientific knowledge that can then be translated back into data. The making of science images is also the making of scientific knowledge (see also Kress and van Leeuwen, 5.5).

REFERENCES

Andrew, J.D. (1976) *The Major Film Theories: An Introduction*. London: Oxford University Press.

Baudrillard, J. (1988) 'The masses: the implosion of the social in the media', in M. Poster (ed.), *Jean Baudrillard: Selected Writings*. Cambridge: Polity Press. pp. 207–19.

Elkins, J. (1999) *The Domain of Images*. Ithaca, NY: Cornell University Press.

Elkins, J. (2003) *Visual Studies: A Skeptical Introduction*. New York: Routledge.

Kudielka, R. (2002) *Paul Klee: The Nature of Creation – Works 1914–1940*. London: Haywood Gallery and Lund Humphries.

McLuhan, M. (1964) *Understanding Media*. London: Routledge & Kegan Paul.

Mitchell, W.J.T. (1986) *Iconology: Image, Text, Ideology*. Chicago: University of Chicago Press.

TAKING A LINE FOR A WALK
PAUL KLEE

An **active** line on a walk, moving freely, without goal. A walk for a walk's sake. The mobility agent is a point, shifting its position forward (Figure 10.1):

FIGURE 10.1

The same line, accompanied by complementary forms (Figures 10.2 and 10.3):

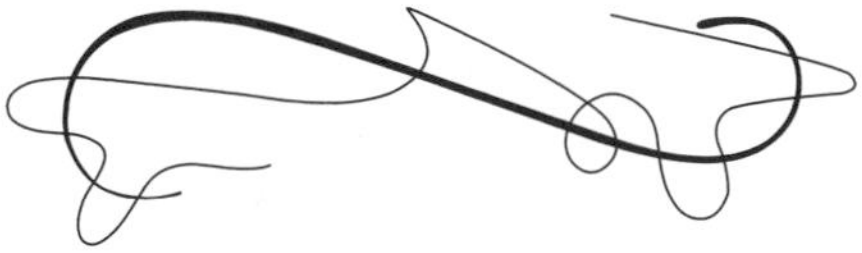

FIGURE 10.2

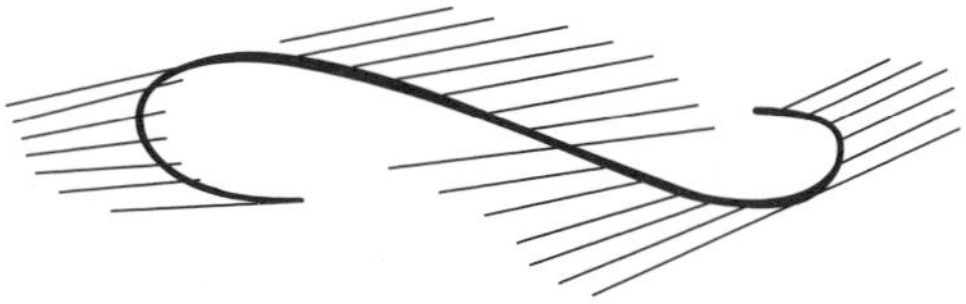

FIGURE 10.3

The same line, circumscribing itself (Figure 10.4):

FIGURE 10.4

Two secondary lines, moving around an imaginary main line (Figure 10.5):

FIGURE 10.5

Paul Klee, from *Pedagogical Sketchbook*. London: Faber & Faber, 1953, pp. 16–21. Reprinted by permission of Faber & Faber.

An **active** line, limited in its movements by fixed points (Figure 10.6):

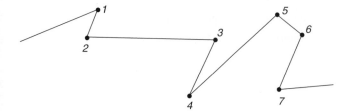

FIGURE 10.6

A **medial** line which is both: point progression and planar effect (Figure 10.7):

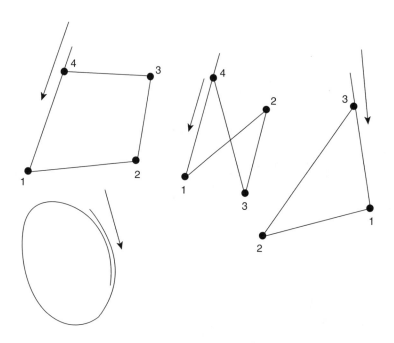

FIGURE 10.7

In the process of being created, these figures have linear character; but once completed, this linearity is replaced by planarity.

Passive lines which are the result of an activation of planes (line progression) (Figure 10.8):

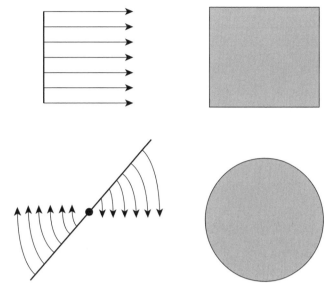

FIGURE 10.8

Passive angular lines and passive circular lines become active as planar constituents.

Three conjugations:

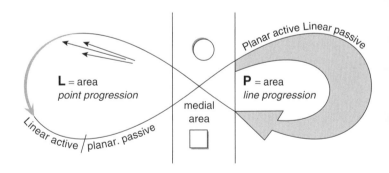

FIGURE 10.9

Semantic explanation of the terms active, medial, and passive:

   active: I fell (the man fells a tree with his ax).
   medial: I fall (the tree falls under the ax stroke of the man).
   passive: I am being felled (the tree lies felled).

10:2

ON MONTAGE AND THE FILMIC FOURTH DIMENSION
SERGEI EISENSTEIN

Orthodox montage is montage *on the dominant*, i.e. the combination of shots according to their dominating indications. Montage according to tempo. Montage according to the chief tendency within the frame. Montage according to the length (continuance) of the shots, and so on. This is montage according to the foreground.

The dominating indications of two shots side by side produces one or another conflicting interrelation, resulting in one or another expressive effect (I am speaking here of a purely *montage* effect).

This circumstance embraces all intensity levels of montage juxtaposition – all *impulses*:

From a complete opposition of the dominants, i.e., a sharply contrasting construction, to a scarcely noticeable 'modulation' from shot to shot; *all* cases of conflict must therefore include cases of a complete *absence* of conflict.

As for the dominant itself, to regard it as something independent, absolute and invariably stable is out of the question. There are technical means of treating the shot so that its dominant may be made more or less specific, but in no case absolute.

[…]

If we have even a *sequence* of montage pieces:

A gray old man,

A gray old woman,

A white horse,

A snow-covered roof,

we are still far from certain whether this sequence is working towards a dominating indication of 'old age' or of 'whiteness.'

Such a sequence of shots might proceed for some time before we finally discover that guiding-shot which immediately 'christens' the *whole* sequence in one 'direction' or another. That is why it is advisable to place this identifying shot as near as possible to the beginning of the sequence (in an 'orthodox' construction). Sometimes it even becomes necessary to do this with a sub-title.

[…]

In distinction from orthodox montage according to *particular dominants*, *Old and New*[1] was edited differently. In place of an 'aristocracy' of individualistic dominants we brought a method of 'democratic' equality of rights for all provocations, or stimuli, regarding them as a summary, as a complex.

Excerpt from *Film Form: Essays in Film Theory* by Sergei Eisenstein, English translation by Jay Leyda. London: Dennis Dobson, 1963, pp. 64–71. Copyright © 1949 by Harcourt, Inc., and renewed 1977 by Jay Leyda, reprinted by permission of the publisher.

The point is that the dominant (with all these recognized limitations on its relativity) appears to be, although the most powerful, far from the only stimulus of the shot. For example: the sex appeal of a beautiful American heroine-star is attended by many stimuli: of texture – from the material of her gown; of light – from the balanced and emphatic lighting of her figure; of racial – national (positive for an American audience: 'a native American type,' or negative: 'colonizer-oppressor' – for a Negro or Chinese audience); of social-class, etc. (all brought together in an iron-bound unity of its reflex-physiological essence). In a word, the *central* stimulus (let it be, for instance, sexual as in our example) is attended always by a *whole complex* of secondary, or the physiological process of a highly nervous activity.

What takes place in acoustics, and particularly in the case of instrumental music, fully corresponds with this.

There, along with the vibration of a basic dominant tone, comes a whole series of similar vibrations, which are called *overtones* and *undertones*. Their impacts against each other, their impacts with the basic tone, and so on, envelop the basic tone in a whole host of secondary vibrations. If in acoustics these collateral vibrations become merely 'disturbing' elements, these same vibrations in music – in composition, become one of the most significant means for affect by the experimental composers of our century, such as Debussy and Scriabin.

[…]

The montage of *Old and New* is constructed with this method. This montage is built, not on *particular* dominants, but takes as its guide the total stimulation through all stimuli. That is the original montage complex within the shot, arising from the collision and combination of the individual stimuli inherent in it.

These stimuli are heterogeneous as regards their 'external natures,' but their reflex-physiological essence binds them together in an iron unity. Physiological in so far as they are 'psychic' in perception, this is merely the physiological process of a *higher nervous activity*.

In this way, behind the general indication of the shot, the physiological summary of its vibrations as a *whole,* as a complex unity of the manifestations of all its stimuli, is present. This is the peculiar *'feeling' of the shot,* produced by the shot as a whole.

[…] The basic indication of the shot can be taken as the final summary of its effect on the cortex of the brain as a whole, irrespective of the paths by which the accumulated stimuli have been brought together. Thus the quality of the *totals* can be placed side by side in any conflicting combination, thereby revealing entirely new possibilities of montage solutions.

As we have seen, in the power of the very genetics of these methods, they must be attended by an extraordinary *physiological* quality. As in that music which builds its works on a two-fold use of overtones. Not the *classicism* of Beethoven, but the *physiological quality* of Debussy and Scriabin.

The extraordinary physiological quality in the affect of *Old and New* has been remarked by many of its spectators. The explanation for this is that *Old and New is the first film edited on the principle of the visual overtone.* This method of montage can be interestingly verified.

If in the gleaming classical distances of the cinematography of the future, overtonal montage will certainly be used, simultaneously with montage according to the dominant indication, so as always at first the new method will assert itself in a question sharpened in principle. Overtonal montage in its first steps has had to take a line in sharp *opposition* to the dominant.

There are many instances, it is true – and in *Old and New*, too – where 'synthetic' combinations of tonal and overtonal montage may already be found. For example, in *Old and New*, the climax of the religious procession (to pray for relief from the drought), and the sequence of the grasshopper and the mowing-machine, are edited visually according to *sound* associations, with an express development which exists already in their spatial 'similarity.'

Of particular methodological interest, of course, are constructions that are wholly *a-dominant*. In these the dominant appears in the form of a purely *physiological formulation of the task.* For example, the montage of the beginning of the religious procession is according to 'degrees of heat saturation' in the individual shots, or the beginning of the state-farm sequence is according to a line of 'carnivorousness.' Conditions outside cinematographic discipline provide the most unexpected physiological indications among materials that are logically (both formally and naturally) absolutely neutral in their relations to each other.

There are innumerable cases of montage joinings in this film that make open mockery of orthodox, scholastic montage according to the dominant. The easiest way to demonstrate this is to examine the film on the cutting table. Only then can one see clearly the perfectly 'impossible' montage joinings in which *Old and New* abounds. This will also demonstrate the extreme simplicity of its metrics, of its 'dimensions.'

Entire large sections of certain sequences are made up of pieces perfectly uniform in length or of absolutely primitively repeated short pieces. The whole intricate, rhythmic, and *sensual* nuance scheme of the combined pieces is conducted almost exclusively according to a line of work on the 'psycho-physiological' vibrations of each piece.

It was on the cutting table that I detected the sharply defined scope of the particular montage of *Old and New*. This was when the film had to be condensed and shortened. The 'creative ecstasy' attending the assembly and montage – the 'creative ecstasy' of 'hearing and feeling' the shots – all this was already in the past. Abbreviations and cuts require no inspiration, only technique and skill.

And there, examining the sequence of the religious procession on the table, I could not fit the combination of its pieces into any one of the orthodox categories, within which one can apply one's pure experience. On the table, deprived of motion, the reasons for their choice seem completely incomprehensible. The criteria for their assembly appear to be outside formally normal cinematographic criteria.

And here is observed one further curious parallel between the visual and the musical overtone: It cannot be traced in the static frame, just as it cannot be traced in the musical score. Both emerge as genuine values only in the dynamics of the musical or cinematographic *process*.

Overtonal conflicts, foreseen but unwritten in the score, cannot emerge without the dialectic process of the passage of the film through the projection apparatus, or that of the performance by a symphony orchestra.

The visual overtone is proved to be an actual piece, an actual element of – a fourth dimension!

   [...]

For the musical overtone (a throb) it is not strictly fitting to say: 'I hear.' Nor for the visual overtone: 'I see.' For both, a new uniform formula must enter our vocabulary: 'I feel.'

NOTE

1. Editor's Note: *Old and New* is the title for the 1930 release in the United States of America of the film otherwise known as the *The General Line*, Генеральная линия aka Старое и новое, 1929).

ELECTRONIC TOOLS
WILLIAM J. MITCHELL   IO:3

Tools are made to accomplish our purposes, and in this sense they represent desires and intentions. We make our tools and our tools make us: by taking up particular tools we accede to desires and we manifest intentions. Specifically, the tools and media of traditional photography – cameras, lenses, tripods, filters, film of various kinds, flashguns, studio lights, enlargers, darkroom chemicals, densitometers, and so on – represent the desire to register and reproduce fragments of visual reality according to strict conventions of perspectival consistency, tonal fidelity, acuity in rendition of detail, and temporal unity. They characterize a way in which we have *wanted* to see the world, and in the world since 1839 they have played a crucial role in the creation of collective memory and the formation of belief. [...]

William J. Mitchell, from *The Reconfigured Eye: Visual Truth in the Post-Photographic Era*. Cambridge, MA: MIT Press, 1992, pp. 59–60, 62, 66–9, 78–80. Copyright © 1992 Massachusetts Institute of Technology.

FIGURE 10.10
Varying the spatial and tonal resolution
of an image. Courtesy of William J.
Mitchell, from *The Reconfigured Eye*,
MIT Press, 1992 p. 68.

Now, after 150 years, we are faced with a discontinuity, a sudden and decisive rupture. The technology of digital image production, manipulation, and distribution represents a new configuration of intention. It focuses a powerful (though frequently ambivalent and resisted) desire to dismantle the rigidities of photographic seeing and to extend visual discourse beyond the depictive conventions and presumed certitudes of the photographic record. Painting has always done this, of course, but it has come to occupy very different territory: the digital image challenges the photograph on its home ground.

*

Usually, digital images are captured through transduction of radiant energy into patterns of electric current rather than through chemical action, but in most cases the capture processes are similarly brief and automatic. Two steps are combined in any digital image-capture procedure. First, intensities in the scene or source image to be captured must be sampled at grid locations. Second, each sample intensity must be converted to an integer value in some finite range process known as *quantization*. [...] This two-stage process of converting scene data near sample points into pixel values is known technically as filtering. An impressionist painter looking at a scene and converting it to discrete brush strokes and a digital image-capture device are both applying sampling and filtering strategies. But, whereas the impressionist painter performs sampling and filtering manually, subjectively, and probably rather inconsistently, the digital device samples and filters mechanically, objectively, and consistently.

*

The pixel values that constitute a digital image can be conceived of in two complementary ways: in relation to the display or print that an artist produces and in relation to the scene depicted by that display or print.[1] In relation to the display or print, a pixel value specifies a small coloured cell on the picture surface – a discrete signifying mark: the density of pixels on the picture surface determines capacity to reproduce fine detail. In relation to the recorded scene, a pixel value is a sample in time and space of light intensities projected onto the picture plane – a discrete datum: the spatial frequency and intensity resolution of samples taken from a scene determine the fidelity of the digital record. If the sampling grid is too coarse, or if intensity differences are not discriminated precisely enough, fine detail will be irretrievably lost. [...]

[...]

How many pixels, and how many intensity values, are necessary to communicate a monochrome image satisfactorily? Clearly this depends to a large extent on the complexity of the image, but Figure 10.10 begins to suggest orders of magnitude. A portrait was scanned at high spatial and tonal resolution, then processed to reduce both kinds of resolution. [...] The highest-resolution version is at the top left of the image array.

Spatial resolution halves at each row, and tonal resolution halves at each column, so that the image with the least amount of information is at the bottom right. Increased tonal resolution can compensate for poor spatial resolution and vice-versa. Even very low-resolution versions are recognizable, but higher-resolution versions tell us more, so there is usually motivation to encode images at the highest resolution possible subject to constraints on storage, transmission, and processing capacity.[2] [...]

Squint your eyes at these images. You will find that the hard edges of individual pixels disappear and that the images of low spatial resolution suddenly look much more lifelike. Surprisingly, there is actually a person lurking behind the pixels. (Technically, squinting amounts to application of a low-pass filter to remove distracting fine detail and leave the broad distribution of tones intact. Painters have long known this trick.)

[...]

Notice how pixels work as signifiers. A single pixel, taken in isolation, depicts nothing in particular – merely 'light thing' or 'dark thing.' But when a pixel is seen in context with other pixels, which narrow the range of likely interpretations, then its significance becomes more precise: it might depict the gleam of an eye or the twinkling of a star in the heavens. Where there are many pixels, they all create detailed contexts for each other, so that each one is read as a depiction of something quite specific. If a pixel, taken in context, has a value that cannot be interpreted in this way, then it is usually seen as visual 'noise' and ignored.

Usually we try to produce images that are of sufficient resolution to render the individual pixels imperceptible, but seeing pixels is not *necessarily* a bad thing. Prominent pixels call attention to the process by which a digital image is actually put together ... and this may be an important part of an image's point: the visible pixels create tensions between actual surface and illusory pictorial space, and between marking process and the object of depiction.

*

The basic principle underlying all display and printing techniques for digital images is nicely illustrated by the story of how the first Mariner IV images of Mars were produced. The spacecraft transmitted back arrays of integers, which were stored on magnetic tape. These numbers were then printed out, and scientists at the Jet Propulsion Laboratory coloured over them, according to a specified colour-coding scheme, with crayons. They would perhaps have been surprised to know that they were employing a technique developed by Paul Klee (Figure 10.11).[3] Today we use computer-controlled display and printing devices to perform this interpretation task automatically and usually at very high speed.

[...]

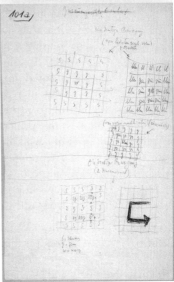

FIGURE 10.11

Interpretation of the raster grid: sketches from Paul Klee's
Notebooks. **Above** Paul Klee, Farbtafel (auf maiorem
Grau), 1930, 83 (Colour table (in grey major));
37.7×30.4 cm. Zentrum Paul Klee, Bern.© DACS London.
Below PKS PN30 M60/101 recto, Paul Klee. Specielle
Ordnung, Bleistift auf Papier; 33×21 cm. Zentrum Paul
Klee, Bern. © DACS, London.

Many digital images, however, are never printed but appear only as transient
screen displays. In other words they are replayed from digital data – using a
personal computer or a specialized player such as Kodak's Photo CD –
exactly as musical performances on digital compact disc are replayed. When
used in this way, digital image files are more closely analogous to recordings
than to negatives or printing plates. They represent the latest stage in the
long evolutionary development of images as objects into images as
performances – a transition away from images realized as durable,
individually valuable, physically rooted artefacts (frescoes, mosaics, and
murals), through portable easel paintings and inexpensive prints, to
completely ephemeral film projections and video displays.

But the now-familiar display screen is still a flat picture plane, still a tiny, glowing window through which we can take a Cyclopean peek at another world. In the late 1960s the computer-graphics pioneer Ivan E. Sutherland realized that electronic displays do not *have* to take the etymological implication of 'perspective' – viewing as 'seeing through' – quite so literally: they can dispense with the bounding frame, break open the plane, and allow redirection of the gaze. Sutherland designed a completely new kind of display [...]. [His] prototype used mechanical linkages to sense the viewer's location and direction of gaze, head-mounted, miniature cathode ray tube displays to place images on the viewer's retinas, and a powerful (for the time) computer to synthesize stereo pairs of perspective images at a sufficiently rapid rate to respond to the viewer's movements without perceptible lag. It was crude and cumbersome, but it opened up the possibility of breaking through the picture plane into a three-dimensional 'virtual reality.' Subsequent research has explored ultrasound and other non-mechanical position-sensing techniques and has sought to miniaturize head-mounted displays still further; by the 1990s the possibility of laser microscanners that painted images directly on the retina was receiving serious attention.[4] Vast increases in available computing power have brought the simulation of complex, detailed three-dimensional worlds within reach. The embryonic technology of virtual reality promises architects the possibility of walking through geometrically modelled proposed buildings, astronomers the possibility of flying through radar-scanned planetary landscapes, and surgeons the possibility of seeing 'through the skin' by superimposing on patients' bodies three-dimensional displays generated from ultrasound or MRI scanner data.

Oliver Wendell Holmes called the Daguerreotype 'a mirror with a memory'[5]: you can think of a digital-imaging or computer-graphics system as a memory with a display. By selecting from among available display and printing processes and by controlling their parameters, you can externally reflect the contents of an internally stored array of intensity values in a multitude of differently rendered and variously inflected ways. There is, then, a fundamental change in our relationship to images. You are not limited just to looking at digital images: you can actively inhabit and closely interact with them.

NOTES

1. Footnote removed.
2. Footnote removed.
3. Footnote removed.
4. Footnote removed.
5. Oliver Wendell Holmes, 'The Stereoscope and the Stereograph,' *Atlantic Monthly* 3 (June 1859).

CAMERA LUCIDA
DAVID HOCKNEY

10:4

The camera lucida is not easy to use. Basically, it is a prism on a stick that creates the illusion of an image of whatever is in front of it on a piece of paper below. This image is not real – it is not actually on the paper, it only seems to be there. When you look through the prism from a single point you can see the person or objects in front and the paper below at the same time. If you're using the camera lucida to draw, you can also see your hand and pencil making marks on the paper. But only you, sitting in the right position, can see these things, no one else can.

*

In early 1991 I made a drawing using a camera lucida. It was an experiment, based on a hunch that Ingres, in the first decades of the nineteenth century, may have occasionally used this little optical device, then newly invented. My curiosity had been aroused when I went to an exhibition of his portraits at London's National Gallery and was struck by how small the drawings were, yet so uncannily 'accurate'. I know how difficult it is to achieve such precision, and wondered how he had done it. [...]

At first, I found the camera lucida very difficult to use. It doesn't project a real image of the subject, but an illusion of one in the eye. When you move your head everything moves with it, and the artist must learn to make very quick notations to fix the position of the eyes, nose and mouth to capture 'a likeness'. It is concentrated work. I persevered and continued to use the method for the rest of the year – learning all the time. I began to take more care with lighting the subject, noticing how a good light makes a big difference when using optics, just like with photography. I also saw how much care other artists – Caravaggio and Velázquez, for example – had taken in lighting their subjects, and how deep their shadows were. Optics need strong lighting, and strong lighting creates deep shadows. I was intrigued and began to scrutinize paintings very carefully.

Like most painters, I imagine, when I look at paintings I am as interested in 'how' it was painted as 'what' it is saying or 'why' it was painted (these questions are, of course, related). Having struggled to use optics myself, I found I was now looking at pictures in a new way. I could identify optical characteristics and, to my surprise, I could see them in the work of other artists – and as far back as the 1430s, it seemed! I think it is only in the late twentieth century that this has become visible. New technology, mainly the computer, was needed to see it. Computers have allowed cheaper and higher-quality colour printing, leading to a great improvement in the last fifteen years in the standard of art books (even twenty years ago, most were still in black and white). And now with colour photocopiers and desktop printers anyone can produce cheap but good reproductions at home, and so place works that were previously separated by hundreds or thousands of

Secret Knowledge, London: Thames & Hudson, 2001, pp. 12–17, 66–7.

FIGURE 10.12
Giotto di Bondone, *Upper Basilica of San Francesco* (detail), 1300. Wall fresco, San Francesco, Assisi. Photograph: Scala.

FIGURE 10.13
Unknown Austrian artist, *Rudolf IV of Austria* (detail), c. 1365. Oil on canvas. Source: Bridgeman Art Library.

miles side by side. This is what I did in my studio, and it allowed me to see the whole sweep of it all. It was only by putting pictures together in this way that I began to notice things; and I'm sure these things could have only been seen by an artist, a mark-maker, who is not as far from practice, or from science, as an art historian. [...]

I discussed my observations with friends, and was introduced to Martin Kemp, professor of art history at Oxford University and an authority on Leonardo and the links between art and science. From the start, he encouraged my curiosity and supported my hypotheses, albeit with reservations. Others, though, were horrified at my suggestions. Their main complaint was that for an artist to use optical aids would be 'cheating'; that somehow I was attacking the idea of innate artistic genius. Let me say here that optics do not make marks, only the artist's hand can do that, and it requires great skill. And optics don't make drawing any easier either, far from it – I know, I've used them. But to an artist six hundred years ago optical projections would have demonstrated a new vivid way of looking at and representing the material world. Optics would have given artists a new tool with which to make images that were more immediate, and more powerful. To suggest that artists used optical devices, as I am doing here,

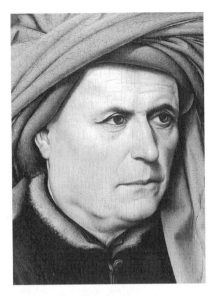

FIGURE 10.14
Masolino da Panicale, *Healing of the Lame Man and Raising of Tabitha* (detail), *c.* 1425. Wall Fresco, Santa Maria del Carmine, Brancacci Chapel. Photograph: Scala.

FIGURE 10.15
Robert Campin, *A Man* (detail), *c.* 1430. Oil and egg tempera on oak. National Gallery, London.

is not to diminish their achievements. For me, it makes them all the more astounding.

[...]

In February 2000, with the help of my assistants [...], I started to pin up colour photocopies of paintings on the wall of my studio in California. I saw this as a way I could get an overview of the history of Western art, and as an aid to the selection of pictures for the book. By the time we had finished, the wall was seventy feet long and covered five hundred years more or less chronologically, with northern Europe at the top and southern Europe at the bottom.

As we began to put the pages of the book together, we were also experimenting with different combinations of mirrors and lenses to see if we could re-create the ways in which Renaissance artists might have used them. The projections we made delighted everyone who came to the studio, even those with a camera in their hands. The effects seemed amazing, because they were unelectronic. The images we projected were clear, in colour and they moved. It became obvious that few people know much about optics, even photographers. In medieval Europe, projected 'apparitions' would be regarded as magical; as I found out, people still think this today.

[…]

It is perfectly clear that some artists used optics directly and others did not, although after 1500 almost all seem to have been influenced by the tonalities, shading and colours found in the optical projection. Brueghel, Bosch, Grünewald immediately come to mind as artists who were not involved in the direct use of optics. But they would have seen paintings and drawings made with them, and maybe even some projections themselves (to see optical projections is to use them); and as apprentices they probably copied works with optical effects. I must repeat that optics do not make marks, they cannot make paintings. Paintings and drawings are made by the hand. All I am saying here is that, long before the seventeenth century, when there is evidence Vermeer was using a camera obscura, artists had a tool and that they used it in ways previously unknown to art history.

*

Finding evidence of the use of optics in northern Europe in the late fifteenth century made me look more closely at early Flemish painting. On my wall a sudden, dramatic change stood out. Here are four portraits painted 130 years apart, Figures 10.12–10.15. Giotto's of 1300 certainly has an interesting expression in the face. Sixty-five years later an unknown artist makes a portrait of Rudolf IV of Austria – like Giotto's, it is awkward. By 1425, in Italy, Masolino has more order in the face; the turban seems to follow the form of the head and looks as though it fits properly. But just five years later, in Flanders, something happens. Robert Campin's face looks startlingly 'modern'; it could be someone from today. There is clear lighting – notice the shadow under the nose – suggesting a strong source of light; the folds in the turban aren't awkward; the man's small double chin is seen clearly; and the mouth and eyes are far more related, giving an intensity to his appearance. This painting has a totally different 'look'.

10:5 IMAGES SCATTER INTO DATA, DATA GATHER INTO IMAGES
PETER GALISON

Stepping back from the specific sciences, a powerful theme running through them comes into view, one central to the arguments and evidence they produce. In brutally short form, it is this: 'We must have images; we cannot have images.'

We *must* have scientific images because only images can teach us. Only pictures can develop within us the intuition needed to proceed further

First published in *Iconoclash: Beyond the Image Wars in Science, Religion, and Art*, Bruno Latour and Peter Weibel (eds), Karlsruhe: ZKM/Center for Art and Media/Cambridge, MA: The MIT Press, 2002, pp. 300–23. Reproduced by permission.

towards abstraction. We are human, and as such, we depend on specificity and materiality to learn and understand. Pictures, sometimes alone, often in sequences, are stepping stones along the path towards the real knowledge that intuition supports. [...] [B]eyond pedagogy or even epistemology, images get at the peculiar – the unique – features of nature in a way that a calculation or verbal description can never do. By mimicking nature, an image, even if not in *every* respect, captures a richness of relations in a way that a logical train of propositions never can. Pictures are not just scaffolding, they are the gleaming edifices of truth itself that we hope to reveal. So goes the brief for the scientific image: pictures are pedagogically, epistemically, and metaphysically inalienable from the goal of science itself.

And yet: we *cannot* have images because images deceive. Pictures create artifactual expectations, they incline us to reason on false premises. We are human, and as such are easily led astray by the siren call of material specificity. Logic, not imagery, is the acid test of truth that strips away the shoddy inferences that accompany the mis-seeing eye. Abstraction, rigorous abstraction, is exactly that which does not depend on pictures. [...] Training, discovery, and truth are all dependent *only* on unambiguous propositions and their logical arrangement. So the scientific iconoclast announces: In the end, the truths of the world will be given to us by the relentless application of logic tied strategically to experiment; truth is something wider and deeper than the pictorial imagination can ever hope to encompass.

For the last hundred and fifty years, and perhaps even longer, the sciences have been caught in this endless struggle. In my field of science studies, before the 1970s, there was a tendency to dismiss the pictorial, to de-emphasize the role of the pictorial in the development and present conduct of science. Then came a reversal: widespread acclimation to the idea that science was overwhelmingly about the visual. Pictures, taken to be both more local and more contingent than propositions, entered as exhibit A in the case against science-as-algorithm. Trying to settle this battle between the picture-local and the proposition-universal strikes me as a losing bet. My goal instead is neither to bury the scientific image nor to sanctify it, but rather to explore the ways in which the sciences find themselves locked in a whirling embrace of iconoclasm and iconophilia.

*

Among the astrophysicists who were inclined to credit the visual with real weight is Margaret Geller. She, as much as anyone, has used images to back a crucial claim about the physical universe. To widespread astonishment, she and her colleagues showed that galaxies seem to be clustered as if on the surface of soap bubbles. But coming to and sustaining that conclusion relied in the first instance on *picturing* what was happening deep in the universe, followed by non-visual statistical studies, followed by more picturing. Recognizing a pattern was one thing. Bringing the broader community of astrophysicists along required a continuing alternation between imaging and more formal analyses: 'Images,' Geller says, 'are not sufficient in themselves.'

[…]

It is worth following the sequence of transformations that lay behind the production of a computer-generated video image that so strikingly showed the flat clustering of galaxies. Geller and her colleagues began with the galaxy catalogs that had been made from the Palomar Sky Survey by the famously irascible Caltech astronomer Fritz Zwicky. Each glass plate covered 36 degrees of the northern sky; from catalogs and plates the astronomers knew where in the sky to look for each of the galaxies in their study.

With those celestial latitude and longitude positions in hand, Geller and her colleagues could then direct the telescope to the right portion of the sky, technicians did the observing and took the data. With those data in hand, Geller and her co-workers then used the red-shift to figure out how far away particular galaxies were from earth (Hubble's law). […] By moving from the Palomar Survey and Zwicky's catalog to the spectrum and then through Hubble's law and the theory of the expanding universe, Geller's group could plot a three-dimensional map of the galaxies' positions. It is these data that they then plotted and inserted into the computer to produce a video clip of a 'walk' through the galaxies.

The astronomers found two remarkable features: first, that the distribution of galaxies was not even approximately smooth throughout space. Instead, the galaxies concentrated as if on the surfaces of vast bubbles. Said another way, there were vast voids in space in which hardly a galaxy was to be found. Second, Geller's group found what they called The Great Wall, a fantastically large and flattened cluster of galaxies exhibiting a filamentary internal structure – spanning a billion-light year swath across the sky with a wafer-thin width of (only) twenty million light years. It was as if you expected a population of miniature galaxies to be scattered evenly through a four-foot cube, but instead found the collection held in strands within a region the shape of a sheet of plywood one inch thick and four feet on a side.

Picturing mattered. To follow the lay of the galaxies it was not enough to have two-dimensional photographs of galaxies, crucial though they were. Nor were the catalogued coordinates of those plates sufficient. Nor were (in and of themselves) the various spectra. Even the thousand three-dimensional coordinates derived by way of Hubble's Law did not yet reveal the pattern. Re-visualization – first by plotting on paper and then by computer – initially forced the clustering to stand out. Then a back and forth between visualizable evidence and statistical analysis: new data meant new possibilities for rendering the information visually striking, and at the same time made possible the computation of new kinds of statistical, non-visualizable, correlations. By the time Geller and her collaborators produced the computer simulation of a walk through the galaxies, and accompanied it by mathematical correlations, the oscillation between the human eye and the statistical calculation made the effect as striking and as evident as the nose on your face. New theories began vying for the honor of explaining this new map of space. Image to data to image to data to image to theory.

At the heart of experimental microphysics lies a not unrelated tension between picture and proposition; on one side the desire to image the microworld; and on the other the equally powerful longing to escape the image. Decorating the cover of textbooks and imprinted into our cultural imagination are the wispy tracks of cloud chambers, nuclear emulsions, and bubble chambers. The cloud chamber, that prototype of all other visualization machines in microphysics, emerged from Victorian technologies that aimed to reproduce nature in miniature. Here was the world *in vitro*, one that displayed miniature storms, table-top volcanoes, room-sized glaciers. At first, C.T.R. Wilson, the inventor of the cloud chamber, had just this in mind: a chamber (that is a controlled space or room) in which he could manufacture clouds, fog, rain. Into the series – camera lucida, camera obscura, dust chamber – came the cloud chamber, the camera nebulosa.[1]

Once Wilson found that he could produce tracks (long trailing clouds) that followed the trajectory of charged particles, physicists began to assemble a new kind of technology, one organized to sort phenomena. This classificatory mechanism relied on a centuries-old tradition of medical atlases: atlases of skulls, atlases of hands, atlases of X-rays. In these compendia the budding physician would, in the simplest case, find 'normal' anatomy. The idea was that by looking at these images, organs, bones, or microscope slides would stand out if they were different, that is if they were pathological. For the physicist the cloud chamber atlas functioned similarly: if the image found departed dramatically from the normal, then pay attention. But while deviation from the normal marked the 'pathological' for the physician, deviation from the normal signaled 'discovery' to the physicist.

Other image-making devices soon followed. Nuclear emulsions were simply sheets of film that particles would traverse leaving tracks to be developed. Bubble chambers were great vats of liquid hydrogen or other liquids that would boil along the tracks of passing particles. As the technologies of image production shifted, much carried forward into the analysis of images.

But almost at once, in every one of these new laboratories, the images themselves begin to dissolve, morphing into other forms. A flash of light and three cameras would capture a complex trail of bubbles in stereo relief. Then a scanner projected the pictures one by one onto a table, where she (almost inevitably *she* during the 1950s and 1960s) clicked a mouse-like device to enter space coordinates. Digitized, the information flowed into a computer which then crunched the data into idealized mathematical curves;

from those curves the computer spat out punch cards with the particles' identities and properties. At first by hand and later by computer, the morass of numbers could finally be reassembled into new images: bar graphs or the so-called Dalitz plots where an entire picture would be reduced to a single black dot. The physicists could then ask: Did the dots cluster? Did the bar graph show one peak or perhaps two? An invisible physical process made bubbling tracks, tracks to numbers, numbers back to pictures. Those pictures in turn could themselves be analyzed back into numbers.

[...]

Even within the image tradition, the picture was always on the verge of being resorbed by the computer, snatched from human eyes and transmuted back into the whirl of numbers. As these new imaging technologies of physics rose to prominence, other competing machines offered data without any pictorial product. Pictures, some physicists lamented, had something nineteenth century about them. Couldn't devices be built that took the world directly to the computer, that fully by-passed the millions of pictures spewing out of cloud and bubble chambers? Geiger counters could click, for example, when a particle passed – sending an electrical pulse to a counter. Spark chambers flashed when particles traversed them, wire chambers became sensitive enough to pick up even the tiny amounts of ionized gas left in the wake of a passing particle. With the help of a computer, machinery could use time and space measurements to reconstruct the event. These were technologies that, in the first instance, produced not images but statistical data, though statistical data quickly converted back into images.

[...]

Image experiments served wonderfully to track individual events; logic experiments often had the edge in treating aggregates. Individual events for some physicists carried persuasive force precisely because they could 'see' into the whole of the process, as if, some said, they could peer directly into the submicroscopic world. They hated not knowing what went on between the counters, resisted the indirect, inferential process of statistical reasoning. The 'logicians' by contrast claimed that arguments by solid statistics stood on vastly firmer ground. 'Anything can happen once,' they grumbled. Science, the anti-imagers asserted, lies in the ability to manipulate and control phenomena, in the behavior of the many, not in the comportment of the few. Science, the image-defenders retorted, lies in the receptive, objective, singular medium of film.

In many ways, this image/logic split highlights, in the laboratory itself, the gulf between the desperate search for the individual image and the equally insistent attempt to avoid reliance on anything pictorial. Epistemically, this is an argument repeated over and over, in field after field. Doctors (and now the courts) slam into each other as they measure case studies versus epistemological studies. Geology had its era of qualitative studies against quantitative ones, seismology opposed to morphology. In the post-World War II years, astronomers often felt that they had to evaluate claims from radio astronomy against the established knowledge of optical astronomy. Do you trust the X-ray or the stethoscope? Would you put your money on the morphology of open faces of rocks or seismological data? Bit by bit over the last few decades there has been a remarkable transformation in all these binaries. In each instance the image followers found themselves manipulating data banks, and the numerical-logicians found themselves gazing into the face of a picture.

NOTE
1. Footnote removed.

11 : VISUAL CULTURE

INTRODUCTION

Since the mid-1990s there has been dramatic growth in scholarship about visual culture. In part this development is a specialisation within British cultural studies, emphasising the anthropological and sociological dimensions of the visual. In America, the field has been somewhat less concerned with ideological analysis and social action, being 'more haunted by art history, and more in debt to Roland Barthes and Walter Benjamin' (Elkins, 2003: 2). Notable exceptions to that tendency include DeLuca's (8.5) work on visual political rhetoric and Mitchell's (1994) pragmatic, de-disciplinary account of the field. It is notoriously difficult to define visual culture, not least because of its interdisciplinary approach and range of interests across all manner of visual objects, histories, theories and practices. The relationship between visual culture and art history has perhaps been the most contentious (see introduction to Section 4). Nevertheless, visual culture studies has gained recognition both within different disciplines and as a subject-area in its own right, evidenced by the development of specific study programmes and numerous primers on the subject (Fuery and Fuery, 2003; Howells, 2003; Mirzoeff, 1999; Rose, 2001; Sturken and Cartwright, 2001).

The most recent and prominent trend in visual culture studies has been to focus on contemporary (transnational) culture as a predominantly visual experience (Mirzoeff, 1999; Robins, 1996). Visual culture is also conceived as its own interdisciplinary, 'networked' object, one *that belongs to no one* (Bal, 2003: 7). It has been defined as an interpretative *tactic*, emphasising a visual *subject* and the various interactions of visual phenomena (Mirzoeff, 1998). Irit Rogoff (1998: 15) considers visual culture as 'a field of vision version of Derrida's concept of *différance*' – a visual mode of intertexuality. Cheng (11.7) illustrates such a post-structuralist approach to visual culture, by both explaining the pertinence of contemporary visual culture for political critique and presenting an image of a new form of criticism. Visual culture has renewed interest in the visual, allowing for the prescience and 'intelligence' of the visual (Stafford, 13.3; see also Section 13). Rather than replicating current writings on visual culture, which are widely available in anthologies (see Evans and Hall, 1999; Mirzoeff, 1998), the selections here also include precursors to contemporary visual culture studies. The social and cultural construction of vision is covered in the next section.

McLuhan's (11.1) famous dictum that 'the medium is the message' is encapsulated by his account of the significance of the electric light. Light does not tell us something specific, but rather as 'a medium without a message', it enables all manner of activities to take place, from brain surgery to night entertainments. However, electric light generally escapes our attention as a communication medium because it has no 'content', leaving no trace of its own. Crary (12.1) reminds us that as modern observers we have been trained to assume that our cultural lives 'will always leave visible tracks', whereas other, often less distinguishable, 'grayer practices and discourses' are equally important.

Lynch (11.2) provides another account of how a new technological base – in this case the design and engineering of the cityscape – has impacted upon (visual) culture. The 'conscious remolding' of city spaces has only been made possible relatively recently, giving rise to a new 'problem of environmental imageability'. We have the means at our disposal not only to respond to images of the city, but also to make them in a fashion which suits us. His concept of 'imageabilility' identifies a complex, multi-sensory experience, reflecting in part Merleau-Ponty's (6.2) phenonemonogical account of vision, as echoed in numerous writings of the *flâneur* or city-stroller (Benjamin, 1999; Gleber, 1999). In contrast to claustrophobic, dsytopian portraits of the city – evident, for example, in films from *Metropolis* to *Bladerunner* – Lynch presents a complex view of the city for practical consideration, his original audience having been urban planners, engineers and architects.

Sontag (11.3) argues that photography transformed twentieth-century expectations of reality, in that photographic images, as copies of firsthand experiences, became 'indispensable to the health of the economy, the stability of the polity, and the pursuit of private happiness'. Her account brings to the fore the double-edged property of the image, as both malady and antidote, provoking both iconophobia and iconophilia (see the introductions to Sections 1 and 3). Sontag readily accepts the significance of our 'image-world,' and the importance of visual culture, closing with the provocative idea that we must allow for 'an ecology not only of real things but of images as well'.

Danto (11.4) neatly presents the paradox of Andy Warhol's pop art, bringing into focus the high/low culture problematic constitutive of much of cultural studies. More particularly, he argues that Warhol offered a form of visual philosophy (see also Section 9), that is not articulated through reasoned argument, but instead embodied as a way of art, or rather a way of living. Warhol 'transformed his life into the image of an artist's life' and demonstrated how the signs and images of cultural life are our reality, not a product of it. Warhol is an 'utterly public artist', drawing upon an immediate shared culture and also re-valuing (or levelling) and immortalising a host of cultural artefacts and personalities, from Campbell's soup to the Empire State Building, from Marilyn Monroe to Chairman Mao, allowing everything to be exchanged on equal terms, as images. In contrast, Jameson (1991: 9) argues that Warhol foregrounds postmodern commodification without criticising it.

Grieve (11.5) takes us away from Western visual culture but is concerned with the limitations of Eurocentric views of religion that value writing but denigrate images, reinforcing the superiority of holy scripture over physical representations of divinity (see 1.2, 1.8, 1.9, 1.10 and Section 8). To unsettle any dominant point of view, Grieve invites us on several occasions simply to look directly at an image of the Indian Stone-God he writes about. His ethnographic work 'suggests that those who worship god-images do not misconstrue human relations by reifying images, but construe the divinity of those images as an aspect of the interaction in the web of their social practices' (Simons, 2003: 2).

As a counter-point to Grieve's account of a 'local' visual culture, Lury (11.6) explains how the 'global' fashions of Benetton clothing have been marketed successfully using racial imagery that transcends racial categories by asserting the ubiquitous 'United Colors of Benetton'. Following from anthropologist Marilyn Strathern's (1992) account of how natural, innate properties combine with artificial cultural enhancement, Lury describes how race is 'created' as a second nature through *cultural essentialism*. In contrast to Gayatri Chakravorty Spivak's (1990) concept of 'strategic essentialism', in Lury's example, instead of a specific cultural identity being upheld for political reasons, a new postmodern, consumerist identity – commensurate with a design-led and brand-oriented image culture – is simulated and sold. Judith Butler (1990) also understands identity in terms of performativity, but rejects strategic essentialism.

REFERENCES

Bal, M. (2003) 'Visual essentialism and the object of visual culture', *Journal of Visual Culture*, 2 (1): 5–32.

Benjamin, W. (1999) *Charles Baudelaire*. London: Verso.

Butler, J. (1990) *Gender Trouble*. New York: Routledge.

Elkins, J. (2003) *Visual Studies: A Skeptical Introduction*. New York: Routledge.

Evans, J. and Hall, S. (eds) (1999) *Visual Culture: The Reader*. London: Sage.

Fuery, P. and Fuery, K. (2003) *Visual Cultures and Critical Theory*. London: Arnold.

Gleber, A. (1999) *The Art of Taking a Walk: Flanerie, Literature, and Film in Weimar Culture*. Princeton, NJ: Princeton University Press.

Howells, R. (2003) *Visual Culture: An Introduction*. Cambridge: Polity Press.

Jameson, F. (1991) *Postmodernism, Or, The Cultural Logic of Late Capitalism*. Durham, NC: Duke University Press.

Mirzoeff, N. (ed.) (1998) *Visual Culture Reader*. London: Routledge.

Mirzoeff, N. (1999) *An Introduction to Visual Culture*. London: Routledge.

Mitchell, W.J.T. (1994) *Picture Theory*. Chicago: University of Chicago Press.

Robins, K. (1996) *Into the Image: Culture and Politics in the Field of Vision*. London: Routledge.

Rogoff, I. (1998) 'Studying visual culture', in N. Mirzoeff (ed.), *Visual Culture Reader*. London: Routledge. pp. 14–26.

Rose, G. (2001) *Visual Methodologies: An Introduction to the Interpretation of Visual Materials*. London: Sage.

Simons, J. (2003) 'Editor's introduction', Special Issue: Images and Text, *Culture, Theory and Critique*, 44 (1): 1–4.

Spivak, G.C. (1990) *The Post-Colonial Critic: Interviews, Strategies, Dialogues*. New York: Routledge.

Strathern, M. (1992) *Reproducing the Future: Anthropology, Kinship and the New Reproductive Technologies*. Manchester: Manchester University Press.

Sturken, M. and Cartwright, L. (2001) *Practices of Looking: An Introduction to Visual Culture*. Oxford: Oxford University Press.

THE MEDIUM IS THE MESSAGE
MARSHALL MCLUHAN

The electric light is pure information. It is a medium without a message, as it were, unless it is used to spell out some verbal ad or name. This fact, characteristic of all media, means that the 'content' of any medium is always another medium. The content of writing is speech, just as the written word is the content of print, and print is the content of the telegraph. If it is asked, 'What is the content of speech?,' it is necessary to say, 'It is an actual process of thought, which is in itself nonverbal.' An abstract painting represents direct manifestation of creative thought processes as they might appear in computer designs. What we are considering here, however, are the psychic and social consequences of the designs or patterns as they amplify or accelerate existing processes. For the 'message' of any medium or technology is the change of scale or pace or pattern that it introduces into human affairs. The railway did not introduce movement or transportation or wheel or road into human society, but it accelerated and enlarged the scale of previous human functions, creating totally new kinds of cities and new kinds of work and leisure. This happened whether the railway functioned in a tropical or a northern environment, and is quite independent of the freight or content of the railway medium. The airplane, on the other hand, by accelerating the rate of transportation, tends to dissolve the railway form of city, politics, and association, quite independently of what the airplane is used for.

Let us return to the electric light. Whether the light is being used for brain surgery or night baseball is a matter of indifference. It could be argued that these activities are in some way the 'content' of the electric light, since they could not exist without the electric light. This fact merely underlines the point that 'the medium is the message' because it is the medium that shapes and controls the scale and form of human association and action. The content or uses of such media are as diverse as they are ineffectual in shaping the form of human association. Indeed, it is only too typical that the 'content' of any medium blinds us to the character of the medium. It is only today that industries have become aware of the various kinds of business in which they are engaged. When IBM discovered that it was not in the business of making office equipment or business machines, but that it was in the business of processing information, then it began to navigate with clear vision. The General Electric Company makes a considerable portion of its profits from electric light bulbs and lighting systems. It has not yet discovered that, quite as much as A.T.&T., it is in the business of moving information.

The electric light escapes attention as a communication medium just because it has no 'content.' And this makes it an invaluable instance of how people fail to study media at all. For it is not till the electric light is used to spell out some brand name that it is noticed as a medium. Then it is not the

Marshall McLuhan, from *Understanding Media: The Extensions of Man*. London: Routledge, 1997, pp. 8–9. Reproduced by permission of the T&F Informa and the MIT Press.

light but the 'content' (or what is really another medium) that is noticed. The message of the electric light is like the message of electric power in industry, totally radical, pervasive, and decentralized. For electric light and power are separate from their uses, yet they eliminate time and space factors in human association exactly as do radio, telegraph, telephone, and TV, creating involvement in depth.

THE IMAGE OF THE CITY
KEVIN LYNCH

11:2

Looking at cities can give a special pleasure, however commonplace the sight may be. Like a piece of architecture, the city is a construction in space, but one of vast scale, a thing perceived only in the course of long spans of time. City design is therefore a temporal art, but it can rarely use the controlled and limited sequences of other temporal arts like music. On different occasions and for different people, the sequences are reversed, interrupted, abandoned, cut across. It is seen in all lights and all weathers.

At every instant, there is more than the eye can see, more than the ear can hear, a setting or a view waiting to be explored. Nothing is experienced by itself, but always in relation to its surroundings, the sequences of events leading up to it, the memory of past experiences. Washington Street set in a farmer's field might look like the shopping street in the heart of Boston, and yet it would seem utterly different. Every citizen has had long associations with some part of his city, and his image is soaked in memories and meanings.

Moving elements in a city, and in particular the people and their activities, are as important as the stationary physical parts. We are not simply observers of this spectacle, but are ourselves a part of it, on the stage with the other participants. Most often, our perception of the city is not sustained, but rather partial, fragmentary, mixed with other concerns. Nearly every sense is in operation, and the image is the composite of them all.

[…]

An environmental image may be analyzed into three components: identity, structure, and meaning. It is useful to abstract these for analysis, if it is remembered that in reality they always appear together. A workable image requires first the identification of an object, which implies its distinction from other things, its recognition as a separable entity. This is called identity, not in the sense of equality with something else, but with the meaning of individuality or oneness. Second, the image must include the spatial or pattern relation of the object to the observer and to other objects. Finally, this object must have some meaning for the observer, whether practical or emotional. Meaning is also a relation, but quite a different one from spatial or pattern relation.

Kevin Lynch, from *The Image of the City*. Cambridge, MA: MIT Press, 1960, pp. 1–2, 8–13. Copyright © 1960 by The Massachusetts Institute of Technology and the President and Fellows of Harvard College.

[…]

This leads to the definition of what might be called *imageability*: that quality in a physical object which gives it a high probability of evoking a strong image in any given observer. It is that shape, color, or arrangement which facilitates the making of vividly identified, powerfully structured, highly useful mental images of the environment. It might also be called *legibility,* or perhaps *visibility* in a heightened sense, where objects are not only able to be seen, but are presented sharply and intensely to the senses.

[…]

A highly imageable (apparent, legible, or visible) city in this peculiar sense would seem well formed, distinct, remarkable; it would invite the eye and the ear to greater attention and participation. The sensuous grasp upon such surroundings would not merely be simplified, but also extended and deepened. Such a city would be one that could be apprehended over time as a pattern of high continuity with many distinctive parts clearly interconnected. The perceptive and familiar observer could absorb new sensuous impacts without disruption of his basic image, and each new impact would touch upon many previous elements. He would be well oriented, and he could move easily. He would be highly aware of his environment. The city of Venice might be an example of such a highly imageable environment. In the United States, one is tempted to cite parts of Manhattan, San Francisco, Boston, or perhaps the lake front of Chicago.

These are characterizations that flow from our definitions. The concept of imageability does not necessarily connote something fixed, limited, precise, unified, or regularly ordered, although it may sometimes have these qualities. Nor does it mean apparent at a glance, obvious, patent, or plain. The total environment to be patterned is highly complex, while the obvious image is soon boring, and can point to only a few features of the living world.

[…]

Since image development is a two-way process between observer and observed, it is possible to strengthen the image either by symbolic devices, by the retraining of the perceiver, or by reshaping one's surroundings. You can provide the viewer with a symbolic diagram of how the world fits together: a map or a set of written instructions. As long as he can fit reality to the diagram, he has a clue to the relatedness of things. You can even install a machine for giving directions, as has recently been done in New York.[1] While such devices are extremely useful for providing condensed data on interconnections, they are also precarious, since orientation fails if the device is lost, and the device itself must constantly be referred and fitted to reality.

[…]

You may also train the observer. Brown remarks that a maze through which subjects were asked to move blindfolded seemed to them at first to be one unbroken problem. On repetition, parts of the pattern, particularly the beginning and end, became familiar and assumed the character of localities.

Finally, when they could tread the maze without error, the whole system seemed to have become one locality.[2] [...]

Shipton's account of the reconnaissance for the ascent of Everest offers a dramatic case of such learning. Approaching Everest from a new direction, Shipton immediately recognized the main peaks and saddles that he knew from the north side. But the Sherpa guide accompanying him, to whom both sides were long familiar, had never realized that these were the same features, and he greeted the revelation with surprise and delight.[3]

[...]

In our vast metropolitan areas [...], like the Sherpa, we see only the sides of Everest and not the mountain. To extend and deepen our perception of the environment would be to continue a long biological and cultural development which has gone from the contact senses to the distant senses and from the distant senses to symbolic communications. Our thesis is that we are now able to develop our image of the environment by operation on the external physical shape as well as by an internal learning process. Indeed, the complexity of our environment now compels us to do so. [...]

Primitive man was forced to improve his environmental image by adapting his perception to the given landscape. He could effect minor changes in his environment with cairns, beacons, or tree blazes, but substantial modifications for visual clarity or visual interconnection were confined to house sites or religious enclosures. Only powerful civilizations can begin to act on their total environment at a significant scale. The conscious remolding of the large-scale physical environment has been possible only recently, and so the problem of environmental imageability is a new one.

NOTES

1. *New York Times*, April 30, 1957, article on the 'Directomat.'
2. Brown, Warner, 'Spatial Integrations in a Human Maze,' *University of California Publications in Psychology*, Vol. V, No. 5, 1932, pp. 123–134.
3. Shipton, Eric Earle, *The Mount Everest Reconnaissance Expedition*, London, Hodder and Stoughton, 1952.

THE IMAGE-WORLD
SUSAN SONTAG

11:3

Reality has always been interpreted through the reports given by images; and philosophers since Plato have tried to loosen our dependence on images by evoking the standard of an image-free way of apprehending the real. But when, in the mid-nineteenth century, the standard finally seemed attainable,

From *On Photography* by Susan Sontag (London: Allen Lane, 1978). London: Penguin, 1977, pp. 153–6, 160–1, 163–5, 167–9, 178–80. Copyright © Susan Sontag, 1973, 1974, 1977. Reproduced by permission of Penguin Books Ltd and Farrer, Straus and Giroux, LLC.

the retreat of old religious and political illusions before the advance of humanistic and scientific thinking did not – as anticipated – create mass defections to the real. On the contrary, the new age of unbelief strengthened the allegiance to images. The credence that could no longer be given to realities understood *in the form of* images was now being given to realities understood *to be* images, illusions. In the preface to the second edition (1843) of *The Essence of Christianity*, Feuerbach observes about 'our era' that it 'prefers the image to the thing, the copy to the original, the representation to the reality, appearance to being' – while being aware of doing just that. And his premonitory complaint has been transformed in the twentieth century into a widely agreed-on diagnosis: that a society becomes 'modern' when one of its chief activities is producing and consuming images, when images that have extraordinary powers to determine our demands upon reality and are themselves coveted substitutes for firsthand experience become indispensable to the health of the economy, the stability of the polity, and the pursuit of private happiness.

[…]

Most contemporary expressions of concern that an image-world is replacing the real one continue to echo, as Feuerbach did, the Platonic depreciation of the image: true insofar as it resembles something real, sham because it is no more than a resemblance. But this venerable naive realism is somewhat beside the point in the era of photographic images, for its blunt contrast between the image ('copy') and the thing depicted (the 'original') – which Plato repeatedly illustrates with the example of a painting – does not fit a photograph in so simple a way. Neither does the contrast help in understanding image-making at its origins, when it was a practical, magical activity, a means of appropriating or gaining power over something. The further back we go in history, as E.H. Gombrich has observed, the less sharp is the distinction between images and real things; in primitive societies, the thing and its image were simply two different, that is, physically distinct, manifestations of the same energy or spirit. Hence, the supposed efficacy of images in propitiating and gaining control over powerful presences. Those powers, those presences were present in *them*.

[…]

The problem with Feuerbach's contrast of 'original' with 'copy' is its static definitions of reality and image. It assumes that what is real persists, unchanged and intact, while only images have changed: shored up by the most tenuous claims to credibility, they have somehow become more seductive. But the notions of image and reality are complementary. When the notion of reality changes, so does that of the image, and vice versa. 'Our era' does not prefer images to real things out of perversity but partly in response to the ways in which the notion of what is real has been progressively complicated and weakened […].

Few people in this society share the primitive dread of cameras that comes from thinking of the photograph as a material part of themselves. But some trace of the magic remains: for example, in our reluctance to tear up or throw away the photograph of a loved one, especially of someone dead or far away. To do so is a ruthless gesture of rejection. In *Jude the Obscure* it is Jude's discovery that Arabella has sold the maple frame with the photograph of himself in it which he gave her on their wedding day that signifies to Jude 'the utter death of every sentiment in his wife' and is 'the conclusive little stroke to demolish all sentiment in him.' But the true modern primitivism is not to regard the image as a real thing; photographic images are hardly that real. Instead, reality has come to seem more and more like what we are shown by cameras. It is common now for people to insist about their experience of a violent event in which they were caught up – a plane crash, a shoot-out, a terrorist bombing – that 'it seemed like a movie.' This is said, other descriptions seeming insufficient, in order to explain how real it was. While many people in non-industrialized countries still feel apprehensive when being photographed, divining it to be some kind of trespass, an act of disrespect, a sublimated looting of the personality or the culture, people in industrialized countries seek to have their photographs taken – feel that they are images, and are made real by photographs.

[…]

Photographs are a way of imprisoning reality, understood as recalcitrant, inaccessible; of making it stand still. Or they enlarge a reality that is felt to be shrunk, hollowed out, perishable, remote. One can't possess reality, one can possess (and be possessed by) images – as, according to Proust, most ambitious of voluntary prisoners, one can't possess the present but one can possess the past. Nothing could be more unlike the self-sacrificial travail of an artist like Proust than the effortlessness of picture-taking, which must be the sole activity resulting in accredited works of art in which a single movement, a touch of the finger, produces a complete work. While the Proustian labors presuppose that reality is distant, photography implies instant access to the real. But the results of this practice of instant access are another way of creating distance. To possess the world in the form of images is, precisely, to re-experience the unreality and remoteness of the real.

The strategy of Proust's realism presumes distance from what is normally experienced as real, the present, in order to reanimate what is usually available only in a remote and shadowy form, the past – which is where the present becomes in his sense real, that is, something that can be possessed. In this effort photographs were of no help. Whenever Proust mentions photographs, he does so disparagingly: as a synonym for a shallow, too exclusively visual, merely voluntary relation to the past, whose yield is insignificant compared with the deep discoveries to be made by responding to cues given by all the senses – the technique he called 'involuntary memory.' One can't imagine the Overture to *Swann's Way* ending with the narrator's coming across a snapshot of the parish church at Combray and the savoring of *that* visual crumb, instead of the taste of the humble madeleine dipped in tea, making an entire part of his past spring into view. But this is not because a photograph cannot evoke memories (it can, depending on the quality of the viewer rather than of the photograph) but because of what Proust makes clear about his own demands upon imaginative recall, that it be not just extensive and accurate but give the texture and essence of things. And by considering photographs only so far as he could use them, as an instrument of memory, Proust somewhat misconstrues what photographs are: not so much an instrument of memory as an invention of it or a replacement.

[…]

Photography, which has so many narcissistic uses, is also a powerful instrument for depersonalizing our relation to the world; and the two uses are complementary. Like a pair of binoculars with no right or wrong end, the camera makes exotic things near, intimate; and familiar things small, abstract, strange, much farther away. It offers, in one easy, habit-forming activity, both participation and alienation in our own lives and those of others – allowing us to participate, while confirming alienation. War and photography now seem inseparable, and plane crashes and other horrific accidents always attract people with cameras. A society which makes it normative to aspire never to experience privation, failure, misery, pain, dread disease, and in which death itself is regarded not as natural and inevitable but as a cruel, unmerited disaster, creates a tremendous curiosity about these events – a curiosity that is partly satisfied through picture-taking. The feeling of being exempt from calamity stimulates interest in looking at painful pictures, and looking at them suggests and strengthens the feeling that one is exempt. Partly it is because one is 'here,' not 'there,' and partly it is the character of inevitability that all events acquire when they are transmuted into images. In the real world, something is happening and no one knows what is *going* to happen. In the image-world, it *has* happened, and it *will* forever happen in that way.

Knowing a great deal about what is in the world (art, catastrophe, the beauties of nature) through photographic images, people are frequently disappointed, surprised, unmoved when they see the real thing. For photographic images tend to subtract feeling from something we experience at first hand and the feelings they do arouse are, largely, not those we have in real life. Often something disturbs us more in photographed form than it does when we actually experience it. In a hospital in Shanghai in 1973, watching a factory worker with advanced ulcers have nine-tenths of his stomach removed under acupuncture anesthesia, I managed to follow the three-hour procedure (the first operation I'd ever observed) without queasiness, never once feeling the need to look away. In a movie theater in Paris a year later, the less gory operation in Antonioni's China documentary *Chung Kuo* made me flinch at the first cut of the scalpel and avert my eyes several times during the sequence. One is vulnerable to disturbing events in the form of photographic images in a way that one is not to the real thing. That vulnerability is part of the distinctive passivity of someone who is a spectator twice over, spectator of events already shaped, first by the participants and second by the image maker. For the real operation I had to get scrubbed, don a surgical gown, then stand alongside the busy surgeons and nurses with my roles to play: inhibited adult, well-mannered guest, respectful witness. The movie operation precludes not only this modest participation but whatever is active in spectatorship. In the operating room, I am the one who changes focus, who makes the close-ups and the medium shots. In the theater, Antonioni has already chosen what parts of the operation I can watch; the camera looks for me – and obliges me to look, leaving as my only option not to look. Further, the movie condenses something that takes hours to a few minutes, leaving only interesting parts presented in an interesting way, that is, with the intent to stir or shock. The dramatic is dramatized, by the didactics of layout and montage. We turn the page in a photo-magazine, a new sequence starts in a movie, making a contrast that is sharper than the contrast between successive events in real time.

[…]

The final reason for the need to photograph everything lies in the very logic of consumption itself. To consume means to burn, to use up – and, therefore, to need to be replenished. As we make images and consume them, we need still more images; and still more. But images are not a treasure for which the world must be ransacked; they are precisely what is at hand wherever the eye falls. The possession of a camera can inspire something akin to lust. And like all credible forms of lust, it cannot be satisfied: first, because the possibilities of photography are infinite; and, second, because the project is finally self-devouring. The attempts by photographers to bolster up a depleted sense of reality contribute to the depletion. Our oppressive sense of the transience of everything is more acute since cameras gave us the means to 'fix' the fleeting moment. We consume images at an ever faster rate and, as Balzac suspected cameras used up layers of the body, images consume reality. Cameras are the antidote and the disease, a means of appropriating reality and a means of making it obsolete.

The powers of photography have in effect de-Platonized our understanding of reality, making it less and less plausible to reflect upon our experience according to the distinction between images and things, between copies and originals. It suited Plato's derogatory attitude toward images to liken them to shadows – transitory, minimally informative, immaterial, impotent co-presences of the real things which cast them. But the force of photographic images comes from their being material realities in their own right, richly informative deposits left in the wake of whatever emitted them, potent means for turning the tables on reality – for turning *it* into a shadow. Images are more real than anyone could have supposed. And just because they are an unlimited resource, one that cannot be exhausted by consumerist waste, there is all the more reason to apply the conservationist remedy. If there can be a better way for the real world to include the one of images, it will require an ecology not only of real things but of images as well.

11:4 THE PHILOSOPHER AS ANDY WARHOL
ARTHUR DANTO

A man sees what looks like an ordinary soap-pad carton in a shop window and, needing to ship some books, asks the shopkeeper if he can have it. The shop turns out to be an art gallery and the shopkeeper a dealer who says: 'That is a work of art, just now worth thirty thousand dollars.'

A man sees what looks like Warhol's Brillo box in what looks like an art gallery, and asks the dealer, who turns out to be a shopkeeper, how much it is. The latter says the man can have it, he was going to throw it away anyway, it got placed in the window temporarily after it was unpacked.

[…]

I have often found myself struck by the irony that someone so outwardly unlikely as Warhol, who seemed to the artworld so little possessed of intellectual gifts and powers, so cool, so caught up in low culture – in kitsch! – should in fact have displayed philosophical intuitions quite beyond those of his peers who read Kant and spouted existentialism and cited Kierkegaard and used the heaviest, most highfalutin vocabularies. When I claimed, in an essay I published at the time of his posthumous retrospective exhibition at the Museum of Modern Art, that he was the nearest to a philosophical genius that twentieth-century art had brought forth, I was looked on with some incredulity by a good many of my friends, who held him in very low intellectual esteem. It is true that one of Warhol's contributions to culture was a certain look – that of the leather-clad, pale, lank night-child, monosyllabic and cool, unmoved by 'art, beauty, and laughter,' to cite de Kooning's trinity. But that persona was itself one of his works – a certain embodiment of 'the artist of modern times.' He achieved something antipodal to the paint-smeared proletarian persona of the Cedar Bar: he became what he did.

[…]

His work and his life were one because he transformed his life into the image of an artist's life, and was able to join the images that composed the substance of art. Unlike Duchamp, Warhol sought to set up a resonance not so much between art and real objects as between art and images, it having been his insight […], that our signs and images are our reality. We live in an atmosphere of images, and these define the reality of our existences. Whoever and whatever Marilyn Monroe actually was is hardly as important as her images are in defining a certain female essence, which,

Arthur C. Danto, from 'The Philosopher as Andy Warhol', in *Philosophizing Art: Selected Essays*. Berkeley, CA: University of California Press, 1999, pp. 65 and 80–2. Copyright © 1999, Arthur C. Danto. Reprinted by permission of the author and Georges Borchardt Inc.

when it was vital, condensed men's attitudes toward women and women's attitudes toward themselves. She *was* her images, on screens and in magazines, and it was in this form that she entered common life. She became part of our own being because she occupied the shared consciousness of modern men and women the world around. Nothing could be hauled up out of the depths of the unconscious that could possibly have the magic and power of Marilyn.

Warhol's art gave objectivity to the common cultural mind. To participate in that mind is to know, immediately, the meaning and identity of certain images: to know, without having to ask, who are Marilyn and Elvis, Liz and Jackie, Campbell's soup and Brillo, or today, after Warhol's death, Madonna and Bart Simpson. To have to ask who these images belong to is to declare one's distance from the culture. This made Warhol an utterly public artist, at one with the culture he made objective. There are connected with this two forms of death – the cessation of life and the obsolescence of one's images. When no one recognizes who a photograph is of, only then is the subject of that photograph irrecoverably dead. True fame in the modern world is to have one image recognized by persons who never knew anything but the image. True immortality is to achieve an image that outlasts oneself, and that continues to be part of the common mind indefinitely – like Charlie Chaplin, or JFK, or Warhol himself. His self-portraits are portraits of his image, and hence as much and as little him as his portraits of Marilyn are 'really' her.

[…]

Warhol invented a form of portraiture that henceforward specified the way stars would appear. Everyone he portrayed became instantly glamorous through being transformed into the unmistakable Warholesque image: Liza Minnelli, Barbra Streisand, Albert Einstein, Mick Jagger, Leo Castelli. The art dealer Holly Solomon commissioned her portrait and exclaimed over the way Warhol turned her into 'this Hollywood starlet.' But in an odd way there was a certain equality in the subjects: just as the Coke drunk by Liz Taylor is no better than the one drunk by the bum on the corner, so Chairman Mao is no more a star than Bianca Jagger, and the black and Latino transvestites of the print series 'Ladies and Gentlemen' are no less – or more – glamorous than Truman Capote or Lana Turner … or the Death Star is no different from the human skull. This is how one looks in one's own fifteen minutes of world fame. 'If you want to know all about Andy Warhol,' he said in an interview in 1967, 'just look at the surface.'

There is more to it than that. He turned the world we share into art, and turned himself into part of that world, and because we *are* the images we hold in common with everyone else, he became part of us. So he might have said: if you want to know who Andy Warhol is, look within. Or, for that matter, look without. You, I, the world we share are all of a piece.

11:5 SYMBOL, IDOL AND MŪRTI: HINDU GOD-IMAGES AND THE POLITICS OF MEDIATION

GREGORY PRICE GRIEVE

When I arrived in Nepal in June 1995 to begin fieldwork, one of the first questions I was asked was 'So just what is (a) god?' It was the early afternoon … and I was drinking a Coke and writing down some scratch field notes. The questioner was one of the ubiquitous high school students-cum-predatory guides who had just peeled himself off a large group of tourists. After I declined a tour, he saw me taking notes, so he sat down next to me and asked what I was doing. I told him I was in Nepal to study religion. He looked at me askance and asked: 'So just what is (a) god?' I could not answer. I was silenced not by a lack of concepts, but rather because as the school student asked the question, he teasingly pointed across the square to the material god-image of the god Bhairava (Figure 11.1).

FIGURE 11.1

God-Image of Bhairava (By Purna Chitrakar (1999), 22.5 × 18 inches). Photograph: G. Grieve, 1999. **See colour Plate 2**

Gregory Price Grieve, from *Culture, Theory and Critique*, Vol. 44, Issue 1, 2003, London: Routledge, pp. 57–72.

One of the most common religious practices in South Asia is *darśan*, which occurs when a devotee gazes upon a material image of a god (Eck, 1996). Stop and take a second look at the god-image of Bhairava, a fierce form of Śiva from the Nepalese city of Bhaktapur. What can you make of this image? Bhairava is a stone god (*loha(n)dya:*) – a humanly constructed concrete deity. *Loha(n)dya:* literally translates from the Newar (Nepal Bhåså) as 'stone (*loha[n]*) god (*dya:*)' and is the local idiom for the pan-South Asian notion of *mūrti*. *Mūrtis* are concrete signs of gods and can be either aniconic or iconic. They are the ritually consecrated images at the center of the chief form of Hindu religious practice, worship (*pujā*).

What occurs when one looks face-to-face with Bhairava's god-image? What can one make of this stone god? If you, like me, find yourself trained in and by 'Western' academic discourses or have been trained in educational systems in other parts of the globe which gain distinction by modeling themselves on elite occidental pedagogy, it is difficult to face up to Bhairava's otherness.[1] This god-image challenges one's understanding. When one gazes at his three fish-like eyes (two large, one small), sharp, fanged teeth, flaming orange-red lips and elaborate, multicolored, snake-encrusted headdress it is hard to escape one's own historical, class and geographic bias. In a skewed Levinasian sense, the 'idol's' face resists our powers to understand (Levinas, 1969: 81). In short, a look at Bhairava shows that there is no innocent 'eye', no naïve viewing. [...] Rather, all social objects are mediated by intervening socially grounded, culturally generated and historically particular mechanisms. Moreover, these intervening mechanisms are not neutral, but are marbled through and through with power relations. For instance, the Bhairava image that hangs on the wall of my office holds a different social meaning than an image of the god *in situ*. In such a case, the image transforms from 'god' to 'art'. That is, the stone-god's *in situ* contextual divine meaning is replaced with a depoliticised aesthetic one.

*

From a scripturalist position, god-images are seen at best as supplements, and at worst as deterrents, to a real understanding of the divine. Mirroring this, scriptural accounts tend toward two mediating strategies: symbolism and idolatry. By mediating strategy, I mean to gloss no particular school, method, or theory, but rather the wider tactics by which god-images are 'turned into' Book-knowledge.

The first interpretative strategy, symbolism, erases the materiality of god-images by positing them as material signs of spiritual transcendental categories. [...] In the broadest sense, the symbolic function has been posed as the general function of mediation by which consciousness constructs all perception and discourse (Cassirer, 1946). In the narrowest sense it means something other than what is said (Ricoeur, 1970: 12). Always, however, the symbol is a vehicle at once universal and particular. Moreover, because symbols' referents are often vague, the symbol is crucial for bringing together abstract scriptural concepts and concrete signs (Firth, 1973: 6–17, 55; Ricoeur, 1976: 53).

The second mediating strategy, idolatry, interprets concrete gods such as Bhairava as material objects of irrational reverence or obsessive devotion.

In the simplest sense, an idol is an image or statue of a deity fashioned to act as an object of worship. Yet, often such worship is perceived as immoral because idolatry gives the name of God to that which is not God. [...] Yet, because all signification is dependent on material signs, all religions must worship matter to some extent. Accordingly, 'idolatry' is not simply the worship of matter, but the accusation of another's 'strange worship' (Halbertal and Margalit, 1992). Lingering in the rhetoric of the idol is one of the most persistent forms of orientalism. [... In] every situation idolatry is a strategy by which a 'community [creates] self-definition through its idea of what is excluded and through its notion of "the other"' (Halbertal and Margalit 1992: 17, 236).

The danger with the two scriptural mediating strategies is [...] that they tend to perpetuate what Bruce Lincoln calls 'immoral discourses,' that is, those that 'systematically operate to benefit the already privileged members of society at the expense of others' (1981: 112). For instance, rather than being an essential object, the 'idol' is created by a constellation of discourses that are linked with the idea of misrepresentation. Similarly, the danger with symbolism is that the material god images are hijacked to reveal a scriptural transcendental signified and to reinforce a dominant view of the world. In both cases, Bhairava is defaced. He is no longer situated in his own domain of social practices, but becomes a signifier of scriptural transcendental categories. In short, both mediating strategies are hypocritical. They hide their own agenda behind the mask of the 'other'.

*

Bhairava is neither an idol nor a symbol. He is a stone god (loha(n)dya:), a humanly constructed material deity which is brought to life in a conversation of gazes. In a stone-god the material component (signifier) is the dominant element. To understand how such concrete images are used to construct the divine, what need be attended to are the local cultural logics in which they are situated.

[...]

Stones are constituted as stone gods (loha(n)dya:) in two ways: descriptively, and through ceremonies and continuing rituals (pujā) which give the stone life (jiva). Descriptively murtis depict the deity. As Līlabhakta Munikarmi said, 'If you believe in (the god) Vishnu then you need a mūrti describing what he looks like. You know him the same way you would know by seeing your father's photograph. That he has two arms, hair and also you can see the fashion of the time' (personal interview, 10 June 1999). In this sense the carved image is seen as an aid to visualizing the god. Yet, not only are there carved statues which are not mūrtis, there are many aniconic stones which are worshipped as gods. The symbolic signification is secondary to the stone god's power (śakti) that is created by its life force (jiva). Mūrti can be both symbolic and have 'power', but it is jiva which transforms the stone (loha(n)) into a stone god (loha(n)dya:). [...] Hence, while the descriptive quality and conceptual levels of a *murti* are important, they are not the defining features. [...] This is especially significant for Bhairavas, most of which are aniconic. What this demonstrates is that instead of an iconic symbolic representation, a *murti's* signification comes from giving life to a stone. In fact, a *mūrti* is 'dead' until life is put into it through ceremonies. Thereafter the image is not merely a symbol of that deity, but it *is* that deity.

[...]

[...One] of the ways that people in Bhaktapur indicate that they are going to worship a god is through the notion of *darśan*, which literally means 'to see'. [...] As Damodar Gautam said: 'To go to the temple and have a face-to-face with the god's image – that is *darśan*' (personal interview, 21 June 1999). When one goes and has a 'face-to-face' with the god, it is not just that the worshiper is seeing the god, but that the god looks back at the worshipers (Eck, 1996: 6). [...] The seeing and being seen between worshiper and god, the investing a *mūrti* with the ability to look at us in return, is a tactic for bringing it into social relations and thus constituting its personhood.

[...] People in Bhaktapur are made. They are constituted through two main social semiotics: rites of passage, and a net of social relations. First, for Newars, creating a person is not a natural process, but a ritual process. The chief set of rituals are the rites of passage (samskāras), a developmental sequence of life starting with writing on the infant's tongue, going through puberty rites, marriage, and ending with funeral ceremonies (Levy, 1990: 658-686; Parish, 1994: 233–275). In Newar culture, the innate, unrefined person is not viewed as sufficient for social life. As Tejeswar Babu Gongah once told me: 'Just as a rough rock is polished smooth, a child must be made into a person by culture' (personal interview, 15 June 1997). The same goes for stone gods (*loha(n)dya:*). [...]

In short, there is no absolute distinction between gods and people (Babb, 1975: 52; Fuller, 1992: 3). As a 'person' Bhairava both creates others, and is in turn created by his social relations with others. Newar society is tied together through a complex web of giving and receiving both goods and favors (Lewis, 1984: 14). Newars in Bhaktapur speak of this web as a net (Parish, 1994: 130). For Newars, the self is not bounded, but created by a net of social relations. [...] Hence, Bhairava is 'alive' (*jiva*) because he is set in a social net (*janjal*) of contingent mutual dependency in which he is treated as if he were a person. Yet, in this net, Bhairava is not just any person; he is extra-ordinary. [...]

*

Take one last look at Bhairava's god-image (Figure 11.1). When a statue is given life, it is said that its eyes have been opened. And during *darśan* once the image's eyes are opened, it gazes back at the worshipers. Up until now, we've been looking at the god. What happens when the stone god looks back? In *Totality and Infinity*, Emmanuel Levinas writes that 'everything that cannot be reduced to an interhuman relation represents not the superior form but the forever primitive form of religion' (Levinas 1969: 79). In a sense Bhairava's god-image both supports and transgresses Levinas' understanding of the divine, and at the very least it qualifies it.

What the god-image qualifies is the scriptural bias of the Western understanding of the divine. Similarly, my encounter with the stone god – initially humiliating or, at best, frustrating – turned out to be serendipitous, for it defamiliarized me from the assumption that scripture must form the foundation of a religious tradition. It showed that in order to properly understand Hindu belief and practice one needs an understanding of situated everyday practice, especially the worship (*pujā*) of god-images (*mūrti*). My encounter indicates that to understand how the concrete god-image is used in everyday Hinduism one must understand that Bhairava is neither a symbol nor an idol, but a *murti*: a divine sign whose material component dominates. To a worshiper of everyday Hinduism, deities are not only transcendental concepts to be imagined, they are tangible practice – gods should be seen, heard, touched, and even tasted. Yet, while the material element is crucial, for the stone to become a stone god it must be situated in *in situ* cultural logics, that is, the mutually contingent net of social relations which give life to the stone. In short, what the god-image demonstrates is that a scriptural understanding of god-images differs from an everyday one, not because of the former's use of material signs, but rather because the material signs are mediated differently.

NOTE
1. Footnote removed.

WORKS CITED

Babb, L. 1975. *The Divine Hierarchy.* New York: Columbia University Press.

Cassirer, E. 1946. *Language and Myth.* Translated by Susanne K. Langer. London: Harper & Brothers.

Eck, D. 1996. *Darsan: Seeing The Divine Image In India.* 2nd edition, revised and enlarged. New York: Columbia University Press.

Firth, R.W. 1973. *Symbols: Public and Private.* Ithaca, NY: Cornell University Press.

Fuller, C.J. 1992. *The Camphor Flame: Popular Hinduism and Society in India.* Princeton, NJ: Princeton University Press.

Halbertal, M. and A. Margalit. 1992. *Idolatry.* Translated by Naomi Goldblum. Cambridge, MA: Harvard University Press.

Levinas, E. 1969. *Totality and Infinity.* Pittsburgh: Duquesne University Press.

Levy, Robert. 1990. *Mesocosm: Hinduism and the Organization of a Traditional Newar City in Nepal.* Berkeley, CA: University of California Press.

Lewis, Todd. 1984. *The Tuladhars of Kathmandu: A Study of Buddhist Traditions in a Newar Merchant Community.* Ann Arbor, MI: University Microfilms International.

Lincoln, B. 1981. *Emerging from the Chrysalis: Studies in Rituals of Women's Initiation.* Cambridge, MA: Harvard University Press.

Parish, S. 1994. *Moral Knowing in a Hindu Sacred City.* New York: Columbia University Press.

Ricoeur, P. 1970. *Freud and Philosophy. An Essay on Mediating.* Translated by Denis Savage. New Haven, CT: Yale University Press.

Ricoeur, P. 1976. *Narration Theory.* Fort Worth: Christian University Press.

THE UNITED COLORS OF DIVERSITY
CELIA LURY 11:6

Benetton's claim to own goodness, if you believe their marketing personnel, has been accepted at face value by all of us: 'If you see five colours together and three different faces, you say "that's Benetton …," even if it really isn't' (Mattei, n.d.: 4). However, it was not until 1984 that the imagery … first began to be used by Benetton to promote its clothing in international advertising campaigns; until then, the company's marketing had been primarily focussed on the representation of the products themselves. The press release accompanying the new campaign described the images as 'Groups of young people, of different races and sizes … photographed jumping and laughing' (quoted in Back and Quaade, 1993: 67). These images are still with us, although the slogan accompanying them changed from 'All the Colors of the World' to the now ubiquitous 'United Colors of Benetton' in 1985. In these photographs, young people, sometimes waving national flags, or bedecked with national emblems such as stars and stripes, hammers and sickles, with accentuated, racially coded physical characteristics, parade in colourful clothes.

[…]

FIGURE 11.2
Swimsuits (Benetton brochure)/*Jumper of many colors* (Benetton brochure). Courtesy of the Benetton Group SPA / *Colors* magazine. **See colour Plate 4**

Celia Lury, from *Global Nature, Global Culture*, eds Sarah Franklin, Celia Lury and Jackie Stacey. London: Sage, 2000, pp. 147–9. Reproduced by permission of Sage Publications and the author.

Certainly Benetton's advertising is distinctive – at least in the UK – for its use of explicitly racially coded models: in general, advertising continues to be remarkably white.[1] In what ways, though, do Benetton's photographic images represent diversity? How do these pictures mediate the relations between the specific and the universal, the cultural and the natural? As Back and Quaade observe, the dominant theme of Benetton's campaign is 'the accentuation of difference coupled with a simple statement of transcendence and global unity' (1993: 68). Applying the work of Stuart Hall, Back and Quaade further argue that this accentuation of difference is generated within a grammar of race:

> [T]he overpowering reference point in their imagery is that *race is real:* racial archetypes provide the vehicle for their message, and racial common sense is overbearingly *present* in the 'United Colors' myth, such that the reality of race is legitimated in Benetton's discourse. (1993: 79, original emphasis)

However, while the legitimation of race in Benetton's campaigns seems beyond dispute, I want to suggest that the novel productivity of these images is missed if it is argued that racial difference is *naturalised* here, if by that is meant that race is presented as an unchanging and eternal biological essence. 'Race', in this imagery, is not a matter of skin colour, of physical characteristics as the expression of a biological or natural essence, but rather of style, of the colour of skin, of colour itself as the medium of what might be called a second nature or, more provocatively, a *cultural essentialism.*

As noted above, 'The idea that's being sold is mainly colour and *joie de vivre* and can be recognised as such' (Mattei, n.d.: 4). So, for example, in Benetton promotional campaigns, young people are colour-coded: they are juxtaposed together to bring out colour contrasts as in Benetton outlets, in which stacks of jumpers are folded and piled up so as to seem as if they are paint colour charts. The overall effect of colour – not any particular colour but colour as such, colour as the medium of difference – is enhanced through the graduations in tone, the suggested compatibility of hues and contrasts in tints created by the endless repositioning of one shade against another. In the creation of this effect, the distinction between cloth and skin is eschewed. In a promotional illustration for tights, for example, the viewer is confronted by a series of legs in profile, each slightly different in shape ('different races and sizes'), completely encased in multi-coloured tights. Here, skin colour is not simply made invisible but displaced and reworked as a stylised act of choice: what colour is your skin going to be today? (The same choice was promoted by Crayola in the production of 'My World Colors', a box of sixteen crayons, supposedly representing the diversity of skin, hair and eye colours, from sepia to raw peach, of the peoples of a colouring-book world.) Similarly, in the publicity images adopted by Benetton of white and black faces daubed with brightly coloured sun-protection creams, the colour of skin is made up/out to be artificial. Race is not not 'real' here, but it is no longer founded in biology but in culture, that is, in culture as a second nature (despite or, rather, precisely because of the play on the white western depiction of 'primitive' tribes through the trope of face-painting).[2]

In yet another example, two eyes, of different colours, look out from a black face. The face is shot in such close-up that only the area surrounding the eyes is visible; the skin appears stretched to the edges of the image such that the contours of the face are flattened: its features and outline are hard to make out. Across this canvas is written, in white capitals, FABRICA, a word which, while taken from the Italian *fabbrica* (factory),[3] also draws on the idea of Andy Warhol's New York City Factory of the 1960s. It resonates with the association of fabrication for English speakers: skin is once again represented as cloth. The promotional slogan 'United Colors of Benetton' is attached, as always, to the side of the image, as if it were a label. This is, in Marilyn Strathern's phrase, nature 'enterprised up' (1992): the natural, innate property and the artificial, cultural enhancement become one. Perusing Benetton's fashion catalogues, the viewer's gaze is drawn from shade to shade, obeying the textual laws of writing rather than the realist ones of verisimilitude, depth and figure. Biology is no longer a referent for race; rather, race is created in the colours constituted in the arbitrary relations between signifier and signified.

NOTES
1. Footnote removed.
2. Footnote removed.
3. Fabrica is also the name of the arts and communication centre of the Benetton group.

WORKS CITED

Back, Les and Quaade, Vibeke (1993), 'Dream Utopias, Nightmare Realities: imaging race and culture within the world of Benetton advertising', *Third Text*, 22: 65–80.

Mattei, Francesa (n.d.) 'A Matter of Style', *News: United Colors of Benetton*: 4–5.

Strathern, M. (1992) *Reproducing the Future: Anthropology, Kinship and the New Reproductive Technologies*. Manchester: Manchester University Press.

THE UNBEARABLE LIGHTNESS OF SIGHT
MEILING CHENG

11:7

How do feminism and visual culture intersect? It is easier to pose an analogy than to answer a complicated question straight on: a set of colors is infused into an undulating pond, a pond of suspended visions. The colors, viscous (in oil-based paint), offer a certain vibrancy to the visions, coating them with an additional texture and seemingly making the phantasmatic floating sights more focused, hence more 'materialized,' especially at the earlier moments when the colors are first introduced to the pond one by one. The visions are gradually awash with yellow, white, pink, green, red, brown, blue, purple, black, and multiple other colors, to the extent that these visions are both reshaped and disguised by the colors and the colors also generate their own floating images. We see a plenitude upon plenitude: their intersection is splendor in disorientation.

HOW IS FEMINISM A SET OF COLORS?

Feminism started out as a simple impulse: to question the patriarchal status quo that presupposed gender inequality. The methods used by feminists in the 1970s to put this redressive impulse into action varied. Some challenged the constraining effects of gender conditioning; some advocated for women's self-determination, economic independence, and political liberation; some attacked the hegemony of masculocentric representations; some asserted the materiality of sexual difference, while pursuing women's right to full citizenship. Each method may be likened to a prime color, with its unique agenda and objectives similar to the particular density and distribution of pigment in each color. As a color tends to saturate and coordinate the surface of an image, so the set of ideological programs associated with feminism functions to orient the words, attitudes, and actions of a feminist.

These 'prime colors,' however, soon proved inadequate matches to the complexity of life. Within feminism, the confrontation with gender oppression alone proved insufficient when the interlocking effects of race, ethnicity, class, age, physical ability, and sexuality were laid open and critiqued. This shift toward greater complexity is not antithetical to the feminist ethos, for its inclusive tendency has prepared most feminists to welcome the intersubjective mandate of self-revision. All-inclusiveness, however, has its side effect of loose proliferation. After three decades' popular dissemination of the term, feminism now becomes a mutable label open to multiple, and often contradictory, censures and applications. A movement that began by exposing the specificity of variegated experiences of subjugation grows to subsume a multiplicity of causes, some of which have little to do with its formative, interventionist impulse. Imagine more and more colors are added to the pond in such rapid intervals that we can no longer discern individual patterns, and least of all evaluate their discord in abstraction. If we, as feminists, desire to tell more stories about the floating visions in our own voices, this may be the moment that we must pause and select more carefully the colors on our palette. Limitation offers us the freedom to intervene with sophisticated clarity.

HOW DO WE COMPARE VISUAL CULTURE TO AN UNDULATING POND OF VISIONS?

Visual culture assembles diverse accesses to a phenomenal world that sustains and envelops us primarily through our senses especially through our optical sense, which extends the reach of our sensory body. The condition of sensory extension is a plus, but also a necessity, as distance is prerequisite for vision. We are capable of seeing only that which stands apart from our eyes. This state of apartness entails that the majority of sights are foreign to, or other than, our being. A dispossessed endowment, our vision can neither own nor transfix the object of its gaze, even though the object under surveillance may feel threatened by this gaze. A certain liquidity distances our act of seeing from the seen; we approach visible sights as if through a watery screen, a pond of visions that keep undulating. Indeed, the saying 'seeing is believing' comments on the impossibility, for us, of verifying a sight purely through seeing, for a belief is born/e precisely to defer the uncertainty of (a) being. We believe what we see in order not to lose (sight of) that to which our visual desire clings. Being unverifiable, the object of our visual desire – as a floating sight in our optical pond – dangles in indeterminacy, glowing in a surfeit of free-ranging signification that resists semantic fixity. But we enact our desire by investing our belief in the visual object, encrypting certain meanings and projecting them onto the image to stop its rippling into invisibility, a disappearance that would register our inability to access the field beyond visuality. Pouring colors onto the floating visions is, then, one way to pre-empt the disappearance of the visible and thus to put in abeyance our mourning for the lost sight.

Like an optical pond that gathers floating images by random accretion, the field of visual culture tends to expand in its inventory of study objects, which are, theoretically, a collection of any visible sight invested with a perceiver's desire. Visual culture, given inherently to multiplicity, triggers the interest in finding ways of comprehending and deciphering the existing images manufactured by contemporary culture. The conundrum hidden in this scenario is the discrepancy of intentionality between the subject of inquiry and the inquiring subject: the image seized for view, however deliberately designed, exists in a state of indifference, whereas the viewer is most likely already overdetermined by her/his interpretive desire. Perhaps the best we can do is to bypass the conundrum by pursuing the liberating potential of that discrepancy, recognizing the being of an image as light/intangible and the core of a desire as heavy/matter-producing. We allow the heavy to impinge upon the light, not to deaden the light, but to turn it into a certain illuminating matter.

Heavy like a set of colors, feminism seeks to produce significant matters that redress the myopia of phallocentric culture. As feminists, we may regard visual culture as a system of commodification heavily encoded with phallocentric values, or simply as a floating gallery of aggregating images phantasmatic in their void of values. The former requires our critique as we challenge the masculinist hegemony that has processed visual representations surreptitiously for its own perpetuation. The latter yields a vast productive space for us to play with subversive colors, those that engender our own narratives, allowing them to radiate from the undulating visions in the pond. When we heed the lightness of sight, we gain the potential of making its lightness as heavy as a commitment.

12: VISION AND VISUALITY

INTRODUCTION

At a most basic level we might suggest that 'vision' refers to what physiologically we are capable of seeing, while the relatively new term 'visuality' refers to how vision is socially, historically and culturally constructed. The term visuality is used somewhat unevenly in visual culture studies (see Section 11, Visual Culture) and is often interchangeable with the phrase 'scopic regime' – originally used by Christian Metz (7.2) in his psychoanalytic studies of cinematic experience. Martin Jay (1993: 149–209) refers to scopic regimes to describe the experiential or phenomenological experience of various dominant and competing 'ways of seeing' that arise through modernist art and its philosophies. Nicholas Mirzoeff (1999) frequently refers to scopic regimes in conjunction with Foucault's (1991) account of the Panopticon, so introducing an explicit notion of relational power on visual terms. Overall, as Hal Foster (1988: ix) argues, visuality is a central concern for visual culture studies, which seeks to socialise vision, 'to indicate its part in the production of subjectivity … and its own production as a part of intersubjectivity'. Yet vision and visuality are not reductively congruent, as the two terms 'are not opposed as nature is to culture: vision is social and historical too, and visuality involves the body and the psyche'. Considered together, vision and visuality lead us to complex issues of how the visual either confirms or transcends acculturation. There is a need both to historicise vision, and to locate the particularities of visual experience and visual knowledge, whether in physiological or cultural terms.

Crary (12.1) historicises vision in order to explore the nature and unfolding of hegemonies of seeing and being seen. In the extract here, he shows how the structural and optical principles of the camera obscura – which from the late 1500s through to the end of the 1700s informed the dominant paradigm regarding the status and epistemology of vision – are suddenly undermined by the privileging of the human body as a visual producer. His study enables, for example, an understanding of how Cartesian perspectivalism (which separates object and subject in vision) is challenged by modernist art, as it brings to attention the distracted viewer, the optical unconscious (Benjamin, 1992: 211–44) and more generally a complex embodied field of vision (Merleau-Ponty, 6.2). However, rather than work from within an art history perspective, which tends to assume 'that an observer will always leave visible tracks', Crary pays attention to 'other, grayer practices', the techniques and discourses about vision 'whose immense legacy will be all the industries of the image'. For Crary the concept of visuality gives rise to a fluid (Foucaultian) genealogy of visual culture, of multiple sites of meaning and perspective, each depending on the current social and cultural matrix surrounding the viewer and viewed. In this vein, we might consider Hockney's (10.4) revisioning of history to add to such a genealogical account. In this case suggesting how the camera obscura, posing an alternative model of artistic skill, undermines received views about the techniques of the 'grand masters' of painting, which subsequently impacts hugely on debates in art history.

Krauss (12.2) develops Crary's archaeological approach and presents two different models of visuality to the dominant modernist ones. In the first case she describes Max Ernst's collage work of a girl placed in a zootrope, which she argues opens up a surrealist model of vision of dreams, evoking a mode of double vision of the dreamer as simultaneously protagonist within and viewer outside of their own world. Krauss then refers to Duchamp's rotorelief artworks, drawing on psychoanalytical concepts of the gestalt and the erotic to suggest a model of imaging as a beat or pulse. Her point is that Duchamp sought to 'corporealise the visual, restoring to the eye (against the disembodied opticality of modernist painting) the eye's condition as bodily organ' (see Damasio, 9.2). In both cases, Krauss is keen to point out how the artists worked in conjunction with forms taken from mass culture.

Dyer (12.3) uses the concept of visuality to suggest that light, as a physical property, has over many years been treated and categorised by media professionals in such a way as to privilege white people. He focuses on the aesthetic or technological construction of beauty and pleasure in film and photography. And, in contrast to much critical, historical reflection on how media construct (deceptive) images of the world (see Section 3, Ideology Critique), Dyer is more concerned we recognise that 'cultural media are only sometimes concerned with reality and are at least as much concerned with ideals and indulgence, that are themselves socially constructed'. More importantly, he shows that whilst media technologies are always social, they are also instruments of technology. On the one hand, cultural historians can frequently underestimate the latter, while on the other hand the more technical-minded can overlook the former. Dyer's suggestion is to bridge the technical and social.

Jay (12.4) counters the claim that images can never be understood as natural or analogical signs with universal capacities, positioning himself against 'the triumph of cultural relativism in visual terms'. He questions the impulse to bring the visual into meaning through its translation into discourse, arguing that there is always an 'excess' of the visual over discourse and cultural boundaries. Jay brings to the fore the potential for vision to transcend 'local' visualities, to offer modes of knowledge and communication that are more directly sensed than discursive ones. His argument can be seen to supplement his thesis in *Downcast Eyes* (1993), which offers an extensive study of the privileging of vision in Western philosophy and social theory. More specifically, however, in demonstrating that the concept of totality in French critical theory is frequently accompanied by scepticism about the possibilities of a totalising gaze, Jay argues that twentieth-century French thought has made a sustained attack on vision to form a tradition he labels as 'antiocularcentric' discourse. Against which, he suggests we need to place more emphasis on the experience of vision in order to open up interrelated questions about natural visual ability, vision and hermeneutics, phenomenological perception, scopic regimes and the relationship of vision to the Enlightenment.

Jay's argument against cultural relativism can certainly be developed and opened up to further possibilities when considered in relation to recent work in neuroscience, which seeks to understand how the sense data of the visual field becomes vision for us. Semir Zeki's (12.5) research suggests that while vision seeks out the essential characteristics of the perceptual field, it is itself 'modular', so that different aspects of our experience, such as motion, colour and shape, are 'processed' by the brain asynchronously. This blur of sensory data is later reconstructed as a mental image by the brain's active processes (see Damasio, 9.2). In contrast to traditional views in neuroscience, Zeki (1999: 68) questions whether seeing and understanding are separate processes and suggests instead that the brain actively seeks out knowledge in the environment. 'The brain ... is no mere passive chronicler of the external physical reality but an active participant in generating the visual image, according to its own rules and programs'. James Elkins (2003) suggests that the proliferation of new visual research in the neurosciences should aid theorists in developing more nuanced views on vision.

REFERENCES

Benjamin, W. (1992) 'The work of art in the age of mechanical reproduction', in *Illuminations*, tr. H. Zohn. London: Fontana Press. pp. 211–44.

Elkins, J. (2003) *Visual Studies: A Skeptical Introduction*, London: Routledge.

Foster, H. (ed.) (1988) *Vision and Visuality*. Seattle, WA: Bay Press.

Foucault, M. (1991) *Discipline and Punish: The Birth of the Prison*, tr. A. Sheridan. London: Penguin.

Jay, M. (1993) *Downcast Eyes: The Denigration of Vision in Twentieth-Century French Thought*. Berkeley, CA: University of California Press.

Mirzoeff, N. (1999) *An Introduction to Visual Culture*. London: Routledge.

Zeki, S. (1999) *Inner Vision*. Oxford: Oxford University Press.

|2:| MODERNIZING VISION
JONATHAN CRARY

It is interesting that so many attempts to theorize vision and visuality are wedded to models that emphasize a continuous and overarching Western visual tradition. Obviously at times it is strategically necessary to map out and pose the outlines of a dominant Western speculative or scopic tradition of vision that is continuous or in some sense effective, for instance, from Plato to the present, or from the Quattrocento into the twentieth century, or to whenever. My concern is not so much to argue against these models, which have their own usefulness, but rather to insist there are some important discontinuities that such hegemonic constructions have prevented from coming into view. The specific account that interests me here, one that has become almost ubiquitous and continues to be developed in a variety of forms, is that the emergence of photography and cinema in the nineteenth century is a fulfilment of a long unfolding of technological and/or ideological development in the West in which the camera obscura evolves into the photographic camera. Implied is that at each step in this evolution the same essential presuppositions about an observer's relation to the world are in place. [...]

These models of continuity are used in the service of both, for lack of better terms, the right and the left. On the one hand are those who pose an account of ever-increasing progress toward verisimilitude in representation, in which Renaissance perspective and photography are part of the same quest for a fully objective equivalent of 'natural vision'. On the other are those who see, for example, the camera obscura and cinema as bound up in a single enduring apparatus of power, elaborated over several centuries, that continues to define and regulate the status of an observer.

*

For at least two thousand years it has been known that, when light passes through a small hole into a dark, enclosed interior, an inverted image will appear on the wall opposite the hole. [...]

But it is crucial to make a distinction between the empirical fact that an image can be produced in this way (something that continues to be as true now as it was in antiquity) and the camera obscura as a socially constructed artefact. For the camera obscura was not simply an inert and neutral piece of equipment or a set of technical premises to be tinkered upon and improved over the years; rather, it was embedded in a much larger and denser organization of knowledge and of the observing subject. If we want to be historical about it, we must recognize how for nearly two hundred years, from the late 1500s to the end of the 1700s, the structural and

From *Vision and Visuality*, ed. Hal Foster, Seattle, WA: Bay Press, 1988, pp. 29–44.

optical principles of the camera obscura coalesced into a dominant paradigm through which was described the status and possibilities of an observer.

[…]

What is striking is the suddenness and thoroughness with which this paradigm collapses in the early nineteenth century and gives way to a diverse set of fundamentally different models of human vision. I want to discuss one crucial dimension of this shift, the insertion of a new term into discourses and practices of vision: the human body, a term whose exclusion was one of the foundations of classical theories of vision and optics […]. One of the most telling signs of the new centrality of the body in vision is Goethe's *Theory of Colours,* published in 1810 […].[1] This is a work crucial not for its polemic with Newton over the composition of light but for its articulation of a model of subjective vision in which the body is introduced in all its physiological density as the ground on which vision is possible. In Goethe we find an image of a newly productive observer whose body has a range of capacities to generate visual experience; it is a question of visual experience that does not refer or correspond to anything external to the observing subject. Goethe is concerned mainly with the experiences associated with the retinal afterimage and its chromatic transformations. But he is only the first of many researchers who become preoccupied with the afterimage in the 1820s and 1830s throughout Europe. Their collective study defined how vision was an irreducible amalgam of physiological processes and external stimulation, and dramatized the productive role played by the body in vision.

[…]

[…T]he privileging of the body as a visual producer began to collapse the distinction between inner and outer upon which the camera obscura depended. Once the objects of vision are coextensive with one's own body, vision becomes dislocated and depositioned onto a single immanent plane. […S]ubjective vision is found to be distinctly temporal, an unfolding of processes within the body, thus undoing notions of a direct correspondence between perception and object. By the 1820s, then, we effectively have a model of autonomous vision.

The subjective vision that endowed the observer with a new perceptual autonomy and productivity was simultaneously the result of the observer having been made into a subject of new knowledge, of new techniques of power. And the terrain on which these two interrelated observers emerged in the nineteenth century was the science of physiology. From 1820 through the 1840s it was very unlike the specialized science that it later became; it had then no formal institutional identity and came into being as the accumulated work of disconnected individuals from diverse branches of learning. In common was the excitement and wonderment at the body, which now appeared like a new continent to be mapped, explored, and mastered, with new recesses and mechanisms uncovered for the first time. But the real importance of physiology lay in the fact that it became the arena for new types of epistemological reflection that depended on new knowledge about the eye and processes of vision. Physiology at this moment of the nineteenth century is one of those sciences that stand for the rupture that Foucault poses between the eighteenth and nineteenth centuries, in which man emerges as a being in whom the transcendent is mapped onto the empirical.[2]

[...]

[One] dimension of the collective achievement of physiology in the first half of the nineteenth century was the gradual parcelization and division of the body into increasingly separate and specific systems and functions. Especially important were the localization of brain and nerve functions, and the distinction between sensory nerves and motor nerves. [...] All of this produced a new 'truth' about the body which some have linked to the so-called 'separation of the senses' in the nineteenth century, and to the idea that the specialization of labour was homologous to a specialization of sight and of a heightened autonomous vision [...]. I believe, however, that such a homology doesn't take account of how thoroughly vision was reconceived in the earlier nineteenth century. It still seems to pose observation as the act of a unified subject looking out onto a world that is the object of his or her sight, only that, because the objects of the world have become reified and commodified, vision in a sense becomes conscious of itself as sheer looking.

But in the first major scientific theorization of the separation of the senses, there is a much more decisive break with the classical observer; and what is at stake is not simply the heightening or isolating of the optical but rather a notion of an observer for whom vision is conceived without any necessary connection to the act of looking at all. The work in question is the research of the German physiologist Johannes Müller, the single most important theorist of vision in the first half of the nineteenth century.[3] In his study of the physiology of the senses, Müller makes a comprehensive statement on the subdivision and specialization of the human sensory apparatus; his fame was due to his theorization of that specialization: the so-called 'doctrine of specific nerve energies'.

[...]

The theory was based on the discovery that the nerves of the different senses were physiologically distinct. It asserted quite simply – and this is what marks its epistemological scandal – that a uniform cause (e.g., electricity) would generate utterly different sensations from one kind of nerve to another. Electricity applied to the optic nerve produces the experience of light, applied to the skin the sensation of touch. Conversely, Müller shows that a variety of different causes will produce the same sensation in a given sensory nerve; in other words, he describes a fundamentally arbitrary relation between stimulus and sensation. It is a description of a body with an innate capacity, one might even say a transcendental faculty, to *misperceive*, of an eye that renders differences equivalent.

[...]

Sight here has been separated and specialized certainly, but it no longer resembles any classical models. The theory of specific nerve energies presents the outlines of a visual modernity in which the 'referential illusion' is unsparingly laid bare. The very absence of referentiality is the ground on which new instrumental techniques will construct for an observer a new 'real' world. It is a question of a perceiver whose very empirical nature renders identities unstable and mobile, and for whom sensations are interchangeable. And remember, this is roughly 1830. In effect, the doctrine of specific nerve energies redefines vision as a capacity for being affected by sensations that have no necessary link to a referent, thus threatening any coherent system of meaning. [...] [W]hat was at stake and seemed so threatening was not just a new form of epistemological scepticism about the unreliability of the senses but a positive reorganization of perception and its objects. The issue was not just how does one know what is real, but that new forms of the real were being fabricated and a new truth about the capacities of a human subject was being articulated in these terms.

*

The collapse of the camera obscura as a model for the status of an observer was part of a much larger process of modernization, even as the camera obscura itself was an element of an earlier modernity. By the early 1800s, however, the rigidity of the camera obscura, its linear optical system, its fixed positions, its categorical distinction between inside and outside, its identification of perception and object, were all too inflexible and unwieldy for the needs of the new century. A more mobile, usable, and productive observer was needed in both discourse and practice – to be adequate to new uses of the body and to a vast proliferation of equally mobile and exchangeable signs and images. Modernization entailed a decoding and deterritorialization of vision.

What I've been trying to do is give some sense of how radical was the reconfiguration of vision by 1840. [...] A new type of observer was formed then, and not one that we can see figured in paintings or prints. We've been trained to assume that an observer will always leave visible tracks, that is, will be identifiable in terms of images. But here it's a question of an observer who takes shape in other, grayer practices and discourses, and whose immense legacy will be all the industries of the image and the spectacle in the twentieth century. The body which had been a neutral or invisible term in vision now was the thickness from which knowledge of vision was derived. This opacity or carnal density of the observer loomed so suddenly into view that its full consequences and effects could not be immediately realized. But it was this ongoing articulation of vision as nonveridical, as lodged in the body, that was a *condition of possibility* both for the artistic experimentation of modernism and for new forms of domination, for what Foucault calls the 'technology of individuals'.[4] Inseparable from the technologies of domination and of the spectacle in the later nineteenth and twentieth centuries were of course film and photography. Paradoxically, the increasing hegemony of these two techniques helped recreate the myths that vision was incorporeal, veridical, and 'realistic'. But if cinema and photography seemed to reincarnate the camera obscura, it was only as a mirage of a transparent set of relations that modernity had already overthrown.

NOTES

1. Footnote removed.
2. Michel Foucault, *The Order of Things* (New York: Pantheon Books, 1971), pp. 318–320.
3. Footnote removed.
4. Michel Foucault, *Discipline and Punish:The Birth* of *the Prison,* trans. Alan Sheridan (New York: Vintage Books, 1975), p. 225.

12:2 THE IM/PULSE TO SEE
ROSALIND KRAUSS

[…In] the central image of his 1930 collage novel, *A Little Girl Dreams of Taking the Veil*, Max Ernst places his heroine at the center of an enclosure, which she calls a dovecot but which we recognize as the drum of a zootrope, he not only presents us with a model of visuality different from that of modernism's, but associates that model quite directly with an optical device which was generated from and spoke to an experience of popular culture. As was the case in many of the components of his collage novels – this one as well as *La Femme 100 Têtes* – the underlying element of the zootrope structuring this image was taken from the pages of the late nineteenth-century magazine of popular science called *La Nature*.

Devoted to bringing its audience news of the latest exploits of technology in a whole variety of fields including engineering, medicine, anthropology,

FIGURE 12.1
Max Ernst. *A Little Girl Dreams of Taking the Veil*, 1930. © DACS, London.

Rosalind Krauss, from *Vision and Visuality*, ed. Hal Foster. Seattle, WA: Bay Press, 1988, pp. 54–5, 58–63.

geology, *La Nature* was particularly obsessed with optical devices – the fruit of recent psycho-physiological research. Inevitably, in these pages, the devices important to this research were lifted from the neutral confines of the laboratory, to be incorporated into the conditions of public spectacle, as the stereoscopic slide was visualized, for instance, in terms of a kind of scenic projection (the static forerunner of the 3-D movie), or the limited, intimate, personal viewing-space of the praxinoscope was enlarged and distanced to fill the screen on an opposite wall.

As Jonathan Crary has pointed out in his own discussions of the archaeology of these optical devices, the obvious drive demonstrated here towards the conditions of modern cinematic projection should not blind us to the particular experience these illustrations still make available, an experience that not only conjures up the effects of a given illusion but also exposes to view the means of this illusion's production.[1] So that the acknowledgement that goes on in these pages is that the spectator will occupy two places simultaneously. One is the imaginary identification or closure with the illusion – as we see, as if they were unmediated, the cow grazing against the hallucinatory depth of the stereoscopically distanced stream, or the bobbing gestures of feeding geese. The second position is a connection to the optical machine in question, an insistent reminder of its presence, of its mechanism, of its form of constituting piecemeal the only seemingly unified spectacle. This double effect, of both having the experience and watching oneself have it from outside, characterized the late nineteenth-century fascination with the spectacle in which there was produced a sense of being captured not so much by the visual itself as by what one could call the visuality-effect.

Now this double vantage, occupied by these early viewers of proto-cinematic devices, was particularly interesting for Ernst's purposes inasmuch as the model of vision he was intent on exploring was the peculiarly mediated perceptual field of the dream. That experience of the dreamer as spectator or witness to the scene of the dream as a stage on which he himself or she herself is acting, so that the dreamer is

FIGURE 12.2
From *La Nature*, 1888.

simultaneously protagonist within and viewer outside the screen of his or her own vision, is the strangely redoubled form of dream visuality that Ernst wants to exploit. And so it is to a sensation of being both inside and outside the zootrope that Ernst appeals in this image.

From outside the revolving drum, peering through the slits as they pass rhythmically before our eyes, we would be presented of course with a succession of stationary birds performing the majestic flexing of their wings in what would appear to be the unified image of a single fowl.[2] From the drum's inside, however, the experience would be broken and multiplied, analyzed into its discrete, serial components, the result of chronophotography's record of a mechanical segmentation of the continuity of motion. But uniting the experience of both inside and outside is the beat or pulse that courses through the zootropic field, the flicker of its successive images acting as the structural equivalent of the flapping wings of the interior illusion, the beat both constructing the gestalt and undoing it at the same time – both positioning us within the scene as its active viewer and outside it as its passive witness.

In a certain way we could think of Ernst's image as configuring within the specific space of the dream many of the effects that Duchamp had in fact put into place throughout his own fifteen-year-long devotion to the turning discs of the devices he collectively called *Precision Optics*. There we find the same tapping into forms of mass culture – in this case both the revolving turntable of the phonograph player and the flickering silence of early film – as we also find an explicit reference to the nineteenth-century optics that underwrote these forms. Further, *Precision Optics* bears witness to Duchamp's commitment to the constitution of the image through the activity of a beat: here, the slow throb of a spiral, contracting and expanding biorhythmically into a projection forward and an extension backward. And here as well the pulse is accompanied by what feels like a structural alteration of the image as it is consolidated only continually to dissolve – the illusion of trembling breast giving way to that of uterine concavity, itself then swelling into the projecting orb of a blinking eye. Yet, to speak of metamorphosis, here, is to miss the dysmorphic condition of this pulse, which, committed to the constant dissolution of the image, is at work against the interests of what we could identify as form.

I have, in another context, spoken about the connection between the pulsing nature of the vision Duchamp constructs and the explicitly erotic theater it stages – the sexual implications of the motions of these discs having escaped no commentator on this aspect of Duchamp's production.[3] I have also described what is clearly Duchamp's concern here to corporealize the visual, restoring to the eye (against the disembodied opticality of modernist painting) that eye's condition as bodily organ, available like any other physical zone to the force of eroticization. Dependent on the connection of the eye to the whole network of the body's tissue, this force wells up within the density and thickness of the carnal being, as, tied to the conditions of nervous life, it is by definition a function of temporality. For the life of nervous tissue is the life of time, the alternating pulse of stimulation and enervation, the complex feedback relays of retension and protension. So that the temporal is mapped onto the figural in the space of Duchamp's

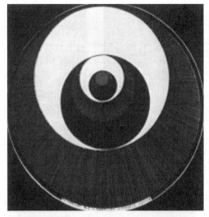

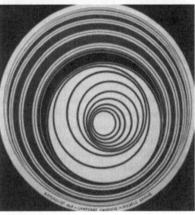

FIGURE 12.3
Marcel Duchamp. **Above** *Rotorelief No. 1,
Carolles*, 1935. **Below** *Rotorelief No. 3,
Chinese Lantern*, 1935. Source: Leeds City Art
Gallery/Bridgeman Art Library © DACS, London.

Precision Optics as the specific beat of desire – of a desire that makes and loses its object in one and the same gesture, a gesture that is continually losing what it has found because it has only found what it has already lost.

[…]

If the gestalt operates as a kind of absolute in the field of vision, as the principle of concordance between difference and simultaneity – that is, the simultaneous separation and intactness of figure and ground – the beat could, from the point of view of a modernist logic, never be anything more than an interloper from the domain of the temporal, the auditory, the discursive. A function of time and of succession, this beat would be something that modernism had solemnly legislated out of the visual domain, asserting a separation of the senses that will always mean that the temporal can never disrupt the visual from within, but only assault it from a position that is necessarily outside, external, eccentric. Yet the power of the works that interest me here – in their contestation of what modernism had constructed as 'the visual' – is that this beat or pulse is not understood to be structurally distinct from vision but to be at work from deep inside it. And from that place, to be a force that is transgressive of those very notions of 'distinctness' upon which a modernist optical logic depends. The beat itself is, in this sense, figural – but of an order of the figure that is far away from the realm of space that can be neatly opposed to the modality of time.

NOTES

1. Jonathan Crary, 'Techniques of the Observer,' *October*, no. 45 (Summer 1988).
2. Footnote removed.
3. See my 'The Blink of an Eye,' forthcoming in *Nature, Sign, and Institutions in the Domain of Discourse*, ed. Program in Critical Theory, University of California (Irvine: University of California Press).

I2:3 LIGHTING FOR WHITENESS
RICHARD DYER

A television company is about to shoot a panel discussion before a studio audience. The producer, from the control room, is discussing with the floor manager in the studio how the audience looks in his monitor. The producer says something about the number of black people at the front of the audience. 'You're worried there are not too many whites obviously there?', asks the floor manager. No, says the producer, it's nothing like that, a mere technical matter, a question of lighting – 'it just looks a bit down'.

This exchange occurred in the preparation of a programme about the street fighting that took place in Handsworth, Birmingham, in September 1985, fighting that was largely understood to be about race and which was the most vivid and controversial of many such incidents throughout Britain that year. The exchange was recorded by the Black Audio Film Collective and included in their film *Hands-worth Songs* (1987),[1] which explores the cultural construction of 'race riots'. That construction is embedded in part in the professional common sense of media production, two items of which are registered in this exchange.

One item [...] is that of 'balance'. The floor manager cannot at first understand what the producer is getting at. Is it perhaps the racial composition of the audience in numerical and representative terms? The topic of the programme has been constructed as race riots, and to have 'balance' one has to think in terms of sides and ensure that equal numbers on each side are represented. This lies behind the floor manager's remark about there perhaps not being 'enough white people obviously there', and the producer understands what he is getting at. However, it is not what concerns him or us here, whereas the second notion at play in the exchange goes straight to the heart of the matter.

Richard Dyer, from *White: Essays on Race and Culture*. London: Routledge, 1997, pp. 82–3, 89–90, 94–8, 102–3. Reproduced by permission.

For the producer it is a purely aesthetic matter. The image looks 'down': dull, dingy, lacking sparkle. There is no reason to presume he is saying this because he finds black people dislikeable or uninteresting. He is, in the terms of professional common sense, right: shoot the scene in the usual way with the usual technology with that audience and it will look 'down'. The corollary is that if you do it the usual way with a white audience, it will look 'up', bright, sparkling.

*

The photographic media and, *a fortiori,* movie lighting assume, privilege and construct whiteness. The apparatus was developed with white people in mind and habitual use and instruction continue in the same vein, so much so that photographing non-white people is typically construed as a problem. All technologies work within material parameters that cannot be wished away. Human skin does have different colours which reflect light differently. Methods of calculating this differ, but the degree of difference registered is roughly the same: Millerson (1972: 31), discussing colour television, gives light skin 43 per cent light reflectance and dark skin 29 per cent; Malkiewicz (1986: 53) states that 'a Caucasian face has about 35 percent reflectance but a black face reflects less than 16 percent'. This creates problems if shooting very light and very dark people in the same frame.

[…]

The technology at one's disposal also sets limits. The chemistry of different stocks registers shades and colours differently. Cameras offer varying degrees of flexibility with regard to exposure (effecting their ability to take a wide lightness/darkness range). Different kinds of lighting have different colours and degrees of warmth, with concomitant effects on different skins. However, what is at one's disposal is not all that could exist. Stocks, cameras and lighting were developed taking the white face as the touchstone. The resultant apparatus came to be seen as fixed and inevitable, existing independently of the fact that it was humanly constructed. It may be – certainly was – true that photo and film apparatuses have seemed to work better with light-skinned peoples, but that is because they were made that way, not because they could be no other way.

[…]

The assumption that the normal face is a white face runs through most published advice given on photo- and cinematography.[2] This is carried above all by illustrations which invariably use a white face, except on those rare occasions when they are discussing the 'problem' of dark-skinned people. Kodak announces on the title page of its *How to Take Good Pictures* (1984) that it is 'The world's best-selling photography book', but all the photo examples therein imply an all-white world (with one picture of two very pink Japanese women); similarly, Willard Morgan's *Encyclopedia of Photography* (1963), billed as 'The Complete Photographer: the Comprehensive Guide

FIGURE 12.4
Ektachrome photograph by L. Burrows illustrating
'special lighting effects.' Source: L. Lorelle *The Colour
Book of Photography* (London: Focal Press, 1955).
See colour Plate 3

and Reference for All Photographers' shows lack of racial completeness and comprehensiveness in its illustrative examples as well as its text [...]. Fifteen years after John Hedgecoe's *Complete Photography Course* (1979), John Hedgecoe's *New Book of Photography* (1994) is neither any more complete or new as far as race is concerned (Hedgecoe is both a bestseller and Professor of Photographic Art at the Royal College of Art in London, in other words a highly authoritative source). Even when non-white subjects are used, it is rarely randomly, to illustrate a general technical point. The only non-white subject in Lucien Lorelle's *The Colour Book of Photography* (1955) is a black woman in what is for this book a highly stylised composition (Figure 12.4). The caption reads:

> Special lighting effects are possible with coloured lamps ... and light sources included in the picture. Exposure becomes more tricky, and should be based on a meter reading of a key highlight such as the dress.

The photo is presented as an example of an unusual use of colour, to which the model's 'colourfulness' is unwittingly appropriate. The advice to take the exposure meter reading from the dress is itself unusual: with white subjects, it is their skin that is determinant. [...] Some more recent guidebooks randomly do include non-white subjects,[3] but even now there is no danger of excesses of political correctness.

[...]

The white-centricity of the aesthetic technology of the photographic media is rarely recognised, except when the topic of photographing non-white faces is addressed. This is habitually conceptualised in terms of non-white subjects entailing a departure from usual practice or constituting a problem.

[...]

In Kris Malkiewicz's book *Film Lighting*, based on interviews with Hollywood cinematographers and gaffers, four of the interviewees discuss the question of lighting for black people (Malkiewicz, 1986: 141). They come up with a variety of solutions: 'taking light off the white person' if there are people of different colour in shot (John Alonzo), putting 'some lotion on the [black person's] skin to create reflective quality' (Conrad Hall), using 'an orange light' (Michael D. Margulies). James Plannette is robust: 'The only thing that black people need is more light. It is as simple as that'. Even this formulation implies doing something special for black people, departing from a white norm. Some of the others (lotion, orange light) imply that the 'problem' is inherent in the technology, not just its conventional use.

Elsewhere, Ernest Dickerson, Spike Lee's regular cinematographer, indicates the importance of choices made at every level of light technology when filming black subjects: lighting (use of 'warmer' light, with 'bastard amber' gels, tungsten lights on dimmers 'so they [can] be dialed down to warmer temperatures', and gold instead of silver reflectors), the subject (use of reflective make-up, 'a light sheen from skin moisturizer'), exposure (basing it on 'reflected readings on Black people with a spot meter'), stock ('Eastman Kodak's 5247 with its tight grain and increased color saturation') and development (using 'printing lights in the high thirties and low forties' to ensure that 'blacks will hold up to the release prints'). Dickerson is explaining his choices against his observation that 'many cinematographers cite *problems* photographing black people because of the need to use more light on them' (emphasis added). Much of his language indicates that he is involved in correcting a white bias in the most widely available and used technology: lights are warmer (than an implied cold norm), they are dialled down (from a usual cooler temperature), they are gold not silver, and the stock has more colour saturation. The whiteness implied here is not just a norm (silver not gold) but also redolent of aspects of the conceptualisation of whiteness [...]: coldness and the absence of colour.

[...]

Movie lighting in effect discriminates on the basis of race. [... Such] discrimination has much to do with the conceptualisation of whiteness. There is also a rather different level at which movie lighting's discrimination may be said to operate. What is at issue here is not how white is shown and seen, so much as the assumptions at work in the way that movie lighting disposes people in space. Movie lighting relates people to each other and to setting according to notions of the human that have historically excluded non-white people.

Movie lighting focuses on the individual. Each person has lighting tailored to his or her personality (character, star image, actorly attributes). Each important person, that is. At a minimum, in a culture in which whites are the important people, in which those who have, rather than are, servants, occupy centre stage, one would expect movie lighting to discriminate against non-white people in terms of visibility, individualisation and centrality. I want however to push the argument a bit further. Movie lighting valorises the notion of the unique and special character of the individual, of the individuality of the individual. It is at the least arguable that white society has found it hard to see non-white people as individuals; the very notion of the individual, of the freely developing, autonomous human person, is only applicable to those who are seen to be free and autonomous, who are not slaves or subject peoples. Movie lighting discriminates against non-white people because it is used in a cinema and a culture that finds it hard to recognise them as appropriate subjects for such lighting, that is, as individuals.

Further, movie lighting hierarchises. It indicates who is important and who is not. It is not just that in white racist society, those who are not white will be lit to be at the bottom of the hierarchy, but that the very process of hierarchisation is an exercise of power. Other and non-white societies have hierarchies, of course; it is not innate to white nature. However, hierarchy, the aspirational structure, is one of the forms that power has taken in the era of white Western society.

Movie lighting also separates the individual, not only from all other individuals, but from her/his environment. The sense of separation from the environment, of the world as the object of a disembodied human gaze and control, runs deep in white culture. The prime reason for introducing back-lighting in film was to ensure that the figures were distinguished from their ground, to make them stand out from each other and their setting. This was regarded as an obvious necessity, so clearly part of how to see life that it was an unquestionable imperative. Yet it expresses a view of humanity pioneered by white culture; it lies behind its highly successful technology and the terrible price the environment now pays for this.

People who are not white can and are lit to be individualised, arranged hierarchically and kept separate from their environment. But this is only to indicate the triumph of white culture and its readiness to allow some people in, some non-white people to be in this sense white. Yet not only is there still a high degree of control over who gets let in, but, [...] the technology and culture of light is so constructed as to be both fundamental to the construction of the human image and yet felt to be uniquely appropriate to those who are white.

NOTES
1. Footnote removed.
2. Editor's Note: Original note removed. Throughout his account Dyer draws upon a wide range of manuals and historical studies of photography, film and video. Space does not permit referencing all of this material. An appendix of this material is included in Dyer's original text.
3. Footnote removed.

WORKS CITED
Hedgecoe, John (1979) *John Hedgecoe's Complete Photography Course*. New York: Simon and Schuster.
Hedgecoe, John (1994) *John Hedgecoe's New Book of Photography*. New York: Dorling Kindersley.
Kodak (1984) *How to Take Good Pictures*. London: Collins.
Lorelle, Lucien (1955) *The Colour Book of Photography*. London: Focal Press.
Malkiewicz, Kris (1986) *Film Lighting*. New York: Prentice-Hall.
Millerson, Gerald (1972) *The Technique of Lighting for Television and Motion Pictures*. London: Focal Press.
Morgan, Willard B. (ed.) (1963) *The Encyclopedia of Photography*. New York: Greystone Press.

12:4 CULTURAL RELATIVISM AND THE VISUAL TURN
MARTIN JAY

> Although vision suggests sight as a physical operation, and visuality sight as a social fact, the two are not opposed as nature is to culture: vision is social and historical too, and visuality involves the body and the psyche. Yet neither are they identical: here, the difference between the terms signals a difference within the visual – between the mechanisms of sight and its historical techniques, between the datum of vision and its discursive determinations – a difference, many differences, among how we see, how we are able, allowed, or made to see, and how we see this seeing or the unseen therein. (Foster, 1988: ix)

Although carefully crafted to resist a reductive congruence between vision and visuality on the one hand, and nature and culture on the other, Foster's distinction within sight raises an important question that touches on the main theme of this article: what is the role of the visual in either confirming or transcending what has come to be called cultural relativism?

[...]

After the recent visual turn ... the claim that images can be understood as natural or analogical signs with universal capacities to communicate has almost entirely come undone. Mitchell, to take a salient example from his influential collection *Iconology*, dismissively calls such a notion the 'fetish or idol of Western culture' (Mitchell, 1986: 90) and insists that images be situated firmly in the world of convention rather than nature. What Norman Bryson has called the 'discursive' as opposed to the 'figural' aspects of images, by which he means their embeddedness in language, has increasingly gained the upper hand in any discussion of their cultural significance. Witness the claim of John T. Kirby (1996) that

> ... *all* images have a discursive aspect, at least insofar as we attempt to consider them cognitively or (especially) to communicate our cognition to another person. And to consider an image cognitively, to engage in discourse about it . . . is to textualize it. (p. 36; emphasis in original)

Or listen to John Tagg (1988), who claims, contra Roland Barthes, that the evidentiary status of a photograph

> ... rests not on a natural or existential fact, but on a social, semiotic process . . . what Barthes calls "evidential force" is a complex historical outcome and is exercised by photographs only with certain institutional practices and within particular historical relations. (p. 4)

[...]

Can we then conclude that along with the new fascination for visual culture has come the triumph of cultural relativism in visual terms, that 'hard, rigorous relativism that regards knowledge as a social product, a matter of

Martin Jay, from 'Cultural relativism and the visual turn', in *Journal of Visual Culture*, 1 (3), 2002, pp. 267–78. Sage Publications. Reproduced by permission of Sage Publications and the author.

dialogue between different versions of the world, including different languages, ideologies, and modes of representation' (Mitchell, 1986: 38) explicitly advocated by Mitchell in *Iconology*? Can we argue that visual experience is always circumscribed by the protocols of the culture out of which it is generated, always an effect of the codes of that culture, and therefore cannot provide a means of transcending its limits? [...] Is the visual no longer separable from visuality, to recall Foster's terms; is it culturally coded all the way down, with no excess beyond what the cultural mediation itself dictates?

[...]

An attempt to topple [the argument for cultural determinism] entirely comes from the historian of science Bruno Latour (1993) in his provocative little book, *We Have Never Been Modern*. In addition to questioning the boundaries separating different cultures, he extends the skepticism to that between the cultural and the natural. Arguing against the assumption that there is a single natural world on which distinct cultures have different perspectives, which in our terms would be the claim that the vision of the natural human eye is always filtered through discursive screens, he notes that the very separation of culture (or plural cultures) from a single nature is itself an historical creation, which he calls the rise of modernity. [...] Without falling back on a universalist notion of a real natural world, which Latour argues is always a conceit of modern Western science claiming to bracket its own cultural moment, he nonetheless challenges the relativist assumption that versions of nature are nothing but the conventional projections of discrete cultures. What he calls the 'hyperincommensurability' argument of post-modernists like Lyotard is based on a simplistic reversal of the modern faith in natural universalism. Latour's alternative is what he dubs relational relativism, rather than absolute relativism, an alternative that sees the world made up of hybrids, quasi-objects that include as much as they exclude. 'How can one claim that worlds are untranslatable', he asks, 'when translation is the very soul of the process of relating? How can one say that worlds are dispersed, when there are hundreds of institutions that never stop totalizing them?' (p. 113).

Ironically, Latour's argument in *We Have Never Been Modern* undermines the function that vision in one of its guises plays in supporting the discourse of cultural relativism. That is, it calls into question the visual metaphor of different perspectives on the real world, which produce different culturally filtered worldviews or phenomenological profiles of an objective real forever beyond our perfect understanding. For if there are hybrids prior to the very split between cultural viewer and natural viewed, the metaphor of perspective is patently inadequate. You can't look, after all, from different angles at an object that no longer exists as an external reality by itself. Hybrid imbrication suggests a more haptic than visual interaction between subject and object – or rather quasi-subject and quasi-object – in what Merleau-Ponty famously called the 'flesh of the world'.

In an even more fundamental respect, Latour can be said to enlist visual experience against the more radical claims of culturalist constructivism. For what he alerts us to with his notion of hybridity is the impossibility of reducing figurality entirely to discursivity, images entirely to texts, the visual to nothing but an effect of the same codes that underlie the linguistic. That is, it is as impossible to reduce natural visual experience to its cultural mediations as it is to disentangle it entirely from them. We need only look as far as the silent film, which swiftly transcended the boundaries of the specific culture out of which it emerged to achieve global success, to see a clear example of the capacity of the visual to break free from linguistic and cultural constraints. Moving images, it was quickly apparent, didn't need dubbing or subtitles to move beyond cultural boundaries. […] Equally telling is the ability of images of human suffering to stir compassion across cultural and linguistic boundaries.

[…]

This is not to say, I hasten to add, that images can once again be seen as natural, unmediated signs, which can shed all their cultural encoding. It is rather that however much they are filtered through such a screen, however much they are connotatively deflected by the magnetic field of culture, they remain in excess of it. Cultural relativism is thus not called into question by a naive return to transcendental universalism in which all mediation is overcome, but rather by the inability of images to be relative to a specific culture understood as a boundaried and coherent way of life. In fact, much of the power of images, we might conjecture, comes precisely from their ability to resist being entirely subsumed under the protocols of specific cultures. […]

[…] As the Australian filmmaker and anthropologist David MacDougall (1998) has noted in his recent analysis of ethnographic film entitled *Transcultural Cinema*, the materiality of images

> … fails to participate in the creation of either narrative or symbol. This excess creates a fundamental psychological disturbance in all human endeavors to construct schemata of the world. It is nevertheless the source of much of the fascination of the photographic media, and a contributor to the underlying erotics and aesthetics of both art and science. Barthes describes this as *figuration*, in contrast to *representation*, for it traverses the grain of significance. (p. 73)

Filming the Other thus leads us away from a simple belief in the pristine sanctity of different cultures espoused by cultural relativists, for it entangles us in more complicated relations with the cultures on view. 'Visual anthropology', MacDougall (1998) writes with a nod to phenomenologists like Merleau-Ponty and Vivian Sobchack,

> … opens more directly onto the sensorium than written texts and creates psychological and somatic forms of intersubjectivity between viewer and social actor. In films, we achieve identification with others through a synchrony with their bodies made possible in large part by vision. (p. 262)

MacDougall's evocation of the psychological dimension of visual experience comes from a largely phenomenological point of view, but one can discern similar implications in the case of those theorists who have found Lacan's thoughts on vision a stimulus to their analyses (Rose, 1986; Brennan and Jay, 1996). That is, by formulating such concepts as the mirror stage or the chiasmic intertwining of the eye and the gaze, Lacan was also asking us to consider the transcultural, perhaps even universal, mechanisms of visual experience. Whether or not one accepts all of his arguments, or inclines to other schools of psychoanalysis (or perhaps to none at all), the recognition that sight is entangled with psyche suggests the limits of an exclusively culturalist approach, and with it the relativism that follows. For even if one discerns cultural biases in psychological discourse, calling into question its universalist pretensions, the tension between psychic interiority and social or cultural exteriority is not thereby effaced. And if we take seriously the idea of the figural moment in psychic life, which Freud himself recognized in the visual representation of the dreamwork, then it cannot be culture all the way down.

WORKS CITED

Brennan, T. and Jay, M. (eds) (1996) *Vision in Context: Historical and Contemporary Perspectives on Sight*. New York: Routledge.

Foster, H. (ed.) (1988) *Vision and Visuality*. Seattle: Bay Press.

Kirby, J.T. (1996) 'Classical Greek Origins of Western Aesthetic Theory', in B. Allert (ed.) *Languages of Visuality*. Detroit: Kritik.

Latour, B. (1993) *We Have Never Been Modern*. Tr. Catherine Porter. Cambridge, MA: Harvard University Press.

MacDougall, D. (1998) *Transcultural Cinema*. Ed. Lucien Taylor. Princeton, NJ: Princeton University Press.

Mitchell, W.J.T. (1986) 'Nature and Convention: Gombrich's Illusions', in *Iconology: Image, Text, Ideology*. Chicago: University of Chicago Press.

Rose, J. (1986) *Sexuality in the Field of Vision*. London: Verso.

Tagg, J. (1988) *The Burden of Representation: Essays on Photographies and Histories*. London: Macmillan Education.

THE MODULARITY OF VISION[1]
SEMIR ZEKI
12:5

The major visual pathway from the retina to the brain is known as the optic pathway. It carries signals to a relatively large part of the cerebral hemispheres, situated at the back of the brain and commonly known as the primary visual cortex, or V1 for short. There are many different kinds of signals – related to colour, luminance, motion, form, depth and much else besides – that are transported to V1. In V1, cells that receive signals related to the different attributes of vision are neatly grouped together into different, anatomically identifiable, compartments […]. The specialised compartments of V1 send their signals to further visual areas, both directly and through an intermediary area surrounding V1 known as area V2. These

Semir Zeki, from *Inner Vision*. Oxford: Oxford University Press, 1999, pp. 59–68. Reproduced by permission.

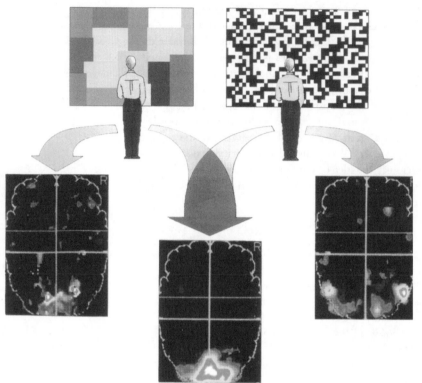

FIGURE 12.5

A simple experiment demonstrates functional specialisation in the human brain. Whilst viewing a coloured scene, area V4 is activated (lower left). Whilst viewing a moving scene, area V5 shows the activation (lower right). Reproduced with permission from S. Zeki, *La Recherche*, 1990, Vol 21, pp. 712–21. **See colour Plate 5**

further visual areas are located in a large expanse of cortex that surrounds V1, and commonly referred to until recently as the 'visual association' cortex [...]. They are themselves specialised for different attributes of the visual scene, partly because of the specialised signals they receive from V1. V1 therefore acts in the office of a distributor of visual signals, much like a central post office: it parcels out different signals to the different visual areas in the cortex surrounding it, although it is also involved in a significant amount of elementary visual processing itself, the results of which it communicates to the visual areas surrounding it. This discrete parcelling of specific visual signals to specific visual areas leads, in turn, to a distinct specialisation for each group of areas, depending upon the type of signals that they receive. What we call the visual brain is, therefore, a collection of many different areas, of which V1, the royal gateway from the retina to the visual areas, is the most prominent. [...]

[...]

The functional specialisation that is so prominent a feature of the visual brain is, then, a consequence of the fact that the individual cells which make up the visual brain are highly selective for the kind of visual signal or stimulus that they respond to. A cell might, for example, be selective for colour, responding to red but not to other colours or to white; other such cells will respond selectively to other colours. These cells are indifferent to the direction in which the stimulus moves, provided it is of the right colour. They are also indifferent to form, that is to say they will respond if a stimulus of the appropriate colour is a vertical or horizontal bar, or if it is a rectangle, circle, or square. [...]

[...]

Cells that are selective for a given attribute, such as form, colour or motion, are concentrated in specific compartments of V1 and in specific visual areas of the surrounding cortex with which the specific compartments of V1 connect, thus conferring their specialisations on the respective areas, and leading to functional specialization. Based on these facts, the theory of functional specialisation supposes that different attributes of the visual scene are processed in geographically separate parts of the visual brain, that there are different processing systems for different attributes of vision (a processing system includes the specialised comparment of V1, the specialised area in the adjoining cortex and the connections between the two). [...]

Functional specialisation is [...] one of the first solutions that the brain has evolved to tackle the problem of acquiring knowledge about the world, of constancy. The kind of information that the brain has to discard or sacrifice in getting to the essence of one attribute, say colour, is very different from the kind of information that it has to discard to get to the essence of another attribute, say size; in the former it has to discount the precise wavelength composition of the light coming from one surface alone and in the latter the viewing distance. The brain has evidently found it operationally more efficient to discount these different kinds of signals in different areas, ones whose entire anatomy and physiology are specifically tailored to the needs for getting to the essentials of particular attributes. It has, in brief, adopted the solution of parallel processing, of processing different attributes of the visual scene simultaneously and in parallel.

*

The demonstration that different attributes of the visual scene are processed separately does not, in itself, prove that the different attributes are also perceived separately; on the whole, visual physiologists and psychologists have assumed that some kind of integration occurs in the brain, whereby the results of the operations performed by the different visual processing systems are brought together, to give us our unitary image of the visual world, where all the attributes are seen together, in precise registration. [...] There is an irony here, at the expense of the visual physiologist; he now seeks to understand how the results of the different processing systems come together to provide the very integration that inhibited him from considering the complexity of the task that the brain has to overcome in providing a visual image in the first place.

There are several hypothetical solutions to this problem. It is plausible to suppose, for example, that the different processing systems 'report' the results of their operations to one or more master areas which would then give us the integrated visual image, where all the attributes take their correct place and are seen in precise spatio-temporal registration. But the facts of anatomy speak against this somewhat simplistic notion, for all the evidence suggests that there is no single area to which all the specialised areas uniquely connect. The concept of a master area faces, in any case, a severe logical and neurological problem. For the problem then becomes one of knowing who or what is 'looking' at the image provided by the master area. Another solution might be an interaction between the different, functionally specialised, visual areas, which are indeed richly connected among themselves, but how these anatomical connections lead to integration is anyone's guess.

Perhaps the best way of approaching this problem scientifically is to begin by asking whether there is such a precise temporal registration of the results of the operations performed by the different processing systems. It is surprising that the visual physiologist, having lost out when enquiring into the complexities of the visual brain for the better part of a century, because of the integrated visual image, should now find himself losing out again, because of the very same factor, by not asking more searching questions about integration. Let us therefore begin by asking the obvious first question: are all the attributes of the visual scene that are processed by the different visual areas brought into precise temporal registration, as almost all of us have too readily assumed? Over a relatively long period of time, from one second upwards, we do see all the attributes in precise temporal registration and this gives us a good reason for wanting to learn how the integrated visual image is generated. But one second (1000 milliseconds) is a very long time in neural terms; it takes an impulse between 0.5 and 1 millisecond to cross a synaptic barrier (point of contact between nerve cells) and about 35 milliseconds for the earliest visual signals to arrive in the cortex, although many reach the cortex later, after about 70–80 milliseconds. If we look, then, into a very brief window of time, would we find the integration which we all assume exists?

In fact, recent experiments that have measured the relative times that it takes to perceive colour, form and motion show that these three attributes are not perceived at the same time, that colour is perceived before form which is perceived before motion, the lead time of colour over motion being about 60–80 milliseconds. This suggests that the perceptual systems themselves are functionally specialised and that there is a temporal hierarchy in vision, superimposed upon the spatially, distributed parallel processing systems. [...] In broader terms, the brain does not, over very brief periods of time, seem to be capable of binding together what happens in real time; instead it binds the results of its own processing systems and therefore misbinds in terms of real time.

One could of course choose to ignore these experiments, because they deal with such brief windows of time and because in the longer term – by which I mean longer than one second – all the attributes are in fact bound together to give us our unitary experience. But the results of these experiments give us powerful hints about the way in which the visual brain works. They provide compelling evidence to show that different processing systems take different times to reach their end-points, which is the perception of the relevant attribute. This in turn suggests that the processing systems are also perceptual systems, thus allowing us to think of several parallel processing-perceptual systems. The results of the operations performed by the separate processing systems are the different percepts; we can therefore speak of a network of spatially distributed processing-perceptual systems. But there is more than that. By definition, perception is a conscious event; we perceive that of which we are conscious and do not perceive that of which we are not conscious. Since we perceive two attributes, say colour and motion, at separate times, it follows not only that there are separate consciousnesses, each a correlate of activity in one of the independent processing-perceptual systems, but that these different consciousnesses are also asynchronous with respect to one another. We are thus led to the conclusion that it is not the activities in the different processing-perceptual systems that have to be bound together to give us our conscious perception of a scene, but rather that it is the micro-consciousnesses generated by the activity of the different processing-perceptual systems that have to be bound together to give us our unified percept.

[...]

Whatever the difficulties in knowing how the final image is assembled together in the brain, functional specialisation has many important implications. It has, among other things, shown us that the process of 'seeing' is far from complete at the level of V1, the 'cortical retina'. It has raised the question of whether 'seeing' and 'understanding' are indeed two separate processes, with separate seats in the cortex [...]. Perhaps most important of all, the discovery of functional specialisation has been instrumental in changing our minds about vision as a process, impelling us to consider it as an active process – a physiological search for constants and essentials that makes the brain independent of continual change, and the servility to it, and makes it independent too of the single and fortuitous view. The brain, then, is no mere passive chronicler of the external physical reality but an active participant in generating the visual image, according to its own rules and programs. This is the very role that artists have attributed to art, and the role that some philosophers have wished that painting could have.

NOTE

1. Footnotes removed.

13: IMAGE STUDIES

INTRODUCTION

In the introduction to this volume, we characterised image studies as we understand it, emphasising both the pertinence of image studies to contemporary image culture as well as historical and philosophical conceptions of imagery, interdisciplinarity and the non-visual character of some images. The selections in this section are by authors who have already made significant contributions to the nascent interdiscipline, bringing their own emphases to it. In fact, it could be argued that calls for the development of image studies have grown more out of a dissatisfaction with the methods and themes of traditional art history and literary analysis, than with any real cultural need outside the discipline itself. The three pioneers in this emerging field – W.J.T. Mitchell (13.1), James Elkins (13.2) and Barbara Maria Stafford (13.3) – have each taken as their starting points the inadequacy of contemporary methodologies for dealing with the complexities of the image. For example, Elkins and Stafford balance their theoretical arguments about applying traditional art historical methods to more contemporary forms of non-art images – such as visual artefacts from science – with the warning that practitioners who fail to do so threaten to make their departments redundant to the educational system (see also Buck-Morss, 4.4). In that interpretation, image studies would be an attempt to update the themes of art history, but not its methodologies. On the other hand, despite obvious differences, these writers appear to be more positively united in the belief that paying close attention to the nature of images and the way that they acquire meaning in their specific cultural settings is central to making sense of our increasingly visual world. Mitchell has characterised this state of affairs as the pictorial turn: 'What makes for the sense of a pictorial turn … is not that we have some powerful account of visual representation that is dictating the terms of cultural theory, but that pictures form a point of peculiar friction and discomfort across a broad range of intellectual inquiry' (Mitchell, 1994: 13). In this more positive interpretation, image studies would both apply and update the methods of traditional art historical, literary and philosophical analysis to the artefacts of the contemporary visual environment because current methodologies are not adequate.

Like visual culture theory, image studies sets itself against dominant linguistic modes of enquiry (see the introduction to Section 11). For example, Stafford (13.3) complains that visual culture programmes are 'governed by the ruling metaphor of reading' – presumably in their use of such methodological techniques as deconstruction, discourse analysis and semiotics. Elkins has also argued that the canon of principal visual culture theorists, such as Walter Benjamin, Michel Foucault and Jacques Lacan, provides the field with a 'very specific, very disciplinary set of interests' that fails to do justice to understanding images on their own terms (Elkins, 2003: 33). By comparison, image studies is interdisciplinary in both the range of images it studies – almost any type of graphic mark, according to Elkins (1999) – and in the methods that it applies to their analysis. It provides a meta-critique of the way that images can be understood by suggesting ways of comparing imaging practices within particular disciplines. In some respects, image studies offers critical frameworks within which such interdisciplinary research can take place.

Given the view that there is no current account of images that does their variety justice, it is not surprising that one of the central concerns of these writers has been to re-categorize images into different groupings that attempt to account for the full range of visual and non-visual images. For example, Mitchell proposes a family tree of images (13.1) and Elkins a diffuse genealogy of image types (13.2). Régis Debray's mediological tables (13.4) categorise societies according to their material mediation of culture and its dominant modes of transmission, including the relative role of words and images (see Section 8). Stressing the mediatory role of images rather than their semiotic codes, Debray argues that the material, technological and institutional conditions of mediation are the key characteristics of any culture. While his critique of politics in the current audiovisual 'mediasphere' bears some relation to Baudrillard's (3.3), Debray approaches images with wonderment rather than ideological suspicion. Closely aligned to these taxonomies is an attempt to give an inclusive account of what types of artefacts might be included in the 'family of images' – from mental images to graphs and charts. That entails looking at different types of images in their original settings and reading contemporary discourses about them in a way reminiscent of art historical, visual connoisseurship (see the introduction to Section 4).

In contrast to traditional iconoclasts who denigrate the meaning of images, these writers emphasise that images embody 'visual intelligence' (Stafford, 13.3). Similarly, Mitchell (13.1) and Latour (13.5) look beyond the ideological critique of images to examine what social and political factors are at stake in the debates that cast such artefacts as either true or false. What makes images the site of such debates and why they arise in particular historical circumstances are central concerns. The point is not to stop critical reflection on images, but to make it more sophisticated and aware of the positive possibilities images provide for understanding (see also Section 9). For example, in *Picture Theory* (1994), Mitchell describes his work as an attempt to unite Erwin Panofsky's iconography (4.1) with the ideological critique of the French structural Marxist Louis Althusser. He says: 'The point of this greeting … is not simply to make iconology "ideologically aware" or self-critical, but to make the ideological critique iconologically aware' (1994: 30). This concept of a critical iconology has been taken up more recently by writers such as Jon Simons (2000), Hans Belting (2005) and Kevin DeLuca (8.5).

While this introduction has emphasised similarities between these writers, there are important differences too. Elkins and Stafford are art historians by training and their work tends to be much less politically motivated than that of Debray, Latour and Mitchell. The formers' sense of interdisciplinarity has led them to look widely for alternative visual practices and they have both drawn extensively on images and metaphors from the emerging cognitive sciences, medicine and scientific imaging practices (see, for example, Elkins, 1999; Stafford, 1993). In devising this *Reader*, we have certainly tried to reflect this broader array of image types and contexts, if only to 'risk' what Elkins (2003: 7) describes as a kind of 'unconstricted, unanthropological interest in vision' – an interest that can go beyond any 'niche in the humanities'. However, Mitchell's concern with what he terms a 'de-disciplinary exercise' can have the effect of theorising the theory and/or discipline of images, rather than images in themselves. It is in line with such an approach that we have brought together a diverse range of writings on the image, from the Bible through to the present. Our aim is to examine what is meant by 'images' across varying intellectual contexts, to consider differences, contrasts and relations. Overall, the willingness of the writers included in this final section to question the nature of images as images suggests a fresh approach to image analysis that makes their relation to visual culture theory at least problematic. It is an approach that we hope invites many new insightful and constructive collaborations and contests.

REFERENCES

Belting, H. (2005) 'Image, medium, body: a new approach to iconology', *Critical Inquiry*, 31: 302–19.

Elkins, J. (1999) *The Domain of Images*. Ithaca, NY: Cornell University Press.

Elkins, J. (2003) *Visual Studies: A Skeptical Introduction*. London: Routledge.

Mitchell, W.J.T. (1994) *Picture Theory: Essays on Verbal and Visual Representation*. Chicago: University of Chicago Press.

Simons, J. (2000) 'Ideology, imagology, and critical thought: the impoverishment of politics', *Journal of Political Ideologies*, 5 (1): 81–103.

Stafford, B.M. (1993) *Body Criticism: Imaging the Unseen in Enlightenment Art and Medicine*. Cambridge, MA: MIT Press.

13:1 THE FAMILY OF IMAGES
W.J.T. MITCHELL

There have been times when the question 'What is an image?' was a matter of some urgency. In eighth- and ninth-century Byzantium, for instance, your answer would have immediately identified you as a partisan in the struggle between emperor and patriarch, as a radical iconoclast seeking to purify the church of idolatry, or a conservative iconophile seeking to preserve traditional liturgical practices. The conflict over the nature and use of icons, on the surface a dispute about fine points in religious ritual and the meaning of symbols, was actually, as Jaroslav Pelikan points out, 'a social movement in disguise' that 'used doctrinal vocabulary to rationalize an essentially political conflict.'[1] In mid-seventeenth-century England the connection between social movements, political causes, and the nature of imagery was, by contrast, quite undisguised. It is perhaps only a slight exaggeration to say that the English Civil War was fought over the issue of images, and not just the question of statues and other material symbols in religious ritual but less tangible matters such as the 'idol' of monarchy and, beyond that, the 'idols of the mind' that Reformation thinkers sought to purge in themselves and others.[2]

If the stakes seem a bit lower in asking what images are today, it is not because they have lost their power over us, and certainly not because their nature is now clearly understood. It is a commonplace of modern cultural criticism that images have a power in our world undreamed of by the ancient idolaters. And it seems equally evident that the question of the nature of imagery has been second only to the problem of language in the evolution of modern criticism. If linguistics has its Saussure and Chomsky, iconology has its Panofsky and Gombrich. But the presence of these great synthesizers should not be taken as a sign that the riddles of language or imagery are finally about to be solved. The situation is precisely the reverse: language and imagery are no longer what they promised to be for critics and philosophers of the Enlightenment – perfect, transparent media through which reality may be represented to the understanding. For modern criticism, language and imagery have become enigmas, problems to be explained, prison-houses which lock the under-standing away from the world. The commonplace of modern studies of images, in fact, is that they must be understood as a kind of language; instead of providing a transparent window on the world, images are now regarded as the sort of sign that presents a deceptive appearance of naturalness and transparence concealing an opaque, distorting, arbitrary mechanism of representation, a process of ideological mystification.

My purpose ... is neither to advance the theoretical understanding of the image nor to add yet another critique of modern idolatry to the growing collection of iconoclastic polemics. My aim is rather to survey some of what Wittgenstein would call the 'language games' that we play with the notion of

W.J.T. Mitchell, from 'What is an Image?', in *Iconology: Image, Text, Ideology*. Chicago and London: University of Chicago Press, 1986, pp. 7–14. © 1986 by The University of Chicago. All rights reserved. Reproduced with permission of The University of Chicago Press and W.J.T. Mitchell.

images, and to suggest some questions about the historical forms of life that sustain those games. I don't propose, therefore, to produce a new or better definition of the essential nature of images, or even to examine any specific pictures or works of art. My procedure instead will be to examine some of the ways we use the word 'image' in a number of institutionalized discourses – particularly literary criticism, art history, theology, and philosophy – and to criticize the ways each of these disciplines makes use of notions of imagery borrowed from its neighbors. My aim is to open up for inquiry the ways our 'theoretical' understanding of imagery grounds itself in social and cultural practices, and in a history fundamental to our understanding not only of what images are but of what human nature is or might become. Images are not just a particular kind of sign, but something like an actor on the historical stage, a presence or character endowed with legendary status, a history that parallels and participates in the stories we tell ourselves about our own evolution from creatures 'made in the image' of a creator, to creatures who make themselves and their world in their own image.

*

Two things must immediately strike the notice of anyone who tries to take a general view of the phenomena called by the name of imagery. The first is simply the wide variety of things that go by this name. We speak of pictures, statues, optical illusions, maps, diagrams, dreams, hallucinations, spectacles, projections, poems, patterns, memories, and even ideas as images, and the sheer diversity of this list would seem to make any systematic, unified understanding impossible. The second thing that may strike us is that the calling of all these things by the name of 'image' does not necessarily mean that they all have something in common. It might be better to begin by thinking of images as a far-flung family which has migrated in time and space and undergone profound mutations in the process.

If images are a family, however, it may be possible to construct some sense of their genealogy. If we begin by looking, not for some universal definition of the term, but at those places where images have differentiated themselves from one another on the basis of boundaries between different institutional discourses, we come up with a family tree something like the following:

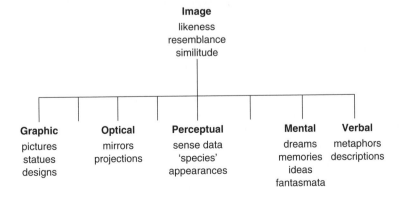

Each branch of this family tree designates a type of imagery that is central to the discourse of some intellectual discipline: mental imagery belongs to psychology and epistemology; optical imagery to physics; graphic, sculptural, and architectural imagery to the art historian; verbal imagery to the literary critic; perceptual images occupy a kind of border region where physiologists, neurologists, psychologists, art historians, and students of optics find themselves collaborating with philosophers and literary critics. This is the region occupied by a number of strange creatures that haunt the border between physical and psychological accounts of imagery: the 'species' or 'sensible forms' which (according to Aristotle) emanate from objects and imprint themselves on the wax-like receptacles of our senses like a signet ring;[3] the *fantasmata*, which are revived versions of those impressions called up by the imagination in the absence of the objects that originally stimulated them; 'sense data' or 'percepts' which play a roughly analogous role in modern psychology; and finally, those 'appearances' which (in common parlance) intrude between ourselves and reality, and which we so often refer to as 'images' – from the image projected by a skilled actor, to those created for products and personages by experts in advertising and propaganda.

[...]

[...] [T]he image is not simply a particular kind of sign but a fundamental principle of what Michel Foucault would call 'the order of things.' The image is the general notion, ramified in various specific similitudes (*convenientia, aemulatio, analogy, sympathy*) that holds the world together with 'figures of knowledge.'[4] Presiding over all the special cases of imagery, therefore, I locate a parent concept, the notion of the image 'as such,' the phenomenon whose appropriate institutional discourses are philosophy and theology.

Now each of these disciplines has produced a vast literature on the function of images in its own domain, a situation that tends to intimidate anyone who tries to take an overview of the problem. There are encouraging precedents in work that brings together different disciplines concerned with imagery, such as Gombrich's studies of pictorial imagery in terms of perception and optics, or Jean Hagstrum's inquiries into the sister arts of poetry and painting. In general, however, accounts of any one kind of image tend to relegate the others to the status of an unexamined 'background' to the main subject. If there is a unified study of imagery, a coherent iconology, it threatens to behave, as Panofsky warned, 'not like ethnology as opposed to ethnography, but like astrology as opposed to astrography.'[5] Discussions of poetic imagery generally rely on a theory of the mental image improvised out of the shreds of seventeenth-century notions of the mind;[6] discussions of mental imagery depend in turn upon rather limited acquaintance with graphic imagery, often proceeding on the questionable assumption that there are certain kinds of images (photographs, mirror images) that provide a direct, unmediated copy of what they represent;

optical analyses of mirror images resolutely ignore the question of what sort of creature is capable of using a mirror; and discussions of graphic images tend to be insulated by the parochialism of art history from excessive contact with the broader issues of theory or intellectual history. It would seem useful, therefore, to attempt an overview of the image that scrutinizes the boundary lines we draw between different kinds of images, and criticizes the assumptions which each of these disciplines makes about the nature of images in neighboring fields.

We clearly cannot talk about all these topics at once, so the next question is where to start. The general rule is to begin with the basic, obvious facts and to work from there into the dubious or problematic. We might start, then, by asking which members of the family of images are called by that name in a strict, proper, or literal sense, and which kinds involve some extended, figurative, or improper use of the term. It is hard to resist the conclusion that the image 'proper' is the sort of thing we found on the left side of our tree-diagram, the graphic or optical representations we see displayed in an objective, publicly shareable space. We might want to argue about the status of certain special cases and ask whether abstract, nonrepresentational paintings, ornamental or structural designs, diagrams and graphs are properly understood as images. But whatever borderline cases we might wish to consider, it seems fair to say that we have a rough idea about what images are in the literal sense of the word. And along with this rough idea goes a sense that other uses of the word are figurative and improper.

[...]

Eventually I will argue that all three of these commonplace contrasts between images 'proper' and their illegitimate offspring are suspect. That is, I hope to show that, contrary to common belief, images 'proper' are not stable, static, or permanent in any metaphysical sense; they are not perceived in the same way by viewers any more than are dream images; and they are not exclusively visual in any important way, but involve multisensory apprehension and interpretation. Real, proper images have more in common with their bastard children than they might like to admit. [...]

NOTES

1. See Jaroslav Pelikan, *The Christian Tradition*, 5 Vols., Chicago: University of Chicago Press, 1974–1991, Vol. 2, Chap. 3, for an account of the iconoclastic controversy in Eastern Christendom.
2. Footnotes removed until section break.
3. Aristotle, *De Anima* II. 12.424a; trans. W.S. Hett, Cambridge: Harvard University Press, 1957, p. 137.
4. See Michel Foucault, *The Order of Things: An Archaeology of the Human Sciences*, New York: Random House, 1970, Chap. 2.
5. Erwin Panofsky, *Meaning in the Visual Arts*, Garden City, NY: Doubleday, 1955, p. 32.
6. Footnotes removed to end of section.

13:2

ART HISTORY AND IMAGES THAT ARE NOT ART[1]
JAMES ELKINS

Most images are not art. In addition to pictures made in accord with the Western concept of art, there are also those made outside the West or in defiance, ignorance, or indifference to the idea of art. In the welter of possibilities two stand out. Non-Western images are not well described in terms of art, and neither are medieval paintings that were made in the absence of humanist ideas of artistic value. Together the histories of medieval and non-Western images form the most visible alternates to the history of art, and they attract most attention in the expanding interests of art history. So far, it has proved useful to describe both medieval and non-Western images using the language of art history, so that they stand partly outside art and partly within it.

In the past few decades, art historians have become interested in a wide variety of images that are not canonical instances of fine art, including anti-art, 'low' art, outsider art, and postcolonial art, as well as images from popular culture (especially television and advertising). Though such images are often described as alternates to art history's usual subjects, they are closely dependent on fine-art conventions even when they are not actively quoting or subverting them. To discuss even the most anarchic anti-art, it is necessary to attend closely to the corresponding practices in fine art. Duchamp's *Fountain* cannot be understood apart from the kinds of sculpture that it is not; when Alfred Stieglitz remarked that the *Fountain* looked like a Buddha, he was naming one way it might be recuperated into fine-art meanings. Postcolonial and outsider art is similarly attached to the practices it works to avoid.

In general, art history tests its boundaries by working with popular, medieval, and non-Western images. But the domain of images is substantially larger. In particular there is another group of images that seems to have neither religious nor artistic purpose, and that is images principally intended — in the dry language of communication theory — to convey information. There is no good name for such images, which include graphs, charts, maps, geometric configurations, notations, plans, official documents, some money, bonds, patents, seals and stamps, astronomical and astrological charts, technical and engineering drawings, scientific images of all sorts, schemata, and pictographic or ideographic elements in writing: in other words, the sum total of visual images, both Western and non-Western, that are not obviously either artworks, popular images, or religious artifacts. In general, art history has not studied such images, and at first it might appear that they are intrinsically less interesting than paintings. They seem like half-pictures, or hobbled versions of full pictures, bound by the necessity of performing some utilitarian function and therefore unable to mean more freely. Their affinity with writing and numbers seems to indicate they are incapable of the expressive eloquence that is associated with painting and drawing, making them properly the subject of disciplines such as visual communication, typography, mathematics, archaeology, linguistics, printing, and graphic design.

Still, it is necessary to be careful in such assessments, because informational images are arguably the majority of all images. If pictures were to be defined by their commonest examples, those examples would be pictographs, not paintings. An image taken at random is more likely to be an ideographic script, a petroglyph, or a stock-market chart than a painting by Degas or Rembrandt, just as an animal is more likely to be a bacterium or a beetle than a lion or a person. The comparison is not entirely gratuitous, and I make it to underscore the final barriers that stand in the way of a wider understanding of images, just as the remnants of anthropomorphism keep the public more engaged with lions than with bacteria. Some images are closer to art, others farther away: In my analogy, fine art, non-Western art, medieval art, outsider art, and popular imagery might be the familiar mammals and other chordates, and informational imagery the many other phyla. It is the distant phyla that are least well known and most numerous sof all.

The variety of informational images, and their universal dispersion as opposed to the limited range of art, should give us pause. At the least it might mean that visual expressiveness, eloquence, and complexity are not the proprietary traits of 'high' or 'low' art, and in the end it might mean that we have reason to consider the history of art as a branch of the history of images, whether those images are nominally in science, art, writing, archaeology, or other disciplines. [...]

*

Art history is centrally positioned in the emerging field of image studies because it possesses the most exact and developed language for the interpretation of pictures. Existing art-historical methods, which are normally trained on art objects, can embrace images of any kind, from graphs to ideographic writing; conversely, art-historical inquiries can be enriched by what is happening in other disciplines. [...]

*

[...] When art history encounters nonart images, it tends to use them to illustrate the history of fine art. In each case, what attracts art-historical interest and gives the images a relatively independent meaning is their closeness to fine art. Those images that have less to do with painting and drawing get less attention. The outlandish distortions of many map projections tend to be overlooked in favor of those projections that resemble the distances and angles of vision common in painting, just as the less naturalistic and intuitive aspects of computer graphics or the less spatially resolved strategies of medical illustration tend to appear less meaningful than their more pictorial instances. There are many studies of gendered figures in the history of medical illustration, fewer of pictures of body parts, and virtually none of histological and sectional anatomies. In general, the supposition behind the art historical studies might be put like this: Some scientific and nonart images approach the expressive values and forms of fine art, but many more are encased in the technical conventions of their fields. Those images are a kind of desert in which interesting pictures are stunted and far between. They are inherently informational and without aesthetic value, and they are properly considered as kin to equations or spreadsheets: They are notations, not images in a deeper sense.

*

It is important to resist this conclusion, both for the sake of the expanding discipline of art history – which would otherwise find itself against an unbreachable barrier at the 'end' of expressiveness, interest, or aesthetic value – and also because it is demonstrably untrue. Especially significant in this regard is a text by the sociologist of science Michael Lynch and the art historian Samuel Edgerton on the ways in which astronomers handle images. Astronomers routinely make two kinds of images: 'pretty pictures' for calendars, press releases, coffee-table books, and popular science magazines such as *Scientific American*; and 'scientific' images, normally in black-and-white, for publications such as the *Journal of Astrophysics*. 'Pretty pictures' are often given strongly chromatic false colors, and initially Lynch and Edgerton hoped to find evidence that expressionist painting might lie behind that practice, making the astronomical images interesting examples of the diffusion of fine art. But according to their informants in the laboratory, fine art influences neither the 'scientific' images nor the 'pretty pictures.'[2] Even though the astronomers might set aside time to make 'pretty pictures,' they do not consider them seriously in terms of the history and meanings of art, or even intend them to be anything more than eye-catching or decorative. On the other hand, they are intensely concerned with their 'scientific' images, because they want to make them as clear, unambiguous, simple, graphically elegant, and useful as possible. To that end they use a range of image-processing tools to 'clean up' the raw data provided by the telescopes. [...] At first it seems this has little to do with anything that might concern a history of art, but Lynch and Edgerton point out that this kind of care is not outside aesthetics. It precisely *is* aesthetics: It is the original, pre-Kantian sense of aesthetics as the 'perfecting of reality' – the very doctrine that governed Renaissance painting. Even when the astronomers use false colors for their scientific images, they do so in order to make natural forms clearer and more susceptible to quantitative assessment. Their images always aim to give what they consider to be the most rational version of phenomena. This, I think, is a fundamentally important result, and no work on nonart images should proceed without taking it into account. What happens in nonart images can be just as full of artistic choices, just as deeply engaged with the visual, and just as resourceful and visually reflective as in painting, even though its purposes might be entirely different. Lynch and Edgerton agree with Leo Steinberg, Thomas Kuhn, and others that not much is to be gained by comparing the scientists' criteria of elegance, clarity, and simplicity with artistic criteria, and that the two senses of images are worlds apart – but in terms of the attention scientists lavish on creating, manipulating, and presenting images, the 'two cultures' are virtually indistinguishable.[3]

Where images are the objects of such concerted attention, then affective, historical, and social meanings – in short, the panoply of meanings that concern art history – cannot be far behind. It is certainly true of the astronomical images that Lynch and Edgerton studied, and it might also be true of even more intractably 'inexpressive' images. [...]

NOTES

1. All footnotes that do not relate to specific texts or quotations have been removed from this section.
2. Lynch and Edgerton, 'Aesthetics and Digital Image Processing: Representational Craft in Contemporary Astronomy,' in Fyfe, G. and Law, J. (eds) (1998) *Picturing Power: Visual Depiction and Social Relations*, pp. 184–220, esp. 193. [...] Sociological Review Monograph, no. 35. New York: Routledge.
3. Steinberg, L. 'Art and Science: Do They Need to be Yoked? *Daedalus* 115, no. 1 (1986)' p. 6. [...] and Thomas Kuhn, 'Comment on the Relation Between Science and Art,' in *The Essential Tension: Selected Studies in Scientific Tradition and Change*, Chicago: University of Chicago Press, 1977, pp. 340–51. [...]

A CONSTRUCTIVIST MANIFESTO[1]   13:3
BARBARA MARIA STAFFORD

Recent academic rhetoric is saturated with terms of rejection, revision, revolution; but manifestos, even of renunciation, remain in short supply. Writing about what is wrong in old optical formats and new imaging technologies is relatively easy. Harder is proposing mind-opening analogies between historical displays of visual intelligence and computer-age information viewed through the eyes. Being digital requires designing a post-Gutenbergian *constructive* model of education through vision. But I am not convinced, with Nicholas Negroponte, that a hypermedia future entails obliterating the past. The crux of the matter, I think, seems more Darwinian

Barbara Maria Stafford, from 'Introduction: Visual Pragmatism for a Virtual World', in *Good Looking: Essays on the Virtue of Images*. Cambridge, MA, and London: MIT Press, 1996, pp. 3–17. © 1996 Massachusetts Institute of Technology. Reproduced with permission of the MIT Press.

than cataclysmic. Today's instructional landscape must inevitably evolve or die, like biological species, since its environment is being radically altered by volatile visualization technologies. This ongoing displacement of fixed, monochromatic type by interactive, multidimensional graphics is a tumultuous process. In the realm of the artificial, as in nature, extinction occurs when there is no accommodation. Imaginative adaptation to the information superhighway, even the survival of reflective communication, means casting off vestigial biases automatically coupling printed words to introspective depth and pictures to dumbing down.

The bound book has led a charmed existence since typesetting was invented in mid-fifteenth-century Mainz. This longevity, no doubt partially owing to a Darwinian flexibility, makes me optimistic about its mutated persistence. Become more virtual informational space than stable artifact, the traditional volume can find another life as an inter-connective environment. Lines of copy interface with users very differently when presented in hybrid Web pages, and acquire unsettling mobility when reformatted, amended, and emended electronically. The digital imaging revolution is crucially reconfiguring how we explore and comprehend ideas from urban planning to photography. Yet in spite of the arrival of what I have termed the 'age of computerism' – rapidly replacing modernism and even postmodernism – a distorted hierarchy ranking the importance of reading above that of seeing remains anachronistically in place. All the while, computers are forcing the recognition that texts are not 'higher,' durable monuments to civilization compared to 'lower,' fleeting images. These marvelous machines may eventually rid us of the uninformed assumption that sensory messages are incompatible with reflection.

I have serious trouble with the deprecating rhetoric that stakes out bookish literacy as a moral high ground from which to denounce a tainted 'society of spectacle.' Contemporary iconoclasm, like early modern versions, rests on the puritanical myth of an authentic or innocent epistemological origin. Clinging to the Rousseauean fantasy of a supposedly blotless, and largely imageless, print ecology ignores not only contrary evidence from the past but the real virtues of colorful, heterogeneous, and mutable icons, whether on or off screen.

These essays, then, are unfashionably positive and frankly polemical. Their perspective is simultaneously pragmatic and theoretical. As practical acts of affirmation, they challenge an implacable system of negative dialectics arcing from the moral denunciations of Plato to the coercive aesthetics of Adorno to the war metaphors of Foucault. In short, they offer case studies, stretching from the lens to the computer era, presenting an alternative view of the pleasures, beauties, consolations, and, above all, *intelligence* of sight. They argue that imaging, ranging from high art to popular illusions, remains the richest, most fascinating modality for configuring and conveying ideas. More broadly, they prismatically interconnect seers and seeing within a sensory web productive of cultural signification.

Yet it is not enough to show the intellectual, spiritual, and physical demands of making, observing, and exhibiting spatialized media, whether pre- or postmodern. I want to combat the sophism that images do only destructive work within our institutions. By engaging the epistemological uncertainties and educational upheavals of an electronic future, I seek to demonstrate their capacity for good interventions. Further, I ask how the practice of image study can regain pertinency at a moment when the traditional visual disciplines, like all the rest, are coming unmoored from their original purposes. From this dual perception of revolutionary opportunity and impending Armageddon, the following essays call on established and aspiring imagists across disciplinary boundaries to confront the fundamental task of remaking the image of images. Freeing graphic expression from an unnuanced dominant discourse of consumerism, corruption, deception, and ethical failure is a challenge that cuts across the arts, humanities and sciences.

As manifestos on the knowingness of visual communication, from scientific illustration to on-line interactivity, these studies have another immediate context. They specifically counter the hierarchical 'linguistic turn' in contemporary thought. The totemization of language as a godlike agency in western culture has guaranteed the identification of writing with intellectual potency. Ferdinand de Saussure, the early twentieth-century founder of structuralism, strengthened the biblical coupling of meaning with naming by formulating the opposition of signifier/signified. These verbalizing binaries turned noumenal and phenomenal experience into the product of language. Not only temporal but spatial effects supposedly obeyed an invisible system, the controlling structure of an inborn ruling *écriture*.

Forcing human cognition to become synonymous both with computational codes or abstruse texts and with the ability to decipher them resulted in downgrading sensory awareness to superficial stimuli and false perceptions. Most damagingly, Saussure's schema emptied the mind of its body, obliterating the interdependence of physiological functions and thinking. It is not surprising that, up to now, an educational economy materially based on language has either marginalized the study of images, reduced it to a subaltern position, or appropriated it through colonization. In most American university curricula, graphicacy remains subordinate to literacy. Even so-called interdisciplinary 'visual culture' programs are governed by the ruling metaphor of reading. Consequently, iconicity is treated as an inferior part of a more general semantics.

[…]

I am arguing that we need to disestablish the view of cognition as dominantly and aggressively linguistic. […]

[…]

It is not hard to see that the multifaceted campaign to establish the primacy and innateness of our linguistic faculty is challenged by the materialist approach to the mind. Intense debates over Darwin's theory that organisms were born of blind chance and evolved according to the quirks of matter have refocused attention on the origin and configuration of all species. Both adaptationist and ultra-Darwinian investigations into human and animal reasoning open up the question of the sensorium's role. The philosopher Daniel Dennett is a spokesman for the latter camp, stating that to have evolved a capacity for awareness, living creatures must have a sophisticated, unified informational organization endowing them with cognitive capabilities. Empirical processes like learning, in this account, are a tool by which natural selection has created complex biological systems. This new turn in the study of consciousness proposes that life is more than selfish genes by bringing the formative powers of perception into productive engagement with a no longer discrete and hierarchical organ of thought. Urging humanity to 'grow up,' he comments that Darwin's great legacy consists in his distribution of design throughout nature. The lesson in this for imagists is that, if there is no hope of discovering an absolute trace or essential mark in life's processes that counts more than the rest, then, similarly, we must select, conserve, invent, and compose our artificial environment so that it becomes humane for all.

Yet, in spite of his Darwinian conviction about the importance of design, Dennett remains strangely language-centered. For him, the unfolding stream of human consciousness occurs in a massively parallel-processing brain, a virtual James Joycean linguistic machine. Only now, with the integrative neuroscientific philosophy of Paul and Patricia Churchland, 'the body-minded brain' of Antonio Damasio, or Owen Flanagan's insistence on 'the missing shade that is you,' is the iron grip of a univocal language-like prototype for cognitive activity starting to erode. Understanding, imagined as a combinatorial and synthetic physical function, has the potential for taking into account a broad range of multisensory endeavors. This suggests that truly enlarging the horizon of the emergent sciences of the mind (cognitive science, neurobiology, linguistics, AI, philosophy) should entail learning from the transactional visual arts about the experiential structures of thought. Ironically, the aesthetic, historical, and humanistic dimensions of perception remain virtually absent from the new interdisciplinary matrix in which cognitive being is about to become embedded.

[…] The much-publicized 'decade of the brain,' bridging the 1980s and 1990s, spectacularly opened a window onto the living mind. Multidimensional medical imaging (CT, PET, MRI) transparently displayed both the permanent neural anatomy and the acrobatics of evanescent emotion. Seeing neurons firing and witnessing localized functions in simultaneous performance suggest that it is more accurate to speak, not of separate art, artists, or art historians, but of interconnective images, imaging, imagists. […] An array of devices, discoveries, and practices, then, are encouraging us to relocate narrowly categorized 'art objects' elsewhere, into what I have termed 'imaging'. In this borderless community without physical territory, spatialized phenomena belong to larger constellations of events. Creating a map of ongoing debates, organized around central issues or substantial questions arising from this evolving geography, will be a major task confronting the new imagist. Such a 'hypermediated' person will have become a reality when we are hard-pressed to say what his or her discipline is.

Optical technology itself is spurring an integrative revolution. Yet it is staggering how loath we visualists have been to transform ourselves. Where are our blueprints, blue-sky or realistic, for guiding media convergence on screen? The conservatism of the supposedly new and old art history, its secondhand reliance on 'discourse,' on recirculating other fields' methodologies, tropes, rhetoric, has meant the loss of any intellectual and moral leadership that we might have exerted. If we have nothing particular to contribute to formerly linguistic fields and professions now undergoing radical *visual* metamorphosis, we confirm our irrelevance both within institutions of higher learning and in a decentralized electronic society.

[…]

All told, when freed from nihilism and liberated from asymmetrical relationships, material artifacts and graphic presentations can regain their rightful cognitive share. In the magical era of ubiquitous computing, art history's mission to retell the story of conventional media without a consideration of their future is over. Even its disciplinary name sounds archaic. But the efficacy of appearances – whether old or new – and the imaginative possibilities of thinking in, through, and with them is not anachronistic. Imaging may even begin to formulate its own questions and confidently say something about its own ends. It might think about itself instead of just being thought about by others. In spite of incessant talk concerning interdisciplinarity, something is wildly out of kilter when, at the end of the twentieth century, no alternative metaphor of intelligence counters the nineteenth-century standard of the printed book.

NOTE
1. All footnotes removed

13:4 IMAGES, NOT SIGNS
Régis Debray

Table 13.1 Mediological tables

	WRITING (LOGOSPHERE)	PRINTED TEXT (GRAPHOSPHERE)	AUDIOVISUAL (VIDEOSPHERE)
STRATEGIC MILIEU (PROJECTED POWER)	THE EARTH	THE SEA	SPACE
GROUP IDEAL (AND POLITICS)	THE ONE (City, Empire, Kingdom) absolutism	EVERYONE (Nation, People, State) nationalism, totalitarianism	EACH ONE (population, society, world) individualism and anomie
SHAPE OF TIME (AND ITS VECTOR)	CIRCLE (Eternal repetition) Archeocentric	LINE (history, Progress) Futurocentric	POINT (news, event) Egocentric: cult of the present
CANONICAL PHASE OF LIFESPAN	THE ELDER	THE ADULT	THE YOUNG PERSON
PARADIGMATIC ATTRACTION	MYTHOS (mysteries, dogmas, epics)	LOGOS (utopias, systems, programs)	IMAGO (emotions and fantasms)
SYMBOLIC ORGANON	RELIGIONS (theology)	SYSTEMS (ideologies)	MODELS (iconology)
SPIRITUAL CLASS (CONTROLS SOCIAL SACRED)	CHURCH (prophets, clerics) Sacrosanct: DOGMA	INTELLEGENTSIA secular (professors, doctors) Sacrosanct: KNOWLEDGE	MEDIAS (broadcasters and producers) Sacrosanct: INFORMATION
REFERENCE OF LEGITIMACY	THE DIVINE (we must, it is sacred)	THE IDEAL (we must, it is true)	THE PERFORMER (we must, for it works)
MOTIVATOR OF OBEDIENCE	FAITH (fanaticism)	LAW (dogmatism)	OPINION (relativism)
REGULAR MEANS OF INFLUENCE	PREACHING	PUBLICATION	VISIBILITY
CONTROL OF INFORMATION	ECCLESIASTICAL, DIRECT (over utterers)	POLITICAL, INDIRECT (over means of sending)	ECONOMIC, INDIRECT (over messages)
STATUS OF INDIVIDUAL	SUBJECT (to command)	CITIZEN (to convince)	CONSUMER (to seduce)
MYTH OF IDENTIFICATION	THE SAINT	THE HERO	THE STAR
MOTTO OF PERSONAL AUTHORITY	'GOD TOLD IT TO ME' (true like words from Gospel)	'I READ IT IN A BOOK' (true like a printed word)	'I SAW IT ON TV' (true like a live broadcast)
REGIME OF SYMBOLIC AUTHORITY	THE INVISIBLE (Origin) of the unverifiable	THE READABLE (Foundation) or true logic	THE VISIBLE (Event) or the plausible
UNIT OF SOCIAL DIRECTION	THE SYMBOLIC ONE: the King (dynastic principle)	THE THEORETICAL ONE: the Head (ideological principle)	THE ARITHMETICAL ONE: the Leader (statistical principle, polls, rating, audience)
CENTER OF SUBJECTIVE GRAVITY	THE SOUL (Anima)	CONSCIOUSNESS (Animus)	THE BODY (Sensorium)

Régis Debray, 'Mediological Tables: Excerpt from *Cours de Médiologie Générale*', in *Media Manifestos*. London and New York: Verso Books, 1996, p. 171. Reproduced with permission of Verso Books.

WHAT IS ICONOCLASH?[1]
BRUNO LATOUR

[…] Icono*clasm* is when we know what is happening in the act of breaking and what the motivations for what appears as a clear project of destruction are; icono*clash*, on the other hand, is when one does not know, one hesitates, one is troubled by an action for which there is no way to know, without further inquiry, whether it is destructive or constructive. […]

*

[Iconoclash] offers … a meditation on the following questions:

- Why have images attracted so much hatred?
- Why do they always return again, no matter how strongly one wants to get rid of them?
- Why have the iconoclasts' hammers always seemed to strike *sideways,* destroying something *else* that seems, after the fact, to matter immensely?
- How is it possible to go *beyond* this cycle of fascination, repulsion, destruction, atonement, that is generated by the forbidden-image worship?

*

[…] As I have claimed, somewhat boldly: are we not after a *re-description* of iconophilia and iconoclasm in order to produce even *more uncertainty* about which kind of image worship/image smashing one is faced with? How could we neatly pull them apart? And yet it might be useful to briefly present … *five types* of iconoclastic gestures … for no better reason than to gauge the extent of the ambiguity triggered by the visual puzzles we have been looking for.

The principle behind this admittedly rough classification is to look at

- the inner goals of the icon smashers,
- the roles they give to the destroyed images,
- the effects this destruction has on those who cherished those images,
- how this reaction is interpreted by the iconoclasts,
- and, finally, the effects of destruction on the destroyer's own feelings.

Bruno Latour, from 'What is Iconoclash Or is There a World Beyond the Image Wars?' in *Iconoclash: Beyond the Image Wars in Science, Religion and Art,* ed. Bruno Latour and Peter Weibel, Cambridge, MA, and London: MIT Press: and ZKM, Center for Art and Media, Karlsruhe, Germany, 2002, pp. 14–15 and 25–32.
© Bruno Latour. Reproduced with permission of Bruno Latour.

This list is rudimentary but sturdy enough, I think, to guide one through the many examples assembled here.

THE 'A' PEOPLE ARE AGAINST ALL IMAGES

The first type – I give them letters to avoid loaded terminology – is made up of those who want to free the believers – those they *deem* to be believers – of their false attachments to idols of all sorts and shapes. Idols, the fragments of which are now lying on the ground, were nothing but obstacles in the path to higher virtues. They had to be destroyed. They triggered too much indignation and hatred in the hearts of the courageous image breakers. Living with them was unbearable.

What distinguishes the As from all other types of iconoclasts is that they believe it is not only necessary but also possible to *entirely* dispose of intermediaries and to access truth, objectivity, and sanctity. Without those obstacles, they think one will at last have smoother, faster, more direct access to the real thing, which is the only object worthy of respect and worship. Images do not even provide preparation, a reflection, an inkling of the original: they *forbid* any access to the original. Between images and symbols you have to choose or be damned.

Type A is thus the pure form of 'classical' iconoclasm, recognizable in the formalist's rejection of imagination, drawing, and models as well as in the many Byzantine, Lutheran, revolutionary movements of idol smashers, and the horrifying 'excesses' of the Cultural Revolution. Purification is their goal. The world, for A people, would be a much better place, much cleaner, much more enlightened, if only one could get rid of all mediations and if one could jump directly into contact with the original, the ideas, the true God.

One of the problems with the As is that they have to believe that the others – the poor guys whose cherished icons have been accused of being impious idols – believe naively in them. Such an assumption entails that, when the Philistines react with screams of horror to pillage and plunder, this does not stop the As. On the contrary, it proves how right they were. The intensity of the horror of the idolaters is the best proof that those poor naive believers had invested too much in those stones that are essentially nothing. Armed with the notion of naive belief, the freedom-fighters constantly misconstrue the indignation of those they scandalize for an abject attachment to things they should destroy even more radically.

But the deepest problem of the As, is that no one knows if they are not Bs!

THE 'B' PEOPLE ARE AGAINST FREEZE-FRAME. NOT AGAINST IMAGES

The Bs too are idol smashers. They also wreak havoc on images, break down customs and habits, scandalize the worshippers, and trigger the horrified screams of 'Blasphemer!, Infidel!, Sacrilege!, Profanity!' But the huge difference between the As and the Bs ... is that the latter do not believe it possible nor necessary to get rid of images. What they fight is *freeze-framing*, that is, extracting an image out of the flow, and becoming fascinated by it, as if it were sufficient, as if all movement had stopped.

What they are after is not a world free of images, purified of all the obstacles, rid of all mediators, but on the contrary, a world *filled* with active images, moving mediators.

They do not want the image production to stop forever – as the As will have it – they want it to *resume* as fast and as fresh as possible.

For them, iconophilia does not mean the exclusive and obsessive attention to image, because they can stand *fixed* images no more than the As. Iconophilia means moving from one image *to the next*. They know 'truth is image but there is no image of truth.' For them, the only way to access truth, objectivity, and sanctity is to move fast from one image to another, not to dream the impossible dream of jumping to a non-existing original. Contrary to Plato's resemblance chain, they don't even try to move from the copy to the prototype. They are, as the old iconophilic Byzantine used to say, 'economic', the word meaning at the time a long and carefully managed flow of images in religion, politics, and art – and not the sense it now has: the world of goods.

Whereas the As believe that those who hold to images are iconophilic and the courageous minds who break away from the fascination with images are iconoclastic, the Bs define iconophilic as those who *do not* cling to one image in particular but are able to move from one to the other. For them iconoclasts are either those who absurdly want to get rid of all images or those who remain in the fascinated contemplation of one isolated image, freeze-framed.

Prototypical examples of Bs could be: Jesus chasing the merchants out of the Temple, Bach shocking the dull music out of the Leipzig congregation's ears, Malevich painting the black square to access the cosmic forces that had remained hidden in classical representative painting, the Tibetan sage extinguishing the butt of a cigarette on a Buddha's head to show its illusory character. The damage done to icons is, to them, always a charitable injunction to *redirect* their attention towards other, newer, fresher, more sacred images: not to do without image.

But of course many icono*clashes* come from the fact that no worshipper can be sure when his or her preferred icon/idols will be smashed to the ground, or whether an A or a B does the ominous deed. [...]

Are neither the As nor the Bs sure of how to read the reactions of those whose icon/idols are being burned? Are they furious at being without their cherished idols, much like toddlers suddenly deprived of their transitional object? Are they ashamed of being falsely accused of naively believing in non-existing things? Are they horrified at being so forcefully requested to renew their adhesion to their cherished tradition that they had let fall into disrepute and mere custom? Neither the As nor the Bs can decide, from the screeching noise made by their opponents, what sort of prophets they are *themselves*: are they prophets who claim to get rid of all images, or the ones who, 'economically,' want to let the cascade of images move again to resume the work of salvation?

But this is not the end of our hesitation, of our ambiguity, of our icono*clash*. As and Bs could, after all, be simply Cs in disguise.

THE 'C' PEOPLE ARE NOT AGAINST IMAGES. EXCEPT THOSE OF THEIR OPPONENTS

The Cs are also after debunking, disenchantment, idol-breaking. They too leave in their trail plunder, wreckage, horrified screams, scandals, abomination, desecration, shame, and profanation of all sorts. But contrary to the As and to the Bs, they have nothing against images in general: they are only against the image to which their opponents *cling* most forcefully.

This is the well-known mechanism of provocation by which, in order to destroy someone as fast and as efficiently as possible, it is enough to attack what is most cherished, what has become the repository of all the symbolic treasures of one people. Flag-burning, painting-slashing, hostage-taking are typical examples. Tell me what you hold to be most dear, and I will wreck it so as to kill you faster. It is the mini-max strategy so characteristic of terrorist threats: the maximum damage for the minimum investment. Box cutters and plane tickets against the United States of America.

The search for the suitable object to attract destruction and hatred is *reciprocal*: 'Before you wanted to attack my flag, I did not know I cherished it so much, but now I do.' So the provocateurs and those they provoke are playing cat and mouse, the first looking for what triggers indignation faster, the others looking eagerly for what will trigger their indignation most fiercely. During this search, all recognize the image in question as a mere *token*; it counts for nothing but an occasion that allows the scandal to unfold. If it were not for the conflict, everyone in the two camps would be perfectly happy to confess that it is not the object that is disputed; it is just a stake for something entirely different. So for the Cs, the image *itself* is not in question at all, they have nothing against it (as the As do) or for it (as in the case of the Bs). The image is simply worthless — worthless but attacked, thus defended, thus attacked …

What is so terrible for idol smashers is that there is no way to decide for good whether they are As, Bs, or Cs. Maybe they have entirely misunderstood their calling; maybe they are misconstruing the screams of horror of those they call Philistines who witness their idols smashed to the ground. They see themselves as prophets but maybe they are mere 'agents provocateurs.' They see themselves as freeing the poor wretched souls from their imprisonment by monstrous things, but what if they were, on the contrary, scandal-mongers looking for ways to shame their opponents most efficiently?

[…]

THE 'D' PEOPLE ARE BREAKING
IMAGES UNWITTINGLY

There is another kind of icon smasher …, a most devious case, those who could be called the 'innocent vandals.' As is well known, vandalism is a term of spite invented to describe those who destroy not so much out of a hatred of images but out of ignorance, a lust for profit and sheer passion and lunacy.

Of course, the label can be used to describe the action of the As, the Bs, and the Cs as well. They *all* can be accused of vandalism by those who don't know if they are innocent believers furious at being accused of naiveté, Philistines awakened from their dogmatic sleep by prophetic calls, or scandal-lovers delighted at being the butt of criticism and thus able to demonstrate the strength and self-righteousness of their indignation.

But the innocent vandals are different from the normal, 'bad' vandals: they had absolutely no idea that they were destroying anything. On the contrary, they were cherishing images and protecting them from destruction, and yet they are accused later of having profaned and destroyed them! They are, so to speak, iconoclasts in *retrospect*. The typical example is that of the restaurateurs who are accused by some of 'killing with kindness.' The field of architecture is especially filled with those 'innocents' who, when they build, have to destroy, when their buildings are accused of being nothing but vandalism. Their heart is filled with the love of images – so they are different from all the other cases – and yet they trigger the very same curses of 'profanation,' 'sacrilege,' and 'desecration' as all the others.

Life is so difficult: by restoring works of art, beautifying cities, rebuilding archeological sites, they have destroyed them, their opponents say, to the point that they appear as the worst iconoclasts, or at least the most perverse ones. […]

And here again, the As as well as the Bs and the Cs can be accused of being Ds, that is, of aiming at the wrong target, of forgetting to take into account the side effects, the far reaching consequences of their acts of destruction. 'You believe you freed people from idolatry, but you have simply deprived them of the means to worship;' 'You believe you are a prophet renewing the cult of images with fresher images, you are nothing but a scandal-monger thirsty for blood;' and similar accusations are frequently leveled in revolutionary circles, accusing one another of being constantly on the wrong foot, of being *horresco referens*, reactionary. What if we had killed the wrong people, smashed down the wrong idols? Worse, what if we had sacrificed idols for the cult of an even bloodier, bigger, and more monstrous Baal?

THE 'E' PEOPLE ARE SIMPLY THE PEOPLE: THEY
MOCK ICONOCLASTS AND ICONOPHILES

To be complete, one should add the Es who doubt the idol breakers as much as the icon worshippers. They are diffident to any sharp distinctions between the two poles; they exercise their devastating irony against all mediators; not that they want to get rid of them, but because they are so conscious of their fragility. They love to show irreverence and disrespect, they crave jeers and mockery, they claim an absolute right to blasphemy in a fierce, Rabelaisian way, they show the necessity of insolence, the importance of what the Romans called 'pasquinades,' which is so important for a healthy sense of civil liberty, the indispensable dose of what Peter Sloterdijk has called kynicism (by opposition to the typically iconoclastic cynicism).

*

Thus, the crucial distinction we wish to draw … is not between a world of images and a world of no-images – as the image warriors would have us believe – but between the *interrupted* flow of pictures and a *cascade* of them. By directing … attention … to those cascades, we don't expect peace – the history of the image is too loaded for that – but we are gently nudging the public to look for other properties of the image, properties that religious wars have completely hidden in the dust blown up by their many fires and furies.

NOTE
1. All footnotes removed

NOTES ON CONTRIBUTORS

Theodor Adorno (1903–69). German Professor of Sociology and Philosophy at the University of Frankfurt and Director of the Institut für Sozialforschung in Frankfurt. His books include: *Negative Dialectics* (1973); *Minima Moralia* (1974); and with Max Horkheimer, *Dialectic of Enlightenment* (1972).

Svetlana Alpers is an art historian and is Professor Emerita at the University of California at Berkeley. She co-founded the progressive art journal *Representations* in 1983. Her publications include: *Art of Describing: Dutch Art in the Seventeenth Century* (1983); and *The Making of Rubens* (1995).

Aristotle (384–322 BC). A student at Plato's Academy and tutor to Alexander the Great, Aristotle later established his own research institute in Athens, the Lyceum. One of the most influential philosophers of all time, Aristotle's writing was of extraordinary range – from biology to metaphysics. His surviving texts include the *Ethics* and the *Politics*.

Mieke Bal is Professor of Theory of Literature and a founding director of the Amsterdam School for Cultural Analysis. Among her many books are *Reading 'Rembrandt': Beyond the Word-Image Opposition* (1991), *Double Exposures: The Subject of Cultural Analysis* (1996), *Narratology: An Introduction to the Theory of Narrative* (2nd edition, 1997), and *The Mottled Screen: Reading Proust Visually* (1997).

Roland Barthes (1915–80). French literary critic and one of the founding figures in the theoretical movement centred around the journal *Tel Quel*. His books include: *Mythologies* (1957); *Elements of Semiology* (1964); *S/Z* (1974); *Roland Barthes by Roland Barthes* (1975); and *A Lover's Discourse* (1977).

Jean Baudrillard is one of France's most well-known intellectuals and a postmodern critic. From 1966 to 1987 he taught sociology at the University of Paris X (Nanterre). His books include: *The System of Objects* (1968); *Symbolic Exchange and Death* (1976); *Simulacra and Simulation,* (1981); and *The Gulf War Did Not Take Place* (1995).

Walter Benjamin (1892–1940). Jewish-German literary critic and philosopher. His writings combined ideas of Jewish mysticism with historical materialism in a body of work which was an entirely novel contribution to Marxist philosophy and aesthetic theory. His works translated into English are mostly collections of essays, including: *Illuminations* (1969); *Charles Baudelaire* (1977); *Understanding Brecht* (1977); *One Way Street* (1979); and the voluminous *The Arcades Project* (1999).

John Berger is a novelist, storyteller, poet, screenwriter and art critic. His books include the novels *A Painter of our Times* (1958) and the 1980s trilogy *Into Their Labour*, as well as theoretical texts, *Ways of Seeing* (1972), based on the 1971 BBC TV series of the same name, and *About Looking* (1980). He was awarded the Booker Prize for his novel *G.* in 1972. Born in England, he has for many years lived in a small rural community in France.

Henri Bergson (1859–1941). French philosopher, professor at the Collège de France and winner of the Nobel Prize for Literature in 1927. While treating major themes in the Western canon of philosophy, such as time, Bergson sought to reformulate philosophy by placing it on intuitive rather than intellectual grounds.

The Bible According to Judaic tradition, the Torah or Pentateuch was given to Moses by God on Mount Sinai, over 3,000 ago. Scholars believe it was mostly compiled from various oral and folkloric sources beginning around the tenth century BC. The King James translation of the Bible, first published in 1611 and commonly referred to as the 'Authorized Version', has had a profound effect on the cultures and literatures of the English-speaking world.

Susan Bordo is Professor of Philosophy at the University of Kentucky. Her books include: *The Flight to Objectivity: Essays on Cartesianism and Culture* (1987); *Unbearable Weight: Feminism, Western Culture, and the Body* (1993); and *Twilight Zones: The Hidden Life of Cultural Images from Plato to O.J.* (1997).

Susan Buck-Morss is Professor of Government at Cornell University, Visiting Distinguished Professor in the Public Intellectuals Program of Florida Atlantic University, and curator of inSITE2000. Her books include: *The Origin of Negative Dialectics* (1977); *The Dialectics of Seeing* (1989); and *Dreamworld and Catastrophe: The Passing of Mass Utopia in East and West* (2000).

Meiling Cheng is Associate Professor and Director of Theater Studies at the University of Southern California. She is a practising poet, performance artist and author of *In Other Los Angeleses: Multicentric Performance Art* (2002).

Joan Copjec is Professor of English, Comparative Literature, and Media Study at the University at Buffalo. Her books include: *Read My Desire: Lacan Against the Historicists* (1994); and *Imagine There's No Woman: Ethics and Sublimation* (2002).

Jonathan Crary is a professor in the Department of Art and Archaeology at Columbia University, New York. His books include: *Techniques of the Observer: On Vision and Modernity in the Nineteenth Century* (1990); and *Suspensions of Perception: Attention, Spectacle and Modern Culture* (1999).

Antonio Damasio is Van Allen Distinguished Professor and head of the department of neurology at the University of Iowa College of Medicine, and Adjunct Professor at the Salk Institute in La Jolla, California. His books include *Descartes' Error: Emotion, Reason and the Human Brain* (1994); *The Feeling of What Happens: Body, Emotion and the Making of Consciousness* (2000); and *Looking for Spinoza: Joy, Sorrow and the Feeling Brain* (2003).

Arthur Danto is Emeritus Johnsonian Professor of Philosophy at Columbia University. His books include: *Nietzsche as Philosopher* (1968); *The Transfiguration of the Commonplace* (1984); *Encounters and Reflections: Art in the Historical Present* (1990); *Embodied Meanings: Critical Essays and Aesthetic Meditations* (1994); and *Philosophizing Art: Selected Essays* (1999).

Guy Debord (1931–94). French political activist, film-maker and key theorist of situationism. Best known for his book *Society of the Spectacle* (1967), which anticipates many aspects of the critique of postmodernity.

Régis Debray is a French intellectual, journalist, government official and professor of philosophy in the Faculté des Lettres at the Université de Lyon III. A former professor of philosophy at the University of Havana and friend of the revolutionary Che Guevara, he later became an adviser to French President Mitterrand. He is the founder of the discipline of médiologie or 'mediology', which categorises societies in terms of their modes of cultural transmission. His books include *Revolution in the Revolution?* (1967); *Media Manifestos* (1996); and *Transmitting Culture* (2000).

Gilles Deleuze (1925–95). A major French thinker of the late twentieth century. He wrote his two most popular books, *Anti-Oedipus* (1983) and *A Thousand Plateaus* (1987) with radical psychoanalyst Félix Guattari. He wrote several other influential works on philosophy, such as *Difference and Repetition* (1968), literature, such as *Proust and Signs* (1964), and fine art, such as *Francis Bacon* (1981). Considering himself an empiricist and a vitalist, his body of work rests upon concepts such as multiplicity, constructivism, difference and desire.

Kevin DeLuca is an associate professor in the Department of Speech Communication and the Institute of Ecology at the University of Georgia. He is the author of *Image Politics: The New Rhetoric of Environmental Activism* (1999) and numerous essays on visual rhetoric, critical theory, environmental activism and the virtues of violence.

René Descartes (1591–1650). French philosopher and a founder of modern philosophy. He rejected Scholasticism in favour of a method of reasoning based on empirical observation and mathematics. His work has enduring influence and has been most criticised for its substance dualism, the concept that mind and matter comprise two distinct substances. His works include *Discourse on Method* (1637) and *Meditations on the First Philosophy* (1641).

Mikel Dufrenne is a French phenomenological philosopher who has written widely on aesthetics. His books include *The Phenomenology of Aesthetic Experience* (1973) and *In the Presence of the Sensuous: Essays in Aesthetics* (1990).

Richard Dyer is Professor of Film Studies at the University of Warwick. He has written on stars, entertainment and representation, and lesbian and gay culture. His books include: *Heavenly Bodies* (1987); *Only Entertainment* (1992); *The Matter of Images* (1993); and *White* (1997).

Anton Ehrenzweig (1908–66). A psychoanalytic art critic whose best-known work is *The Hidden Order of Art* (1967).

Sergei Eisenstein (1898–1948). Russian film director and film theorist. His early films, *Strike* (1924), *Battleship Potemkin* (1925) and *October* (1927), are among the greatest classics of the silent cinema. *Alexander Nevsky* (1938) marked a successful transition to sound and in the second part of the unfinished *Ivan the Terrible* (Part 1, 1944; Part 2, 1946) he was equally successful in using colour stock for the first time.

James Elkins is Professor of Art History, Theory and Criticism at the School of the Art Institute of Chicago. His writing focuses on the history and theory of images in art, science and nature. His books include: *Our Beautiful, Dry, and Distant Texts* (1997); *On Pictures and the Words That Fail Them* (1998); *What Painting Is* (1998); *Why Are Our Pictures Puzzles?* (1999); and *The Domain of Images* (1999).

Friedrich Engels (1820–94). A German industrialist and social critic, best known for his association with Karl Marx, whom he supported both financially and intellectually. They collaborated on *The Communist Manifesto* (1848), although Marx wrote the text, and Engels edited *Das Kapital*, ensuring its publication after Marx's death.

Ernest Fenollosa (1853–1908). In turn Professor of Philosophy at Tokyo University, Curator of the Imperial Museum of Japan, and Curator of Oriental Art at the Museum of Fine Arts, Boston. His promotion of Chinese and Japanese art resounded throughout the United States, but his legacy is still uncertain, with some considering him a pioneer and others a fraud.

Michel Foucault (1926–84). Social scientist, philosopher and historian of ideas. As Professor of History and Systems of Thought at the Collège de France, he became a much celebrated and controversial figure of the French intellectual establishment. His books include: *Madness and Civilisation* (1961); *The Order of Things* (1966); *The Archaeology of Knowledge* (1969); *The Birth of the Clinic* (1973); *Discipline and Punish* (1975); and the three-volume *History of Sexuality* (1976–84).

Sigmund Freud (1856–1939). Founder of the therapeutic technique of psychoanalysis, the 'talking-cure' for mental illness. A trained doctor from the Vienna Medical School, Freud was a prolific writer, producing many highly influential works, including *The Psychopathology of Everyday Life* (1905) and *Civilization and Its Discontents* (1930).

Peter Galison is Mallinckrodt Professor of the History of Science and of Physics at Harvard University. His work explores the interaction between the three principal subcultures of twentieth-century physics: experimentation, instrumentation and theory. His books include: *How Experiments End* (1987); *Image and Logic: A Material Culture of Microphysics* (1997); and *Einstein's Clocks, Poincaré's Maps* (2003).

Paul Gilroy is Professor of Social Theory at the London School of Economics. He is the author of *There Ain't No Black in the Union Jack* (1987), *The Black Atlantic* (1994) and *Between Camps: Nations, Cultures and the Allure of Race* (2000). His latest book is *After Empire: Melancholia or Convivial Culture* (2004).

Ernst Gombrich (1909–2001). An Austrian-born art historian who moved to England in 1937, enjoyed a long association with the Warburg Institute, including a period as its director, and was Professor of the History of Classical Tradition at the University of London until his retirement in 1976. His many publications include *The Story of Art* (1950) and *Art and Illusion: A Study in the Psychology of Pictorial Representation* (1960).

Gregory Price Grieve is an assistant professor in the Department of Religious Studies at the University of North Carolina, Greensboro. His area of study is South Asian religions with an emphasis on Himalayan traditions.

Martin Heidegger (1889–1976). German philosopher and a one-time student of Edmund Husserl, the founder of phenomenology. Highly influential, particularly on post-war French thought, and controversial because of his association with the Nazis and the difficulty of his work. His books include: *Being & Time* (1927); *What is Called Thinking* (1952); and *Nietzsche* (4 vols) (1961).

Thomas Hobbes (1588–1679). Originally an English classicist, Hobbes turned his attention to philosophy, politics and science. His most controversial and influential works were on politics and included *The Elements of Law, Natural and Politic* (1640), *De Cive* (1642) and *Leviathan* (1651).

David Hockney is an English painter, printmaker, photographer and stage designer who became internationally famous in the early 1960s as one of the leaders of the British pop art movement. He emigrated to the United States and was known for his 'swimming pool' paintings during the 1960s, for elaborate stage sets during the 1970s and for photo collages during the 1980s.

Iconodules and iconoclasts in Byzantium. John of Damascus Often called the last Greek father and the first Christian Aristotelian, St. John Damascene became a monk and wrote three treatises in defence of the use of icons in worship in opposition to the iconoclasm of Byzantine Emperor Leo III the Isaurian. These works led to John's condemnation by Leo's successor at the **Council of Hieria** in 754. His later rehabilitation at the **Second Council of Nicaea** in 787 came five years after his death and four years after Empress Theodora had re-allowed the worship of icons. His most famous work, *The Source of Knowledge*, is sometimes translated as *The Fount of Wisdom*.

Don Ihde is Distinguished Professor of Philosophy and Director of the Technoscience Research Group at Stony Brook University in the USA. He is author of many books including *Technics and Praxis* (1979), *Technology and the Lifeworld* (1990) and *Expanding Hermeneutics: Visualism in Science* (1998).

Fredric Jameson is generally considered to be one of the foremost contemporary Marxist literary critics writing in English. He has published a wide range of works analysing literary and cultural texts and developing his own neo-Marxist theoretical position. His many works include *Marxism and Form* (1970); *The Prison-House of Language* (1972); *The Political Unconscious: Narrative as a Socially Symbolic Act* (1981); *Postmodernism, or, The Cultural Logic of Late Capitalism* (1991); *Signatures of the Visible* (1991); and *The Geopolitical Aesthetic* (1992).

Martin Jay is Professor of History at the University of California, Berkeley. His books include: *The Dialectical Imagination* (1973); *Marxism and Totality*

(1984); and *Downcast Eyes: The Denigration of Vision in Twentieth-Century French Thought* (1993).

Immanuel Kant (1724–1804). A German philosopher and professor of logic at the University of Königsberg, Kant led an orderly, punctual but uneventful private life. Philosophically he has been ranked with Plato for his range and originality. His major works include *Critique of Pure Reason* (1781); *Critique of Practical Reason* (1788); and *Critique of Judgement* (1790).

Paul Klee (1879–1940). Swiss-born painter and graphic artist of extraordinary formal inventiveness whose art combined a childlike, primary vision and the utmost sophistication. He was a member of *Der Blaue Reiter*, an expressionist group that contributed much to the development of abstract art. He wrote numerous books and essays on formal and aesthetic issues and, after the First World War, he taught alongside fellow painter Wassily Kandinsky at the well-known Bauhaus school.

Rosalind Krauss is co-editor and co-founder of the journal *October* and a Professor of Art History at Hunter College in New York. Her publications include: *The Originality of the Avant-Garde and Other Modernist Myths* (1986); *The Optical Unconscious* (1994); and *The Picasso Papers* (1998).

Gunter Kress is Professor of English and Education at the Institute of Education, University of London. His publications include: *Social Semiotics* (1989); *Language as Ideology* (1993); and *Learning to Write* (1994).

Jacques Lacan (1901–81). French psychoanalytic theorist and psychiatrist who reworked Freud's ideas by drawing on linguistic structuralism, philosophy and topography. His publications are largely transcriptions of his seminars, including: *Écrits: A Selection* (1977); *The Four Fundamental Concepts of Psycho-Analysis* (1977); and *Television* (1990).

Bruno Latour is Professor at the Centre de Sociologie de L'innovation at the École des Mines in Paris, with appointments at the London School of Economics and the History of Science Department at Harvard University. His books include *Science in Action* (1987) and *Pandora's Hope* (1999).

Michèle Le Doeuff is a Director of Research at the National Centre for Scientific Research in Paris and has been Professor of Women's Studies at the University of Geneva. She is the author of *The Philosophical Imaginary* (1989), *Hipparchia's Choice, An Essay Concerning Women, Philosophy, etc.* (1991) and *The Sex of Knowing* (2003).

Gotthold Lessing (1729–81). Perhaps the first German dramatist to write about the contemporary life of his fellow countrymen in his play *Minna von Barnhelm* (1767). He is sometimes credited as being the 'father of German criticism' for essays including the *Laöcoon* (1766) on poetry and painting and *Hamburg Dramaturgy* on theatre (1769).

John Locke (1632–1704). A prolific English author who produced highly influential works on philosophy, political theory, education and religion. *An Essay Concerning Human Understanding, Two Treatises of Government* and his *Second Letter on Toleration* were all published in 1690, although they had been many years in preparation.

Celia Lury is Lecturer in Sociology at Goldsmiths College, University of London. Her research is concerned with aspects of visual culture and the commodity character of contemporary culture. Her books include: *Consumer Culture* (1996); *Prosthetic Culture: Photography, Memory and Identity* (1998); and *Brands: The Logos of the Global Economy* (2004).

Kevin Lynch (1918–84). Educated at Yale University, Rensselaer Polytechnic Institute and, most notably, Massachusetts Institute of Technology (where he earned professor emeritus status), Lynch was a significant contributor to city planning and city design in the twentieth century. In his most famous work, *Image of the City* (1960) he describes a five-year study that reveals what elements in the built structure of a city are important in the popular perception of the city.

Karl Marx (1818–83). German philosopher and political theorist who spent most of his life exiled in poverty in London. He was supported by Friedrich Engels, a close collaborator. Major works include *The Communist Manifesto* (1848) with Engels and *Capital,* the first volume of which was published in 1867, while the remaining two volumes were edited and published posthumously by Engels.

Marshall McLuhan (1911–81). Critic and cultural commentator, who in the last years of his life worked from the Centre for Culture and Technology, University of Toronto, Canada. He wrote prolifically on media criticism, cultural perception and the American advertising industry. Following the publication of *Understanding Media* (1964), McLuhan gained international fame and a cult status. Other books include: *The Mechanical Bride* (1951); *The Gutenberg Galaxy* (1962); *The Medium is the Message* (1967); and *War and Peace in the Global Village* (1968).

Maurice Merleau-Ponty (1907–61). French philosopher who undertook an in-depth study of the work of Edmund Husserl while a prisoner of war during the Second World War. His major work, *The Phenomenology of Perception* (1945), is largely a result of these studies and his interest in Gestalt psychology.

Christian Metz (1941–93). A French film theorist. His early writings in the 1960s represent an attempt to establish a semiotics of cinema, but by the mid-1970s his work changed direction as he began to elaborate a psychoanalytic theory of film. His books include: *Film Language: A Semiotics of Cinema* (1968); *Language and Cinema* (1971); and *Psychoanalysis and Cinema* (1977).

Midrash Rabbah is a collection of rabbinic commentaries on parts of the Hebrew Bible, including the Pentateuch. A mixture of homily and exegesis developed orally and compiled over time, the section about Genesis is believed to have been edited in Palestine around the end of the fourth or early fifth century AD.

William J. Mitchell is Professor of Architecture and Media Arts and Sciences and Dean of the School of Architecture and Planning at the Massachusetts Institute of Technology. His books include: *Computer-Aided Architectural Design* (1977); *The Poetics of Gardens* (1988); *The Logic of Architecture* (1990); *The Reconfigured Eye: Visual Truth in the Post-Photographic Era*

(1992); *Digital Design Media* (1995); *and Me++: The Cyborg Self and the Networked City* (2003).

W.J.T. Mitchell is the Gaylord Donnelley Distinguished Service Professor of English and Art History at the University of Chicago, and editor of the journal *Critical Inquiry*. His books include: *Iconology* (1986); *Picture Theory* (1994); *The Last Dinosaur Book: The Life and Times of a Cultural Icon* (1998); and *What Do Pictures Want? The Lives and Loves of Images* (2005).

Laura Mulvey is a film-maker, critic and feminist cultural theorist. She is Professor of Film and Media Studies at Birkbeck College, University of London. Her publications include: *Visual and Other Pleasures* (1989); *Fetishism and Curiosity* (1996); and the BFI Film Classic *Citizen Kane*.

Friedrich Nietzsche (1844–1900). German philosopher appointed philology professor at Basle University at the young age of 24. He retired in ill-health in 1879 and wrote a series of aphoristic and narrative books including *Thus Spake Zarathustra* (1883–85) and *Beyond Good and Evil* (1886). He became insane in 1889.

Erwin Panofsky (1892–1968). A highly prominent German-born art historian who fled to the United States when removed from office by the Nazis in 1933. His publications include: *Early Netherlandish Painting: Its Origin and Character* (1953); *Studies in Iconology: Humanistic Themes in the Art of the Renaissance* (1939); and *Perspective as Symbolic Form* (1991).

Charles Sanders Peirce (1839–1914). American philosopher, best known for his contributions to debates on logic, pragmaticism and semiotics. His numerous essays and voluminous unpublished writings are collected in eight volumes, *Collected Writings*, published by Harvard University Press (1930).

Plato (427–347 BC). Along with his pupil Aristotle and his executed friend and teacher Socrates, Plato helped shape the intellectual tradition in the West. Over 20 of his philosophical dialogues are extant, such as the *Protagoras and Meno,* many featuring Socrates as the main protagonist.

Marcel Proust (1871–1922). French novelist who ranks as one of the greatest literary figures of the twentieth century. Proust's work, *À la recherche du temps perdu* (1913–27) – (or *Remembrance of Things Past*) is a seven-volume novel, which abandons plot and traditional dramatic action for the vision of the first-person narrator confronting his world.

Paul Ricoeur (1913–2005). A French philosopher who combined phenomenological description with hermeneutic interpretation. He was a professor at the University of Strasbourg, the Sorbonne, the University of Nanterre and the University of Chicago. Among his books are: *Freud and Philosophy: An Essay on Interpretation* (1970); *The Rule of Metaphor* (1977); and the three-volume *Time and Narrative* (1984–88).

Robert D. Romanyshyn is a Jungian psychotherapist who teaches at Pacifica Graduate Institute, California. He is the author of *Technology as Symptom and Dream* (1989); *Soul in Grief* (1997); *Mirror and Metaphor* (2001); and *Ways of the Heart* (2002).

Jean-Paul Sartre (1905–80). French novelist, dramatist, critic and philosopher, often associated with post-war existentialism and communism. His philosophical books include *Being and Nothingness* (1943), *Existentialism and Humanism* (1946) and *Words* (1964); his novels include *Nausea* (1938) and *The Age of Reason* (1945).

Ferdinand de Saussure (1857–1913). Swiss linguist, regarded as the founder of modern linguistics and the forefather of structuralism and semiology. His celebrated *Course in General Linguistics* (1916) was published posthumously, based on students' notes from his lectures given at the University of Geneva between 1907 and 1911. His central role in the modern human sciences is due to his influence on the work of anthropologists, philosophers and psychoanalysts.

Susan Sontag (1933–2005). American literary critic, cultural commentator and novelist. Her books include: *Against Interpretation* (1966); *On Photogaphy* (1977); *Illness as Metaphor* (1978); and *Regarding the Pain of Others* (2003).

Barbara Maria Stafford is the William B. Ogden Distinguished Service Professor of Art History at the University of Chicago. Her books include: *Body Criticism: Imaging the Unseen in Enlightenment Art and Medicine* (1993); *Good Looking: Essays on the Virtue of Images* (1996); and *Visual Analogy: Consciousness as the Art of Connecting* (1999).

Theo van Leeuwen has worked as a film and television producer and is Director of the Centre for Language and Communication at Cardiff University. His books include: *The Media Interview – Confession, Contest, Conversation* (1994); *Multimodal Discourse – The Modes and Media of Contemporary Communication* (2001); and a co-edited volume, *Handbook of Visual Analysis* (2000).

Ludwig Wittgenstein (1889–1951). Austrian-born philosopher, widely regarded as one of the twentieth century's most influential thinkers, who made ground-breaking contributions to the philosophy of language and logic. He published only one book in his lifetime, *Tractatus Logico-Philosophicus* (1922), but several books were published posthumously, notably *Philosophical Investigations* (1953); *The Blue and Brown Books* (1958); and *On Certainty* (1969).

Semir Zeki is Professor of Neurobiology at the University of London. He is a Fellow of the Royal Society and a Member of the American Philosophical Society. His books include: *A Vision of the Brain* (1993); and *Inner Vision: An Exploration of Art and the Brain* (1999).

NOTES ON EDITORS

Sunil Manghani is a lecturer in the School of Arts at York St John University, where he teaches critical and cultural theory. His publications appear in *Theory, Culture & Society, Invisible Culture, Journal of Visual Art Practice,* and *Culture, Theory and Critique*. He is currently working on a book about visual semiotics, which brings together his long-term interest in Roland Barthes' late writings and post-structuralist theories of visual culture.

Arthur Piper teaches image studies and visual culture at the University of Nottingham. His doctoral research centres on connections between neuroscience, visual studies and phenomenology. He is a professional journalist and writer.

Jon Simons is Associate Professor of Communication at Indiana University, Bloomington. He has authored *Foucault and the Political* (1995) and edited *From Kant to Lévi-Strauss* (2002) and *Contemporary Critical Theorists* (2004).

INDEX

401217